OUR HIDDEN HERITAGE

PENNSYLVANIA WOMEN IN HISTORY

EDITED BY

Janice H. McElroy, Ph.D.
Pennsylvania Division
Project Director

ASSISTANT EDITORS
Mary Ann Stangil and
Margaret D. Druse

*To Mother –
our special
Pennsylvania woman.!!
Love,
Lois and Ken
11/24/83*

**AA
UW**

A PROJECT OF THE PENNSYLVANIA DIVISION
AMERICAN ASSOCIATION OF UNIVERSITY WOMEN

2401 Virginia Ave., N.W.
Washington, D.C.
20037

COVER: The counted cross-stitch cover design was created and stitched by Barbara Zinck Mendola, a certified craftsman of the Embroiderers' Guild of America. The five figures illustrate the change in women's costumes over the 300-year span of Pennsylvania history. Artistic assistant for the overall cover layout was Judy Haase, Art Department Chairman at The Swain School. Barbara and Judy are both members of the Allentown Branch of AAUW.

This project was funded in part by a Research and Projects Grant from the Educational Foundation Programs of the American Association of University Women.

Library of Congress Catalog Card Number: 83-71272

ISBN 0-961-14760-1

Printed in the United States of America

First Edition

ACKNOWLEDGEMENTS

The Division Project, Pennsylvania Women in History, has required thousands of woman-hours to complete, and I am sure that for all of us it has been truly a labor of love. Getting to "know" these special women in our state has been a source of pride and inspiration to everyone involved. A Project of this magnitude required the cooperation and coordination of hundreds of individuals and organizations. I am most grateful to Martha Zeller, past president of the Pennsylvania Division, for giving me the opportunity to direct this effort.

Initial support and advice on this undertaking came from the Brookville Area Branch which had proposed this as the Division Project. With help from the AAUW network, names of members with background experience in researching and writing local histories were proposed to me and a Division Project Committee was established. Its members represented various regions of the state and they served as resource persons to their areas. I wish to thank the following committee members for their assistance: Loretta Coltrane, Sabina Freeman, Patricia Gill, Nada Gray, Margaret Tenpas, Donna Schaefer, and Mary Ann Stangil.

The key figures in this Project have been the branch chairmen. They had the responsiblity for developing the local organization to research, write, document and submit materials to the division. The names of the fifty-five branches which contributed to the Project and their chairmen, or other submitting agents, are indicated in APPENDIX D. I am truly grateful to them for their enthusiastic response and diligence in making this Project so successful and to their committee members, many of whom are acknowledged as the researchers and writers of the biographies.

The selection committee, which I chaired, performed the very important task of choosing the individuals included in this volume from the two hundred and fifty-nine entries. The committee members' knowledge of history and sense of written communication greatly facilitated a very difficult task. I wish to express my appreciation to them for assisting me in this sensitive area: Margaret D. Druse, Donna Schaefer and Mary Ann Stangil.

Special and regional division editors performed an invaluable service in the preparation of the biographical materials for publication. In instances where it was necessary to combine entries because of multiple submissions, or where extensive revisions of materials were required, the special division editor who performed this function is noted in the credits. I am extremely grateful for the editorial efforts of the following: Catherine Barrett, Joan Boyce, Anne Dayton, Margaret D. Druse, Lois Follstaedt, Judith Furlow, Marilou L. Gary, Patricia McCoy Gill, Cynthia

Gordon, Barbara Klaczynska, Ph.D., Karen Methlie, Betty B. Moorhead, Janet O'Keefe, Margaret Reid, Christine C. Ritter, Donna Schaefer, Marion Schlack, Anne Stakelon, and Mary Ann Stangil.

During the research stage, many, many people and institutions assisted the local branches. I wish to acknowledge our indebtedness to all the organizations who helped and all those individuals who gave special assistance with the biographical and photographic materials contained in this volume. Listed below are those known to me who are not otherwise credited in References and Notes in APPENDIX B. The order corresponds to an alphabetical listing of the submitting communities.

Beaver County Historical Research Center, Margaret Ross, coordinator, Beaver; Old Economy, Dan Reibel, former curator, Beaver County; *The Call-Chronicle Newspapers,* Allentown; Lehigh County Historical Society, Allentown; *The Bethlehem Globe Times;* Bethlehem Public Library; Reeves Library, Moravian College, Bethlehem; Central Moravian Church, Bethlehem; Administrative Office for the Bradford Area Schools; Zelienople Historical Society, Gertrude Ziegler, executive director; Joseph and Elizabeth Shaw Public Library, Clearfield; Clearfield Hospital; Clearfield County Historical Society; Pennsylvania Medical Society Auxiliary, Clearfield; Easton Area Public Library; *The Express,* Easton; American Anthropological Association, Washington, D.C.; Department of Treasury, Washington, D.C.; U. S. Department of Labor, Women's Bureau, Washington, D.C.; Northampton County Historical and Genealogical Society, Easton; Singing City, Philadelphia; Hazel Larsen Goetz, St. Marys; Pennsylvania Room Collection, Carnegie Library of Pittsburgh; *Valley News Dispatch,* Audrey Lang, Tarentum; The National Museum of American History, The Smithsonian Institution, Washington, D.C.; New Kensington Chamber of Commerce; New Kensington Library, Janet Malik, reference librarian; The Homestead Association, Springdale; Wilson College Alumnae Office, Chambersburg; Adams County Library, Gettysburg; Adams County Historical Society; Westmoreland County Historical Society, Greensburg; The Sisters of Mercy, Pittsburgh; *The Patriot News,* Paul Beers, Harrisburg; Wayne County Historical Society, Honesdale; *The Wayne Independent,* Honesdale; *The News Eagle,* Honesdale; Hazelton Public Library; *The Daily News,* Huntingdon; Huntingdon County Historical Society; Historical and Genealogical Society of Indiana County, Indiana, PA.; Stapleton Library, Indiana University of Pennsylvania; Indiana Free Library; Lancaster County Historical Society; The Mennonite Heritage Center, Lansdale; Pennsbury Manor, Morrisville; Sisters of the Blessed Sacrament, Cornwells Heights; The Woods School and Residential Treatment Center, Langhorne; Temple University Library, Philadelphia; University of Pennsylvania Library and Annenberg Center at the University of Pennsylvania, Philadelphia;

Historic Langhorne Association, Langhorne; Historic Fallsington, Inc., Fallsington; Bucks County Historical Society, Doylestown; Pennwood Branch of the Bucks County Free Library; The Spencer Hospital, Meadville; Oil City Library; Allegheny College Library, Margaret Moser, Meadville; Alpha Tau Chapter of Delta Kappa Gamma, Oil City; Philadelphia Area Cultural Consortium; The Rosenbach Museum and Library, Philadelphia; Philadelphia Mayor's Commission for Women; Historical Society of Pennsylvania Library, Philadelphia; Hunt Library of the Carnegie-Mellon University; Hillman Library, University of Pittsburgh; Carnegie Library, Squirrel Hill and Oakland Branches; Western Pennsylvania Historical Society, Pittsburgh; St. Peter's Village, Pottstown; *Reading Eagle;* Boston College; State University of New York, New Paltz; Lackawanna Historical Society, Scranton; *The Scranton Tribune,* Maureen Garcia Pons and Ge'ne' Brislin; Bucknell University Archives, Lewisburg; Laurelton Center Library, Laurelton.

This Project was partially funded by a Research and Projects Grant from the Educational Foundation Programs of the American Association of University Women. Service-in-kind assistance with the photocopying of materials was provided by Mack Trucks, Inc., Rodale Press, Inc. and The Swain School, all of Allentown. I especially thank these institutions for the support they have given the Project.

Special words of gratitude go to Barbara Zinck Mendola for the hours of researching, designing and stitching required to create the counted cross-stitch cover design and to Judy Haase for the brainstorming sessions that went into the selection of the book's name and the preparation of the cover.

I wish to express my sincerest appreciation to Barbara Klaczynska, Ph.D., of the University of Pennsylvania, whose scholarly research and analyses served as the foundation for *Part One.* Her overview of Pennsylvania history and insights into women's history provided the contextual perspective for these biographies. The many hours of work she has invested in this effort have made a significant contribution to our better understanding of women's role in Pennsylvania history.

Barbara Herman gave technical information and assistance on the publication phase of this project and I am most grateful for her professional guidance. Josephine Mountain handled the book orders and distribution of the copies, and I am very appreciative of her supportive effort.

I would like particularly to acknowledge the dedicated work of my two assistant editors, Mary Ann Stangil and Margaret D. Druse. Mary Ann is a journalist, who reads extensively in women's history, and Margaret is a history "buff" who studied manuscript preparation. Mary Ann has been the main copy editor in this effort and Margaret has done much of the extra research needed to clarify or verify, as far as possible, questionable parts of submitted text. They have both assisted me in the task of proofreading copy. Their knowledge and cooperation in every phase of this Project have been invaluable in ensuring its success and I am deeply grateful to them both.

A special "thank you" goes to my friends and members of the Division Board for their suggestions and personal encouragement and to my family who have had to share me with all these others for two years. I especially thank my mother, Josephine Kern Jilka; my children, Helen Elizabeth and Bryan Douglas McElroy; and my husband, Jim, who have patiently supported me in this effort.

I hope that all who contributed to this project have the same sense of satisfaction that I have in knowing what a major achievement we have accomplished through our collective efforts. May our hidden heritage become our proud heritage of proclamation.

Janice H. McElroy, Ph.D.
Editor and Project Director
Allentown, Pennsylvania

June, 1983

DEDICATION

This book is dedicated to the struggle to guarantee constitutionally that "Equality of rights under the law shall not be denied or abridged by the United States or by any state on account of sex."

TABLE OF CONTENTS

PREFACE

Women have been the faceless, forgotten figures of history. The goal of the AAUW-Pennsylvania Division Project has been to reconstruct for women the fabric of their past heritage and to show the threads of continuity weaving texture and substance through their lives.

Our Hidden Heritage: Pennsylvania Women in History is a state-wide collection of women's biographies. They reveal a fascinating record of what it has meant to be a woman through the three hundred years of Pennsylvania's history. These accounts provide remarkable snippets of real life where, at times, the extraordinary is combined with the commonplace. They teach many valuable lessons about the versatility, resourcefulness and stamina of women. The struggles that women have gone through to maintain their families, develop their communities, gain access to education, win their political rights and obtain admission into various fields of work are clearly documented in this collection.

This Project was undertaken by the Pennsylvania Division of the American Association of University Women in June 1981 as a salute to the Pennsylvania tricentennial. It was designed to raise public awareness of the roles that women have played in our state's history and to provide documented reference materials for future research. The Division Project Director implemented and coordinated both the research and publication phases of the Project through the locally appointed branch chairmen and their committees. Members of the Division Project Committee served as regional consultants.

Fifty-five of Pennsylvania's seventy-eight AAUW Branches contributed to the Project, submitting two hundred and fifty-nine biographies for this publication. One hundred and sixty-five entries were selected for inclusion. The other submitted names are listed in APPENDIX C. All the original manuscript materials are filed in the AAUW archives with the Pennsylvania Historical and Museum Commission in Harrisburg. Many branches have also provided references to local archives where additional sources are available.

Branches were encouraged to select and research in their communities women whom they felt had made a significant contribution at either a local, state or national level. The Project chairman in each branch (listed in APPENDIX D) was responsible for overseeing the preparation and submission of the biographies. The chairman was generally assisted by members of a committee. Their job was a very difficult one since the sources were often scarce and of varying quality. They were frequently charting new areas of investigation, and, through their volunteer efforts, they have opened the way for further historical research.

Because of the many different people involved in this collection process, there was, expectedly, a wide variation in the approaches taken to the biographies. Each reflected the unique research and writing style of the person(s) who originally worked on it. That element of variation is still evident in this volume.

A division selection committee screened all entries on the basis of the established merit of the individual's contribution, the general interest and appeal of the written presentation, the geographic representation of the individual and the comparative spectrum of roles represented. In the selection process, living women, over a specified age, were considered only if the long-term merits of their achievements were readily recognized at a state or national level. Other women of accomplishment were chosen from each of the three categories; i.e., local, state or national. Regional and special division editors helped in the initial editing and/or researching and rewriting of the biographies.

The first significant work to analyze woman's historical position was Mary Beard's *Woman as Force in History*, published in 1946. She demonstrated that women have been active, competent and recognized in their own times in a wide range of endeavors and circumstances. However, historians traditionally neglected women because they defined history primarily by issues of power, influence, violence and visible activity in the world of political and economic affairs. Those institutions, such as social relationships, marriage and the family, which have affected individuals most intimately have been outside the scope of historical research. During the 1960s, as an egalitarian approach became more important, women's history emerged as a legitimate field of analysis.

The scholarship which has emerged in the last two decades in women's history has provided a context for the one hundred and sixty-five diverse and impressive women present in this collection. *Part One* of the book gives a brief review of Pennsylvania history, followed by an overview of the history of women in Pennsylvania as encompassed by these biographies. Examples of historical trends and developments are drawn with illustrations from the lives of the women included in this volume, whenever possible. In some instances, however, in order to preserve the coherency of the account, it was necessary to refer to a significant figure not represented in this collection. The names of the included women are designated by an asterisk(*), and the resource materials for all the contained biographies are listed in APPENDIX B. A selected bibliography on Pennsylvania and women's history is given in APPENDIX A.

The history of women in Pennsylvania as revealed by these biographies is actually the history of women's work in and outside the home. An analysis of what these women were doing during the period in which they lived tells a great deal about their society. The fact that work patterns changed slowly over time, in response to larger societal needs and social values about the proper sphere of women, allows the tracing of the historical forces influencing women's lives. It is hoped that *Part One* will provide a perspective against which the lives of these Pennsylvanian women and of all women, past, present and future, may be set.

The arrangement of the biographies in *Part Two* reveals an interesting historical perspective in itself. The women are divided into sixteen sections by their prime area of involvement or occupation. Their biographies are arranged chronologically within sections which, in turn, are ordered chronologically. The *overall* sequence of these sections reflects the temporal evolution of women's roles in society, while the sequence of the biographical accounts *within* each section traces the changes overtime that have affected and been effected by women in that role.

The biographies in *Part Two* also attest to the multifaceted lives most women have led. The women are grouped according to the interest or occupation for which they are best known; however, this was often very difficult to do. Many of the women had significant achievements in several areas. They excelled as homemakers and volunteers as well as in occupations or professions for which they were paid. At various stages of their lives, women pursued different interests; for example, combining writing with social causes, homemaking with politics, religion with education or paid with volunteer work. It is often easier to stereotype and generalize than to analyze individually the variety, the ambiguity and the difficult choices which define women's lives. These biographies begin to do this.

This project was not designed to document the lives of all the "outstanding women" in Pennsylvania's history, but rather to provide a statewide view of the lives of selected women. Many previously documented Pennsylvania notables may have escaped this survey, but many women who were very special within the framework of their own, perhaps small, communities have been discovered and their stories shared. This provides a textured view of the roles women have played in our state. The life of the western frontier was quite different from colonial life in Philadelphia; life in a mining town was different from life in a farming community. The demands of each time and place called forth new and different skills and strengths, and these are revealed in the lives set forth in *Our Hidden Heritage: Pennsylvania Women in History.*

Janice H. McElroy, Ph.D.
June, 1983

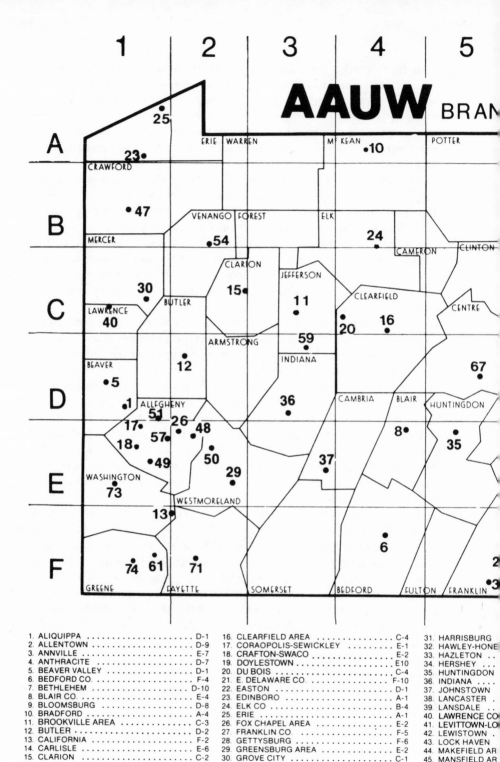

ES IN PENNSYLVANIA

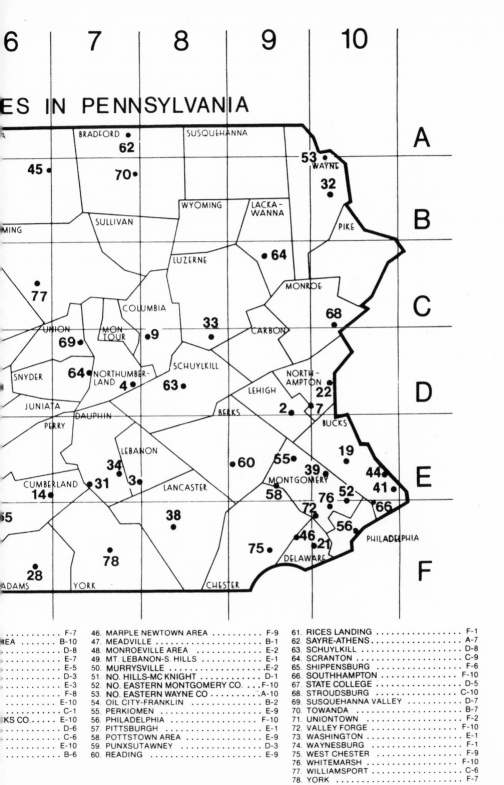

PART ONE

A PERSPECTIVE ON PENNSYLVANIA WOMEN IN HISTORY

A BRIEF OVERVIEW OF PENNSYLVANIA HISTORY

For centuries Pennsylvania had been an ancestral home for tribes of the Algonquian and Iroquoian Indians. Many tribes lived near waterways which would eventually also attract European exploration and settlement. In 1609 the British explorer Henry Hudson sailed into Delaware Bay while trying to find a trade route to the Far East for the Dutch East India Company. He left the region, but his reports led to further exploration by others. The Swedes established the capital of their New Sweden colony on Tinicum Island, near Philadelphia, in 1643. The Dutch captured the Swedish colony in 1655, only to have the English take control of it in 1664.

Pennsylvania, because of its central location along the eastern shore of the country and excellent river ports, was a significant colony from the time of earliest European settlement. Once William Penn received a charter from the King of England, Charles II, for the colony in 1681, his Quaker beliefs set a tone for religious and political tolerance which marked the colony as unique. Early Pennsylvania contained a combination of more Roman Catholics, Jews and radical Protestant sects than any other colony. In eighteenth century Pennsylvania, one was as likely to hear German as English as the spoken language. The most numerous German settlers included the Mennonites in Lancaster County, the Moravians in Bethlehem and the German Baptist Brethren in Germantown and Lancaster County.

Philadelphia became the premier commercial center of the colonies. This port city stimulated the rapid development of the frontier, which began as early as the seventeenth century as a westward expansion of civilization and continued into the twentieth century with the development of small communities in the western part of the state. During the pioneer development of each area, first trappers and traders, and later farmers and merchants, began to settle the edges of civilization. The more urban, eastern commercial cities were often locked in controversy with the western and more rural areas, which viewed their goals as incompatible with the metropolitan areas. These differences existed when settlers spilled out of Philadelphia to relocate only a few miles away or to establish small towns and rural areas all over the state.

The push to settle the state came from the southeast as settlers journeyed slowly westward and northward. By 1729 settlers reached the Susquehanna River and spread to the Cumberland and Juniata Valleys. By 1785 the eastern slopes of the Allegheny Mountains were settled in Bedford County. While the mountain barriers temporarily halted westward progress, settlers from New England and Virginia, often soldiers who had fought in the French and Indian and Revolutionary Wars in that area, began to settle the western section of the state including Fayette, Greene, Washington and Westmoreland Counties.

Pennsylvania's leadership in a commercial and educational sense made it a natural place for the breeding of revolutionary fervor against English colonial rule and a battleground between local American patriots and English soldiers during the War of Independence. The two most significant American documents, the Constitution and the Declaration of Independence, were written in Pennsylvania. Philadelphia served as the national capital from 1790 to 1800. Pennsylvania's position as a centerpiece of the colonies made the capital a focal point of education, art, religious organization, architecture, journalism, law and science.

Turnpikes, canals and railroads helped Pennsylvania's commercial development in the nineteenth century. The expanded transportation systems and use of anthracite coal by 1840 led to improvements in Pennsylvania's iron-making industry which had flourished in the state since the 1750s. In 1859 the nation's first commercially successful oil well was drilled near Titusville. By 1860 Philadelphia and Pittsburgh were established as major manufacturing cities. Pittsburgh was known as the *Gateway to the West.*

Pennsylvania became a center for protest against the inequities of slavery through the abolitionist movement which eventually led to the Civil War. During the War Pennsylvania once again became a significant battlefield in 1863, when the bloody battle at Gettysburg broke the strength of the Confederacy.

Industrial development, stimulated by the Civil War, expanded and a new industrial, urban society emerged, buttressed by increasing immigration of European laborers and the migration of American farmers to the cities. But this rapid growth brought serious labor problems which led to the formation of worker unions and destructive railroad strikes in 1877. Pennsylvania became a leading producer of oil and aluminum and, by the 1900s, was producing most of the coal and sixty per cent of the steel in the United States. This industrial system, and the state's natural resource of coal, made Pennsylvania an important commercial center during World Wars I and II. Pittsburgh, Philadelphia, Allentown-Bethlehem, Reading, Scranton-Wilkes Barre, and Erie all became major industrial areas stimulated by developing technology and consumer demands.

Much of this industrial system has been weakened in recent years with changes in the demand for coal and competition from other products and other countries in the production of steel. The state and its workers have been struggling to overcome this economic dislocation. However, new types of jobs have evolved in certain parts of the state making Pennsylvania a leader of new technological developments in the production of nuclear power, electricity, chemicals, and electric and electronic equipment. The state is a leading food processor, and its farmlands continue to be some of the richest producers in the world.

Women were an important part of the development of the colony and state of Pennsylvania. The Quaker religion fostered a positive attitude toward women which gave them authority in religious and worldly spheres unlike any other group in the early colonies. The openness of the society led to a wide ranging mixture of cultures with varying attitudes toward women, but the coexistence of many ethnic and religious groups in close proximity led to a cross-fertilization which tended to expand rather than to limit the potential for women's achievement in each group.

Up until the twentieth century, some of the small towns in the state still maintained pioneer status. There were significant differences in the politics and social situations which impacted women's lives. A prominent example of this was played out during the struggle for the state's suffrage amendment. The eastern part of the state had a much more flamboyant and political approach to this issue than the western, central and northern areas. And at the federal level, Pennsylvania, as a whole, was a much more conservative state. Because of its years of existence, the deeply ingrained traditions and social structures excluded women from participating in professions and organizations that would have been available in the younger, less organized areas of the country.

The vastness and great variety in the state underlie the difficulty of generalizing about women's experiences. A woman's ethnic group, social background, geographic region, economic circumstances and religious traditions dramatically influenced her opportunities and achievements. However, women throughout the state shared much in common in their life cycles, family responsibilities, participation in the work force, involvement in organized activities and general approach to life. By examining the lives of women in Pennsylvania over a period of time, these differences are highlighted, while, at the same time, the threads of similarity running through the lives of all the women are clearly revealed.

PENNSYLVANIA WOMEN IN HISTORY

In the early history of the American colonies, a pre-industrial society existed which required the full efforts of each person, whether man or woman, in order to survive. In early Pennsylvania, women held significant roles as merchants, doctors, apothecaries, midwives, farmers and educators. Women ran mills, farms, taverns, schools and printing establishments.

The earliest settlers throughout the state were fur trappers and traders, and women were included in these numbers. Elizabeth Kinsey, a Swede, was one of the first settlers in Philadelphia. She fought so well for her right to some pelts that she began to represent other trappers in local disputes. *Mary Ferree and *Ann Letort were French Huguenot landholders and traders in Lancaster County during the eighteenth century. *Jane Frazier set up a tavern in Bedford County outside Fort Bedford. *Zelie Passavant, the wife of an early nineteenth century merchant, had a significant influence on the western frontier of the state, promoting culture and religion in the area near Butler.

Hostilities between frontier settlers and Indians were inevitable, and *Massa Harbison and *Margaret Wotring are significant in the bravery they displayed when they were captured by the Indians. *Susanna Wright took the unpopular position of defending the rights of the Indians at the time of the massacre of the Conestoga Indians in Lancaster County. *Queen Alliquippa, a Seneca tribal leader, showed that same type of courage in siding with the English against the French in the period prior to the French and Indian War on the western edge of the state.

Women's influence was also significant in fields most difficult to document: that is, their work in the home or as volunteers. The services women provided, caring for the young, the elderly and other employed family members, raising and perserving food, cooking, cleaning, and producing clothing and household items, were vital economic functions officially unrecorded and, formally, not acknowledged. It was not until women began to leave these pursuits to participate in the paid work force that the importance of such efforts was recognized. Women also played a more subtle, but significant, set of roles in the home by maintaining group identity, religious traditions and ethnic customs, such as food, language and moral codes. They provided these for their own and extended families and for fellow countrymen, who often lived with families as boarders, or who bought other services like meals and tutorial help from them.

Women acquired their work skills in early Pennsylvania in much the same way as men: that is, through apprenticeships. However, for women these were frequently informally directed by members of their own families such as fathers, husbands or brothers. *Hannah Penn learned in her father's home the administrative and financial skills she would later use in directing her husband's land grant for fourteen years after he was incapacitated. Later women, like *Ann Wood Henry, *Betsy Ross and *Sarah Finney, when widowed, would also take over their husbands' work, having learned the requirements of the position by working together with them.

The Revolution provided additional opportunities for women to assume new responsibilities since the men of the communities were drawn away by military and diplomatic interests. Women were allowed,

*This indicates the name of a woman whose biography appears in this volume.

if not obliged, to run businesses, organize fund-raising campaigns and even to participate in the fight for independence as soldiers and spies. The colonial women represented in these accounts were brave and rugged women without fear or reservations about their lives. A number of Pennsylvania women served in the military during the Revolutionary War, following their husbands into the battle zones, cooking, nursing the injured, assisting in the battles and often taking the places of the men as they fell. The actions of *Margaret Corbin, *Molly Pitcher and *Sarah Benjamin demonstrated the bravery and determination of these women.

Women were active protestors against the English. Philadelphia homemakers were responsible for tarring and feathering British representatives who carried out unfavorable taxation policies. The women of Philadelphia raised the equivalent of $300,000 to provide shirts to clothe the patriot soldiers. The same spirit of defiance against government interference in citizens' rights was exemplified at a later period by *"Grandy Miller," who reportedly rose from her bed of childbirth labor to lead a tax rebellion.

In post-Revolutionary America, a tightening of regulations and licensing procedures, in many instances, forced women of power out of their positions. Mary Katharine Goddard, the courageous Philadelphia printer who had published the first signed version of the Declaration of Independence, was forced to resign as a Maryland postmistress when the position became more formal and lucrative. *Elizabeth "Mammy" Bell Morgan, twice widowed, set up an inn and store at a crossroads in Easton and became a resource for surrounding counties in law and medicine. She developed her expertise through self-study of law and medical books. People came from great distances for her to settle their disputes, but the legal profession was displeased at the competition and allegedly attempted to force her out of practice.

Although some forms of higher education were denied women until the twentieth century, a tradition of education for women was a strongly held belief among Quaker families. The Young Ladies Academy was founded in Philadelphia in 1789 to "implement fresh ideas" about women's education and had, by the end of two years, an enrollment of over one hundred pupils. A woman's education was deemed significant, not so much for the personal benefit she would derive as for the impact she could have on her sons. In a republic undergoing transition, women were believed to represent stability and had to be educated. Women's academies, often established by female school mistresses, were an important part of the lives of many accomplished women in the nineteenth century. Young women, including suffrage leader Susan B. Anthony who attended a Quaker school, came to Philadelphia to obtain an education.

In 1833 Oberlin College in the neighboring state of Ohio became the first institution of higher education in the United States to admit women. Three years later the first all women's college, Mount Holyoke, was founded in Massachusetts. Beaver College in Jenkintown, Pennsylvania, was founded in 1853 and was joined by a number of sister colleges following the Civil War. The most notable of these early women's colleges in Pennsylvania were Wilson College, founded in 1869 through the estate of *Sarah Wilson; Chatham College, also in 1869; and Bryn Mawr, in 1880.

The first employees of early industrialization were women. The tasks that women traditionally performed at home, like spinning, weaving and sewing, were transformed first into a "putting out" system. The women organized themselves as a work group in which each would specialize in a particular part of the process. This system evolved into small workshops and, later, into mills. However, during the nineteenth century, as the work became more dangerous and complicated, the workplace became an unsafe environment. Class, ethnic and racial distinctions were intensified and it became unacceptable for middle-class women to engage in work outside the homes. Work for women came to be seen as something to hide rather than to encourage. The "cult of womanhood" was explained and emphasized in publications like *Godey's Lady's Book* published by *Sarah Josepha Hale in Philadelphia. She made her career in journalism by telling women that their only career lay in the home. This emphasis on woman's role as being a "lady," sweet and seclusive, tending the home fires and children, changed the image of middle class women's stature as workers for a long time.

Industrialization and the subsequent attitude toward work freed middle-class women to become more involved in the tasks of community development. With increased leisure time, women could work at the tedious and time-consuming tasks of providing services for the less fortunate, developing educational opportunities, organizing religious services, protesting for moral causes, and establishing cultural and artistic organizations. By the latter part of the nineteenth century, this was a well-established pattern for middle-class women and would continue to be a dominant theme in women's lives well into the twentieth century.

Despite the fact that work was viewed as an unbecoming experience by women in the nineteenth century, this should not hide the fact that middle-class women did work inside and, sometimes, outside the home. Economic reversals, an unbalanced sex ratio, widowhood or desertion and a conscious choice to be single made it important that women have opportunities to work to support themselves. Teaching, nursing, social service and, eventually, positions in the expanding federal bureaucracy were natural extensions of women's volunteer work and, thus, were some of the acceptable fields for these women. However, these factors and increasing access to higher education led women to enter other areas as well.

The field of medicine provides one of the best documented examples of the barriers women faced in moving in new directions. In colonial Pennsylvania women were the primary health care providers. Their knowledge of anatomy, gained from butchering livestock for meat, administering herbal cures, and managing childbirth, made them an essential part of the health care of the community. As medical education became more formalized through college and medical school requirements, women were entirely excluded from the process. Medical schools refused admissions even to the most determined and gifted women. However, a group of enlightened Pennsylvania Quaker physicians, influenced by a sister-in-law of one of their members, saw a need to change this attitude. In 1850 they founded the Woman's Medical College of Pennsylvania and provided the first opportunities for women to study and practice medicine. Thus, some of the first women trained to practice medicine in the United States studied in Pennsylvania. *Hannah Longshore, whose persuasiveness brought the school into existence, and *Anne Preston were members of its first graduating class. The school itself and its students encountered harsh prejudice and opposition from doctors, medical students and potential patients. Hannah Longshore's children were taunted because their mother was a physician interested in gynecological and obstetric medicine, a speciality ignored by the male physicians of her day.

Throughout the state women eventually began to participate as physicians. *Esther Marbourg, a young widow, studied medicine at Woman's Medical College after deciding that was the best way to support herself and her child. After graduating, she practiced in Johnstown. *Mary Montgomery Marsh went to Mount Pleasant to practice medicine in 1895. She treated the people scattered in the remote Laurel Mountains. Notes left on her door by loggers would alert her to ailing people in the mountain area and she would respond by going to them in her buggy. Her operating theater was often the dining room table.

The Civil War opened up the field of nursing to women. Pennsylvania became an important source of nurses and a center for nursing education as well. *Kate Scott from Jefferson County was one of the first of many women to answer the call to attend the sick and wounded during the war between the states. *Anne Wittenmyer of Pottstown saved the lives of thousands of Civil War soldiers by organizing diet kitchens on the battlefields. For many women, these auxiliary health fields were the only alternatives available to them to continue their interest in medicine. The struggle of women to enter the profession of medicine paralleled changes that were occurring in each of the professions during the nineteenth and early twentieth centuries.

For years the legal profession in Pennsylvania systematically excluded and discriminated against women who attempted to enter that field. Finally, in 1897, *Isabel Darlington became the first woman to receive the Bachelor of Law Degree from the University of Pennsylvania. Since no woman had been admitted previously to study law, she had encountered strong resistance to her acceptance, but perseverance and ability carried her through. Later, she became the first woman to practice before both the Pennsylvania Superior and Supreme Courts. *Sara Soffel was the first woman to receive a law degree from the University of Pittsburgh. She finished first in her class in 1916. This position traditionally carried with it the offer of a teaching position at the law school and a monetary reward. Sara received only the money. *Anne X. Alpern, also a graduate of the University of Pittsburgh (1928), was assigned only the routine office chores at her first law office, since those were the tasks deemed suitable for women. When she pleaded for a case in court, she was assigned cases the men refused to handle. Her diligence and success were recognized when she was appointed the first woman city solicitor of Pittsburgh.

Teaching was a career many young women pursued in the early years of this country since there were no formal educational requirements for it. If a woman had been a good student and was from a "good family," she could be judged suitable to teach. Even after women gained access to higher education and the requirements to teach became more formal, teaching was still a preferred position for them. A survey of 8,000 women college graduates in the 1880s showed that 5,000 had married and did not work outside the home, while 2,000 of the remaining 3,000 taught.

Pennsylvania women pioneered in education in a number of ways. *Ella Boyce was the first woman school superintendent in the United States, a position still rarely held by women. *Victoria Lyles was an early advocate of racial integration in schools; *Mollie Hare was a dedicated educator of the mentally retarded; and *Helen Beebe became known internationally for her speech and hearing work with the profoundly deaf.

The social pressure against employment for married women was very strong, even after World War I when women increasingly began to combine careers and marriages. Sometimes women were forced to make painful decisions between marriage and a career. Although nearly forty per cent of the women in this volume were not married, the number of women who did successfully combine career and family are significant and reveal a great deal about the versatility and stamina of these women. This is well exemplified in the life of *Margaret Kerr Bell Miller, who held a teaching position at Waynesburg College, taught six hours a day, administered for the college and raised eight children.

During both the World Wars, tremendous demands were placed upon women to enter the labor force both to increase production and to take the place of men who went to war. Industrial areas such as Pittsburgh, and military centers, like Philadelphia, became concentrated areas of employment for women. Women were exhorted through the media of magazines and newspapers and, by the Second World War, through motion picture newsreels and radio broadcasts to enter factories producing war items. After women responded to this high pressure blitz in unprecedented numbers during the War, equally strong pressure was exerted on women after the War to leave the work force and produce large families in order to increase post-war consumption. This did occur, but not without protest, in the 1940s and 1950s. However, large scale social and economic trends, such as expanded education for women, an increased sense of personal rights for women, demographic trends toward smaller families, increasing life expectancies, time-saving domestic items, inflated prices and a need for more educated white collar workers, made women's increased participation in the labor force inevitable.

This background is significant in relationship to the women's lives described in this volume as we examine the work they pursued in their lives. For, despite significant efforts to exclude women from paid work in all occupations and professions, women's tenacity, talent, intelligence and, in some cases, the good fortune of inheritance allowed them to make their mark in a variety of occupations. *Rebecca Lukens took over her father's business and converted the dilapidated Brandywine Slitting Mill to a successful producer of rolled iron plate. The special quality of her product and her keen business sense gave her a market in all major east coast cities as well as Mississippi River ports. *Katharine Beecher transformed her cottage industry of making butter mints into a major candy factory. *Ella Mountz owned and operated coal and oil businesses in Pennsylvania. Other women developed businesses ranging from small post offices and undertaking establishments to a major urban department store.

Women served not only as employees and entrepreneurs but also as labor researchers and organizers. Some of the significant women labor leaders who were associated at some time with Pennsylvania include: Frances Perkins, who became Secretary of Labor under the administration of Franklin D. Roosevelt and, thus, the first woman Cabinet member in the United States; Mary Anderson, the first Director of the Women's Bureau of the Department of Labor; *Frieda Miller, an internationally known authority in labor law administration; and *Dorothea de Schweinitz, an expert on labor-management relations.

In many cases, when women were excluded from paid occupations and the professional world dominated by men, they sought both paid and volunteer work in their own sphere of influence. These interests were generally in areas involving children, the sick, the poor, the elderly, the oppressed, as well as in general community and cultural improvement. This led to the active involvement of women in many religious, social, ethical and political causes through the years.

Volunteerism as a significant American tradition can be traced in the histories in this volume. Religious traditions set the tone for philanthropy of time and money. The Quaker women organized charitable institutions including model hospitals and schools. *Rebecca Gratz, the daughter of a devout Jewish family, established schools and homes for her community's children during the early nineteenth century. Orders of Roman Catholic sisters founded nursing schools, colleges for women, and hospitals throughout the state. *Mother Francis Warde, Mother Superior of the Sisters of Mercy Order in Pittsburgh after 1845, founded hospitals and schools across the country. *Mother Mary Katharine Drexel founded the Sisters of the Most Blessed Sacrament dedicated to providing education and social services for Blacks and American Indians. *Mother Mary Agnes Spencer was the leading force in the establishment of the first hospitals in Meadville and Erie.

Times of crises generated unprecedented volunteer support. Women provided the services which the government could not organize during the Revolutionary and Civil Wars in Pennsylvania by feeding, clothing and housing the soldiers. In later years, *Martha McKeen Welch organized the first overseas United Service Organizations (USO.) to provide services for soldiers. Red Cross workers such as *Gabriella Gilbert prepared medical supplies for the First World War wounded and volunteers like *Marie Tarnapowicz coordinated extremely profitable bond drives in ethnic communities during the Second World War.

The years following 1830 saw the beginning of women's involvement in national and international causes such as the anti-slavery and women's suffrage movements and, later, temperance, labor and social welfare movements. The involvement of women in the abolitionist movement strengthened their leadership and organizational skills. After the Civil War, women began to form organizations which helped them meet their personal needs and those of the women in their communities. In the United States, the Young Women's Christian Association was begun in 1866. In 1874 the Woman's Christian Temperance Union was formed and *Annie Wittenmyer was elected its first president. The American Association of University Women was founded in 1882, the General

Federation of Women's Clubs in 1890 and the National Federation of Business and Professional Women's Clubs, in 1919. These were among the first of many organizations which provided support and solidarity to women and, simultaneously, served as mechanisms to accomplish tasks that formal establishments and over-burdened governments were unable either to identify or to address.

Ethnic groups organized women into fraternal associations beginning in the 1890s. At first these were designed to provide financial assistance to spouses and families in times of death and illness. There were no workmen's compensation and death benefits for the immigrant worker at this time, and these organizations, lead by women, responded to this vital need. These associations also served to solidify ethnic awareness, religious practices and group visibility. The Union of Polish Women in America and the First Catholic Slovak Ladies Association are examples of such organizations. *Elizabeth Lipovsky of Bethlehem joined this latter association in 1914 at the age of six and later was to serve as its president for eleven years.

Working class and middle-class women, in most instances, lived in separate spheres oblivious to each others' causes. However, it was middle-class women who were first to offer recognition and assistance to working class women. Their efforts were frequently awkward and ineffective; however, they attempted to do something to improve the conditions for working women when men, particularly men in organized labor, refused to assist. The two most significant efforts were the National Consumers League, founded in 1899, and the National Women's Trade Union League of America, founded in 1903. Both formed with active chapters in Pennsylvania. The Consumers League attempted to influence producers and retailers to provide fair employment opportunities to women, while the Women's Trade Union League attempted to organize women workers into trade unions. Both organizations began with middle-class leadership and gradually turned over authority to working women leaders.

For most of American history, war was perceived by the overwhelming majority of the American public as a patriotic duty. However, a substantial number of citizens in Pennsylvania were strongly opposed to America's participating in any war. Many of the strongest proponents for this position were women who feared the losses of sons, brothers and husbands or who were simply committed to the position that war is morally wrong. This movement was strong in colonial times because of the Quaker beliefs against wars and continues in groups like the Women's International League for Peace and Freedom. College educated women were an important part of the early twentieth century movements. Leaders from women's colleges like M. Carey Thomas, president of Bryn Mawr, were followed by student protesters from other colleges such as Temple, University of Pennsylvania and West Chester. In the 1930s women in colleges throughout the state formed auxiliaries to an existing organization and called themselves "Future Gold Star Mothers." Such positions were often publicly painful and socially unacceptable, but women were convinced of the moral worth of these causes and had the time and energy to devote to such activities.

A tradition of protest for social reform was demonstrated in other ways. Women workers were involved with the socialist movement in Reading. Others were leaders of radical colonies such as *Gertrud Rapp of the New Harmony Movement. Mother Jones (Mary Harris Jones) was a dynamic labor organizer who helped promote strikes by the garment workers, coal miners and textile workers throughout the state. Tens of thousands of women in the Women's Trade Union League participated in the labor strikes in the garment industry in Philadelphia from 1909 through the 1920s. Throughout the state women struggled to gain acceptance in male-dominated industrial unions, and by the 1930s, they had won incorporation. Bryn Mawr Summer School for Women Workers in Industry was a model training ground for women labor leaders from across the country in the 1920s and 1930s.

Women were excluded from formal participation in the government's political processes both by custom and by law since the early days of the founding of the Commonwealth. The state, however, served as a focal point in attempting to bring about changes in this system. Two important reform movements which involved women, abolition and women's suffrage, had their beginnings in Pennsylvania.

The strong Quaker traditions of the area made it a natural center for the anti-slavery movement in the nineteenth century. The home of Quaker *Hannah Gibbons in Lancaster County sheltered some 1,000 escaped slaves as they passed through the state on the way to freedom. Together with her husband and children she lived in constant danger as a "station" on the "underground railroad" which attempted to aid runaway slaves. After the Civil War, *Martha Schofield went south to help feed, clothe and educate the former slaves. She established a school, meagerly supported by the Freedman's Bureau. After that support was withdrawn, she ran her program with the help of a group of Germantown friends. *Fanny Coppin, herself a Black, provided education for Blacks in Philadelphia after the War.

Women who played a major role in dramatizing and supporting the abolitionist cause soon found themselves involved in women's rights issues. When Quaker women attempted to speak out against slavery, they discovered that they could not do so because women were not permitted to speak in public. The exclusion of New York's Elizabeth Cady Stanton and Pennsylvania's *Lucretia Mott from the World Anti-slavery Conference in London in 1840 signaled the beginning of a campaign for women's rights. The battle for women's suffrage did not end until the passage of the National Women's Suffrage Amendment in 1920, while the struggle for broader rights still continues in the drive for passage of the Equal Rights Amendment. *Lucretia Mott, *Hannah Longshore, *Anna Dickinson, *Ann Dorris Chisolm, Angelina and Sarah Grimke, among others, all worked for women's suffrage. The radicalism of these women offended certain segments of the Quakers and, on occasion, they found themselves rejected from the very tradition that spurred their interest in reform.

The strength of the fight for women's suffrage ebbed and flowed over its eighty-year history. A Pennsylvania high point occurred at Independence Hall on July 4, 1876, on the occasion of the American Centennial, when a dramatic protest was staged in Philadelphia by the National Women's Suffrage Association. The organization requested the opportunity to present a petition of women's rights at the Independence Hall ceremony. As the audience rose to greet the Emperor of Brazil, Susan B. Anthony and four followers went up to the podium and presented a petition to Thomas W. Ferry, president pro tem of the Senate, who presided over the ceremony. The startled senator accepted the petition and the women left expecting to be arrested. Instead, they were allowed to walk out to Independence Square and read the Declaration of Women's Rights. The suffragists then marched to the First Unitarian Church for a five-hour rally.

The history of obtaining suffrage in the state, however, was a much less dramatic, less flamboyant struggle than that day in 1876. Efforts were made by the Pennsylvania Women's Suffrage Association for two successive years to secure an amendment to the state constitution by a majority vote of the legislature. The suffrage movement was linked to the temperance movement, which helped develop rural support but hindered efforts with the "saloon lobby" in the cities. The absence of a state-wide system for effecting any legislative action was recognized. New chapters were established throughout the state, and by 1912 the entire state was organized. Hannah Jane Patterson of Pittsburgh was elected chairman of the state-wide organization. By 1912 the balance of power in the suffrage movement had shifted from Philadelphia to Pittsburgh. The westerners understood the small town groups better and stressed a quieter, less activistic approach, more acceptable in the conservative areas of the state.

Finally, the Pennsylvania House in 1913 and Senate in 1915 approved a suffrage amendment to the state constitution; but fifty-four per cent of the male Pennsylvania voters rejected the amendment. It could not be resubmitted to the voters for five years, so the suffragists quickly turned their attention to the national effort.

On January 10, 1918, the United States House of Representatives voted in favor of the amendment and on June 4, 1919, the Nineteenth Amendment to the Constitution was approved by the Senate and sub-mitted to the states for ratification. Ten days later Pennsylvania became the seventh state to ratify it, and by August 1920 women had won the right to vote.

Three years after the Nineteenth Amendment was ratified, an Equal Rights Amendment (ERA) was introduced in Congress, authored by Alice Paul, a Pennsylvanian by virtue of her doctoral study at the University of Pennsylvania. Reformers were divided in their support of the amendment; some activists saw it as a way of violating the protec-tive legislation that brought about better working conditions for women, while others saw it as the only means of bringing about necessary and permanent reforms in women's status. There was a great deal of organ-ized opposition to the ERA and its passage failed. The federal amend-ment had languished for nearly fifty years when Pennsylvania decided to act, and in 1972 it became the first state to add an equal rights amendment to its constitution. The resulting reform in existing laws and the direction it gave to future laws has made Pennsylvania a national model for implementing such legislation.

Once suffrage was passed, this same energy and organizational skill was translated into women's political activity. The first women to hold political positions in the state were those who had been active in the suffrage movement. *Helen Stone Schluraff was elected as an Erie County Commissioner, the first woman in the state to be elected com-missioner. *Sarah McCune Gallaher was elected to the state legislature during the first term that women were eligible to serve in it. She ran because she felt that most women were too timid to serve in this capacity and she wanted to be an example for them to follow. *Alice Marie Bentley was one of the first three women elected to the state assembly in 1922. She once presided as Speaker of the Pennsylvania State House, becoming the first woman in the United States to have this honor. Women are still pioneering in politics in the state. Gene-vieve Blatt became the first woman elected to a statewide office when she was elected Secretary of Internal Affairs in Pennsylvania in 1954 and the first women elected to a state judicial post in 1973. In 1967 *Jeanette Reibman became the first and only woman elected to a full term in the Pennsylvania Senate, and *Elizabeth Marshall was elected in 1978 as the first woman mayor of York.

By the 1890s social work, which had its roots in the volunteer sphere, developed as an acceptable profession for middle-class women. Pennsylvania women held key positions in the development of social welfare programs. *Adena Rich from Erie served with Jane Addams at the model of all settlement houses, Hull House in Chicago. When Jane Addams died in 1935, Adena became head resident, fulfilling a promise she had given to Jane. Hull House served an average of 1500 people a day. At the turn of the century, social workers serviced many of the communities of Pennsylvania, and settlement houses were located in most major cities to provide education, medical assistance and material aid to the poor, especially recent immigrants to the United States.

Florence Kelley, a social worker from Philadelphia, was a militant opponent of the harsh working conditions for women and children. As the Secretary of the National Consumers League for thirty-four years, she was perhaps the single most influential force in the United States in bringing about changes in the laws to protect women and children.

On the local level as well, women worked tirelessly for social reform causes such as the establishment of the first Children's Aid Society in Pennsylvania by *Jessie Barclay of Bedford County. Other examples include the dedicated life of *Laura "Nan" Rossiter, who took dozens of foster children into her home in Erie and the effort of *Sarah Ann Reed, who founded the Erie Association for Improving the Conditions of the Poor and a Home for the Friendless, which provided needed services for women and children.

Accomplishments in the arts were generally more acceptable for women since they were not clearly linked to monetary reward and were a vehicle of expression for traditional female skills. Women in colonial and early federal Philadelphia set the tone for artistic achievement. They wrote poetry, shared dramatic readings and held salons in their homes where literature and art were discussed, analyzed and created. The first women artists in America were members of artistic families where sons as well as daughters were trained in painting. Anna Claypoole Peale, Margarette Angelina Peale, and Sarah Miriam Peale were the daughters of James Peale and nieces of Charles Willson Peale. Sarah (1800-1885) was probably the first professional woman portrait painter in America.

Two of America's most important artists are women from Pennsylvania. *Mary Cassatt was born in Pittsburgh and lived on Philadelphia's Main Line, although she worked most of her life in Paris. She is most significant as an American artist who was able to combine the techniques of the impressionist style of painting with a more American style and interest in drawing. She is best known for her delicate portrayals of women and children. Because she influenced her family and friends to buy art from her struggling impressionist colleagues, Pennsylvanians were able to acquire many of the works of these important artists. Pennsylvania still remains a world resource for art from that period.

Cecelia Beaux, a member of a prominent Philadelphia family, was faced with discrimination when she wanted to obtain training using live models. However, she persisted and developed as one of the more important painters of the nineteenth century. She became a teacher at the Pennsylvania Academy of Fine Arts and had a significant influence on the training of other American artists.

*Blanche Nevin was a sculptor of national recognition. Her marble work is displayed in the Hall of Fame in Washington, D.C. Other women artists presented more local perspectives, painting their homes and regions in special ways. *Rachel McClelland Sutton did so in Pittsburgh and *Ida Jones, the daughter of a slave, became known as Chester County's "Grandma Moses" with her work on local subjects.

Pennsylvania's women artists have expressed themselves in many ways. *Maya Schock translated her Japanese experience into important paintings such as the Yin Yang series. She established the Doshi Gallery in Harrisburg to exhibit her work and that of other artists. *Ruth Eleanor Newton of Erie was a more practical artist who illustrated children's books, designed special dolls and produced greeting cards.

Women discovered journalism as a means of creative expression as well as public influence. *Anne Newport Royall entered this profession at the age of fifty-four when she failed to inherit her husband's money in 1823. She wrote travelogues that were sold on a subscription basis; however, her political opinions caused her difficulties. She became an editor of a major newspaper and earned the title, "Grandmother of All Muckrackers." *Ida Tarbell, perhaps the most famous "muckracker," was from western Pennsylvania. Her two-volume *History of Standard Oil*, published in 1904, exposed corporate corruption and led to new legislation to prevent some of the abuse.

*Grace Greenwood (Sarah Lippincott) was a journalist noted as an abolitionist and advocate of the Union cause. She was the first woman foreign correspondent, writing articles from Europe for *The New York Times*. *Nellie Bly (Elizabeth Cochrane Seaman) was an early female investigative reporter. She entered her profession with an article advocating women's right to work. She made an international reputation for herself by reporting on her less-than-eighty-days trip around the world.

Women's experiences often formed the bases of their publishing interests. Two Pennsylvania teachers founded and published two significant national educational publications which have influenced generations of American school children. *Caroline Clark Myers published *Highlights for Children* and *Eleanor M. Johnson originated the idea for, and later edited, *My Weekly Reader*. *Margaret Maze Craig, *Ruth Nulton Moore and *Elsie Singmaster wrote children's books.

These biographies are replete with the stories of women writers who provided a broad perspective on life from the provincial to the international. Some of the most well-known women writers were Pennsylvanians: Gertrude Stein, Willa Cather, *Mary Roberts Rinehart, *Pearl S. Buck, *Catherine Drinker Bowen, *Agnes Turnbull and *Jean

Kerr. Others, lesser known, are also significant, such as *H. D. (Hilda Doolittle Aldington), a colleague of Ezra Pound and representative of the Imagist Movement. The writings of *Helen Reimensnyder Martin reflected her interest in socialism and women's rights, two relatively unpopular topics. She disguised these themes in her popular but satirical descriptions of traditional Pennsylvania German society.

The history of Pennsylvanian women in the performing arts began in the latter part of the nineteenth century. *Belle Archer from Easton was one of the best known actresses of the period. She had to overcome both family and societal prejudices against women performers. Later Pennsylvanian stage and motion picture personalities included: *Evelyn Nesbit, known as "The Girl in the Red Velvet Swing;" *Ardelle Ford, for whom Sigmund Romberg composed a song; and *Grace Kelly, an Academy Award winning actress. Women served the performing arts in other disciplines as well. *Marjorie Fink of Bethlehem pioneered in bringing a high standard of ballet into the Lehigh Valley. *Alvina Krause brought her love of theater and talent as an educator and director to the central area of the state. And Philadelphia-born singer *Marian Anderson broke racial barriers for all Black performers and won the heart of the world with a "voice that comes along once in a century."

During the twentieth century, Pennsylvania women made significant contributions in the natural and social sciences. These scientists have included: *Florence Seibert, who isolated the protein in the tubercle bacillus making possible the early detection and eradication of tuberculosis; *Mildred Hicks-Bruun, an industrial chemist who pioneered in petroleum chemistry; *Sister Doloretta Thorn, a national officer of the American Chemical Society; and *Sophie Gordon, who founded a pharmaceutical company. *Margaret Mead, a pioneering anthropologist, was one of the most recognized women in the world. Her studies of primitive tribes contributed not only to the field of anthropology but to our basic understanding of human behavior. *Rachel Carson, a biologist, has also had a worldwide impact with her work in ecology. Through her book, *Silent Spring*, she sensitized the world to the dangers of pesticides and launched the whole era of environmental consciousness.

The biographies in this model collection are a foundation for the major processes of women's history research: identifying women in the past, legitimizing their work, characterizing their exceptional accomplishments, initiating critical examinations of their lives and analyzing them in a comparative perspective. The clearest generalization from this material is that women were making significant accomplishments in Pennsylvania in areas such as the arts, literature, education, journalism, medicine, science and social reform when it was uncommon, if not unpopular to do so. The exclusion of these accomplishments from history was primarily a result of the emphasis on military and political history. Although women were also involved in wars as soldiers, nurses and fund-raisers and in politics in the early years of the nation as initiators of protests, managers of social-political gatherings, and writers and publishers of materials which shaped political opinions, it is seldom acknowledged. A close analysis of the intricate operations of society by looking specifically at the women in the fabric of its history creates an intriguing story of determination, courage and conviction.

Stereotypes of women as passive creatures, lacking in initiative and drive, fade as one reviews these accounts. A small proportion of women periodically in American history might have valued docility and passivity, but women's work of providing goods and services was conducted both inside and outside the home. Women's family and kin networks extended beyond their individual homes into a wider community of relatives and neighbors. Paid and unpaid labor were sometimes blurred and combined as women worked along side men to build a better society. Women's lives in a rapidly evolving state often spanned several areas of accomplishments, both of a volunteer and a career nature, along with a wide variety of family roles and responsibilities.

This research, painstakingly compiled "from the bottom up," suggests the existing wealth of primary resources (letters, diaries, wills, census data, oral history interviews) and published secondary sources available to reveal our hidden heritage. The identification of themes and approaches provides topics to guide further exploration of women's history. This material suggests the need for more systematic comparisons and contrasts of women's lives from rural and urban-suburban areas, east and west, mountainous and plains regions. In the same way, other occupational groupings such as the factory workers and farmers, homemakers and office workers need to be researched. Increased historical understanding of issues such as family life, child care, work, poverty, aging, organizational analysis and cultural accomplishments will help clarify the perspective on the lives of women, as well as men, today. This understanding provides the essential background against which ways to address the future may be realistically conceptualized.

PART TWO
BIOGRAPHIES

1
WOMEN
AT THE
FRONTIER

1

Queen Alliquippa

16?–1754 ————————————————————————————

Queen Alliquippa was one of several influential Indian women who were prominent in the early history of Pennsylvania. She is remembered today in the place names at sites where she lived: Alliquippa Borough near Legstown, an Indian village and trading post; Alliquippa's Rocks below McKeesport; and Queen Alliquippa's Cornfield on the Youghiogheny River in North Huntington Township. It is more important that she be remembered for her part in the political and military struggle that determined that England and not France would rule America. Her history parallels the demise of the Indians and the conquest of the continent by Europeans.

For most of her life, Queen Alliquippa was the leader of some thirty families, a tribe of Seneca Indians who were dependents of the Iroquois Nation. It was not unusual for women to assume leadership among the Indians. Scaroyady, the Half King, said in 1756, "Women have great influence on our young warriors. It is no new thing to take women into our councils, particularly among the Senecas."

The first written record of Alliquippa is from the Quaker Thomas Chalkey, who visited a tribe of Conestoga (Seneca) Indians living in Chester County ruled by Queen Alliquippa and reported that ". . . the tribe gave much heed to what she wished." As Quaker settlements spread westward in the 1730s on lands sold to them by the Iroquois, the dependent Seneca tribes moved ahead of the settlements, crossing the Allegheny Mountains to western Pennsylvania. Alliquippa made contact with the representatives of France, Pennsylvania and Virginia, and, in the journals and letters that have survived, she is mentioned as living variously along the Ohio, Allegheny, Monongahela and Youghiogheny Rivers. Conrad Weiser, Pennsylvania's ambassador to the Indians, found her at the Forks of the Ohio (Pittsburgh) in 1748, a "Seneca woman who reigned with great authority."

The next year, Celoron de Brenville, acting for the French governor of Canada, traveled down the Allegheny and Ohio Rivers to warn the Indians not to trade with the English. He reported that "Iroquois inhabit the place and an old woman of that nation is their leader. She looks upon herself as a queen and is entirely devoted to the English." As a result of de Brenville's trip, the French established a line of forts from Niagara to Pittsburgh.

Alarmed at the French intrusion in 1753, Governor Robert Dinwiddy of Virginia sent a young surveyor to deliver a message to the French to leave the area. That young man was George Washington, at twenty-one years of age, making his first visit to the country that would figure significantly in his later career. On this trip he met Queen Alliquippa and recorded the December meeting in his journal. "I went up about three miles to the mouth of the Youghiogheny to visit Queen Alliquippa, who had expressed great concern that we passed her in going to the fort. I made her a present of a watchcoat and a bottle of rum, which the latter was thought much the better present of the two."

In April Washington returned with two hundred soldiers to try to drive the French from the Ohio region. He called the Indians of the vicinity to a conference, seeking their support. The French prevailed, however, and on July 4, Washington was forced to surrender Fort Necessity at Great Meadows. The English with their Indian allies retreated to Augswich in Huntington County. Generals Braddock and Washington returned the next year to be defeated decisively on the Monongehela River above Pittsburgh. Thus began the French and Indian War.

This eventful year of 1754 was Queen Alliquippa's last. Washington reported in a letter to Dinwiddy that "Queen Alliquippa desired that her son . . . might be taken into council . . . and that he should have an English name given him. I then called the Indians together by the advice of the Half King, presented one of the medals, and desired him to wear it in remembrance of the King of England, and called him by the name of Colonel Fairfax . . . This gave him great pleasure."

After Fort Necessity fell, some of the Indians joined the French, and others stayed in western Pennsylvania as neutrals. Queen Alliquippa and her Senecas fled to George Crogan's plantation at Augswich where she died before the year ended. Crogan reported, "Alequeapy, ye old quine is dead."

Aliquippa Branch
Researcher/Writer: JoAnne Walker

2

Mary Warenbauer Ferree

1653? – 1716 _____

Mary Ferree and her Huguenot family were the kind of people that William Penn was seeking to help when he founded Pennsylvania as a haven for the oppressed. He was especially interested in those who had suffered religious persecution and insisted that absolute religious freedom, as well as civil and political rights, be granted to settlers in his province. Penn and his agents traveled widely in Europe to advertise his colony and his beliefs, hopes and ideals.

Word of Penn's message undoubtedly reached French Protestants who, in the latter part of the seventeenth century, were fleeing their native land to avoid tyranny and persecution. The Edict of Nantes (1598), a document guaranteeing the religious freedom and civil rights of French Protestants, was revoked in 1685, thereby formalizing the practice of anti-protestantism begun in the 1670s. Among the Huguenots who emigrated to Germany in 1685 were Mary Ferree, her husband, Daniel, and their children. She was widowed in 1686, the same year the family moved to the Rhenish Palatinate town of Steinweiler.

Although she lived in Germany twenty-one years, Mary dreamed of beginning a new and better life in America. In 1708 the family obtained passports to emigrate from Steinweiler, via Holland and England, to Pennsylvania. Mary and her unmarried children arrived in England in 1709. (Her married children and their families had already emigrated to a French colony in Esopus, New York.)

In London "armed with a spirit of resolution superior to her sex," she set out to meet William Penn. She received from him a promise to recommend her to his agents in Pennsylvania and also to introduce her to Queen Anne. The Queen, too, was most favorably impressed by Mary. "She arranged for her to go to America with the privileges of British citizenship and ordered plans made for the transportation of the Ferree family on an English ship."

After waiting many months for a vessel sailing to New York, the Ferree family finally reached America. They joined the French colony in Esopus, but moved to Pennsylvania in 1712, settling near the Pequea Creek, not far from Paradise. Here her son and son-in-law took title to

2,000 acres of land for her, the custom of the time frowning upon female ownership of land rights.

As other Huguenots arrived in Paradise, they took up land within the Ferree grant. Tradition claims that Mary Ferree was an excellent leader who "ruled" over her community with grace, fairness and uncommon wisdom during her four years in Pennsylvania. Her relationship with the local Indians was most friendly, the chief of the Pequea Indians was very impressed with the "paleface squaw." Before long she was looked upon as the advisor, legal counselor, doctor and pastoral leader by the community on the Pequea.

Lancaster Branch
Researcher: Frances Keller
Writer: Gladys Baldwin

3

Susanna Wright

1697 – 1784 _____

Susanna Wright was a woman of considerable intellectual and practical attainments. She assisted her father and other community leaders and, after her father's death, became virtual "ruler" of the settlement of Wright's Ferry (re-named Columbia).

Her Quaker father, John Wright, is credited with naming Lancaster County after his home county in England. He brought his family to Penn's territory in the early years of the eighteenth century. Susanna, who completed her education in England, joined her family on the frontier in Hempfield Township in 1722. At that time the area was inhabited only by Indians, with whom Penn had negotiated for land rights at an earlier time.

Having had the advantage of an education, she willingly used it for the benefit of the community in legal, medical and social concerns. She was certainly the most celebrated woman of her day in Lancaster County.

The Wright home was a center for hospitality, and many of the neighbors depended upon Susanna for legal and medical assistance and advice. As the community grew, she became more and more respected as a leader in her own right.

She was also a champion of the local Indians. At the time of a shameful massacre of the Conestoga Indians by the "Paxton Boys" (1763), she took the unpopular position of defending the rights of the Indians.

She was well-educated and well-read, and was familiar with French, Latin and Italian. Her poetry, some of which was published in magazines of the time, showed "piety united with constant introspection." She also was widely known for her interest in silkworm culture. Her skill in this area won her a prize from King George III.

Susanna, who chose never to marry, met and corresponded with distinguished scientists, philosophers and politicians of her day, including John Dickinson, Dr. Benjamin Rush and Benjamin Franklin. Many of the letters from her extensive correspondence with Franklin still exist.

Lancaster Branch
Researchers: Frances Keller
and Betty Duncan
Writer: Sally Wiker

4

Jane Ball Frazier

1735?–1815?

Jane Ball married Edward McClain when she was eighteen. McClain was an English officer stationed in Will's Creek, Maryland. There Jane thrived on the pioneer life, but her husband died shortly thereafter.

Jane met John Frazier, a frontiersman, trader and gunsmith and found that his pioneer spirit matched her own. A short time after their marriage as she and her servant, Bradley, were enroute to Evitts Creek where John was building a trading post, they were attacked by Miami Indians. Bradley was killed, and Jane was captured and taken to Ohio. She was named Red Morning, adopted by the chief, and forced to marry an Indian brave, Pesquitomen.

After thirteen months of capitivity, she and two male captives managed to escape while the braves were on a hunting trip. The three suffered many hardships and hunger on the long journey home. They managed to kill a rabbit which the men ate before it was properly cooked, and, as a result, both men died. Luckily, Jane had refused to eat her share. She finished the rest of the trip back to Will's Creek alone. There she discovered that, thinking her dead, John had remarried.

John and Jane were reunited and moved to Fort Bedford, where the third of her ten children, a son, was born. He is said to have been the first white child born in Bedford County. Jane set up a tavern called Frazier's Inn just outside of the fort. The tavern still stands on the corner of Pitt and North Richard Street in Bedford. Jane managed the tavern while John carried out his duties as justice of the peace and judge of several courts. He died in 1773.

In 1775 Jane married Richard Delapt, but was widowed for the third time in 1781 when her son Benjamin Frazier and Delapt were killed and scalped by Indians in a raid near Frankstown.

Bedford County Branch
Researcher/Writer: Mary Sue Whisker

5

Massa White Harbison

1770 – 1837

In the late 1700s when the frontier was still in western Pennsylvania, attacks by Indians were common occurrences. Many a white settler lost his life, but the stories of those who dared to escape their captors, like Massa Harbison, show the courage, determination and resourcefulness of those who moved west with the frontier.

Massa White was born in Amwell Township, Somerset County, New Jersey, on March 18, 1770. Her father was a Revolutionary War soldier who, in 1773, settled in Brownsville, Fayette County, Pennsylvania. There, in 1787, Massa married John Harbison, who was a scout on the Allegheny frontier.

Early on the morning of May 22, 1792, while her husband was on duty, a party of Seneca and Munsee Indians entered Massa's house. She and her three sons, ages five, three and one, were dragged from their beds. Some Indians plundered the house, while others attacked the nearby Reed's Blockhouse.

When Massa refused to leave, she was flogged. Her middle son, crying, was grabbed by his feet, his head dashed against the doorstep, stabbed and scalped. The Indians forced the other Harbisons to go with them, Massa clutching the baby in her arms. As the Indians tied up their booty, she counted thirty Indians and two white men painted as Indians. They crossed by canoe to Todd's Island in the Allegheny River across from Freeport. When Massa's oldest son complained of a slight injury incurred when he tumbled off a horse and lamented his younger brother's death, an Indian promptly tomahawked and scalped him.

As the journey continued, Massa, weary and afraid, decided to force the Indians to kill her. Three times she threw away the powder horn she was ordered to carry, expecting the tomahawk to fall, but an Indian who had claimed her for his squaw protected her.

Heading toward the Connoquenessing Creek, they reached the Indian camp, near where Butler now stands. Massa spent two nights in the camp. There was no fire and her only food was a small piece of venison which she fed to her child. After sunrise on the third day, May 25, she stuffed a cloth into the child's mouth to stifle his cries and escaped with him while her guard slept. Guided by birds, she headed toward

Connoquenessing Creek, but chose a direction away from her home to mislead her captors.

On May 27 Massa reached the Allegheny River near her home. A neighbor, who did not recognize her at first because of her haggard appearance, crossed to pick her up in a canoe. With her baby still in her arms, she received a joyous welcome at the settlement on the other side. On May 28 Massa Harbison was taken to Pittsburgh, where she made an affidavit recounting her experiences. A scout went to Todd's Island to bury her murdered son.

Massa bore thirteen children altogether, then was abandoned by her husband when she refused to accompany him on a move farther west. They were divorced in 1820; the property was granted to her eldest son and Massa was given a stipend of $30 per year. Her last years were spent living in the homes of her children. She died in 1837 and is buried at Freeport.

Butler and Fox Chapel Area Branches
Researcher/Writer: Ruth B. Jones
Researchers: Evelyn Conti and Ruth Weir
Writer: Patricia Demase
Special Division Editor: Mary Ann Stangil

6

Fredericka Wilhelmina Basse Passavant

1786–1871 _____

A touch of elegance is what Fredericka Wilhelmina Basse Passavant brought to the former wilderness area which is now named for her—Zelienople, Pennsylvania. Born in 1786 and known as Zelie, she lived in Paris with her family for ten years where she had excellent teachers and numbered among her friends the governess to King Louis XVI. Her family moved in literary circles and had many authors as friends.

Zelie left that life of culture to travel from Amsterdam to Philadelphia. From Philadelphia, she traveled to Pittsburgh by Conestoga wagon—a five-week trip—where she took up residence in her father's castle, Bassenheim, overlooking the Connoquenessing Creek.

Zelie returned to Germany and married Philipp Louis Passavant in Frankfurt, in 1807. Highly respected, he became the first merchant in Zelienople, providing goods for the early settlers. Zelie bore seven children; the first two, who were girls, died in infancy.

Education was important to Zelie and she taught her children to read, write and to speak three languages. She also believed a prime requisite in education was beautiful handwriting.

Deeply religious, Zelie taught Sunday School and was instrumental in getting materials for the Sunday School. When her daughter Emma was in Pittsburgh, Zelie sent her lists of periodicals and tracts to buy, with instructions to leave the tracts on the mantels at the stage coach stops.

Her son, William A. Passavant, D. D. (1821–1894), was one of the outstanding Lutheran religious leaders in America according to Dr. Robert J. Marshall, former president of the Lutheran Church in America. William would occasionally preach "off the cuff," upsetting his mother who said, "God's word demands more thought and should be written." She considered it a sin for people to lavish goods on themselves rather than on people in need. When William visited the penitentiary, Zelie sent books to start a library for the prisoners. She also sent potatoes and other garden produce to the Pittsburgh Infirmary, the forerunner of today's Passavant Hospital.

Zelie was very thrifty. Old clothing which was beyond mending was saved for carpeting. When her son Sydney was at school, he bought books of which they had copies at home. His mother scolded him, saying, "You do not spend money for things you have at home." However, Zelie was fashion conscious and had booklets of the latest Paris styles sent to her from which she could get ideas for her own clothes. Pages from these booklets are on exhibit at the Passavant House.

Zelie died on December 29, 1871, at the age of 85. Her home, the Passavant House in Zelienople, has been restored and is listed in the National Registry of Historic Places in the United States. The Zelienople Historical Society maintains its headquarters there.

Butler Branch
Researcher: Gertrude Ziegler
Writer: Jane M. Davis

2

WOMEN IN GOVERNMENT AND POLITICS

7

Hannah Callowhill Penn

1671–1726 ─────────────────────────────────

Hannah Callowhill Penn, the second wife of William Penn, provided the leadership necessary for the early development of the Colony of Pennsylvania. Her excellent diplomatic and business skills were revealed throughout her husband's life and especially during his trip abroad. After his illness and death, for fourteen years she was the absolute proprietor of a crown grant which stretched west of the Delaware River between New York and Maryland.

Born in Bristol, England, the sixth child of nine, Hannah was familiar with her father's business in overseas trade. Watching her Quaker parents, Thomas Callowhill and Hannah Hollister, she learned how to market, gauge the value of money and keep accounts.

At twenty-four years of age, Hannah's good business sense was viewed by fifty-four-year-old widower, William Penn, as one of the many qualities necessary in a woman to accompany him to America and to be a stepmother to his three youngsters. Letitia, Penn's daughter, recalled a change in her father when he came home from a Quaker meeting. He had met Hannah Callowhill. They were married and set out with his children on a three-month trip to the New World on the "Canterbury." Hannah was pregnant during the journey which was made more difficult by salty food, insufficient water, lice, the threats of pirates and bad weather. They sailed into the Delaware Bay in December 1699.

John, the first son of Hannah and William, was born in Philadelphia, a town of 1,000 houses and 5,000 people, in 1700. In the spring the Penn family moved up the Delaware to Pennsbury Manor in Bucks County. A six-oared boat was used for the twenty-five mile trip to Philadelphia.

The big house was furnished with an oak table in the main hall for meetings, chairs with satin or leather seats in the parlor and walnut panelling on the walls. The women, dressed in white petticoats, ivory or lavender silk dresses and chains of gold around their necks, welcomed the arriving guests who had traveled to the manor by rough roads, the river or through the fields. The lifestyle of the Penns was lavish for the day. Penn was given two thousand pounds by the assembly of the proprietory association but he spent twenty times that amount in the colony. Pennsbury Manor, alone, cost approximately six thousand pounds to build and furnish.

Hannah Penn's responsibility was to maintain the manor by supervising its large staff. She oversaw weaving, growing, harvesting and preserving food, brewing medicine, beer and ale, making marigold wine and mead, as well as taking charge of the servants' conduct and manners. Her role became more social when they moved into the city in winter.

Penn found it necessary, after a short stay, to return to England when the crown attempted to remove his proprietary rights. Hannah Penn, convinced by her stepdaughter, Letitia, that life in the wilderness was one of self-denial and hardship, persuaded her husband to take the family back to England for a year. The Penns moved in with the Callowhills.

Hannah, who during the time bore eight children, realized her husband was a dreamer and an idealist. She wrote "slowing him down, was like trying to hold on to a tail of a whirlwind." She knew by this time that he was a poor family financier, for she had lost her inheritance after loaning him the money, and that he was also a poor judge of men. She felt that her role was to protect him from his friends' criticism and the slanderous backbiting of his enemies.

When a stroke in 1712 left Penn unable to speak, Hannah assumed the role of proprietor of Penn's Woods until her death fourteen years later. James Logan and she worked together to protect her husband's lands and discouraged the movement of the Maryland boundary ten miles north to Philadelphia.

Hannah Penn's budgetary administration of the colony, her ability to deal with the early political problems encountered and her effective management of the diplomatic and political operations of the colony made her a valuable contributor to the early growth of Pennsylvania.

Levittown-Lower Bucks County Branch
Researcher: Ann Clements
Writer: Audrey B. Pappenberger

8

Ann Wood Henry

1732 – 1799 _____

In an age when women had few financial and legal rights, Ann Wood Henry served as Treasurer for Lancaster County. She probably had no inkling that she would someday fill such an important government position, but circumstances, patriotic duty and her proven abilities brought her into the formal service of the county.

Ann Wood was born in Burlington, New Jersey, and moved with her family to Lancaster. In 1775 she married William Henry, a prominent Lancaster citizen, who had originally come to the town to learn a trade as a gunsmith. Henry was active in local and state affairs, serving as Justice of the Peace, and taking part in the Braddock and Forbes expeditions. In 1778 he became Assistant Commissary for the Continental Army and was a member of Congress from 1784 to 1786. In addition, he was armorer-general for Pennsylvania, New Jersey and Delaware.

Fully in sympathy with her husband's patriotic work, Ann was a typical revolutionary wife. Their home was open to many important men of the day. She was hostess to such guests as author Thomas Paine, artist Benjamin West and the acting State Treasurer, David Rittenhouse. The Henrys' sense of patriotic duty was instilled in their family as well; a son was a volunteer in a Lancaster County regiment and a Judge of the Lancaster Court.

In 1777 William Henry began serving as Treasurer of Lancaster County. When her husband was occupied with other duties, Ann assisted in this work. After his death in 1786, she was appointed to serve the remainder of his term. The Supreme Executive Council of Pennsylvania then appointed her to an additional four-year term in her own right. There have been other cases where a colonial woman assisted her husband during absences and illnesses. It was, however, a testament to her abilities to receive an official appointment as the Treasurer of Lancaster County.

Lancaster Branch
Researchers: Frances Keller and
Betty Duncan
Writer: Mantana Pratt

9

Harriet Lane Johnston

1830 – 1903 ⎯⎯⎯⎯⎯⎯⎯⎯⎯⎯⎯⎯⎯⎯⎯⎯⎯⎯⎯⎯⎯⎯

The responsibility for the official entertaining of guests at the White House normally belongs to the wife of the President of the United States. First Ladies are usually mature women with years of experience in this kind of undertaking since it is a necessary part of their husbands' political careers. Every president, but one, has had a wife to assume most of the hostess duties. When her unmarried uncle, James Buchanan became president in 1857, his twenty-seven-year-old niece, Harriet Lane, took on the duties of the First Lady.

Harriet Rebecca Lane was born May 9, 1830, at Mercersburg, Pennsylvania, the youngest of four children of James Buchanan's sister, Jane, and Elliot T. Lane. When the children were orphaned at an early age— Harriet was just nine—their Uncle James became their guardian. Harriet came to live with him in Lancaster, and Buchanan's housekeeper, Miss Hetty, became her friend and companion.

As a schoolgirl, Harriet was described as "a merry and mischievous girl, never so happy as when ringleader of schoolgirl pranks." She attended some of the best private schools then available, two in Lancaster and one in West Virginia, and graduated with high honors from Georgetown's highly regarded Visitation Convent in Washington, D.C. Her Uncle James supervised her education and wrote to her frequently about her activities, her friends and her progress. He was especially concerned with her manners, deportment and inner character.

From girlhood, Harriet became accustomed to meeting distinguished visitors, both at the Washington, D.C., home of her uncle, who was Secretary of State under President James K. Polk, and at Wheatland, Buchanan's country estate located just west of Lancaster. Harriet was an accomplished and admired young hostess for local friends and foreign visitors alike. She was described as "a blonde with deep violet eyes, golden hair, a vivacious expression and a mouth of peculiar beauty, and withal distinguished for dignity and grace in every movement." Such attributes held her in good stead when, in 1854, she accompanied her uncle on his mission to England as Minister to the Court of St. James. The years in England were a happy time for the young woman, and social activities included dinners with Queen Victoria and dances with Prince Albert.

Returning from England, Buchanan began campaigning for the presidency. Harriet's skill as a hostess was again called upon as a seemingly endless stream of delegations of politicians visited Wheatland. In 1857 Buchanan became the nation's fifteenth president. Harriet's charm, tact and experience made her an exemplary hostess for her uncle during his White House years. Although wealthy and fashionable, she retained a belief in the importance of public service and intellectual pursuit. She initiated in Washington some of the cultural and social standards she had observed in Europe; however, she never forgot her American heritage and foreign guests were always entertained at least once at Mount Vernon.

Two highlights of Harriet's White House experience were the entertaining of the Japanese ambassadors, the first ever to visit this country, and the historic week-long stay of Edward Albert, Prince of Wales. (Harriet received a personal invitation to his coronation as King Edward VII in 1902.) Harriet's popularity in those years was underlined by tributes such as the popular song, "Listen to the Mockingbird," which was dedicated to her, and the naming of the revenue cutter, which was often used for shipboard entertaining, the "Harriet Lane," in her honor by the Secretary of the Treasury.

Aside from her official duties, Harriet was genuinely concerned with social welfare and worked on behalf of the American Indians in an effort to improve their living standards. One of the first influential persons to do so, she was hailed as "the Great Mother of the Indians" and many named their daughters after her.

After Lincoln's inauguration in 1861, Harriet returned to Wheatland with the former president, glad to be free of the cruel criticisms Buchanan had drawn. In 1865 she became engaged to Henry Elliot Johnston, a lawyer and friend of long standing. With her uncle's enthusiastic consent, they married at Wheatland on January 11, 1866, with another uncle, Reverend Edward Buchanan officiating. The couple had two sons, James and Henry, both of whom died in childhood.

Social and cultural efforts filled Harriet's later years. She established a hospital for children's diseases, the first of its kind in this country, as a memorial to her sons. The Harriet Lane Home in Baltimore is now associated with Johns Hopkins Hospital. After the death of her husband and uncle, she sold her home in Baltimore and the Wheatland estate and moved to Washington, D.C., where she worked toward the building of the National Cathedral and planned a school for boys to be trained as choristers, which became a reality as the result of a bequest in her will. The school, St. Albans, is a preparatory school for college-bound students.

A collector and supporter of the arts for many years, she encouraged the idea of a national art gallery. After her death, the Smithsonian Institution accepted her art collection and established the National Gallery of Art. She also bequeathed $100,000 for a monument in memory of her Uncle James, which was unveiled in 1930 in Washington's Meridian Hill Park.

Harriet Lane Johnston died at Narrangansett Pier, Rhode Island, in 1903. She is buried, along with her husband and sons, in Greenmount Cemetery in Baltimore.

Franklin County and Lancaster Branches
Researcher/Writer: Rachel Minick
Researcher: Frances Keller
Writer: Betty Duncan
Special Division Editor: Mary Ann Stangil

10

Mary Scott Lord Dimmick Harrison

1858 – 1948 _____

Mary Scott Lord Dimmick Harrison was the second wife of the twenty-third president, Benjamin Harrison. She was a niece of his first wife, Caroline Lavinia Scott Harrison.

Born in Honesdale, Pennsylvania on April 30, 1858, she was the daughter of Russell F. Lord, a Delaware and Hudson Canal Company engineer. She received her post-high-school education from Elmira College in Elmira, New York.

In 1881 Mary married her first husband, Walter E. Dimmick, a lawyer in Scranton, Pennsylvania. Six months later she was widowed when her husband died of typhoid fever.

When her Aunt Caroline became ill while living in the White House, Mary went to her aid and managed it during the remainder of President Harrison's term in office. Mary Dimmick married Harrison in New York on April 6, 1896. Her marriage to the widowed former president, twenty-five years her senior, caused great comment in the press at the time.

Mary Harrison survived the president as a widow for forty-seven years. In 1914, while visiting Europe with her daughter, Elizabeth, she became stranded in Germany when World War I broke out but later was able to effect a safe return to her home in New York.

During the years following the president's death Mary Harrison was an ardent Republican who regularly attended the National Conventions until she became too infirmed to do so. She died in New York City on January 5, 1948, and was buried in Indianapolis, Indiana.

Hawley-Honesdale Area Branch
Researcher: Mary Todd
Researcher/Writer: Marie Casper

11

Alice Marie Bentley

1859 – 1949 _____

Alice Bentley, one of the first women to be elected to Pennsylvania's General Assembly, is an example of what can be accomplished when a woman begins a third career at the age of sixty-three.

Alice Bentley was born and raised on a farm near Sugar Lake, Pennsylvania. She attended Edinboro State Normal School and the Chautauqua Literary and Scientific School. After graduation, she began a career as an elementary school teacher. She taught in Guys Mills and in Meadville for twenty years. She then began a second career as the area representative for the Mutual Life Insurance Company of New York and held this position for another twenty years.

In 1922 she announced that she was running for the Republican nomination for the Pennsylvania State Assembly and would conduct her own campaign, without party backing. This outgoing, energetic woman gained office in her first bid for election, at a time when women had only recently received the right to vote. Her capabilities led to three consecutive terms as Crawford County's representative, from 1923 to 1928.

In the State Assembly, she took an important part in efforts leading to the construction of a consolidated school in her home district. She also was active in enacting legislation for the construction of the Pymatuning Dam. During her first term she once presided as Speaker of the House, becoming the first woman in the United States to have this honor. In 1925 she became the first woman in Pennsylvania to act as chairman of a committee. She handled her Committee on Education with such efficiency "as to win praise from the entire House of Representatives." While in office, she helped found the National Council of Republican Women.

In 1925 United States Senator George Pepper selected Alice as vice-chairman of his re-election campaign committee, partly because she was known as an independent rather than as a party machine adherent. One newspaper account of her political views stated that she did not believe in political bosses and "wanted more justice for the masses."

In 1929 she retired from public life, enjoying family and friends for the final twenty years of her long and fruitful life. Alice Bentley once said that she believed women would make politics better. She carried out that conviction in her own contributions to political life, where she was recognized as a woman of ability, integrity and commitment.

Meadville Branch
Researcher/Writer: Rebecca Borthwick

12

Photograph courtesy of the *Butler Eagle*, Butler, PA

Emma Guffey Miller

1874–1970 _____

Emma Guffey Miller was the Democratic National Committee member from Pennsylvania from 1932 until her death in 1970. Her thirty-eight-year tenure in this position was the longest in the party's history. She was an influential figure in both state and national politics and made the seconding speeches for the presidential nominations of both Al Smith and Franklin Delano Roosevelt.

Emma's father, John, was a descendant of a Scotsman who settled in Westmoreland County before 1760. John Guffey was a sheriff in this same county, when Emma was born on July 6, 1874.

Emma Guffey's interest in politics began during her years as a student at Bryn Mawr College. She graduated in 1899 with a degree in history and politics. Throughout her political career, her interests included education, women's suffrage, equal rights, social welfare and prohibition repeal.

In 1901 while on a year's visit to Japan, Emma met Carroll Miller, a consulting engineer. They were married in 1902 and had four sons. They traveled extensively, making several visits to Japan and living in many different areas of Pennsylvania, including Pittsburgh. In 1932 Emma's husband was appointed to the Interstate Commerce Commission, where he served three terms until his death in 1949.

At her first Democratic National Convention in 1924, Emma became the first American woman to receive a vote for the presidential nomination. She was a long-time advocate of an Equal Rights Amendment and spoke before the platform committees at the Democratic conventions of 1936 and 1938. In 1940 as a delegate to the Pennsylvania electoral college, she cast her vote for Franklin D. Roosevelt. She was later invited to his inauguration in 1941. As an active member of the National Woman's Party, she served as vice-chairman and as acting chairman in 1956. In 1964 she represented the National Woman's Party and spoke before the platform committee of the Democratic Party. She said, "I am convinced more than ever that women will never take their rightful place in our country or the world until we have an Equal Rights for Women Amendment in our National Constitution." At the age of ninety, she was still proving herself a strong supporter of women's rights and of the Democratic Party.

Her interests included local history, and she wrote an article for a 1927 issue of the *Western Pennsylvania's Historical Magazine*, entitled, "The Romance of the National Pike." She also wrote the Indian history chapter for the *Souvenir History of Slippery Rock's 100th Anniversary.* She served on the board of trustees of Slippery Rock State College from 1933 to 1939 and from 1956 to 1968. In 1960 the college dedicated Miller Auditorium in her honor. For many years she resided on a farm north of Slippery Rock, along Wolf Creek, and, prior to her death, this property was given to the college.

Sometimes known as "The Old Gray Mare," Emma Guffey Miller was an outspoken but cherished character in Pennsylvania politics. Her active involvement in and commitment to the Democratic party and political and social issues continued throughout her long life. In 1969 just months before her death, she received a Certificate of Honor from the Democratic National Committee.

Grove City Branch
Researcher: Jean Willis
Writer: Carol Ann Gregg
Local Editor: Anne Dayton

13

Photograph by Bradford Bachrach, Scranton, PA

Marion Margery Warren Scranton

1884–1960

Marion Margery Scranton had a presence about her that commanded respect and attention. It was probably a natural attribute which was polished by attending Miss Potter's School in Connecticut and by her long-time association with wealth. She was born in 1884 to Everett and Ellen Willard Warren. Her mother was a daughter of an attorney, and her father, a prominent Scranton attorney, enjoyed taking young Margery to political meetings, which may have set the stage for her later interest in politics.

The Warrens resided in the "hill section" which in other towns might be described as the "right side of the tracks." She had a younger brother and sister. As a young woman, she seemed to have a flair for flamboyant clothes which lasted at least until 1912, when an oil painting shows her in a dramatic costume which almost calls attention away from the handsome face and intelligent eyes of a sympathetic and mature woman.

Tall and quite attractive, she must have been a beautiful bride when she married Worthington Scranton in 1907. The young couple lived for years just two and one–half blocks away from the original Scranton estate which had been built by Worthington's grandfather, Joseph Scranton.

Margery and Worth had four children: Marion, born in 1908; Katherine, 1910; Sarah called Sally, 1913; and William II, 1917. Although her children were young, Margery balanced the tasks of mother, wife and society matron with a new role in 1918. She became deeply involved in politics and especially with the women's suffrage movement. Shortly after the suffrage amendment was passed in 1920, she became the first woman to serve on the Lackawanna County Republican Committee. She was also a delegate to the Republican National Convention and continued to attend every convention through 1948.

During World War I, she served three times as chairman of Lackawanna County's Liberty Loan drives selling war bonds and helped establish the Mothers' Assistance Fund. She was an early member of the Business and Professional Women's Club, the Century Club, and the Daughters of the American Revolution (through the Warrens and Williards).

In 1922 Margery held several political positions. She was State Representative Committee Member and was elected treasurer of the Pennsylvania Council of Republican Women, an office she held until 1928 when she was elected its vice–president. In that year she was also elected National Committee Woman from Pennsylvania, an office she held until 1951. From 1936 to 1938 she served as vice-president of the Republican National Convention.

In between her other duties, she also was attending local meetings. It was a common occurrence for her to appear at meetings in private homes, lodge halls and other places from Old Forge and Wilkes-Barre to Carbondale and Honesdale, and tiny places in between. She went wherever she felt she could be of use. Despite her wealth and social position, Margery Scranton was never too important or set apart in her own world to attend meetings in out-of-the-way places, often traveling over rough, muddy roads to get there. It was at this time that her son, William II, was introduced to politics, when he was often recruited to drive her.

Margery always dressed in good taste. She wore beautiful, expensive clothes and was fond of wearing hats. She also liked jewelry, and her children often teased her for wearing too much. People were compelled to look at Margery Scranton; but while their attention was caught, she made the most of it with her charm and her intelligent and eloquent speaking.

In addition to Margery's political involvement, the Scrantons were always interested in and sympathetic to the plight of the poor. One of their lesser known philanthropic actions is a million dollar trust fund set up in 1954 called the Scranton Area Foundation.

Worthington died in 1955 at their winter residence of Hobes Sound in Palm Beach, Florida. Margery died five years later in 1960. Her children donated a pipe organ to St. Luke's Church in Scranton in her memory.

Scranton Branch

Researchers: Brenda Williams and
Georgianna Cherinchak Cole
Writers: Ethel DeVirgilis, Ann Costello and
Judith Evans

14

Helen Stone Schluraff

1884 – 1964 _____

A businesswoman who ran her own floral shop, Helen Schluraff was the first woman in Pennsylvania to be elected a county commissioner, a post she held for three consecutive terms.

Helen's involvement in business was thrust upon her when she and her husband Verne separated in 1915. In order to support their two children, she took over his floral shop in Erie, learning the business on the job. Within a few years, it had become the second largest floral shop in the city and the only one run by a woman.

As a woman in business, Helen saw a need for working women to exchange ideas and concerns. She placed ads in the Erie papers inviting women to meet each weekday at the Young Women's Christian Association for lunch. The noon meetings continued for several years, cancelled only during the influenza epidemic in 1918. By October 1920 the group had organized and was chartered as the Business and Professional Women's Club (BPW) of Erie. Helen Schluraff remained active in this group throughout her career, serving three separate terms as president and holding state offices in the organization as treasurer, vice-president and president. She also served as national vice-president.

Helen's involvement with women's organizations was not limited to the BPW She was an active suffragist and became president of the Erie County chapter of the League of Women Voters when it was formed in 1920, immediately after the ratification of the Nineteenth Amendment. She held leadership positions in the Daughters of the American Revolution and the Daughters of the American Colonists and served two terms as president of the local chapter of Zonta International a year after its organization in 1919.

Politics was an exciting venture for Helen Schluraff. Republican Gale Ross, who was running for mayor of Erie, appointed her chairman of the Women's Division of his campaign. Ross was not expected to win the election, but thanks to Helen and the women, he achieved an upset victory, which he gratefully attributed to their votes.

When the stock market crash of 1929 brought a decline to many businesses, including Helen's floral shop, her friends urged her to run for county commissioner, an office never before held by a woman in

Pennsylvania. The position was regarded as a directing rather than a working one, which would require only part of Helen's time while she struggled to rebuild her business. She was elected to office in 1931, during the worst of the Depression, and soon found herself involved full time in helping the unemployed find work and various forms of assistance.

During her twelve years as a county commissioner, Helen advocated strict economy in an effort to reduce taxes. She was instrumental in getting the Erie County Tuberculosis Hospital built out of current tax funds without a bond issue; it remains the only county building so financed. She worked for a better airport, to have elevators installed in the County Courthouse, and to change the requirements for voter registration. Her humor and honesty combined to earn her the respect of her constituents, whom she worked tirelessly to assist.

Helen was sixty years old when she left office, but politics remained one of her most avid interests. She was known as "Mrs. Republican," serving on the State Council as president of Pennsylvania's Republican Women and as vice-president of both the county and state Republican Committees. Under Governor Pinchot, she was a member of the Board of Public Assistance.

She always believed strongly in the capabilities of women. In October 1946, when the Business and Professional Women celebrated their national recognition week, Helen wrote for the local newspaper:

> Women have proved themselves in every line of business and in all the professions as well. Any year is a suitable year to pay tribute to the women who proved their worth in industry when our country had need of them. From pioneer days to the present time, women have successfully met the situation, whatever the challenge, and they always will.

Helen Schluraff died at eighty years of age. She was praised as an active member of nearly every women's and service organization in the city and county of Erie, having held office or board positions in many. In 1976 Zonta International of Erie presented a portrait of Helen Schluraff to be hung in the Erie County Courthouse. It is the only woman's portrait so displayed in the building.

Erie Branch
Researcher/Writer: Sabrina
Shields Freeman

15

Kathryn O'Hay Granahan

1895 – 1979

Kathryn O'Hay Granahan, the fourth woman to be appointed United States Treasurer, was born in Easton, Pennsylvania, on December 7, 1895, the daughter of James B. and Julia Reilly O'Hay. Kathryn graduated from Easton High School in 1912 and from St. Joseph's College in Philadelphia, where she majored in sociology.

After college, she became politically active within the Democratic party. She was Supervisor of Public Assistance in the Attorney General's Department in the Commonwealth of Pennsylvania and the liaison officer between the Auditor General's Department and the Department of Public Assistance.

On November 20, 1948 she married William Thomas Granahan, who served five terms in Congress as representative for Philadelphia's Second District. When he died in 1956, Kathryn was elected to complete his term and she was also elected to her own term. She was the first Congresswoman to be elected from Philadelphia.

During her five years in Congress, Kathryn O'Hay Granahan was involved in the fight against pornography. She was a staunch advocate for stronger penalties for the distribution of pornographic materials. She was also interested in securing better Social Security benefits for women.

While in Congress, Kathryn served on two committees—the House Government Operations Committee and the Post Office and Civil Service Committee. In 1959 she received an honorary Doctor of Laws degree from St. Joseph's College.

In 1962 Kathryn Granahan lost her congressional seat by realignment. At this time, Representative William Green, Jr., recommended her for the treasury post. In September 1962 President John F. Kennedy appointed Kathryn O'Hay Granahan United States Treasurer. She succeeded Elizabeth Smith Gatov, who resigned from the position to work for the re-election of Governor Edmund G. Brown of California. As treasurer, one of Kathryn's interests included the possibility of printing different denominations of bills in different colors.

Kathryn Granahan received many awards for her charitable as well as for her political works. Pope Pius XII honored her as an outstanding Catholic woman, and the late Cardinal Spellman presented her with a gold cross for her fight against pornography. In 1961 she received the Distinguished Daughter of Pennsylvania award and in 1962 was made an honorary member of Theta Phi Alpha National Catholic fraternity. On April 5, 1963, she was also honored by Easton High School at the fifteenth annual Easton High School Day.

In 1964 she suffered a severe head injury in a fall. The following year she was stricken by a blood clot in the brain while in Atlantic City to address a convention of Pennsylvania and New Jersey bankers. Brain surgery followed, but her memory capacity was reportedly impaired afterwards. She resigned from the Treasury in 1966 and died in July 1979.

Easton Branch
Researcher: Margaret D. Druse
Writer: Suzanne Gallagher

16

Ruth Grigg Horting

b. 1900 ──

From a background of teaching and volunteer work, Ruth Grigg Horting made a career for herself in politics and social administration. Her work not only resulted in several firsts for Pennsylvania women in county and state government but also included appointments on the national level.

The Lancaster native was an elementary school teacher following her graduation from Millersville State Teachers College in 1920. After marriage and the birth of a son, she became heavily involved in volunteer efforts. Extremely active in music, religious organizations and women's clubs, she became president of the Four County Women's Missionary Society (Lancaster, Lebanon, Cumberland and Dauphin Counties) and the third president of the Lancaster Federation of Women's Clubs.

These and other activities brought her to the attention of Pennsylvania Governor Earl who appointed her to the Board of Trustees for the Thaddeus Stevens Industrial School in 1936. The Lancaster County Democratic party then selected her as the first Lancaster woman to be nominated for a state-wide office. She won the race for the House of Representatives and was one of two women serving there in 1936-38.

As a Democrat in Lancaster County's Republican delegation to the Democratic Legislature, she received important committee assignments: The House Committees on Agriculture, Education, Public Welfare and Cities, as well as the Committee on Public Health and Sanitation.

After completing her term of office, she remained very active in Democratic politics, serving as vice-chairman of the Lancaster County Democratic Committee for seventeen years and as vice-chairman of the Pennsylvania State Democratic Committee for fifteen years. During her term on the State Committee, she was a member of the Democratic National Committee's Speakers' Bureau (Women's Division) and traveled with Franklin Roosevelt, Harry Truman, Alben Barkley and Adlai Stevenson on campaign trips. She attended all Democratic National Conventions from 1936–1968 and was on the executive committee of the convention held in Philadelphia in 1938.

Her most significant contribution to Pennsylvania came with her appointment by Governor Leader as Secretary of Public Assistance in

1955. Having helped establish the Department while in the Legislature, it was most unusual then to administer the program. When this Department was combined with the Department of Welfare, she became Commissioner of Public Welfare and then was appointed by Governor Lawrence to be Secretary of Public Welfare in 1959 for a four-year term.

During her term of office, she served as Pennsylvania's chairman of the first White House Conference on Children and Youth. She was on the Governor's Intergovernmental Committee on Migratory Labor, and during her term, Pennsylvania conducted the pilot program for Food Stamps. She was also appointed to the State Civil Defense Council in 1959.

Ruth considers her religious life possibly more satisfying than her political activities. Serving as Sunday School superintendent at the Trinity Lutheran Church of Lancaster for eighteen years, she was the first women elected to the vestry. She was an incorporator of the Lutheran Inner Mission of the Lancaster Conference in 1948, secretary of the Lutheran Service for Older People, and was appointed in 1956 to the Board of Christian Higher Education of the United Lutheran Church of America. From 1956 to 1962 she was a representative of the Lutheran Church of America to the National Lutheran Council. In June 1966 she became the first woman to serve on the fifteen-member Executive Council of the Lutheran Church in America. At the Helsinki meeting of the Lutheran World Federation, she was a discussion leader and the only woman speaker at an evening session.

Named a Distinguished Daughter of Pennsylvania, her biography appeared in the first edition of *Who's Who of American Women* in 1958. She has received numerous awards including an honorary Doctorate of Humane Letters from Gettysburg College and has been named an honorary member of Quota Club, Soroptomist Club and the Pennsylvania State Kappa Gamma. Sponsored by the Lancaster County Federation of Women's Clubs, she was named Pennsylvania Merit Mother of the Year in 1967.

Ruth Horting retired from public office in 1963, but continued to be active on issues which concerned her. She was always in demand as a public speaker and stayed involved in many community endeavors.

Lancaster Branch
Researcher/Writer: Frances K. Keller

17

Grace McCalmont Sloan

b. 1903? ————————————————————

Grace McCalmont Sloan was the second woman to be elected to a state-wide office in Pennsylvania and the first woman to be elected to the offices of State Treasurer and Auditor General.

Although Grace Sloan was born in Dayton, Armstrong County, she graduated from high school in Clarion and spent much of her adult life there. She married John E. Sloan, a former sheriff of Clarion County and United States Marshall for the Western District of Pennsylvania. They had two daughters, Mary Kathryn and Jacqueline.

Before her election to a state office, Grace was active in civic and political affairs. She was co-founder in 1935 of the Clarion County Chapter of the Foundation for Infantile Paralysis and served for years as secretary. She was a member of the Red Cross, the American Cancer Society, the Heart Association and the Clarion Civic Club, and was also affiliated with the Presbyterian Church.

In the political area she was an active member of the Pennsylvania Federation of Democratic Women, becoming a member of its board of directors in 1949 and serving as its president from 1957 to 1961. She was also a member of the Democratic State Committee of Clarion County from 1944 to 1960 and served three terms on its Policy Committee. She was a delegate to all Democratic National Conventions from 1952 through 1976. Grace Sloan was her party's candidate for Congress from the 23rd District in 1956. She also served for many years as co-chairman of the Statewide Democratic Registration Committee. Governor Leader in 1957 and Governor Lawrence in 1965 appointed her to the State Employees' Retirement Board.

Grace Sloan was no novice in politics when she ran for and was elected State Treasurer in 1961. At the end of her term in 1964, she was elected Auditor General of Pennsylvania. Again in 1968 she was elected State Treasurer, an office she held until 1977.

Clarion Branch
Researcher/Writer: Helen Knuth

18

Senator
Jeanette Reibman

b. 1915 _____

State Senator Jeanette Reibman has the distinction of being the first, and *only*, woman ever to be elected to a full term in the Pennsylvania Senate.

In her numerous speeches across the state, she frequently quotes the Biblical description of a good woman and her work activities found in the Book of Proverbs. Jeanette, herself, is a woman whose worth, through her important legislation benefiting all citizens of the Commonwealth, "is far above rubies."

Born in Fort Wayne, Indiana, the daughter of Meir and Pearl (Schwartz) Fichman, she was educated at Hunter College and at Indiana University Law School, one of only two women students there at that time. Following her graduation she spent six months job-hunting in Washington, D. C. where she found herself hampered by two biases: being a woman and not having a degree from an Ivy League college. However, through the assistance of a friend—early "networking"—she was hired by the Director of the Office of Emergency Management who was also a woman lawyer.

After her marriage she moved to Easton, Pennsylvania and with three young sons at home, she was concerned about the local educational system. Through her membership in the American Association of University Women (AAUW) and in the League of Women Voters, she became interested in campaigning for the candidacies of others to the school board. Her husband and law partner, Nathan Reibman, encouraged her to run, not on the local level, but for the State House of Representatives. Elected in 1955, she served there continually, except for one term, until 1966, when she was elected to the State Senate. In the election of 1974 she received more votes than any other candidate for the Pennsylvania Senate.

As chairman of the Senate Education Committee, her most valuable contributions have been in that area. She sponsored the legislation which established and developed area vocational-technical schools; the community college system; the Pennsylvania Higher Education Assistance Agency which provides financial aid to students attending colleges, nursing or trade schools; and special education for gifted and exceptional children. In addition she sponsored legislation regarding health examinations for students and for constitutionally permissible aid to non-public schools for transportation and instructional materials.

Senator Reibman is the vice-chairman of the Labor and Industry Committee and a member of the Judiciary, Local Government, Rules, and Executive Nominations Committees. She has achieved a remarkable ninety-nine per cent attendance and voting record.

Jeanette was active in the successful passage of the State Equal Rights Amendment and was one of the sponsors for the legislation that established Pennsylvania's Human Rights Relations Commission. These achievements clearly reflect her deep egalitarian and humanitarian spirit.

Many honors have been bestowed upon Jeanette. She received honorary Doctor of Laws degrees from Lafayette College (1969), Wilson College (1974) and Cedar Crest College (1977). She was elected a member of the Hunter College Alumnae Hall of Fame in 1974 and was named a Distinguished Daughter of Pennsylvania in 1969. In 1977 the Government of Israel presented to her the "Jerusalem City of Peace Award," and she was given the Myrtle Wreath Award by the Eastern Region of Hadassah in 1979. Numerous other organizations have also honored her.

Jeanette is an intelligent, hard working legislator. Both politically and educationally, she has made a significant impact on Pennsylvania laws and schools. Her areas of legislative reform are diverse and important as shown by her contributions to industrial development, unemployment compensation, mental health, agriculture, consumer protection and anti-discrimination legislation. Pennsylvania is very fortunate to have such an outstanding legislator.

Easton Branch
Researchers/Writers: Ann L. Peaslee and
Margaret D. Druse

19

Elizabeth Nath Marshall

b. 1918 _____

By her own admission, Elizabeth Nath Marshall might have been considered the "least likely person" to become the top administrator and primary spokesman for a city of over 44,000 people. However, in 1978 she became the first woman mayor of York, Pennsylvania.

A native of Chelmsford, Massachusetts, Elizabeth attended business college in her home state during the Depression and married a high school schoolmate. They settled in York in 1948 where they raised their two sons and a daughter. Although she "always tended to avoid controversy," she held a strong interest in politics, at least as an observer. During the 1960s she took an active role in volunteer work within the community, beginning her relatively brief progress toward becoming an elected official.

She served on the Young Women's Christian Association board and the board of the League of Women Voters and became involved in the planning of York's first "Charrette:" a symposium which addressed itself to many of the crucial urban issues of the day including health, law enforcement, community relations, education, housing and employment. The Charrette articulated the problems within the city and proposed solutions via "brainstorming" with local, state and federal government officials as well as private agencies. The programs proposed were to be implemented through city government. Urging from her friends and a desire to see the Charrette programs carried through prompted her to run for city council. In 1972 she became the first woman ever to be elected to that body. Two years later she was elected by her fellow councilmen as council president.

During her years on city council, much of the initial planning for York's urban renewal took place. Officials and citizens were confronted by a city devastated by riots in the 1960s and by widespread flooding and destruction in the downtown area from Hurricane Agnes in 1972. A federal grant was proposed through the local Redevelopment Authority for the Codorus River basin flood control project and for badly needed housing rehabilitation. By 1977 renewal was underway in the inner city and Elizabeth Marshall felt once again the need to be in a position to see her projects through to completion. She ran against two male opponents for the office of mayor and won.

Her administration was characterized by the many changes that took place in the heart of the city. By encouraging cooperative efforts of the public and private sectors, she initiated changes that were not only cosmetic but beneficial to the economic health of the city. Revitalization of the downtown area included a mini-park, the narrowing of a major traffic route (Market Street) through center city to encourage pedestrian shoppers, two additional parking garages and the "back to the city" residential movement. A seven-million-dollar bond issue made possible complete restoration of buildings in the square for residential and commercial uses. An industrial park was also created.

During her four-year term as mayor, Elizabeth Marshall was also an active participant in the United States Conference of Mayors and the National League of Cities. She frequently visited Washington to testify at hearings concerning cuts in federal aid to cities, demonstrating her conviction that unless this country continues to encourage our cities to prosper, it will be a tragic loss to us all.

York Branch
Researcher/Writer: Joan R. Schumacher
Writer: Natalie Baturka

20

Kathryn Fourhman Olewiler

b. 1930

Kathryn "Kitty" Fourhman Olewiler was the first woman coroner in the Commonwealth of Pennsylvania. Originally from Williamsport, she moved to York to attend nursing school at York Hospital. After two years of training, she married and, while her five children were growing up, she took a job with a physician who was also the county coroner. As his "Girl Friday," she handled everything from billing to medication to the paperwork that came through the coroner's office.

In 1971 after the coroner's death, a new coroner, also a physician, was appointed who soon found himself too busy to handle the responsibilities of over 400 cases a year in addition to his personal practice. He appointed Kathryn deputy coroner, and she began to go out on cases as well as handling paperwork duties. The coroner soon resigned from his post, recommending that Kathryn be appointed coroner for the remainder of his term; the county commissioners agreed. In 1973 she ran for the office, defeating a physician, after campaigning on the platform that she could give full-time service as coroner. She was victorious again in 1977, defeating an osteopathic physician and, in her bid for office in 1981, she ran unopposed.

Pennsylvania has no specific training requirements for the position of coroner. However, a coroner must be knowledgeable in anatomy, physiology and ethics, all subjects which Kathryn had studied in nurses' training. When she first took over the coroner's position, she had two major prejudices to overcome: she was not a doctor and she was a woman. "A doctor for a doctor's job" was an argument she had to contend with, but her training as a nurse helped counter that complaint. She was often the only woman at an accident scene with ambulance crews, police and firemen. However, the most difficult part of the job—that of telling the families that a loved one had been killed—was where Kathryn's quality of compassion became valuable. She said, "You're sharing with that family probably the most traumatic thing that's happened to them."

In her years as coroner, Kathryn Olewiler saw many things which were "staggering," many needless deaths which moved her to speak out and go even beyond her official duties as coroner. She urged awareness of legal drug abuse by the elderly and taught driver education students about the horrors of accidents caused by alcohol intoxication. Kathryn felt that her ability to speak up for the things which she considered important came from her upbringing. Her grandfather always said that "if you feel strongly about it, you must learn somehow to have a backbone and stand up for what you believe." In 1981 Kathryn Olewiler was appointed to the Governor's Task Force on Driving Under the Influence of Alcohol and Other Controlled Substances. This task force, composed of legislators, judges and citizens, worked on legislation to make the penalties for driving under the influence of drugs or alcohol more severe and to make the testing for drivers' alcohol levels more easily attainable.

"You're as good as the time you give," is the attitude Kathryn Olewiler carried with her throughout her career as coroner, and it earned her the respect and appreciation of her colleagues and those she served as Pennsylvania's first woman coroner.

York Branch
Researcher/Writer: Joan Schumacher

3
WOMEN IN BUSINESS AND LABOR

21

Ann Letort

16-?–1728 _____

Ann Letort was a Huguenot (French Protestant) who came to America with her husband in 1686. The Edict of Nantes, a document guaranteeing the religious and civil rights of French Protestants, had been revoked the year before. Fleeing the resultant religious persecution, the Letorts went first to London where they met William Penn. Penn granted them acreage on the Schuylkill River upon which to settle with a group of Huguenots. A few families came with the Letorts and settled there. Because of the remoteness, most colonists soon left, but Ann and her children remained while her husband went back to England to arrange passage for more settlers to his colony. While in London he contracted with the West Jersey Company to trade furs for them and to have goods provided by their agents.

There was great competition among entrepreneurs in the lucrative fur trade. The French Letorts were often under suspicion by their English neighbors in Pennsylvania. Sometime before 1704 they moved their trading post to Conestoga, Indiantown, Lancaster County, where they lived in the forest and made friends with the Indians in the region. Ann kept the trading post while her husband was west of the Susquehanna River on long trips.

The Letorts, of strong character and high principles, dealt fairly with the Indians, exchanging useful goods—blankets, pots and hardware—for the furs. It is recorded that, with a horsewhip, Ann drove away from her doorstep other traders who tried to rob the Indians by providing them with rum. She corresponded with the governor of the province when he wanted accounts of the colonists' relations with the Indians. Charges brought by jealous Swedish and English traders against her and her husband were quickly dismissed at a trial in Philadelphia.

The politics of the fur trade combined with the politics of religious differences continued to harass the Letort family as long as they lived. A woman of gentle birth, Ann showed remarkable stamina and endurance in coping with the exile from her birthplace, the long voyage to America, the rigors and real dangers to her life in the wilderness and the loneliness of carrying on during the absences of her husband.

After her husband's death in 1696, she apparently went to Kent County, Delaware, to live for a time, since there is a record of the registration of her cattle there. While her son followed his father's footsteps along the paths to the west, she carried on vigorously for as many as fifteen more years as a trader in Conestoga and lived close to the spot which still bears her name, the little village of Letort.

Lancaster Branch
Researcher/Writer: Mary Krogman

22

Sarah Finney

170?–1743? (1754?) ————————————————————————

A typical, colonial day for Sarah Finney began before dawn when she added more wood to the drafty kitchen fireplace and began kneading the dough for the numerous loaves of bread she would serve to her customers that day.

Sarah and her husband, Joseph, were Reading's earliest settlers, having come from Philadelphia to the vast Berks' wilderness prior to 1733 to clear the land for their early homestead. The house they built became the area's first inn.

Although Reading wasn't officially founded until 1748 by Thomas and Richard Penn, the Finneys developed their land, and Sarah's good cooking and baking attracted weary travelers, including merchants, land surveyors, trappers and even the Penn brothers.

A survey map done by Benjamin Lightfoot in 1732 pinpointed the Finney homestead. The Finney lot was later laid out in the Penns' 1748 plan for the city.

Sketchy accounts note that Joseph was eager to leave Philadelphia and strike out on his own as a pioneer homesteader. Sarah, believed to be of genteel, English upbringing from a respectable Philadelphia family, apparently followed him out of a sense of wifely duty.

In 1734 Joseph died, leaving Sarah to fend for herself and their two young daughters. Why she chose to remain in her home along the Schuylkill River, rather than return to the security of her family's home in Philadelphia, is unknown. However, she decided to dig in her heels and make the Finney farm a landmark for travelers. The area became known as "the Widow Finney's place."

The Penns tried to reclaim the property, but Sarah held out. The land was a choice piece of property, and Sarah apparently had more than one run-in with Thomas Penn and Thomas Lawrence, a Philadelphia businessman who dealt with Penn and owned the land adjacent to the Finney's.

One can speculate that some of Sarah's overnight lodgers may have included George Boone, Daniel's grandfather, who settled in nearby Oley Township in 1718; Conrad Weiser, a land and Indian agent, who settled the Weiser homestead near Womelsdorf; and Mordecai Lincoln, great-great-grandfather of President Lincoln, who built a sturdy, stone house near the Boone property near Baumstown in 1733.

Besides the rugged trappers and crafty merchants, the Widow Finney held her own with the neighboring Lenni Lenapes, a tribe of the Delaware Indians who were, for the most part, friendly to her.

Records show Sarah's two daughters married the sons of Conrad Weiser and of Governor Joseph Hiester. Some records indicate that Sarah, before her death in 1743, passed the deed to her land to daughter, Rebecca. Other accounts, which place Sarah's death in 1754, note that the deed somehow was reclaimed by Thomas Lawrence, the conniving, land-hungry neighbor.

Regardless of the outcome of the land ownership, the Widow Finney held a place of distinction in the early annals of Reading.

Reading Branch
Researcher/Writer: Carole Simpson

23

Betsy Ross (Elizabeth Griscome Ross)

1752–1836 ─────────────────────────────────────

Betsy Ross is best known as the legendary maker of the first United States flag. She was a talented entrepreneur who conducted a successful upholstery business in Philadelphia. Betsy was brought up as a Quaker and was educated at the Friends School in Philadelphia. She married John Ross, an apprenticed upholsterer, and together they worked in an upholstery business.

When her husband was fatally injured in a gun powder explosion in 1776, Betsy continued to run the business, supplementing her income by making flags for the Commonwealth of Pennsylvania. According to the tax records, she was successful enough in this venture to have acquired 190 acres of property in Philadelphia and Cumberland Counties as well as some livestock. She married a second and a third time—to Joseph Ashburn, who died in an English prison in 1782, and finally to one of Ashburn's fellow prisoners, John Claypoole—and raised seven children while continuing to run her upholstery business.

The Betsy Ross legend tells of how she was visited by George Washington, Robert Morris and George Ross, members of a secret committee of the Continental Congress authorized to design a flag. She convinced them that a five-pointed star was easier to make than a six-pointed star and was given the commission to make the first flag. The legend goes on to say she then became the manufacturer of flags for the government and continued in business until her death.

While the flag legend acknowledges the contribution of women to the revolutionary cause through their domestic activities, it glosses over the substantial business and professional activities that many women such as Betsy Ross engaged in during the absences, or after the deaths, of their husbands. Betsy Ross' life was more in keeping with the addendum to the flag story—that she secured a contract to manufacture flags for the government and successfully ran that business until her death in 1836.

Philadelphia Branch
Researcher/Writer: Ellen H. Moore
Special Division Editor: Dr. Barbara Klaczynska

24

Maria A. Harvey

1792–1884 _____

Maria A. Harvey was the first woman west of the Allegheny Mountains to become a pharmacist. As an independent business woman, she strove for excellence in her profession and acquired a sizeable fortune in the frontier village of Waynesburg, Pennsylvania.

Born in Philadelphia in 1792, Maria moved with her family to Center Township, Greene County, in 1807 or 1808. The land was later referred to as the "Old Harvey Farm." There she assisted in operating a post office and managing a small hotel on the old mail route from Morgantown to Wheeling, West Virginia. After a time Miss Harvey sold her interest in the family farm and business and moved to Waynesburg.

Clearly a woman of many talents, Maria taught in a select school for a time and later opened a millinery establishment. She was noted for her needlework. When something in the bleaching process in the making of hats endangered her health, she was obliged to give up millinery and try other work.

Encouraged by two area doctors, she opened a drug store and became a pharmacist. Over the next thirty years she made what in those days amounted to a fortune. She declared at the beginning that she knew nothing about pharmacy but that she wasn't too old to learn.

When she retired, she stated that she had never filled a prescription incorrectly and had positively refused to sell whiskey unless she knew it was prescribed by the physician for medicinal purposes.

Maria Harvey was described as having a "bright, sunny disposition, being exact in business methods, possessing kindly ways, and being very interested in education." She encouraged her nieces and nephews to attend Waynesburg College. She was a member of the Cumberland Presbyterian Church for over fifty years.

This pioneering woman pharmacist left an indelible mark on the Waynesburg community. Her zeal for education, her dedication to her profession and her zest for life made her a rare leader in southwest Pennsylvania.

Waynesburg Branch
Researcher/Writer: Anna Meighen

25

Rebecca Pennock Lukens

1794–1854 _____

"Rebecca Lukens, Ironmaster" is incised on the front of the Chester County Courthouse. Rebecca is the only woman included among nine "founding fathers" honored under a prominent bas-relief depicting early life in the county. She received this recognition because she managed the Brandywine Slitting Mill from 1825 to 1847, building it up from a dilapidated, debt-burdened mill which converted iron slabs into rods for blacksmiths' use to a producer of boiler plates. The mill was located near what is now Coatesville and was later renamed Lukens Steel Company.

Rebecca's formal education at a girls' boarding school in Wilmington, Delaware, included French and chemistry, indicating that it was more extensive than that of many girls of the period. She acquired a background in management by accompanying her ironmaster father to the Federal Slitting Mill which he had started in 1793 at their home on Bull Run, about five miles from what is now Coatesville. She also learned much about the iron business during twelve years of marriage to Dr. Charles Lukens. He had given up medicine to work for her father at the mill, and later leased and renovated the Brandywine Slitting Mill.

In 1825 Rebecca was widowed at the age of thirty-one. Although it had been agreed that the mill would be Rebecca's after her father's death, her father died before her husband and left an ambiguous will which gave her mother his estate for her lifetime. Charles's death left Rebecca with large debts, a rent of $450 a year for the mill and five children to support with a sixth expected. Her mother disapproved of Rebecca's attempt to continue managing the mill but offered her no alternative support.

Rebecca Lukens assumed management of the business aspects of the mill, while her brother-in-law and, later, other relatives managed production. Charles had agreed to provide iron for the S. S. Codorus in a contract stating "that thou will deliver sheet iron to me at York, Pennsylvania, at $140 per ton rolled 2 feet wide and from 7 to 10 feet long." The Codorus was the first metal-hulled vessel built in the United States, and this was the first time such plate was produced in this country. Under Rebecca's management, the contract was filled, helping to establish a market for the iron plate which Charles had been adapting the mill to produce.

Rebecca overcame many problems as manager of the mill. Competitors' dams on the Brandywine and water fluctuations caused by excessive rain or drought interrupted her power supply. Failure of the antiquated machinery and debts were constant worries. By astute bidding for contracts, careful quality control and efficient use of her workers, Rebecca was able to repay all creditors in nine years. At one time she was ordered by a Committee of the Orthodox Order of Friends to lower her mill dam six inches because of the difficulty it caused a competitor who had built a dam upstream. The competitor's dam had lessened her water supply, necessitating her building up her dam the extra six inches. Although she was a Quaker, she kept her dam intact. During the economic panic of 1837, she wrote that she "was in constant fear and have even forbidden my agents to sell, not knowing who would be safe to trust."

Although the management of the mill claimed much of her time and she reported for work at the mill office early each morning, Rebecca was devoted to her children. She took time to tell them stories, to ride with them to the docks at Chester, Wilmington or Philadelphia, to purchase pretty dress fabrics with them and to picnic in the meadows with them. The childhood deaths of her two sons and one of her daughters were deep personal tragedies.

By employing mill hands on her farm when orders for iron did not require their labor, she was able to pay them partially in produce they harvested and meat they butchered. As the mill prospered, she improved the stone houses adjacent to the mill which were provided for workers.

Politics, especially as it affected her business, claimed some of her attention. She wrote the inscription for a silk banner which the ladies of Coatesville made for the presidential campaign of 1840, when tariffs had been reduced and mill hands were working half time.

> Let patriots from each wooded height
> And freemen from our fair vale, come
> To rear this banner broad and bright,
> And rally round brave Harrison.

With the coming of the railroad to the Brandywine Valley in 1834, iron plate could be shipped beyond the range of horse-drawn wagons which had taken loads to the ports in Wilmington, Delaware and York, Pennsylvania. As demand for boiler plates increased, Rebecca's superior quality product gained a market in all major East Coast cities as well as in New Orleans. It was used to construct Mississippi river boats and Baldwin locomotives.

At the age of fifty-three, Rebecca sold an interest in the mill to a son-in-law and turned management over to him, subject to her approval. Later another son-in-law joined the firm. Due to the controversy over her father's will, Rebecca was involved in a lengthy court case which was finally settled in 1853. The court's decision required her to pay substantial amounts to other heirs to clear ownership of the mill. Even though her title to the mill had not been clear, she had managed it so successfully that it had brought her wealth, recognition of her ability and the satisfaction of providing jobs in her community and material for progress in her country.

West Chester Branch
Researcher: Claire C. Etherton
Writer: Mary S. Pinkney

26

Ella J. Mountz

1869–1938

Ella J. Mountz has been described as one of the foremost business women who ever lived in Clearfield County. In 1910, according to one source, she was operating one of the largest coal mining enterprises in the area, which produced 144,380 tons in one year.

Ella Dore was born in Sharon, Pennsylvania, in 1869. When she was seven, her family moved to Ramey, where her parents ran a general store. After completing her schooling, Ella taught school for one year.

In 1885, at the age of sixteen, Ella married Seth J. Mountz, a native of Vail, and they opened a store in nearby Morann. In 1892 Ella was appointed postmistress of Morann, a post she held for eighteen years. While the Mountzes lived at Morann, they became involved in the coal-mining business and ultimately owned several mines in the Whiteside-Morann-Hale area.

Eventually, the Mountzes moved to Janesville near their Viola mining operation, which they had named for their daughter. There they opened a company store. The Mountz Store supplied treats for the local Sunday School every Christmas, a practice continued as long as the store was in existence, until 1976.

A niece said Ella was a "very aggressive woman—all business." She was also a very determined woman. As a strong supporter of the Janesville Methodist Church, she is said to have deducted one dollar per month from each employee's salary to pay the church minister.

Ella was active during World War I equipping a Red Cross unit and maintaining thirty-two war orphans. After the war she gave a job to every returning soldier who applied.

She was an ardent Republican, serving on committees of the Republican state organization and using her influence in the party to have the main street of Janesville paved. She was a delegate to the 1924 Republican National Convention in Cleveland and was chosen by the electors to cast the state's vote at the meeting of the electorate in Washington, D.C.

Ella bought an interest in the *Clearfield Raftsmen's Journal* newspaper and served as board president for several years. In time she acquired oil wells in Texas and Louisiana. By the 1920s she had become the first millionaire in the Clearfield area. However, she lost most of her money in the stock market crash of 1929.

In February 1937 Ella suffered a heart attack while on a business trip to Texas. She was bedridden for a year and died February 18, 1938. She was buried in Beulah Cemetery, Ramey.

The *Houtzdale Citizen Standard* called her one of the foremost businesswomen in the country and one of the most successful individual bituminous coal operators in Pennsylvania." In her honor the Mountz Memorial Community Park in Janesville was dedicated in 1971.

Clearfield Area Branch
Researcher: Gretchen Hiller
Writer: Susan D. Berlin

27

Nelle Sweeney Hayes

1876?–1953 _____

Nelle Sweeney Hayes was one of the first women in Pennsylvania to be licensed as an undertaker. The business had been founded by her father, John Sweeney, who was one of the first undertakers in the state to be licensed and, eventually, became one of the oldest active undertakers in the United States. Nelle's brother, Harry, also worked in the business.

Nelle Sweeney was a member of Houtzdale High School's first graduating class, the class of 1891. After graduation she attended Lock Haven Normal School. Around 1917 she married Morgan Hayes, a widower from Stillwater, Minnesota, who opened a garage in Houtzdale.

The Sweeney-Hayes business on Hannah Street in Houtzdale was a combination funeral parlor and furniture store. (This was not uncommon at that time since the same wood-working skills were used on furniture and coffins.) Nelle spent much of her time there. When she was not involved in the business work, she knitted, crocheted and talked to persons who stopped to visit.

She served as president of the then newly organized Houtzdale High School Alumni Association, was a member of the Mothers' Assistance Board of Clearfield County and served as Red Cross chairman in the Houtzdale Presbyterian Church and its Ladies Aid Society.

Nelle also became quite active in politics. According to one story, Nelle's influence was so important that a newly elected mayor stopped in early on his first day in office to find out what she wanted him to do. When the new state road, Route 53, which goes through Irvona and Coalport to Ashville in Cambria County, was opened, Nelle Hayes was asked to ride in the front car of the procession with Governor Gifford Pinchot and Ella Mountz of Janesville.

Nelle Hayes died June 2, 1953. She never revealed her age, but it was believed that she was seventy-seven at the time of her death. She is buried in the Odd Fellows Cemetery in Brisbin.

Clearfield Area Branch
Researcher: Gretchen Hiller
Writer: Susan D. Berlin

28

Mary Sachs

1888-1960 _____

Harrisburg has been touched by Mary Sachs since she moved to the area in the early 1900s. Born in Lithuania on March 10, 1888, she emigrated to the United States with her family and grew up in Baltimore. After moving to Harrisburg as a young woman and working for others in various positions, Mary found her calling in the world of retail fashion.

Although she received no formal education, Mary had a deep appreciation for learning and an insatiable interest in culture and the arts. She was a keen observer and quickly learned the likes and dislikes of those she served. When she was fired from a job as a salesclerk, Mary convinced a local investor to back her in a special business undertaking that proved to change the fashion scene of central Pennsylvania.

The odds were against Mary. She was young, single, in debt and Jewish, a near fatal combination in 1918. But she was enthusiastic and believed she could satisfy a need missing in other retail establishments in the area. Her small store was short on inventory but long on personal service. Much like the current boutiques of today, Mary's store featured dressing booths where patrons received personal attention directly from the owner. She made weekly trips to New York City by train, often to pick up a single piece of merchandise for a customer. When her salesclerks would accompany her on her buying trips, she would treat them to dinners in the finest restaurants so that they could learn what the latest fashions were among the trend setters.

Times were tough at first. It is rumored that she sent herself flowers, signing the names of clothing manufacturers, to enhance the store's image. But the gamble paid off and her business flourished. By the early 1930s the name of Mary Sachs was synonomous with high fashion. Her store was "the" place to shop in central Pennsylvania.

Disaster struck in 1931 when the store was destroyed by fire, but Mary was not one to give up so easily. After seeing a building she particularly admired in New York, she hunted down the architect, Eleanor Lemaire, and commissioned her to build a new store on the site of the old one. This landmark decision was also an enormous success and the store was operated by Mary until her death on June 14, 1960. It was sold in 1968 and eventually closed in 1978.

As an employer Mary was extremely generous to her staff. She instituted a free-of-charge pension fund for her employees. All of the charitable giving for which she is still remembered was made in the name of her employees. She was loved and respected by those she served and by those who served her.

Perhaps Mary Sachs is best remembered for her philanthropy. She was quoted as saying "I am a collector of helping. It makes me feel more alive." Her overwhelming generosity and charity assisted a long line of needy individuals and organizations. Mary compensated for her own lack of advanced education by providing scholarships for all the colleges and universities in the area. Her money helped provide for cancer research at Hershey Medical Center, for the Cooper Cleft Palate Institute, for Einstein Medical College and for all the hospitals in Harrisburg and Lancaster. Even her death in 1960 did not stop the effect she had on the area since her estate continued to be a factor in most of the local schools and her foundation provided additional scholarship money to Harrisburg Area Community College and to the newly created Museum of Scientific Discovery in downtown Harrisburg.

Mary was also known for her elegant style of entertaining, an extremely important quality in the Harrisburg of her time. During World War II she opened her home to the troops stationed nearby, and

Army students such as Josh Logan and Burgess Meredith were boarders in her home. She hosted the best—Eleanor Roosevelt, Abba Eban, Elizabeth Arden, and Golda Meir—yet she had that quality of making everyone she touched feel at ease, from the commoner to the aristocrat.

Her life and her legacy might well be described in a quote from Eleanor Roosevelt: "I surmise she has been inspiring others through her own generosity to be as generous as possible. However, I imagine few can match her."

Harrisburg Branch
Researcher/Writer: Sally Chamberlain

29

Frieda Segelke Miller

1889–1973

Frieda Segelke Miller was an internationally known expert in labor law administration.

Born April 16, 1889, in LaCrosse, Wisconsin, she was the older of two daughters of Erna and James Miller. With the deaths of both her parents when she was quite young, she was raised by her grandparents.

A 1911 graduate of Downer College in Milwaukee with a Bachelors of Arts in Liberal Arts, Frieda laid the groundwork for her chosen career by studying labor economics and political science at the University of Chicago from 1911 to 1915. Her work in labor relations began in 1916 when she accepted a position as a research assistant and teacher in the department of social economy at Bryn Mawr College near Philadelphia. From 1917 to 1923 she worked for the Philadelphia Women's Trade Union League. In this position, she participated in the organization of the Trade Union College in Philadelphia, helped found the Workers' Education Bureau of America and was a member of the administrative committee that set up the Bryn Mawr Summer School for Women Workers in Industry in 1920.

In 1924 Frieda worked as a factory inspector for the International Ladies' Garment Workers Union. In 1929 she was appointed to head the New York State Labor Department's Division of Women in Industry. In 1936 she became a delegate to the League of Nations' International Labor Organization (ILO) and was the first woman elected to the ILO's executive board.

By this time, she was well-known internationally as well as in the United States. She was appointed to complete an unexpired term as the Industrial Commissioner of New York in 1938. In this position, she reorganized the state's Employment Service, increasing job placements by over fifty percent in one year. She also implemented a system of collecting unemployment insurance from employers, which was instrumental in getting benefits for three million workers in New York, both men and women.

In 1942 Frieda Miller became a special assistant on labor to the United States Ambassador to Great Britain. From 1944 to 1952 she served at the federal level as the Director of the Women's Bureau, dealing with the problems of reemployment of women after World War II. In this position, she was the highest ranking woman in the United States Department of Labor and worked diligently there to achieve equality for working women until 1952 when she returned to her work with the ILO. Among her many projects were a study of the conditions in which women worked worldwide and a survey of the status of child welfare for the United Nations' International Union for Child Welfare.

Although she traveled extensively in her work, Frieda kept a residence south of Easton on Coffeetown Road. She was an active member of the Easton Branch of the American Association of University Women from 1955 to 1967. She returned to New York City in retirement and died there in 1973. Her work in the field of labor was significant and left a lasting impact on the lives of working women.

Easton Branch
Researcher: Margaret D. Druse
Writer: Susan Berkowitz

30

Marjorie Allison

1890–1964 ———————————————————

Through her achievements, Marjorie Allison assured a place in banking for future Allentown women. Marjorie was the daughter of successful industrialist and two-term Allentown Mayor Henry Willard Allison and Clara Unger Allison. As a young woman she attended schools in Bethlehem and served as personal secretary to her father. She graduated from the Drexel Institute in Philadelphia.

In 1913 she began her association with the Lehigh Valley Trust Company and became the first woman in Pennsylvania to hold an executive position in banking. She became a member of the American Institute of Banking and was regional vice-president of the Pennsylvania Association of Bank Women.

Co-workers and lifelong friends recall that Marjorie Allison was involved in nearly every facet of banking, from trusts and estates to the stock transfer department. She eventually became the assistant secretary and treasurer.

"I'm a friendly ambassador of all the banks in Allentown," she once said. This genial quality was exemplified in every aspect of her life. She brought her unique energy and enthusiasm to bear in the fields of education, health, welfare and the arts.

Of great importance to her was the education of the community. She was active in developing The Swain School and was chairman of the school's board of directors.

"She was our great benefactress," said Dr. Esther Swain, founder and headmistress *emerita* of The Swain School. "There would be no physical plant without her." When Dr. Swain contemplated closing the school because it had outgrown its existing quarters and she had difficulty finding a satisfactory facility, Marjorie, a member of the advisory committee at that time, purchased twenty-three acres of open fields near Allentown. She donated the land to The Swain School and engaged an architect to design a new facility. As a testimonial to her caring and giving, the auditorium at the school was dedicated Allison Hall– the only gesture she would permit as recognition of her generosity.

Marjorie was honored frequently for her many accomplishments during her lifetime. During the 1960 graduation exercises at Muhlenberg College, she was given an honorary degree of Doctor of Humane Letters. At Drexel Institute's 60th Anniversary celebration in 1951, she was awarded an alumni citation for "Civic Contribution and Professional Accomplishments."

Her tireless attention to community activities marked her as one of Allentown's most generous volunteers. She was a director of the Allentown Art Museum and of the Allentown Symphony Association. She was a member of the Lehigh Valley Heart Association and a treasurer of the Heart Fund campaign. She was also a member of the United Fund, the Lehigh Valley Chapter of the American Red Cross, and advisor and treasurer of the Children's Theatre School of Civic Little Theatre of Allentown. Numerous individuals, as well, benefited from her generosity. She provided the funds to educate many young men and women from the community.

Her accomplishments in both her business life and in community activities did not go unnoticed. In 1959 she was named a Distinguished Daughter of Pennsylvania, an award conferred on her personally by Governor David Lawrence in honor of her contributions to community and state.

Allentown Branch
Researcher/Writers: Kae Tienstra and
Camille S. Bucci

31

Dorothea de Schweinitz

1891–1980 ——————————————————————————————

Dorothea de Schweinitz of Bethlehem, Pennsylvania, a pioneer in the field of labor-management relations, demonstrated throughout her life her great interest in people, their backgrounds and their needs.

The third child of Bishop and Mrs. Paul de Schweinitz, Dorothea was born September 5, 1891, in Nazareth, Pennsylvania. As a young child, she moved with her family to Bethlehem, where she attended the Moravian Parochial School (now Moravian Academy.) She was graduated from Smith College in 1912 and did graduate work in economics and political science at the University of Chicago. She received her Master of Arts degree at Columbia University in 1929.

The first twenty years of her career were spent in employment and guidance work, beginning with the development of a junior employment service in the public schools of Philadelphia. She then worked at the Young Women's Christian Association in New York City and later in the Industrial Research Department of the Wharton School at the University of Pennsylvania.

Dorothea assisted in the development of a demonstration office, the Model United States Employment Bureau of Pennsylvania in Philadelphia, for the Pennsylvania State Employment Service. While working in research at the U.S. Employment Service, Washington, D.C., she wrote two books: *How Workers Find Jobs, a Study of 4,000 Hosiery Workers in Philadelphia,* published by the University of Pennsylvania Press, and *Occupations in Retail Stores,* published by the U.S. Employment Service and the National Vocational Guidance Association (NVGA). She served as president of the Philadelphia Vocational Guidance Association from 1924 to 1925 and from 1925 to 1926 as president of the NVGA.

During the next twenty years, her career positions were largely in the field of employer relations, initially as regional director of the National Labor Board of St. Louis. She was a member of the War Production Board in Washington during World War II. After the war she obtained a grant from the Wertheim Committee of Harvard University. In 1949 her book on the war period, *Labor and Management in a Common Enterprise,* was published by Harvard University Press.

During the Korean War period she served as an industrial relations specialist on the Wage Stabilization Board. In 1966 another work, based on a year's independent research, *Labor-Management Consultation in the Factory; the Experience of England, Sweden, and Germany,* was published by the Industrial Relations Center of the University of Hawaii.

After her retirement Dorothea de Schweinitz turned her attention to the Georgetown section of Washington, D.C. She had been influential in the passage of the 1950 "Old Georgetown" Act, by which the United States Congress made Georgetown a Historic District under its Commission of Fine Arts. Until her resignation in 1970, she was chairman of the Historic Preservation Committee of the Citizens Association of Georgetown. She died November 13, 1980.

Bethlehem Branch
Researcher/Writer: Polly Hinder

32

Katharine Beecher

1892–1952 —————————————————————————

During the Great Depression many women tried to help their families by making some money, but few were as successful as Katharine Beecher.

Katharine Beck Jacoby was born in York, Pennsylvania, on August 4, 1892. She grew up in York and worked for a short time in a camera store before she married Henry W. Beecher in 1913.

The Beechers lived in Jefferson, Indiana, for about a year and then moved to Greensboro, North Carolina. Katharine made many friends and became active in her church. She was an excellent cook and housekeeper and learned to make butter mints, a regional Southern candy, while she lived in Greensboro.

In 1930 the Beechers moved to York County. After living in York for a year, they bought a home in Manchester, a small town northeast of York. There was a summer kitchen behind the house, and there Katharine Beecher began making butter mints for her friends and neighbors. The mints were very popular among York Countians, who had never tasted anything like them, and the demand for them grew.

Mr. Beecher, who was working for a furniture company, decided to quit his job to help his wife in the candy business. By purchasing some additional equipment, he helped to increase the efficiency of the business and was thus able to expand its sales area.

One of the Beecher's new customers was the Harrisburg Hotel. While staying there, J. Bruce Wallace, a specialty foods salesman, tasted the mints and was so impressed by their quality and uniqueness that he insisted on finding out where they were made. Wallace made several trips to Manchester and eventually persuaded the Beechers to produce mints for distribution in the Midwest. The mints were packaged for freshness in the plain green tins, which later became so famous.

World War II caused a shortage in an essential ingredient—sugar. The Beechers began to sell to Army PX stores and Navy ships' stores and commissaries in order to get government certificates so they could buy more sugar. In this way, the product was introduced to men and women from across the United States.

By 1949 the small business had grown into a $300,000 a year operation, and the Katharine Beecher Company moved into a modern new factory in Manchester.

"She was a very dynamic individual who had a tremendously captivating personality, and people just loved to meet her and to be with her and to talk with her," said Katharine's oldest son, Henry Beecher. "She was right on top of everything . . . She was at home among the salesmen. She could meet with them and discuss the business and the problems with customers and she always came up with an answer. She always had a good answer, too, and they respected her. She was a strong individual who knew how she wanted things."

Katharine Beecher died on October 10, 1952.

York Branch
Researcher/Writer: Betty K. Hooker

33

Elisabeth Surowski Blissell

b. 1912 _____

Elisabeth Blissell is recognized as one of the most vital members of the New Kensington community. Her career in business and community service began in 1938 when she was hired by the New Kensington Chamber of Commerce. In 1947 she became the first and only woman to be elected president of the Pennsylvania State Chamber of Commerce Executives.

Elisabeth attended Duff's Iron City Business School and the University of Pittsburgh Evening School. She completed the Academy of Organization Management at Michigan State University in 1965 and did postgraduate studies at Syracuse University.

After attending institutes in organizational management at Northwestern University, Yale, Michigan State and Syracuse, Elisabeth contributed her own knowledge by providing instruction in management in each of these schools over a fifteen-year period.

In her nearly forty years with the Chamber of Commerce, she worked energetically for the development and recognition of New Kensington, involving herself personally as well as professionally in a broad variety of projects including education, senior citizens, politics, human services, industrial development, economic development, nursing and the Easter Seal Society. In each of these endeavors Elisabeth rose to a leadership position and helped set goals and policies.

In 1978 Pennsylvania State University honored Elisabeth for her community service and participation on the campus advisory board by naming the library on the New Kensington Campus the Elisabeth S. Blissell Library.

Though her laurels were many, Elisabeth Blissell remained a modest woman who, after retiring from the Chamber of Commerce in 1977, continued to work as Public Relations Director for New Kensington's People's Library and as a member of the Downtown Improvement Group (DIG) and the Westmoreland County Industrial Development Authority.

In October 1982 Elisabeth was made an honorary member of the American Chamber of Commerce Executives. She was the first woman chamber manager so designated by this national professional association in its fifty-year history.

Fox Chapel Area Branch
Researcher/Writer: Patricia Demase

4
WOMEN IN THE MILITARY AND SUPPORT SERVICES

34

Sarah Matthews Benjamin

1745—1859? _____

Sarah Matthews Benjamin, a Revolutionary War patriot, was born on November 17, 1745, in Goshen, New York. Her family moved to Pennsylvania from New York while she was very young; she vaguely remembered crossing the Delaware River. She spent many years in the midst of border warfare and the Revolutionary struggle and had distinct recollections of many events from those times.

During the Revolution she never doubted its success and never feared danger. Her first husband, William Read, served in the Revolutionary War and died of a wound he received while in Virginia. Her second husband, Aaron Osborne of Goshen, was also in the Revolution but survived.

She accompanied her second husband during the war and on the marches made herself useful in preparing food or sewing. She was ready to do anything that was required. In one instance when the army was preparing to attack New York, which was in the hands of the enemy, she relieved her husband as a sentinel so that he could aid in the loading of the heavy artillery. General George Washington, inspecting the outposts, sensed an unusual person in her and asked,"Who placed you here?" to which she replied, "Them that had a right to, Sir!" That pleased him and he passed on.

She was with her husband at Yorktown for the surrender of General Cornwallis. During the battle she tried to relieve the suffering of the wounded. She again met General Washington who said, "Young woman, are you not afraid of bullets?" She replied, "The bullets will never cheat the gallows." He smiled and went on.

Sometime after the war Osborne died, and she married John Benjamin. They resided in Pleasant Mount, Pennsylvania. Benjamin died in 1826.

Sarah had five children, and some of her descendants still live in the area of Pleasant Mount. She received a pension from a grateful government; but even so she never sat still and was renowned for her carding, spinning and knitting of triple yarn. Some of her fine work was exhibited at the 1853 World's Fair in New York and a sample of her work, completed when she was one hundred years old, was on display at the Crystal Palace in London in 1851.

At the age of one hundred Sarah still made a yearly trip into town to visit her elderly friends—on foot. Sarah died in Pleasant Mount about 1859 at the age of 114 or 115 and was buried in the Green Grove Cemetery of the Old Methodist Church near Pleasant Mount.

Hawley-Honesdale Area Branch
Researcher: Mary Todd
Writer: Marie Casper

35

Margaret Cochran Corbin

1751–1789

During the American Revolution, some military wives chose to accompany their soldier husbands to war. They did the cooking, washing, sewing and nursing for their husbands' units. In the heat of battle, they often carried pitchers of water to refresh the weary fighting men and, thus, earned the nickname "Molly Pitcher." Legends abound concerning the heroic actions of "Molly Pitcher."

Margaret Cochran Corbin was the Cumberland Valley of Pennsylvania's "Molly Pitcher." Born November 12, 1751, near Rocky Spring Presbyterian Church, Margaret was orphaned at the age of five when Indians killed her father and captured her mother, who was never heard from again. Margaret and her brother were raised by an uncle.

About 1772 Margaret married John Corbin of Virginia, and they lived in Franklin County. At the beginning of the Revolutionary War, when John enlisted with the Pennsylvania Artillery, Continental Line, Margaret accompanied him. John was with George Washington's troops at Fort Washington, near the northern tip of Manhattan Island, New York. On November 16, 1776, following the capture of New York by the British, the Hessians attacked Fort Washington, and John Corbin was mortally wounded while manning his cannon situated on a five-bastioned earthwork. Seeing her husband lying on the ground near his cannon, Margaret quietly walked over his body and took over his cannoneer duties. When the cannon crew saw her, they cheered and called her "Captain Molly," a nickname that would follow her to the grave. Margaret helped to swab, load and fire the cannon until wounded herself.

Margaret was taken prisoner and sent to Philadelphia. She was only partially recovered from her wounds when released and could never use one of her arms again.

On June 29, 1779, when Margaret was about twenty-eight years old, the Pennsylvania Supreme Council awarded her a $30 widow's allowance and recommended her for consideration by the Board of War of the Continental Congress. The Congress, in July, declared her a disabled soldier and granted her one-half a soldier's pay for life and a complete outfit of clothing or its value in money. Thus, Margaret Corbin became the first woman pensioner of the United States.

In 1780 Margaret was assigned to the Invalid Regiment which was stationed at old Fort Montgomery near West Point. Two years later she remarried, although nothing is known of her second husband. Even with the pensions, it was hard to get along and Margaret petitioned for further allowances; she asked to receive the whisky or rum ration (which was usually forbidden to women) and was granted it. The extra money helped make life a little more bearable.

Her disabilities, her strenuous experiences and the financial hardship had taken their toll; "Captain Molly" was known as a haughty, disagreeable eccentric. She insisted on being saluted and returned the salute. A small artillery coat was her regular attire.

In 1783 when the Invalid Regiment was officially disbanded, Margaret chose to remain near West Point where she was provided for by the Commissary of the military establishment. "Captain Molly" died in 1789 and was buried in the Highland Falls Cemetery, New York. In 1926 through the efforts of the Daughters of the American Revolution, her remains were reinterred in the cemetery at the U.S. Military Academy at West Point.

Franklin County and Shippensburg Branches
Researcher/Writer: Rachel Minick
Researcher/Writer: Carol Hozman
Special Division Editor: Mary Ann Stangil

36

Molly Pitcher
(Mary Ludwig Hays McCauley)

1754–1832 ──────────────────────────────────

It was at the decisive Battle of Monmouth in the Revolutionary War that "Molly Pitcher" earned the name by which she is known and ensured that she would be known centuries later. Throughout a hot day's battle, she carried water from a spring to her husband's gun crew and, when he fell, she took his place at the gun.

Born near Trenton, New Jersey, on October 13, 1754, Mary Ludwig was the daughter of an immigrant German farmer or dairyman. In 1769 she moved to Carlisle, Pennsylvania, where she worked as a servant for Dr. William Irvine. On July 24, 1769, she married a local barber, John Caspar Hays, by whom she had at least one child, a boy named John L. Hays.

When the Revolutionary War began, her husband joined Thomas Proctor's First Company of Pennsylvania Artillery, on December 1, 1775. In January 1777 he reenlisted in the Seventh Pennsylvania Regiment, which Molly's ex-employer, Dr. Irvine, later commanded. Almost from the first, Molly joined her husband as a camp follower, washing, cooking, and nursing the soldiers. This was not a life for a fastidious woman, and there are contemporary reports that she was far from fastidious; she chewed tobacco and swore as well as the seasoned soldiers.

In late June 1778 Molly was present with her husband's regiment during the long, hot battle of Monmouth. Although the British and American armies suffered about the same number of losses (some 350 dead, wounded and missing), and although the two sides ended up about where they had been months earlier, this was a decisive battle. The American army halted its retreat long enough to allow for reorganization of the line, and that controlled maneuver proved how well-trained the new army was. Not only had the British failed to win in the North, but they had also learned that the American army was a worthy opponent.

Molly Pitcher is known for bringing water to the troops; it is less well-known that when her husband fell, either wounded or overcome by heat, she took his place at the battery. She then loaded the cannon and performed a soldier's job for the rest of the battle.

Joseph Plumb Martin, then a soldier, later described the scene in his memoirs, quoted by Henry Steele Commager and Richard B. Morris:

> While in the act of reaching a cartridge and having one of her feet as far before the other as she could step, a cannonshot from the enemy passed directly between her legs without doing any other damage than carrying away all the lower part of her petticoat. Looking at it with apparent unconcern, she observed that it was lucky it did not pass a little higher, for in that case it might have carried away something else, and continued her occupation.

After the war Molly returned to Carlisle, In 1792 she married another veteran, John McCauley (variably spelled McAuley, M'Kolly). She worked as a cleaning woman both in private homes and in the county courthouse.

There are few reliable sources for the story of Molly's involvement in the battle, and those which exist contain contradictions.

Still, the Pennsylvania Legislature passed an act to pay "Molly M'Kolly" an annuity, not because she was a soldier's widow, but because of "her services during the Revolutionary War." That act, passed on February 21, 1822, authorized payment of $40 at once and the same amount annually for the rest of Molly's life.

Molly Pitcher is buried in the Old Graveyard in Carlisle. During the Centennial of 1876, a tombstone was added to the site, and a quarter of a century later, a cannon, flag and flagstaff were also added. Molly and her acts in the war are commemorated in paintings such as one by D. M. Carter and in a bronze bas-relief at the battle monument in Monmouth, New Jersey.

Carlisle Branch
Researcher/Writer: Susan Rubinow
Gorsky

37

Annie Wittenmyer
(Sarah Ann Turner Wittenmyer)

1827–1900 ─────────────────────────────────

Sarah Ann Turner Wittenmyer, known as Annie, is credited with saving the lives of thousands of Civil War soldiers by organizing diet kitchens on the battlegrounds. She began her work as executive secretary of the Soldiers' Aid Society of Keokuk, Iowa, where she lived as a young woman. Carrying a pass signed by U.S. Secretary of War Edwin M. Stanton, she toured the army hospitals, bringing food, clothing and compassion to the soldiers.

Distressed with the type of food served to the sick and wounded, in December 1863 she proposed the establishment of diet kitchens in each hospital. By the close of the war, she was supervising one hundred of these kitchens. Wholesome food prescribed by doctors for individual patients had replaced such menus as greasy bacon, beans and strong black coffee.

Her work won the personal attention of President Abraham Lincoln, who wrote on October 20, 1864, "Let this Lady have transportation to any of the Armies, and any privileges while there, not objected to by the commanders of the Armies respectively."

After the war she helped to found homes for children left fatherless. One of these homes, which also served mothers and widows of soldiers, was located in Brookville, Pennsylvania.

Annie Wittenmyer was elected the first president of the National Woman's Christian Temperance Union, holding this office from 1874 to 1879. She served as president of the national Woman's Relief Corps, auxiliary of the Grand Army of the Republic, in 1889.

After spending several years in Philadelphia, she moved to Sanatoga, near Pottstown, in 1889, where she spent her remaining years. Here she wrote a book about her war experiences entitled, *Under the Guns,* and other books including *The Women of the Reformation, History of the Temperance Crusade, Women's Work for Jesus* and *Jeweled Ministry.* Active in the Methodist church, she wrote a number of hymns published in the denominational hymnbook.

Annie Wittenmyer's grave in a Pottstown cemetery is marked by a large monument erected by the Woman's Relief Corps and is inscribed with these words: "In loving memory of her services on battle-fields (sic) and in hospitals during the Civil War."

Pottstown Area Branch
Researcher/Writer: Muriel E. Lichtenwalner

38

Kate M. Scott

1837–1911 ——

During the winter of 1861-62, the first one of the Civil War, the 105th Pennsylvania Regiment was stationed at Camp Jameson, Virginia. Many of the men were sick and dying of fever and pneumonia. In desperation, the regiment commander, Colonel Amor A. McKnight, sent out a call for nurses. Back in Jefferson County, Pennsylvania, Kate Scott heard that call and volunteered.

Kate M. Scott, daughter of John and Hannah Gray Scott, was born in Ebensburg, Pennsylvania, on October 5, 1837. In 1857 the Scott family moved to Jefferson County, and, thereafter, Kate occupied an important place in the affairs of her hometown and county. She was a woman of unusual ability and energy, and her entire life was devoted to activity and usefulness.

The days of Kate's service in Virginia were discouraging. Twice during the winter she was quarantined because her associate nurse, Ellen Guffey, was stricken with scarlet fever. In honor of the services performed by these pioneer nurses during the Civil War, Liberian elms were planted on the Brookville Hospital grounds in 1931.

After the war Kate Scott was closely identified with her regiment and was secretary of the Regimental Association from 1879 to 1891. She was also the author of a history of the regiment and was many times honored by the members of that historic command.

For many years Kate was prominently identified with the work of the Woman's Relief Corps in the county and the state, and she was instrumental in the establishment of the Brookville Soldiers' Home, now known as the Pennsylvania Memorial Home.

Kate took a great interest in the work of the Association of Army Nurses of the Civil War and served as the national secretary. At the time of her death, she was working on a comprehensive history of that association. She also assisted in arranging entertainment for the nurses and veterans at the annual encampments of the Grand Army of the Republic. During the summer of 1910, she spent some time at Atlantic City assisting Executive Director Colonel Frank M. Sterrett in the preparations for the 1910 encampment.

In addition to these activities, Kate served as postmistress of Brookville under appointment from President Benjamin Harrison. *The Brookville Republican* was founded by Miss Scott's father, and for many years she was a valued contributor to its columns. Many of her historical articles later appeared in metropolitan papers. She was the editor of the comprehensive *History of Jefferson County*, published in 1888, a work involving extensive research, which stands as a monument to her ability and energy.

Kate Scott died April 15, 1911, and is buried in the Brookville Cemetery. Her obituary stated:

> Miss Scott was perhaps the most widely known woman in Jefferson County, and in many respects one of the most noted women which the county has ever produced. Her life was a busy and useful one, unselfish and devoted to the friends and causes she so loved, and her death takes from the community one of those of whom it can well be said, "None knew her but to love her, none named her but to praise."

Brookville Area Branch
Researcher: Kathryn I. Wachob
Writer: Judith Brady

39

Marie Tarnapowicz

1900–1983 ————————————————————————————

In a remarkable feat, a Pittsburgh woman was responsible for selling some $300 million worth of war bonds between the years of 1942 and 1945 to help the young men who were serving on the battlefields of World War II. Marie Tarnapowicz, fondly known as "Tarney," accomplished this and more. She is also credited with raising another $34 million for the construction of two veterans' hospitals in the Pittsburgh area during a ten-week drive.

One of six children of a strong Polish immigrant family, Marie was born on July 5, 1900, in Mt. Pleasant, a mining town in Westmoreland County. All her siblings were college-educated; Marie received a bachelor's degree from the University of Pittsburgh. This "extremely practical Polish girl," as she described herself, married Francis Tarnapowicz, a physician on the staff of St. Francis Hospital. Marie loved people and was equally at home at a society benefit or the local fire hall. Her charitable work led to her appointment as Associate State Administrator of the U.S. Department of the Treasury at a token salary of $1 a year; her job was to sell war bonds.

Marie mustered her charm and her determination—nothing discouraged her—and got the job done. Her bond-selling caught the attention of Washington, and an official was sent to Pittsburgh to learn her secrets. The only secret was "Tarney" herself. She had inexhaustible energy, a flair for getting attention, a love for people and a "nothing is impossible" attitude.

One of her ideas was to get the many ethnic groups in Pittsburgh involved and working together in the bond-selling effort. "Impossible," she was told, but she went ahead and organized the U.S. Treasury's Nationality Groups Division. She held rallys, set up booths on street corners with girls in national costume selling bonds, had luncheons and teas. Every promotional idea she could think of she put in the works, from auctioning nylons and cigarettes, to having bombers and ships named for nationality groups holding successful bond drives. She brought Hollywood stars, including Victor Mature and Linda Darnell, to her rallies. Her love of hats and her large wardrobe of more than 200 millinery creations served to attract attention to her. She was one of the most publicized women during the war years, second only to Eleanor Roosevelt.

It was "Tarney" who originated the idea of having a streetcar, painted red, white and blue, carry the message to the people through all sections of Allegheny County to support the bond drives. Her promotional ideas were so outstanding that they were frequently reported in *Minute Man Magazine*, the national promotional magazine of the U.S. Treasury Department, and often featured on the cover. She was also written up in *Home Front Journal*, a monthly publication of the Women's Section of the War Savings Staff, produced by the *Ladies Home Journal*. Her articles appeared in newspapers all over the country.

Marie Tarnapowicz was a success that translated into some $300 million in war bond sales. Her efforts made possible the construction of two Veterans' Administration (VA) hospitals in Pittsburgh, as well as numerous Liberty Ships, bombers and overseas hospitals. She was offered a full-time job by the Treasury Department which she turned down because she did not want to leave her husband, to whom she was married for forty-four years at the time of his death. She received many honors for her accomplishments including a citation from the Treasury Department, numerous gold and silver medals, among them the Gold Legion of Honor in 1980 from the Polish Falcons of America, a key to the city of Pittsburgh and recognition as a "Great American" by the U.S. Congress on November 19, 1945.

A gold bracelet was presented to her by the 107 nationality units in the Pittsburgh area. It held four gold medals: two were given her at testimonials by the groups, the third commemorates her breaking of the ground for the VA hospital at Leech Farm, and the fourth was presented to her at the dedication on September 16, 1954, of Room EL-27 of the VA General Hospital in the Oakland section of Pittsburgh. The room was furnished in her honor by the Nationality Groups. Her book, *The Origin and Development of the Nationality Groups in the Volunteer War Bond Effort,* which details her experiences, was deposited in the library at Hyde Park at the direction of President Franklin D. Roosevelt.

Into her eighties, Marie Tarnapowicz remained active in volunteer work in Pittsburgh, taking part in a variety of community projects and causes.

Mt. Lebanon-South Hills and Pittsburgh Branches

Researcher/Writer: Elizabeth West
Researcher/Writer: Marie Iwanczyk
Special Division Editor: Mary Ann Stangil

40

Lieutenant Colonel
Frances J. Coble

1911–1968

Although she was a capable civilian nurse and rose to the position of assistant head nurse of New York's Roosevelt Hospital Operating Room, Frances Jane Coble is more noted for her military career.

Frances Coble was born in DuBois, Pennsylvania, on August 23, 1911. She graduated from Punxsutawney High School and the Graduate Hospital of the University of Pennsylvania in Philadelphia. She received her Bachelor of Science and Master of Arts in Nursing Administration from New York University.

From 1942 to 1943 she was Chief Nurse of the 9th Evacuation Hospital, a unit affiliated with Roosevelt Hospital. She went to England in October 1942 and then to North Africa in November 1942. She was Chief Nurse of the 9th Evacuation Hospital and the William Beaumont General Hospital Annex. After World War II she remained on reserve status and was called to active duty again in 1950. She helped develop the air inflatable tent which is still in use today.

She served at Walter Reed Hospital and at Ft. Hamilton before becoming Chief Nurse Hq. MAAG Taiwan and Consultant to the Chinese Army Corps. In this capacity, she became a personal friend of General and Mrs. Chiang Kai-Shek.

After service as Supervisor of the Pulmonary Disease Service at Valley Forge Army Hospital and Chief Nurse Hq. 7th U.S. Army, she became Chief Nurse Hq. USCONARC, Ft. Monroe, Virginia. She retired September 30, 1964. During retirement ceremonies, Lieutenant Colonel Coble was awarded the Army Commendation Medal for her successful coordination of nursing services programs in hospitals and field installations assigned to the Army areas throughout the continental United States.

Lieutenant Colonel Frances Coble died at Walter Reed Hospital on May 9, 1968.

Punxsutawney Branch
Researcher/Writer: Miriam Cokely

5
WOMEN
IN
MEDICINE

41

Margaret Frantz Wotring

1745–1823 ─────────────────────────────────

Margaret Frantz, a twelve-year old lass from Heidelberg Township, had lived a rather uneventful life until one fall day in 1757. She and a young friend had been sent to a nearby creek to wash flax. They were accompanied by an armed guard because Indians had been spotted in the area. Apparently the guard dozed off in the warm September sun. A stealthy band of Indians crept up behind the girls, and Margaret was captured before the guard could come to his senses. She was lost for seven years.

In 1764 she returned unharmed to grateful family and friends and related the incredible story of her life with the Lenni Lenape Indians near the Delaware Water Gap. She married Nicholas Wotring in 1769 and re-established her place in the "civilized community." But the knowledge she had gained from the Indians was not forgotten. Apparently she was an astute pupil of the Indian healing arts, because her services in curing various ailments were in great demand.

She became a legendary figure as she rode on horseback from town to town with her herbs and natural medicines, ministering to the sick and wounded.

Allentown Branch
Researcher/Writer: Kae Tienstra

42

Anne Preston, M.D.

1813–1872 _____

Anne Preston grew up on her Quaker father's farm in West Grove, Chester County, Pennsylvania, a stop on the Underground Railroad. As the eldest of nine children with a mother in poor health, Anne had to assume much of the housework. She soon became aware of the unhealthful circumstances forced upon women: restrictive clothing, confinement indoors and lack of recreation. It was a contrast to the out-of-doors life with healthful exercise which seemed to free men from many of the illnesses which afflicted their mothers and sisters. The deaths of her mother and two sisters further fostered her interest in preventive medicine.

When her duties at home permitted, she applied for admission to four Philadelphia medical schools and was refused. In 1848 she began to study in a private clinic under the guidance of a qualified physician, an acceptable type of medical training at that time. After a Philadelphia businessman and philanthropist, William Mullen, and Dr. Joseph Longshore obtained a charter to open the Female Medical College (now Woman's Medical College of Pennsylvania), she studied there. The requirements were two years' study under a practicing physician followed by four months of lectures, including some pharmacy. Anne continued another year to better prepare herself for practice, although she was one of eight candidates fully qualified for degrees in the first graduating class. She was offered a chair of physiology and hygiene which she held for nineteen years, later she became dean for six years and then a member of the board.

In lectures and speaking engagements, she proposed ideas quite new at the time but accepted now: that drugs are secondary in importance to pure air, proper diet and well-regulated exercise; that fashion in clothing should be in harmony with nature, not distorting a woman's figure; that doctors should keep careful records; that they should spend time reading medical journals; that they should consult other doctors to aid in diagnosis, and that women should have the choice of a male or female doctor.

After spending a year in Paris at Maternity Hospital, Dr. Preston returned to Female Medical College in Philadelphia and helped establish a hospital for women and children, with a training course for nurses. By 1858 the general public was recognizing the ability of women doctors; yet the Board of Censors of the Philadelphia Medical Society recommended that members refuse to consult with any graduate of the Female Medical College because of the "irregularity" of their instruction. Dr. Preston defended her College's graduates in a response published in the *Philadelphia Medical and Surgical Reporter* by saying that the Board of Censors were discriminating against them because they were women.

At her death in 1872, she left an interest of $4,000 a year for the benefit of a female medical student. By then 138 women had received their M.D.'s from the Female Medical College. It and the hospital she had helped to establish were internationally recognized for their high standards of teaching and patient care.

West Chester Branch
Researcher: Claire C. Etherton
Writer: Mary S. Pinkney

43

Hannah E. Myers Longshore, M.D.

1819–1902 ⸻

Hannah E. Myers Longshore was one of the first women to practice and teach medicine in Pennsylvania. Born in Sandy Spring, Maryland, on May 30, 1819, she came from a strong Quaker tradition which emphasized reform sentiments. Because of their opposition to slavery, the Myers family moved from Washington, D.C. to New Lisbon, Ohio. The family highly valued education of women, and Hannah attended a Quaker school in Washington and the New Lisbon Academy. Their home provided a stimulating atmosphere for discussions on all current and important topics of the day. Hannah was especially interested in science and medicine but was not able to go to Oberlin College for lack of money.

On March 26, 1841 she married Thomas Ellwood Longshore of Attleboro (now Langhorne), Bucks County, Pennsylvania, a philosopher who was teaching at the New Lisbon Academy. The couple shared a great interest in social reform, education and women's rights. They had two children, Channing and Lucretia. When Thomas lost his teaching job in New Lisbon because of his anti-slavery stand, the family moved back to Attleboro. Hannah apprenticed herself to her brother-in-law, Joseph Skelton Longshore, a graduate of the University of Pennsylvania Medical School and successful doctor in Attleboro. Along with her sister-in-law, Anna Mary Longshore, Hannah read her brother-in-law's medical books, listened to his lectures and observed his care of patients.

Dr. Joseph Longshore applied for and received a charter for the Female Medical College (now Woman's Medical College of Pennsylvania) from the state legislature in March 1850 and became the first professor of obstetrics and diseases of women and children. In 1850 at thirty-one, Hannah enrolled for the first four-month session at the College. Among her seven classmates were her sister-in-law, Anna Longshore, and Ann Preston, future Dean of the College. In the second session, September to December 1851, Hannah's name appears below the faculty as demonstrator of anatomy; because of this, she has been called the first woman to hold a faculty position (not a professorship) in an American medical school. She received her Doctor of Medicine degree on December 31, 1851.

From February to June 1852, Hannah Longshore was demonstrator of anatomy at the New England Female Medical College in Boston under a faculty-exchange system arranged between the two medical schools. In 1853 Dr. Longshore joined a newly formed department of the University of Pennsylvania Medical School and taught there for four years. As Philadelphia's first woman doctor she struggled to develop a practice while overcoming hostility and scorn. Her children were taunted, as it was considered immoral for women to practice medicine. However, as a result of a series of lectures to women on hygiene and physiology, she was able to attract an estimated 300 patients. This number of patients allowed her to practice medicine on a full-time basis, and eventually she gave up teaching.

Dr. Longshore retired in 1892, after forty years of successful practice. Hannah's son became a physician, and her daughter, Lucretia, active in civic affairs and in women's rights, married a reformer who would become mayor of Philadelphia in 1911. Dr. Longshore died in 1902 in Philadelphia.

Levittown-Lower Bucks County Branch
Researcher/Writer: Martha Czop

44

Phoebe Jane Teagarden, M.D.

1841–1921 ─────────────────────────────────

Few women in the nineteenth century challenged the male-dominated ranks of American physicians. Phoebe Teagarden was the first woman doctor in Waynesburg and for many years the only female physician in Greene County.

Familiarly known as "Doctor Jennie," Phoebe Teagarden graduated with honors from Waynesburg College and then taught school in Iowa while living with relatives. Legend has it that after her sweetheart died of typhoid fever while serving in the Union Army in the last days of the Civil War, she decided upon a medical career, believing that reasonable care and treatment would have prevented his death. Another version says that the young man was wounded and died on the battlefield without care. She always wore a gold locket containing a lock of hair and a picture of a "dashing young man in uniform."

Phoebe earned her medical degree at the Female Medical College in Philadelphia and immediately began practice in Waynesburg. At this time women physicians were generally regarded as freaks. Doctors John Iams and John Ullom recognized her ability as a diagnostician and began to call her in on cases. The help of these doctors gave her standing, and soon she acquired a large practice. Always elegantly dressed, she was a familiar sight in her spanking horse and buggy in good and bad weather and at any time of day or night.

She also contributed regularly to *The Republican*, a local newspaper. One of her most interesting columns tells of the visit to Waynesburg of Susan B. Anthony when she lectured at the college on May 10, 1880.

Because of Dr. Jennie's efforts, the Children's Aid Society was established in Waynesburg. She financed the education of many needy children as well as some in her own family. She became a member of the Waynesburg College faculty, was president of the Greene County Medical Society and was a staunch and active member of the Cumberland Presbyterian Church. Dr. Teagarden also belonged to the National Society of the Daughters of the American Revolution and the United States Daughters of 1812.

Her home was the repository of the family antiques, some of which dated back six generations to the ancestral home in Prussia. As a member of the Centennial Committee, she helped plan the centennial year celebrations of Waynesburg and Greene County in 1896.

Dr. Teagarden died at her home in Waynesburg at the age of eighty, leaving behind her a memory of "bright blue eyes, high intelligence, a cultured mind, great energy, beautiful and stylish clothes, wide interests, and deep kindness and compassion." She was widely acclaimed for her humanitarian efforts for neglected children, her pioneering leadership in historical preservation and for her contributions to the Waynesburg College faculty.

Waynesburg Branch
Researcher/Writer: Anna Meighen

45

Esther Marbourg, M.D.

1844?–1900? ─────────────────────────────

In the late 1800s women were shielded from many things, including higher education, exercise and even the facts of life. They were not permitted to serve on juries, testify in court or cast ballots in an election. Yet, in spite of such a climate, Esther Marbourg launched a career in medicine.

Born Esther Lukens Wright, her father was William Wright, a civil engineer and professor of languages in Philadelphia, and a man of prominence. Her mother was Rachel Lukens Wright. Esther was raised in Philadelphia and educated in the city's public schools.

She married Chester W. C. Nippes, a farmer in Indiana County, and they had one child. Shortly after the child was born, Esther's husband was killed at the Battle of Gettysburg (July 1863). Finding herself a young widow with no financial prospects to support herself and her child, she decided to study medical lore with Dr. Benjamin B. Wilson of Philadelphia. In 1869 she entered the Woman's Medical College of Pennsylvania in Philadelphia.

Soon after graduating, Esther went to live in Johnstown, Pennsylvania, where she practiced her profession with courageous success. She was married a second time in March 1872 to Dr. H. W. Marbourg, a Johnstown physician.

For almost thirty years Esther Marbourg practiced medicine in Johnstown. She was an honored member of the American Medical Association and was a delegate to the Chicago meeting of the Association in 1887. She was the only woman among the incorporators of the Conemaugh Valley Memorial Hospital in Johnstown and served on the staff of the hospital. She was also a permanent member of the Pennsylvania Medical Society. She was a member of the Methodist Episcopal Church of Johnstown, and it is said that "she did good work and spread good influence in the community."

Johnstown Branch
Researcher/Writers: Pauline Horwin,
Mary Jo Novelli and
Anne McDonald

46

Charcoal portrait by Erling Roberts

Elizabeth
McLaughry, M.D.

1865–1967

On July 18, 1895 the state of Pennsylvania issued a license to practice medicine to a young woman who became a familiar figure in New Castle and Lawrence County. Elizabeth McLaughry, M.D., with her satchel, horse, buggy and driver could be seen on main streets, country roads, at the doors of mill workers, at the gates of mansions or the homes of the impoverished. She was the first woman doctor in Lawrence County and a medical pioneer.

Elizabeth was born in New Wilmington on September 29, 1865, the twelfth of thirteen children. She graduated in 1887 from Westminster College and for two years taught school in the mill town of Braddock. While recuperating from diphtheria, she tutored in a lumber camp school and had time to consider a long-held desire to become a medical missionary. During college a young man had asked her to go to India as his wife, but she replied she didn't want to be the wife, she wanted to be the real missionary.

"I had no money and not very good health," she later wrote. She borrowed the money and entered the Woman's Medical College in Philadelphia in 1891, graduating in 1894. Although internships for women were hard to find, she was accepted at the New England Hospital for Women and Children in Boston. Her training completed, she applied to go to India. However, the mission's medical board ruled that her health would not stand the rigors of life in India. She came home to Lawrence County to practice in New Castle.

As a woman she was not welcomed by the community or by most male doctors. A breakthrough came when the son of a retired physician, Dr. George W. Veach, became seriously ill. He was attended by a highly respected doctor. When Dr. Veach requested a consultation with Dr. McLaughry, the senior doctor retorted, "I do not want to consult with that young girl!" Dr. Veach said he would then give the case to Dr. McLaughry. The doctor reconsidered. After the consultation he apologized and thereafter asked her to assist in a number of consultations and operations.

Years later when asked how she got along with male doctors, she replied with a twinkle, "I never let them get ahead of me." When an epidemic of typhoid fever struck in New Castle, Dr. McLaughry risked being the first to use the newly developed serum, and she lost no cases.

When she was called to deliver one of the 2,000 babies she helped bring into the world, Charlie, her driver, held the horse. On election day, the illiterate driver voted. "But I, being a woman," she writes, "did not have a vote. I held the horse while he voted. How low I felt."

Elizabeth did graduate work at Johns Hopkins University where she was the only woman in the class. Deeply influenced by Dr. Howard Kelly and Sir William Osler, she later wrote, "These great men gave me extra advantages and profoundly influenced my professional life."

In 1905 Elizabeth worked in the clinic for children's diseases at Ormond Street Hospital in London. Later in Vienna she studied operative obstetrics and gynecological diagnosis at the famous Altgemeine Krankenhaus and received her diploma from the University of Vienna.

Numerous patients with mental disorders created a longing in Dr. McLaughry to have a sanitarium where psychiatric patients could be cared for. She sold her New Castle home, and construction for the new building began in New Wilmington.

In 1911 this medical care facility, "The Overlook," became reality, a "healthful environment for overtired minds and bodies." The Overlook was built by sheer will, determination and the assistance of a supportive family. She wrote, "I felt the nervous patient was the least understood by the medical profession and their families. I wanted to help them fall in love with life again."

In 1932 Dr. McLaughry's niece, Dr. Elizabeth Veach, came to The Overlook to practice; she was eventually named Medical Director in 1945. Dr. Veach described Dr. McLaughry's philosophy of psychotherapy:

It was based upon the principles of re-education. Well-grounded in the analytical concepts of Sigmund Freud, in the teachings of Carl Jung, Alfred Adler, and Adolph Meyer, she herself chose the direct approach of re-education in her therapy . . . She laid great stress upon group activities because she knew it was important for patients to learn how to work and live together . . . To the best of my knowledge she was one of the first advocates of what is now called "group psychotherapy."

To Dr. McLaughry no healing process was complete without a spiritual reorientation . . . She believed that the most rapid road to achieving such changes in thinking, feeling and acting was through man's relationship to his Maker . . . Over and over again in her notes she calls attention to the importance of knowing the whole man and in having the courage to treat the whole man.

In 1937 Westminster College conferred on her the honorary degree of Doctor of Science for her pioneering work in nervous diseases. She was named a diplomate of the American Board of Psychiatry in 1938.

The concepts of Moral Re-Armament were a strong influence in her life, and she participated actively in this worldwide force. She was a member of national and international medical boards and societies and a founder and member of women's professional and business organizations in New Castle.

The physical, mental and spiritual discipline of Dr. Elizabeth McLaughry provided the stamina for a long productive life. She died on December 7, 1967, age 102, at her beloved Overlook.

Lawrence County Branch
Researcher/Writer: Mary Beth McLaughry
Special Division Editor: Patricia McCoy Gill

47

Mary Montgomery Marsh, M.D.

1872–1966 ──────────────────────────────

Mary Montgomery was born December 28, 1872, in Lancaster County, Pennsylvania. She attended Swarthmore College one year and graduated from the Woman's Medical College in Philadelphia in 1895. After serving her internship in New England, she moved to Mt. Pleasant on the advice of a fellow graduate, Dr. Ida Blackburn of Greensburg. Dr. Blackburn told her of the need for a young female physician in the area. Mary's father had encouraged her to leave the Lancaster area because he felt that a young female doctor could not develop a large medical practice in such a conservative community as Lancaster. In 1896 she began to practice general medicine and obstetrics in the Mt. Pleasant vicinity, where she continued her work for over fifty years.

In 1900 Mary Montgomery married Dr. William Marsh, a noted physician who shared a practice with his father, Dr. F. L. Marsh. Through the efforts of these three physicians and the women of the Mt. Pleasant churches, the Mt. Pleasant Memorial Hospital, later known as the H. C. Frick Community Hospital, opened in 1904.

Dr. Mary Montgomery Marsh and other women in the community organized the Hospital Aid Society, which evolved into the first auxiliary group to support the new hospital. The Aid Society sponsored a day annually called "Donation Day" when community members brought food, bandages, bedding and other items to the hospital to keep it operating. This was a way to help the hospital when monetary gifts dwindled because of difficult financial times.

Drs. Mary and William Marsh resided at 729 Main Street, Mt. Pleasant, where they had their offices and reared their children: Jean, Rebecca, Louise and William. The doctors cared for injured miners from the local bituminous coal mines and treated the "mountain folks" from the Laurel Mountains. Mary and William frequently had notes left on the door of their home by timber haulers regarding ailing mountain people. They would load up their buggy and drive into the mountains to care for the sick and perform operations—on a dining room table if necessary.

Dr. Marsh had young immigrant women known as "patch girls" from the mining patches work in her home as housekeepers. While the women worked in her home, she taught them "American ways."

She was a member of many civic groups. She organized the Mt. Pleasant Business and Professional Women's Club and served as a director of the group. She was an active member of the American Medical Association and the County Medical Society as well as her church and Missionary Society. She participated in the Civic Club and Music Club in Mt. Pleasant.

On Sunday, September 6, 1964, at the age of 91, Dr. Mary Montgomery Marsh, then an honorary medical staff member, addressed the audience at the cornerstone-laying ceremony of the new Frick Community Hospital, recounting events leading to the founding of the new hospital. This dedicated woman, who was a good doctor, a fine mother and a community leader throughout her life, died at the age of ninety-three on October 27, 1966.

Greensburg Area Branch
Researcher/Writer: Susan Steinbrenner

48

Mary Moore
Wolfe, M.D.

1874–1962

Mary Moore Wolfe was born in Lewisburg, Pennsylvania, on March 31, 1874, into a family that exemplified intellectual pioneers. Five of her immediate ancestors were among the founders of Bucknell University and her aunt was one of the first women to graduate from the Woman's Medical College of Pennsylvania in 1856. Mary Wolfe, herself, became a pioneer in mental health and the education of mentally deficient women. Her ideas for helping the mentally defective develop to their fullest potential are only now, almost sixty years later, widely accepted and implemented.

Perhaps inspired by stories of her aunt, Mary Wolfe's girlhood ambition was to become a doctor—almost a dream at a time when women doctors were few. She graduated from Bucknell University in 1896 and received her medical degree from the College of Medicine and Surgery of the University of Michigan in 1899, the only woman in her class. Her first position was that of assistant psychiatrist at the Norristown State Hospital for the Insane. After two years she advanced to chief physician of the women's department, with 1200 women under her care. From 1910 until 1914 she headed her own sanitarium at Stonyhurst, near Philadelphia. In 1907 she was accorded the singular honor of being the only woman among five delegates from the United States to the Congress of Nervous and Mental Diseases in Amsterdam, Holland.

The years from 1914 to 1919 were spent in preparation for her greatest professional work: the establishment and development of Laurelton State Village. Although an act of the Pennsylvania Legislature had authorized an institution for "feeble-minded" women in 1913, the appropriation of funds lagged, delaying the opening until December 1919, when Mary Wolfe assumed the superintendency, a post the law required be held by a woman.

In the meantime she served with distinction as a physician at the U.S. Industrial Camp at Muscle Shoals, Alabama, from 1914 to 1915. At home she showed herself an ardent feminist, leading the cause for women's suffrage by speaking in many localities in the county. When the Woman's Suffrage Party of Union County was formed, she was elected its first president. She was also actively involved in the Woman's Christian Temperance Union.

During her twenty-year tenure at Laurelton, Mary Wolfe, with the able assistance of the resident psychologist Mary Vanuxem, was able to develop a progressive institution that was innovative beyond its basic requirement to remove mentally deficient women of child-bearing age from the general community in order to prevent the increase of these deficiencies. In an address to the American Association for the Study of the Feeble-Minded in 1925, entitled "The Relation of Feeble-Mindedness to Education, Citizenship and Culture," she proposed a system of education that recognized the limits of the mentally deficient. After determining these limits on an individual basis, education should be provided, either academically or vocationally, that would develop the abilities of each individual to the fullest. She advocated an educational system that would allow "every child in our Country an opportunity to make the most of all its inherent capacities," encompassing both ends of the spectrum of mental capabilities. In 1935 her presidential address to the American Association on Mental Deficiency was an exposition that the problems of the mentally defective are not primarily medical but must be approached, first and foremost, through psychological, educational and sociological methods.

This was precisely the course of action followed in Laurelton. First, the population was divided into two groups. Those with very low mentality and strong anti-social behavior would always require institutional care. They were trained mainly in agricultural activities, helping to make the institution self-supporting. Those who gave evidence of being able to live in the outside world were given instruction in practical job skills, such as sewing, cooking or laundering, that would enable them to earn a living. In 1925 a community placement program was initiated for these women to lead "supervised extra-institutional lives." It proved eighty-five per cent successful during its first thirteen years; "Dr. Mary's girls" were much in demand as efficient workers. Laurelton became a nationwide model for mental institutions.

Mary Wolfe's role as the head of a state institution required character traits that commanded the respect, if not the personal devotion, of her associates. She proved a most competent administrator and ruled with authority. Her position, a political appointment, made her involvement in party politics inevitable. In order to keep her job, she changed her party affiliation—a matter of expediency during the Depression, rather than a change of philosophy. Thus, it was for political reasons that she was forced to resign in 1940.

Until her death in 1962, she lived in Lewisburg, actively working as a trustee for the advancement of her alma mater, Bucknell University, which had honored her with a Doctor of Science degree in 1933.

Susquehanna Valley Branch
Researcher: Lois Kalp
Researcher/Writer: Elsbeth S. Steffensen

49

Elizabeth Fair Lewis, M.D.

1874–1969

On February 9, 1874, Elizabeth Fair Lewis was born on a farm near Frostburg, Pennsylvania. One of fourteen children, she was destined to become one of Jefferson County's first women physicians.

Elizabeth Lewis taught in the Punxsutawney school system for three years before entering Grove City College, from which she was graduated in 1898. Upon graduation she returned to teaching in Aspen, Colorado, before she entered Woman's Medical College in Philadelphia. After receiving her medical degree in 1905, she served as a resident physician at the Jewish Maternity Hospital in Philadelphia before going to China in 1905.

Dr. Lewis remained in China for twenty-one years. For five of those years, she worked with her brother, Dr. Charles Lewis, a distinguished surgeon. Both served under the Presbyterian Board of Foreign Missions.

In 1915 Dr. Lewis was appointed superintendent of the Talcott Memorial Hospital in northern China. For twelve years she not only managed the hospital but performed surgery and examined as many as one hundred patients in an afternoon. She was forced to leave China in 1927 because of an ongoing civil war and the advance of Communism. Her exit from China was made by a three-day boxcar ride to the coast and, then, by boat to Japan and the United States.

The following year, Dr. Lewis opened a practice in Grove City where she continued to treat patients until she entered a convalescent home at the age of eighty-nine in 1963.

Over the years Dr. Lewis received many honors. In 1955 she received the American Medical Association's award for fifty years of service to the medical profession. Governor Raymond P. Shafer issued a proclamation in 1967, recognizing Dr. Lewis's efforts in making it possible for more women to enter the medical profession. In addition, Dr. Lewis was honored by the Commonwealth Committee of the Women's Medical Association of Pennsylvania.

Dr. Elizabeth Lewis died in Harrisville, Pennsylvania, on December 4, 1969 at the age of ninety-five.

Punxsutawney Branch
Researcher/Writer: Irma P. Stein

50

Geneva E. Groth, D.D.S.

b. 1898 _____

Dr. Geneva Groth was the first female orthodontist in Philadelphia. She also taught at the University of Pennsylvania and maintained a successful practice in Philadelphia for twenty-three years.

She was born in 1898, the daughter of Charles and Matilda Groth, both of whom were practicing dentists. Geneva's mother served as an example of commitment to the profession. Matilda Groth had trained at the Pennsylvania Dental School, the first school of dentistry in Philadelphia. During the course of her studies there, she still managed to run a busy household and raise three daughters. At that time, women dentists were barred from attending professional meetings and, although she was a member of the American Association of Women Dentists, Matilda was obliged to pay one of the male dentists to lecture her on the topics discussed at the professional meetings. Once a University of Pennsylvania professor opined to the Philadelphia press that "women dentists do sloppy work." Matilda Groth and her female colleagues wrote a formal protest to the university and succeeded in gaining a public retraction of the professor's remarks. Matilda was a strong role model for her daughter, Geneva, to follow.

Geneva Groth was not yet twenty-one when she finished her dental training. Although the University of Pennsylvania would not allow her to graduate until she reached her twenty-first birthday, she passed the State Boards and worked as an assistant to a Philadelphia orthodontist until she received her diploma. This was finally granted to her in 1920, in the third class that had admitted women. She stayed with the orthodontist for another five years, while also commuting to New York for graduate courses in dentistry. She then decided to open her own practice and, at the same time, accepted a teaching position in the Dental School of the University of Pennsylvania. For the next twenty-three years, she taught orthodontia and dental hygiene, as well as working in her Philadelphia practice.

With her mother as an example, it is not surprising that Geneva Groth pursued her profession so zealously. The knowledge that the practice of dentistry would be difficult for a woman in the 1920s did not deter Geneva Groth from achieving her ambitions. Her sister gave some insight into Geneva's professional success. "Geneva had a slight advantage in competing in a man's world. She was tall and that meant men had to look her straight in the eye. They *couldn't* overlook her."

Lansdale Branch
Researcher/Writer/Interviewer:
Margrett Beckett
Local Editor: Diane Brouillette

51

Dorothea McClure Gilmore, M.D.

b. 1900 ———————————————————————————————

Neoplasia—the formation of tumors; clinical pathology—the use of laboratory tests to diagnose disease; pediatrics—a branch of medicine dealing with the child, its development, care and diseases: in these words and definitions can be found the heart and life of Dorothea Frances McClure.

Dorothea was born in Freeport, Pennsylvania, March 11, 1900. She was one of eight children of Bertha Gilson and William Lincoln McClure. After graduating from nearby Jeannette High School, she attended Grove City College. She entered the University of Michigan Medical School and was one of only eight women to graduate from it in 1926.

Dorothea joined Western Pennsylvania Hospital in Pittsburgh as an intern in 1926. In 1927 she passed the National Board examinations and was licensed to practice medicine in Pennsylvania. Dr. McClure served residencies in pathology at Western Pennsylvania Hospital and at Children's Hospital, Pittsburgh, where she became interested in the study of children's diseases. She was chief resident in pediatrics at Children's Hospital from 1928 to 1930.

In August of 1930 Dr. McClure went to Clearfield Hospital as chief pathologist. She was also the only pediatrician in Clearfield and its only woman physician for twenty years. At Clearfield Hospital's School of Nursing, it became her responsibility also to teach pathology to the nursing students. She taught for many years until her diversified and many clinical commitments did not permit the time necessary for the instruction.

From the late 1940s until the early 1960s, Dr. McClure was visiting pathologist for the Andrew Kaul Memorial Hospital at St. Marys, Pennsylvania.

Noting the great need for health care in the community, Dr. McClure established a local Well-Baby Clinic. She was also one of the organizers of the Red Cross Blood Bank in the area and served as its local chairman. She organized the first Tumor Clinic at Clearfield Hospital.

Dr. McClure was a member of many organizations and medical societies, attending seminars and meetings to keep up on innovations in her areas of specialization. She participated in the Clearfield Medical Society, the Pennsylvania Medical Society, the American Medical Society, the Pittsburgh Pediatric Society, the American Association for the Study of Neoplastic Diseases and the Pennsylvania Association of Clinical Pathologists. She was a Founding Fellow of the American Society of Clinical Scientists and a member of the Wainwright Tumor Clinic Association and the American Cancer Society.

In a way, Dr. McClure could be called a "first lady." She was the only female member of the National Research Organization for the Study of Neoplastic Diseases. When she served as president of the group during 1957 and 1958, she was the first woman to do so. She attended the first meeting of the Pennsylvania Clinical Pathologists at Pocono Manor, April, 1947, and was the only female member.

Dorothea McClure married Colonel John Pruit Gilmore in 1961. He died a year later.

In recognition of her work in the Tumor Clinic of Clearfield Hospital, the Wainright Tumor Clinic Association presented her with a special award the "Diploma of Honor" of the Association of Clinical Scientists for distinguished and meritorious contributions in clinical science in 1968. The Clearfield Business and Professional Women's Club recognized her contributions to the community and her interest in civic affairs by naming her Woman of the Year in May, 1968.

The Clearfield County Medical Society honored Dr. McClure Gilmore for fifty years of service in the profession; she was only the third person in the state to be so cited. A banquet was given by Clearfield Hospital in recognition of her years of exemplary service and the new laboratory wing of the hospital was dedicated in her honor.

The last few years of her work were devoted to cancer research and cytology. Dr. McClure Gilmore retired in April, 1982 after completing fifty-two years of professional service to Clearfield Hospital and the community.

One of her greatest attributes was that she was a person who would listen to and try to help anyone who came to her, but she was happiest looking through her microscope. In this way, she contributed to the health care of the citizens of the Clearfield area. In a manner typical of one who has spent much of a lifetime in service to others, she wondered, "Where did all those years go?" Time passes quickly for those who are giving of themselves for others.

Clearfield Area Branch
Researcher/Writers: E. Jane Kinkead,
John F. Kennard, M.D.,
and Ann Dotts

52

Lois Irene Platt, M.D.

1908–1979 _____

Despite many promising breakthroughs, a definitive cause and cure for cancer still eludes us. However, research procedes painstakingly slowly—all too slowly for those who number their days by the disease's progress. Dr. Lois Platt was one of the researchers who probed the mysteries of cancer cells for nearly thirty years of her medical career.

Born on March 10, 1908, in Oil City, Lois Platt graduated from high school there in 1926. She attended Goucher College in Baltimore and, for nine years after her graduation in 1931, taught biology in Towson, Maryland. During the summers of her teaching career, she worked as a research assistant in cytology, the study of cells, at the Carnegie Institution in Baltimore. From this experience, her interest in and dedication to the study of cancer cells arose. She enrolled in the University of Maryland and received her medical degree in 1946.

The following year Dr. Platt began to work at the National Cancer Institute of the National Institutes of Health. In 1948 she founded the Cytology Society of Washington, D.C. and soon began teaching at George Washington University. From 1949 to 1954, she was cytologist and instructor of surgery at the University's cancer clinic.

Dr. Platt joined the pathology department at George Washington University in 1954, where she remained until her retirement. She was in charge of the university's cytology laboratory, taught in the School of Cytotechnology and was a lecturer in post-graduate education for physicians. Because of her ability to communicate in sign language, she was lecturer to the deaf both at the School of Cytotechnology and at Gallaudet College in Washington, D.C.

After her retirement in 1974, Dr. Platt was an active volunteer for the American Cancer Society which she served as vice-president until her death. Several days a week she gave lectures on breast cancer. For her dedication, she was made a fellow of the Public Health Cancer Association and, in 1973, received the American Cancer Society's highest honor, the St. George Medal, for her work in cancer detection. She was also named professor *emerita* by George Washington University.

On January 2, 1979 Dr. Lois Platt died in Northern Virginia Doctors' Hospital, a victim of the cancer cells which she had so zealously studied for several decades.

Oil City-Franklin Branch
Researcher/Writer: Lois E. Follstaedt

6
WOMEN IN THE LEGAL PROFESSION

53

Elizabeth "Mammy" Bell Morgan

1761–1839 _____

"Mammy" Morgan lived a long life during which she was described as "mother to the whole township." Although legend and fact are now intertwined, it is known that the twice-widowed Elizabeth Morgan raised two daughters and ran a successful tavern for forty-six years, while providing legal, medical and educational assistance to her neighbors in Williams Township, south of Easton.

Elizabeth Bell was born November 2, 1761, in Philadelphia. In her teens she fell in love with an American Revolutionary War soldier. Her peace-loving Quaker parents objected to the romance on religious grounds. Despite their disapproval of both war and the relationship, legend says that Elizabeth removed the weights from her father's expensive clock and had them cast into bullets. Her parents tried to discourage these activities by sending her to Europe for a university education.

When Elizabeth returned to Philadelphia four years later, in 1781, she married Hugh Bay despite her parents' disapproval, although eventually they accepted her marriage. The following year Elizabeth and Hugh had a daughter, Ann (whose descendents can be found in the Easton area.) Hugh Bay died three years after the marriage, and six years later, in 1790, Elizabeth married Dr. Abel Morgan. Dr. Morgan was a surgeon in the Revolutionary War and later became a private physician in Philadelphia. He and Elizabeth had a daughter, Hannah, in 1793.

In that year an epidemic of yellow fever raged through Philadelphia. Dr. Morgan took his wife and daughters to a hunting lodge in Williams Township, Northampton County, overlooking the Forks of the Delaware, for their safety. When Elizabeth received no word from her husband for two months, she grew concerned and took a stagecoach to Philadelphia, where she learned that her husband had died earlier in the epidemic. To make matters worse, their Philadelphia home had been ransacked, and the only thing of value left behind was her father's clock.

Elizabeth decided to return to the hunting lodge on the hill in Williams Township and to start a business. She built a log addition to the stone lodge and on one side of the building she ran a hotel and a store. The lodge became the headquarters for stagecoaches running to Philadelphia from Easton.

In her new home Elizabeth had two complete sets of law and medical books. She studied them and became a legal and medical adviser to her neighbors in the surrounding areas. Both young and old respected her knowledge and judgment. For many years, according to legend, she was the arbiter of all the disputes in Williams Township, and it was rare that an appeal to a higher tribunal was made. People came from miles around, and even as far as Bucks County, to have their differences settled by her.

Lawyers and historians are intrigued by tales of her assumption of judicial authority and practice of law without proper credentials. Evidence is scant, and some conclude that her law career is legendary aside from her being a good neighbor and a well-read chief counselor in the Township. However, few bar members had a better education or a more genuine concern for people than she, and the power of those qualities should not be discounted.

Elizabeth was a refined, generous, and highly regarded woman, whose advice was widely sought. Because of her services as lawyer and doctor, her predominantly German neighbors called her "Die Mommie." It was a title of reverence, which eventually evolved to "Mammy" Morgan.

"Mammy" Morgan valued education, and in 1820, fourteen years before Governor George Wolf established public schools in Pennsylvania, she contributed land and money for the Hope School House in Williams Township, with the understanding that it was to be free to all children. When she died in October 1839, her funeral cortege was almost two miles long. She was buried in the Reformed Church Cemetery on Mount Jefferson, which later became the site of the Easton Area Public Library—her tombstone is one of just two remaining on the front lawn of the library. In her honor, the hill and the road she lived on still bear her name.

> **Easton Branch**
> Researcher: Margaret D. Druse
> Writer: Ann L. Peaslee
> Special Division Editor: Catherine Barrett

54

Isabel Darlington

1865–1941

Isabel Darlington broke many precedents as the first woman lawyer in Chester County. She was the first woman to receive the Bachelor of Laws Degree from the University of Pennsylvania Law School and the first woman to practice before both the Pennsylvania Superior Court and the Pennsylvania Supreme Court. Her competence and diligence in the pursuit of her career helped her overcome the prejudices of many of her male contemporaries and maintain a highly successful legal practice.

Isabel Darlington received her Bachelor of Science, *magna cum laude*, from Wellesley College. After graduation, she traveled extensively in Europe and the western United States. While her father served as a Congressman from Pennsylvania, she lived in Washington, D.C. and assisted her mother and sisters in entertaining many national and foreign officials. She also acted as private secretary for her father, learning a great deal about politics, people and world events. At a time when ladies were separated from the men after dinner, she must have been irked at missing the full range of conversation.

In 1894 at the age of twenty-nine, she passed an examination administered by the Chester County Bar Association which qualified her to begin the study of law. After reading Blackstone in her uncle's West Chester law office in 1894 and studying for the summer at Carlisle Law School, she decided to enter the University of Pennsylvania Law School. Since no woman had previously been admitted to the school, she had to persist in applying to the dean, who finally allowed her to take an entrance examination. The examination was reported to have been more difficult than those given male applicants, but Isabel demonstrated such superior ability, that the dean had to admit her. She said that during her legal training, her fellow students went out of their way to be kind and friendly, indicating that she knew how to get along with men in a competitive situation.

In 1897 Isabel Darlington received her Bachelor of Law degree, *cum laude*. She began practicing in the office of her brother-in-law, Thomas S. Butler, at times being the only active lawyer in the firm. In 1900 she became the first woman admitted to practice before the

Pennsylvania Superior Court, and in 1902 she appeared before the Pennsylvania Supreme Court.

Throughout her career, she disdained the use of "feminine wiles" to influence jurors, believing that they should be allowed to decide on the merits of the case. She also abhorred the way some aged lawyers played upon the sympathies of jurors. When she grew older, she no longer made court appearances, but specialized in handling estates, wills and legacies of friends and depositors in her father's bank

Isabel retired from the practice of law at the age of sixty. In retirement, she continued to break precedents by her election as the first woman president of the Chester County Bar Association. She was also the first woman in the county to be appointed as receiver of a closed bank, the Parkesburg National Bank. She continued her involvement in the community through service as vice-president of the Chester County Historical Society, assisting at the Orphans' Court as Director of the Poor and working in the Women's Republican Club.

Isabel Darlington believed that "every woman should have some business or professional training. They need it if only to keep from being imposed on. . . ." She also realized that women would be more effective and influential if they earned more money. She advised them to "get into law, as it affects those with money." Her success in her precedent-breaking career encouraged women to believe that they too could enter professions previously closed to them.

West Chester Branch
Researcher: Claire C. Etherton
Writer: Mary S. Pinkney

55

Judge Sara Mathilde Soffel

1886–1976 _____

Sara Mathilde Soffel achieved many "firsts" for Pennsylvania women. With quiet individualism, she distinguished herself by her academic accomplishments and notable judicial career.

Born on October 27, 1886, Sara Soffel was the youngest of eight children. Her father, a German immigrant, was a court tipstaff and an interpreter. Her mother died when she was only four years old.

A native of Pittsburgh, Sara graduated as valedictorian of her Central High School class and earned Phi Beta Kappa honors when she graduated from Wellesley College in 1908. Her career choice to study law drew her father's strong objections which was probably typical of the common reaction at that time: "Two-thirds of the men can't make a living at it," he said. "What do you expect to do?"

Sara taught high school Latin while attending classes at the University of Pittsburgh School of Law. In 1916 she finished first in her class and earned the distinction of being the first woman to receive her entire legal training at that school.

Despite her credentials, she did not receive the customary awards and job offers given to the outstanding male graduates. It was the University of Pittsburgh's custom to award the highest ranking law graduate money and a teaching appointment. Sara Soffel received only the money. No law firm in Pittsburgh offered her a position, so she opened her own law office.

In 1922 she became the first woman to serve as assistant city solicitor, and in 1930 she was appointed by Governor John Fisher to fill a one-year vacancy on the County Court, the first woman to be so appointed. The next year she won election to a full ten-year term, leading the field of thirty-one candidates with the highest vote ever given a judicial candidate in Allegheny County up to that time.

Judge Soffel was the first woman to seek nomination to the state Supreme Court. In 1939 she polled 742,000 votes. Although this total was 300,000 greater than the closest Democratic candidate's and 28,000 greater than the closest Republican candidate's, she failed to win the nomination from either party.

Judge Soffel was the first Pennsylvania woman elected to the Court of Common Pleas. She served there from 1941 until her retirement in 1962. Then, instead of relaxing, she practiced law with a Pittsburgh firm for six years.

Throughout her thirty-two-year career as a judge, Sara Soffel addressed controversial issues with courage and integrity. During a national steel strike in 1946, she ruled against the steelworkers' union when she granted an injunction to limit picketing. The decision was upheld by the state Supreme Court. Judges now routinely rule against mass picketing. This case was so controversial that it has been suggested that her decision might have been different if she had put her political future first.

Judge Soffel had the distinction of being the first woman appointed to the board of trustees by the University of Pittsburgh. Her personal life also reflected quiet individualism. She never married and her tastes included unconventional female pursuits: mountain climbing and fishing.

Just three weeks before her ninetieth birthday, Judge Soffel died on October 5, 1976. Her life was an example of pioneer achievement for women in Pennsylvania's judicial arena.

Mt. Lebanon-South Hills Branch
Researcher/Writer: Heather Stewart Kijowski

56

Judge Anne X. Alpern

1904–1981 ──────────────────────────────────

In an era when men monopolized politics and the legal profession, Anne X. Alpern broke through that man-made barrier. After graduating from the University of Pittsburgh School of Law in 1928, she undertook legal public service and remained in that field for forty years, serving on the bench for eighteen of those years.

Anne Alpern's interest in the law was fostered by her father, who taught school and was a great admirer of Clarence Darrow. Anne graduated from law school and obtained a position with a law firm, but she was assigned all the routine office chores, the only ones a woman was considered capable of handling. Pleading to be allowed to try a case in court, she was finally handed one which the men in the firm refused to tackle. She worked diligently and was able to win the case by her knowledge of the fine points of the law.

Public officials took notice of this capable young woman, and in 1932 she was appointed assistant city solicitor in Pittsburgh. Ten years later she became solicitor, the only woman in the country to hold that title.

While she was still assistant city solicitor, she married Irwin Swiss, an employee of the city's legal department. They had been fellow students in law school. Though becoming a public figure in Pittsburgh, Anne Alpern managed to keep her personal life private. Her marriage to Mr. Swiss in New York was not made public, and the couple sailed on the *Aquitania* for a honeymoon in England, France and Switzerland without fanfare. In time a daughter, Marsha, was born, and she lived a normal life, away from the public gaze. In 1960 Irwin Swiss was killed by a truck while crossing a busy boulevard. Anne hid her grief and put all her energies into the law, winning higher and higher legal positions.

In 1958 she had been elected to the Allegheny County Court of Common Pleas, and Govenor David Lawrence had appointed her to the office of Pennsylvania Attorney General in 1959. As the state's first female attorney general, Anne had empathy for people and their welfare. She fought for decent housing, lower gas rates, and better hospitals.

In 1961 Governor Lawrence appointed Anne Alpern to fill a vacancy on the Pennsylvania Supreme Court, the first woman in its 240-year history. The swearing-in took place in the Pennsylvania House of Representatives before about 500 spectators. The oath of office was administered by Judge Michael Musmanno. After lauding her legal ability, Musmanno said there was a mystery about Judge Alpern: no one knew what her middle initial, X, stood for. Forced to accept her silence, he concluded that the X stood for "extraordinary."

Judge Alpern was appointed in September and the term expired in November, and although she ran for a full term, she was defeated by Common Pleas Judge Henry X. O'Brien. Governor Lawrence appointed Judge Alpern to O'Brien's former place on the Common Pleas Court, a position she held until 1973.

In 1973 Judge Alpern announced that she would retire at the end of the year, just before she reached the mandatory retirement age of seventy.

Judge Anne Alpern died in 1981, having ploughed a deep furrow for women in the legal and judicial fields. The first woman solicitor in the country, the first woman state attorney general and the first woman justice on the Pennsylvania Supreme Court are all landmarks she attained. A newspaper account of her death included this statement:

> She won case after case and won them on legal points and oratory and a stage presence that would have graced Broadway. And she won on pure nerve.

Pittsburgh Branch
Researcher/Writer: Dr. Ann Quattrocchi

57

Judge Genevieve Blatt

b. 1913 ⎯⎯⎯⎯⎯⎯⎯⎯⎯⎯⎯⎯⎯⎯⎯⎯⎯⎯⎯⎯⎯⎯⎯⎯⎯⎯⎯⎯⎯

Genevieve Blatt has had a long and distinguished career in Pennsylvania politics and government. She was the first woman in the state to be elected to a state-wide office, the first to be chosen by a major political party as its candidate for the office of United States Senator and the first woman to be elected to a state judicial post.

Genevieve was born in East Brady, Pennsylvania, on June 19, 1913, the daughter of George F. and Clara Laurent Blatt. Her active participation in Pennsylvania politics began when, as a seventeen-year-old student at the University of Pittsburgh, she served as a volunteer "doorbell ringer" in the 1930 campaign. Her bachelor's degree from the University of Pittsburgh with a major in political science and her master's in 1934 helped to reinforce her interest in government. From 1934 to 1938 Genevieve taught political science at the University of Pittsburgh while she studied for the law degree which she received in 1937. In 1938 she was admitted to the Pennsylvania Bar and became a practicing attorney. While a student, she helped to organize the Pennsylvania Intercollegiate Conference on Government, and she served as its volunteer executive director from 1934 to 1972.

With her strong interest in politics and government, it is not surprising that she should seek work in the public sector. From 1938 to 1942 she was the secretary and chief examiner of the Pittsburgh Civil Service Commission. In 1942 she became the assistant city solicitor of Pittsburgh, a position she held until 1945 when she became executive director of the State Treasury Department and deputy state treasurer. In 1948 she served as secretary of the Democratic State Committee.

Elected Secretary of Internal Affairs in Pennsylvania in 1954, Genevieve Blatt was re-elected in 1958 with the largest plurality of any candidate on either ticket and was the voters' choice again in 1962, in spite of the fact that Republicans won the other state offices. In 1964 Genevieve Blatt defeated the other Democratic candidates in a close race in the primary election for United States Senator but lost to her Republican opponent in the general election by a small margin. In 1972 she was commissioned Judge of the Commonwealth Court, and in 1973 she was elected for a full term on the Court.

In addition to the state offices she has held, Genevieve Blatt has been active in other areas. She was a delegate-at-large to the Democratic National Conventions of 1956, 1960 and 1964 and served as vice-chairman of the delegation in 1956. She was appointed to the State Reorganization Committee in 1956 and to the State Constitutional Revision Commission in 1958. President Kennedy appointed her to the National Advisory Committee on the United States Bureau of Standards and to the Defense Advisory Committee on Women in the Services. In 1965 President Johnson placed her on the President's Commission on Law Enforcement and the Administration of Justice and on the President's Consumer Advisory Council. She was also appointed Assistant Director of the Office of Economic Opportunity by Johnson in 1967.

Judge Blatt has received many honors and awards during her career. She is a member of Phi Beta Kappa and of the National College of State Judiciary and received twelve honorary degrees. In 1956 she was named "Woman of the Year in Government" by *Who's Who of American Women*. In 1964 she was among those named "Most Admired Woman of 1964" in the annual Gallup Poll and was also awarded the Mother Gerard Phalen Gold Medal, the League of Women Voters National Citizenship Award and the Pennsylvania League for Civil Service Career Service Award. In 1966 she was presented the *Pro Ecclesia et Pontifice* Medal by Pope Paul VI.

Judge Blatt is a member of the American, Pennsylvania and Dauphin County Bar Associations, the National Association of Women Lawyers, the American Judicature Society, the American Association of University Women, the League of Women Voters, the Business and Professional Women's Clubs and the National Council of Catholic Women.

Clarion Branch
Researcher/Writer: Helen Knuth

58

Judge Madaline Palladino

b. 1924 _____

For twenty years, until 1969, Attorney Madaline Palladino was the only woman attorney in the Lehigh County Bar. In spite of occasional jests about "the lady lawyer," she was well-received and, in fact, served as secretary-treasurer of the Bar Association.

Madaline Palladino was salutatorian of her Allentown High School graduating class. Subsequently, she attended the University of Pennsylvania where she was elected to Phi Beta Kappa and where she received a bachelor's degree in 1944. At the Columbia University Law School, she was admitted under the quota of two women per year and earned her Bachelor of Laws degree in 1947. She received her Doctor of Jurisprudence degree in 1969, also from Columbia University.

Madaline is a member of the Pennsylvania Bar Association where she served as the first woman chairman of the Public Relations Committee. She is a charter member and past president of the Conference of County Legal Journal Officers of the Pennsylvania Bar Association. In addition, she has lectured for the Pennsylvania Bar Institute. She is a member of the American Bar Association as well as of the American Arbitration Association National Panel. In 1982 she was made a fellow of the American Bar Foundation.

Madaline Palladino served her community in a number of legal positions, frequently as the first woman to hold the office. Between

1952 and 1980 she served, for varying periods of time, as the Allentown assistant city solicitor, and as solicitor to the Lehigh County Recorder of Deeds, solicitor to the Register of Wills and as assistant district attorney. She was appointed Judge of the Commonwealth Court and served during 1980-1981.

Along with her legal duties, Judge Palladino has served her community in the area of education on the board of trustees of Cedar Crest and Muhlenberg Colleges and as president of the advisory board to the Allentown Campus of Pennsylvania State University. In the area of community health care she has been a member of the board of directors of Blue Cross of the Lehigh Valley and a trustee of Sacred Heart Hospital of Allentown. She also served on the board of the United Way, as the chapter chairman of the Lehigh County Red Cross, and as a board member of the Klein-Baum Art School, the Civic Little Theater and the Lehigh Valley Guidance Clinic. Judge Palladino has shown a long-term interest in the Girls Club of Allentown and has served as president of their governing board. She has been president of the Quota Club of Allentown (1954-1955), of the Allentown Branch, American Association of University Women (1958-1960) and of the Allentown Business and Professional Women's Club (1977-1981).

Women's issues have always been a high priority for Judge Palladino. She recalls when representing a male client before a judge in another county, the judge interrupted her remarks and said, "Young lady, would you please be quiet and let your lawyer speak for you." The memory of having had to enter law school as part of a minority quota, and the recollection of incidents such as that of the judge who assumed that the man must be the attorney have made Madaline Palladino a strong proponent of equal rights for women.

Along with her deep commitment to civic and professional organizations, Madaline Palladino maintained a private law practice until her appointment to the Commonwealth Court. She remains in the vanguard of Pennsylvania women in the legal profession.

Allentown Branch
Researcher/Writer: Margaret G. Smart

7
WOMEN
IN
JOURNALISM
AND
PUBLISHING

59

Anne Newport Royall

1769–1854 _____

Anne Newport Royall was a pioneer female journalist and social reformer in the nation's capital for two decades before the Civil War. As one of the first women newspaper editors, she was a recognized crusader against graft and corruption in government.

Born Anne Newport on June 11, 1769, in Baltimore, Maryland, she soon moved to Westmoreland County, Pennsylvania. She spent her childhood there and saw her father die during troubles with the Indians.

Anne and her widowed mother migrated on foot to Virginia where they became servants in the household of a Revolutionary War veteran, Major William Royall. Major Royall educated Anne and shared with her his admiration for the works of George Washington and of Thomas Jefferson and his free-thinking ideas. Anne readily embraced those ideas and the Major himself; they were wed and spent several happy years together.

When Major Royall died, Anne inherited his entire estate, but a lateral heir challenged the will in a court case that dragged on for several years. During that time, thinking that she would surely inherit the estate, Anne traveled throughout the southern part of the country and resided for some years in Alabama. In 1823 in Huntsville, Alabama, Anne learned that she had lost the court case and was penniless. At age 54, alone and ill, she had to find a new means of support.

Traveling to Washington, D.C., she was successful in having legislation introduced in the United States Senate that would guarantee a pension to widows of Revolutionary War veterans. This legislation was debated in Congress over the next twenty-five years. During that time, Anne traveled and wrote travelogues that were sold on a subscription basis to interested readers. One of her subscribers was John Quincy Adams, then Secretary of State. However, Anne got into trouble with her travelogues because she used them to attack persons and politics with which she disagreed. She was arrested and convicted as a "common scold." Although the conviction carried only a ten-dollar fine, Anne's subscription career was finished.

Returning to Washington, D.C., she once again changed careers, becoming the first woman in American to edit a newspaper in a major city. The first edition of her paper, *Paul Pry,* appeared in Washington on December 3, 1831. In it, Anne attacked all those in authority and in government positions whom she felt were involved in graft and corruption and pressed for the elimination of corrupt officials, the abolition of bank monopolies and for tolerance for Roman Catholics and foreigners. She also published a literary magazine, *Huntress,* for eighteen years.

After twenty-five years of continuous reintroduction, Anne's pension bill finally got through Congress. It earned her a lump sum of $1200, but after her debts were paid, she received only $10.

A story suggests that Anne Newport Royall was the first person to be granted a presidential press interview with John Quincy Adams. Adams had a habit of bathing nude in the Potomac River. Legend has it that Anne sat on his clothes and refused to allow him out of the water until he answered her questions!

Because of her crusading spirit, Anne Newport Royall is considered the "Grandmother of all Muckrakers." As an editor, Anne was a figure to be reckoned with by all members of the government because she was so widely read and devoutly believed. She died on October 1, 1854, and was buried in an unmarked grave in the National Congressional Cemetery.

Greensburg Area Branch
Researcher: Susan Steinbrenner
Writer: Trish Smithson

60

Sarah Josepha Buell Hale

1788-1879 ————————————————————————————————

Sarah Josepha Buell Hale was an important publisher of a magazine which influenced American fashion, thinking and lifestyle in the nineteenth century. She was born in New Hampshire in 1788. When her husband died in 1822, she was thirty-four years old and had four small children to support. Forced into the business world by economic necessity, she chose journalism as a means of her livelihood. In 1828 she became the editor of the Boston "Ladies' Magazine," the first women's periodical published in America. In 1837 the magazine merged with a Philadelphia publication, and the name was changed to "Godey's Lady's Book." In 1841 the publication moved to Philadelphia where Sarah served as editor. The magazine provided literature, as well as domestic and fashion advice for women. Under Sarah's leadership, the magazine broke all circulation records, rising from 10,000 in 1837 to 150,000 in 1860. "A tireless author and shrewd business woman, Sarah Hale wrote or edited over fifty books, including recipe collections, etiquette manuals, children's books and floral gift annuals."

She urged the celebration of Thanksgiving Day uniformly throughout the United States, advocating this in her magazine for twenty years. Finally, in 1864 President Lincoln adopted her suggestion and the observance had its national inception.

"Throughout her long career Sarah Hale promoted an unconventional view of the cult of true womanhood and women's sphere. Although she never abandoned her conviction that marriage and maternity comprised women's true destiny, she was an ardent advocate of higher education, especially medical education and professional training for women." These ideas were advocated by the Women's Union Missionary Society, of which she was president for several years. But Sarah Hale opposed suffrage believing women should control through persuasion and example. She was, however, a supporter of property rights for women and, contrary to the prevailing customs of the day, Sarah Hale advocated sensible dress, regular exercise and healthy diets for women. Following her own advice, she lived to be ninety-one.

Philadelphia Branch
Researcher/Writer: Ellen H. Moore
Special Division Editor: Dr. Barbara Klaczynska

61

Grace Greenwood (Sara Jane Clarke Lippincott)

1823–1904 ─────────────────────────────────

Photograph courtesy of the University of Michigan Museum of Art, Ann Arbor, MI

Readers of *The New York Times* in the mid 1850s were treated to lively reports from Europe written by a young woman reporter, Grace Greenwood. Her articles might recount her experiences, such as a dinner with Charles Dickens, or a meeting with Queen Victoria and Prince Albert, or discuss the latest social and political developments of the day. Sent abroad by *The Times,* Grace Greenwood was probably America's first woman foreign correspondent.

Grace Greenwood was the pen name of Sara Jane Clarke, who was born in Pompey, New York, in 1823. At a young age, Sara moved with her family to New Brighton, Pennsylvania, which she considered her hometown all her life. She attended the Greenwood Institute, a girls' academy, directed by an enlightened woman name Myra Townsend. Sara's educational experience there must have had a profound influence on her, for she chose the name Grace Greenwood in honor of the school.

She was an established writer when *The New York Times* sent her on a fifteen-month assignment to Europe in 1852. Her articles had appeared in New York newspapers and magazines including the *Saturday Evening Post, Harper's Monthly* and the *New York Mirror.* Armed with letters of introduction to the famous of the day, Grace Greenwood wrote about the European scene as seen through an American's eyes. She was a keen observer and a competent journalist, whose comments on the social aspects of the period hold interest for today's historians. Her dispatches are collected in book form in *Haps and Mishaps of a Tour in Europe,* published in 1854.

In 1853 Sara Jane Clarke married Leander Lippincott of Philadelphia and, for several years, they published a juvenile magazine, *The Little Pilgrim.* Poet John Greenleaf Whittier wrote "The Barefoot Boy" for the magazine.

As the Civil War was approaching, Sara moved to Washington, D.C. to observe the political life of her own country. Grace Greenwood's reports from the galleries of Congress were of such help to the cause of the North that Lincoln dubbed her "the little patriot." A hard-working abolitionist, she lectured widely. She visited the camps and, after the Battle of the Wilderness, witnessed the devastation of Virginia. *The Record of Five Years* recounts her war experiences.

After the war she returned with her husband to the Little White Cottage in New Brighton, but not for long. To publicize their new railroad, officials of the Union Pacific sent Grace Greenwood to California. Her enthusiastic letters are collected in *New Life in New Lands.* In 1883 she published her *Life of Queen Victoria,* in hopes that it would have "a happy and enobling effect" on young Americans. Among her other works are: *Forest Tragedy, Legends of Travel, Stories from Home Folks,* and *Stories and Sketches.*

The life and works of Grace Greenwood provide a good view of the early Victorian age. Having had a mother who carefully explained to her how each of her pets should be cared for, Grace published *History of My Pets.* She is said to have been a fearless horsewoman who claimed the best remedy for a sagging spirit or a drooping mind was a good gallop. Always greatly interested in social problems, she was an early proponent of equal pay for equal work. She said she "would like to see adopted the German plan of Kinder-Garten," enabling the children of the poor to spend vacations in the country. Prison reform was another of her interests, and she twice visited the state prison in Columbus, Ohio. She also hoped for reform in women's clothing, wistfully suggesting loose Turkish-style trousers for walks in the country.

Sara Jane Clarke Lippincott died in 1904 and is buried in Grove Cemetery, New Brighton. The Little White Cottage, which was her home, still stands on Third Street in New Brighton and has been designated an historical site by the Pennsylvania Historical and Museum Commission. A portrait of *Grace Greenwood* painted in 1849 hangs in the Smithsonian Institution's Portrait Gallery in Washington, D.C.

Aliquippa and Beaver Valley Branches
Researcher/Writer: JoAnne Walker
Researcher/Writer: Sarah P. Kenah
Special Division Editor: Mary Ann Stangil

62

Ida Minerva Tarbell

1857–1944

Photograph through the courtesy of Allegheny College, Meadville, PA

A slim, brown-haired, young woman approached the desk of the editor of *The Chautauquan,* a magazine published by the Chautauquan Literary and Scientific Circle of Meadville, Pennsylvania, where she had worked for the past eight years. At age thirty-three, Ida Tarbell had decided it was time for a big change in her life.

"I'm leaving," she announced. "I'm going to Paris."

Her boss was surprised. "How will you support yourself?" he inquired.

"By writing," she replied.

"You'll starve. You're not a writer," he retorted.

The year was 1890. Always strongly independent and determined to make something useful of herself, Ida Tarbell's "whole nature was against the acceptance of limitations." In 1891 she took a daring step for a woman of her day: she went to Paris to become a free-lance journalist.

Ida Tarbell was born in a log house in Erie County in 1857. The panic of that year and its subsequent depression brought her carpenter father back from a venture in Iowa to the oil fields of western Pennsylvania, where he began making wooden oil tanks. As the tank business flourished, the family moved to Titusville in 1870, and there, young Ida graduated from high school with highest honors. She was one of the first dozen women to attend Allegheny College in nearby

Meadville and the only female in her class. She received her bachelor's degree in 1880 and, after a short, unsatisfying stint as a school teacher in Poland, Ohio, returned to earn a master's degree in 1883. She then joined the staff of *The Chautauquan.*

Having made her move to Paris, Ida began to write. Her work soon attracted the attention of *McClure's* magazine, and she joined its staff. She wrote articles based on interviews with such notables of the day as Alexandre Dumas, Louis Pasteur and Emile Zola and conducted her own extensive research for the ·biographies she wrote of Napoleon Bonaparte and Abraham Lincoln.

The History of the Standard Oil Company, which first appeared in nineteen installments in *McClure's* and then was published as a book in 1904, firmly established Ida Tarbell as one of the first and foremost "muckraker" journalists of that era. As a teenager, Ida had been a firsthand witness to Standard Oil's excesses in its takeover of the Pennsylvania oil fields. Because of her carefully documented, fearless exposé of this powerful corporation, an investigation of the company was conducted, leading to federal regulation of monopolies and big business. John D. Rockefeller, himself, refused to reply to Ida Tarbell's charges, calling her a "misguided woman."

In 1906 Ida Tarbell joined the *American Magazine* as co-editor, where she remained for nine years. She then returned to free-lance work, producing numerous articles and her autobiography, *All in a Day's Work,* and lecturing widely. During World War I she was appointed to the Women's Committee of the Council of National Defense by President Woodrow Wilson. She was the first woman elected to the Authors Club and, for thirty years, was president of Pen and Brush, a group of women authors and artists. When she was in her eighties, she taught at Bucknell University, at the University of Arizona and at her alma mater, Allegheny College, where she was a trustee for thirty years. Her writing seminars were conducted sitting at a table when she was no longer able to stand. She was awarded honorary degrees from Allegheny and Knox Colleges.

Although she chose a career over marriage, Ida Tarbell considered home and family of vital importance to a strong society. She was always interested in woman's role in society but disagreed with the militant views of the women suffragists. Her later writings and lectures stressed the need for world peace and understanding.

Ida Tarbell died in 1944 at the age of eighty-six and is buried in Woodlawn Cemetery, Titusville.

Meadville and Oil City-Franklin Branches
Researcher/Writer: Rebecca Borthwick
Researcher/Writer: Lois E. Follstaedt
Special Division Editor: Mary Ann Stangil

63

Nellie Bly
(Elizabeth Cochrane
Seaman)

1867–1922 ──────────────────────────────

In the memory of her living descendants, pioneer investigative reporter Nellie Bly was just an ordinary girl who grew up in a small western Pennsylvania town and who did extraordinary things. But some of the experiences Nellie endured to get the story indicate that she was somewhat more than an ordinary woman.

Nellie Bly was born Elizabeth Cochrane on May 5, 1867, at Cochran's Mills, Armstrong County, the daughter of Michael Cochran, a mill owner and later an Associate Judge of the county. (Elizabeth added the final "e" to her name as an extra touch.) Attending school in Indiana, Pennsylvania, Elizabeth was nicknamed "Pink," because of the pink calico ruffles she often wore and her fragile appearance.

After her father died, she and her mother moved to Pittsburgh so Elizabeth could find work. At the age of 18, she responded to an editorial in the Pittsburgh *Daily Dispatch,* which criticized the "new fad" of hiring women in offices and shops. Indignant that the editorial suggested that "a respectable girl stay home until someone offers to marry her," Elizabeth wrote a scathing reply stating that girls should take their rightful place in society alongside men where they could lead interesting, useful and profitable lives. When editor George Madden met Elizabeth in person he was surprised to find her an attractive young woman, fashionably dressed. He was also impressed with her writing. He hired her to write for the *Dispatch* and gave her the pen name, Nelly Bly, taken from a then-popular Stephen Foster song. The typesetter mispelled it "Nellie" and it stuck.

Nellie's first series for the *Dispatch* was on divorce, a topic taboo in polite society of the Victorian 1880s. The articles published in the newspaper caused a sensation and curious readers wondered if the writer was really a woman or a male reporter in journalistic disguise.

Other series took Nellie into the steel town's factories and tenements to observe the appalling working conditions for women, the starvation wages and poverty in the slum areas. Since no picture of Nellie Bly was ever published while she worked in Pittsburgh, she could do her investigating freely without being recognized. Her articles, however, attracted a great deal of attention. Nellie spent six months in Mexico, traveling widely to do a series of articles on the government and living conditions. The articles appeared in several newspapers. Her revelations of the extreme poverty which existed there so embarrassed the Mexican government that they asked Nellie to leave the country.

In 1888 Nellie joined the staff of Joseph Pulitzer's New York *World* and, as her first assignment, feigned insanity and had herself committed to the insane asylum on Blackwell's Island for 10 days. Her published accounts of the horrors she observed there—and perhaps experienced—in "Ten Days in a Mad House" led to the allocation of over $1 million for the improvement of mental health treatment in state facilities. The articles in the *World* under Nellie's bylines exposed social injustice and political corruption and, in many cases, led to government action and reform.

Stunts were a specialty of Pulitzer's *World,* and one of its most famous was Nellie Bly's around-the-world trek designed to beat the eighty-day record of Jules Verne's character, Phileas Fogg. Nellie, in a blue broadcloth dress, wool coat and matching hat and carrying her belongings in a satchel, embarked from New York on a trip around the world as the *World* launched a contest for the nearest guess on the exact time of Nellie's trip. Throngs of people greeted Nellie when she arrived in San Francisco from Japan. She boarded a special train which took her across the country, with crowds and brass bands saluting her all along the way. She reached New York after seventy-two days, six hours and eleven minutes, beating Fogg's time by eight days. The story of her adventures appears in *Nellie Bly's Book: Around the World in Seventy-Two Days,* published in 1890.

By the age of twenty-eight Nellie had turned down numerous marriage proposals and was earning $25,000 a year, when she met and married Robert Seaman, a seventy-two-year-old millionaire industrialist. She retired from newspaper work and enjoyed a happy married life helping her husband run his business. When Seaman died in 1904, Nellie managed the company. She equalized wages and benefits for women and men employees and improved working conditions, but the treachery of some of her employees led to financial reverses and the eventual bankruptcy of the company in 1912.

Nellie returned to her writing, joining the staff of the New York *Evening Journal.* Her final story was another sensation: she was the first newspaper woman to give an eyewitness account of an electrocution at Sing Sing prison. Her story was a plea against capital punishment.

Nellie contracted pneumonia and died at the age of fifty-four early in 1922. The New York *Journal's* obituary called her "the best reporter in America." With her perseverance, audacity and ingenuity, Nellie Bly exposed social evils which begged for reform; she also helped open the field of journalism—until then a man's domain—to women.

Butler, Fox Chapel Area, Mt. Lebanon-South Hills and Pittsburgh Branches

Researcher/Writer: Ruth B. Jones
Researcher/Writer: Patricia Demase
Researcher/Writer: Debbie Popp Gilbert
Researcher/Writer: Marie Iwanczyk
Special Division Editor: Mary Ann Stangil

64

Florence Fisher Parry

1886–1974

Although it is through her writing that her influence was most broadly and keenly felt, her dynamic involvement in a variety of other fields is testimony to the creative vitality of Florence Fisher Parry. A look at her accomplishments—as an actress, as an early-widowed wife and mother, as a woman establishing her own successful business, as a lecturer, broadcaster, drama critic and daily newspaper columnist— makes her life seem to be not one, but many lives. A fiery individualist before it was a seemly or popular trait for women, she approached each challenge of her life with energy, enthusiasm and talent.

Born May 7, 1886, and always possessed of an overwhelming desire to learn, Florence cajoled her father, a Punxsutawney lawyer, into sending her to boarding school at Washington Seminary in Washington, D.C. As much as she loved Punxsutawney, she wanted to expand her horizons.

By the time she graduated from Washington Seminary five years later, she was committed to the prospect of becoming an actress. In view of her background and the times, this was tantamount to announcing a desire to join the circus as an acrobat, but she was finally able to prevail upon her parents to send her to Wheatcroft Dramatic School in New York City. When she had been at the school only a few months, the leading lady of *Pygmalion and Galatea* fell ill. Florence, understanding the role, was rushed into the part of Galatea. That night, producer Thomas Dixon was in the audience and was so impressed with her performance that he booked her immediately to be a part of his new company. Her career as an actress had begun.

This engagement was soon followed by other successes: summer stock with Amelia Bingham, an association with Russian star, Alla Nazimova, leading lady to Walker Whiteside and, later, to Otis Skinner. Her lifetime success as an actress seemed assured. Then, in 1913, she met David Parry, a handsome young banker, and she made her choice; she abandoned the stage for marriage.

Adapting quickly to her new role as wife and mother, Florence lived with her young family in New York, Pittsburgh, San Francisco and Los Angeles. She realized early in the marriage that, because of poor health, David would not live long. In California, while he was in a diabetic sanitarium, she starred with Nazimova in a movie version of *A Doll's House*, which they had performed in together many times on the stage. Nazimova's personal photographer photographed Florence Parry with her children as a gift for her dying husband. As David Parry's condition worsened, Florence brought him to Punxsutawney where he soon died.

In corresponding with the photographer and his wife, Florence learned that they were eager to find someone to invest in a photographic studio in the east. At her father's urging she invested in the business, hoping to lessen her grief. Knowing nothing about either business or photography, she opened a tiny studio in Pittsburgh, only to discover, some months later, that the photographer was embezzling the profits. She was ready to abandon the studio altogether and return to Punxsutawney, but her father persuaded her to hire another photographer and to run the business herself. Starting on a shoestring, in 1923, she established a business which at its peak had expanded to four studios in Pittsburgh.

Although her family and business consumed her time, she had not lost her great love for the theatre, and in 1925, when she wrote a letter to a Pittsburgh newspaper about a particular production of *Hamlet*, she was invited by the editor to write on a regular basis.

Over the next twenty-five years, Florence Fisher Parry wrote approximately 10,000 words a week for *The Pittsburgh Press*, not only for a theater column, "On With the Show," but for a daily column, "I Dare Say," as well. As drama critic, she wrote about plays and movies, while in her daily column she discussed a variety of topics including her family, and frequently, her beloved Punxsutawney. Both columns attracted a wide and faithful following for many years. At the same time she continued to run the Parry Studios, lectured and broadcast frequently and was an active participant in many civic groups and enterprises.

After her retirement from the studios and *The Pittsburgh Press*, she maintained apartments in Los Angeles and in Kenosha, Wisconsin, near her children and their families. Her writing energies were now directed to her extensive memoirs, family history, short stories, and regular and frequent letters to the local papers.

Florence Parry died on August 22, 1974, at the age of eighty-eight.

Punxsutawney Branch
Researcher/Writer: Florence Parry Heide

65

Caroline Clark Myers

1887–1980 ————————————————————————

Caroline Myers was well-known for her work with her husband, Dr. Garry C. Myers, in the founding of the highly regarded children's magazine, *Highlights for Children*. Under her guidance *Highlights* became an effective blend of games, facts and realistic fiction which, since 1946, has helped children grow into sensitive, reasoning and patriotic adults.

Born in Morris, Pennsylvania on July 14, 1887, Caroline was the daughter of Charles and Elizabeth Boyd Clark. She graduated from Bloomsburg State Teachers College in 1905 and later attended Ursinus and Juniata Colleges, finishing her graduate work at Teachers College, Columbia University in 1934.

In 1930 Caroline Myers received the Laura Spellman Rockefeller Scholarship for study in child development and family life at the Merrill-Palmer School in Detroit, Michigan. She served as the director of parent education and family life at the Cleveland Welfare Federation from 1931 to 1941. She was also an instructor in family life and child development at Cleveland College, Western Reserve University, and was an instructor at several other institutions of higher learning.

From 1941 to 1946 she served as the associate editor for *Children's Activities* and, in 1946, co-founded *Highlights for Children* with her husband. She was the vice-president and director for Highlights for Children, Inc., which has its home office in Honesdale, Pennsylvania, until her death on July 3, 1980.

Through the years Caroline Myers received many awards and recognition for her work including: the Distinguished Service Award from Bloomsburg State Teachers College in 1953, the Special Citizenship Award for community contributions and the B'nai B'rith Citizenship Citation in 1971 and the National Recognition Award from the Freedoms Foundation in 1976. She received the National Freedoms Foundation Award because she furthered "two basic elements of America: a fundamental belief in God and the idea that constitutional government was devised to serve the people."

Caroline co-authored more than a dozen research articles and worked on a series of arithmetic workbooks in the 1920s as well as *Myers Mental Measure* (1920), *Language of America* (1921), and *Homes Build Persons* (1950).

Highlights is read and used by over 1.5 million children every year. Through the magazine, Caroline Myers has motivated America's children to high ideals and a constructive life.

Hawley-Honesdale
Researcher: Sally Stanton
Writer: Marie Casper

66

Eleanor Murdoch Johnson

b. 1892 ───────────────────────────────────

The idea for the newspaper which became *My Weekly Reader* came to Eleanor Murdoch Johnson when she was the Director of Elementary Schools in York, Pennsylvania.

"I saw children reading folk and fairy tales and myths," she said, "which I adore, and to which there is no objection; but the pupils had no idea of what was happening in the world—not a flicker. The idea came to me that school children needed a newspaper of their own, specially written, so they could read it."

Eleanor Johnson was born on December 10, 1892, in Frederick, Maryland. After teaching in Oklahoma for six years, she served as the Director of Elementary Schools in Drumright, Oklahoma from 1918 to 1922 and in Oklahoma City from 1922 to 1926. She graduated from the University of Chicago with a bachelor's degree, with honors, in 1925 and received her master's degree in 1932 from Columbia University, Teachers College.

Eleanor Johnson came to York as Director of Elementary Schools in 1926 and from 1930 to 1934 served as assistant superintendent of schools in charge of Curriculum at Lakewood, Ohio. She co-authored *Child Story Readers*, (1927), *Junior Language Skills*, (1935), *Treasury of Literature Readers*, (1954), and *Spelling for Word Mastery*, Books 1-8, (1956).

It was in 1927 that Eleanor Johnson met William C. Blakey, the publisher of a newspaper called *Current Events*, which was used in many high schools.

"I told him of my idea for a children's newspaper for grades one to six," continued Miss Johnson. "Then in August, 1928, I was teaching at the University of Chicago in the summer session when a telegram came from Mr. Blakey: 'Save Sunday. Ready to start your children's newspaper.'"

"We sat in the old Blackstone Hotel there on Michigan Avenue all day, and it was hot as blazes. There was no air conditioning—no air, hot, humid—and we mapped out the name, the format, and the promotion, all based on material I had submitted to him."

"Are you ready to become editor-in-chief?" Blakey asked.

Eleanor replied that she had a very good job, at that time, assistant superintendent in charge of curriculum in Lakewood, Ohio. "I wasn't quite sure *My Weekly Reader* would make a go of it, whether it would succeed. However, the American Education Press sent editors to Lakewood on weekends, and I trained them and helped to write *My Weekly Reader* until 1934 when I joined them permanently as their editor-in-chief." She served as editor-in-chief until 1971 and, then, continued as a consultant.

Another of Eleanor Johnson's ideas was realized in 1956 when she helped to found the Weekly Reader Children's Book Club. "Children's books were costing parents too much and they weren't buying enough, so my next dream—and I had dreamed of it for almost thirty years—was to offer books that parents could afford to buy." She explained that because of Weekly Reader Book Club's high volume of sales, they can sell their books at much lower prices than traditional publishers. "So that was another dream of mine that came true," she said.

Eleanor kept up with all the studies on students' reading interest for many years. She spent her spare moments at night in York keeping up with the very best magazines and in touch with the universities where research was going on. Through those years she built a background without which she could never have conceived of *My Weekly Reader* and brought it into being. After more than fifty years of supplying news of interest and value to pupils in grades one to six, *My Weekly Reader* is still the leader in children's newspapers.

York Branch
Researcher/Writer: Betty K. Hooker

67

Eve Garrette

1896–1969 _____

Eve Garrette was highly regarded as a traveler, lecturer, author and critic.

After graduating as a Greek major from Wilson College, she studied privately in New York, Washington, D.C., Paris, Vienna, London and Berlin. She remained "a life-time student of world literature in seven languages."

In 1930 and 1931 she was in Russia working for the *Saturday Evening Post.* She and her husband, an engineer who helped industrialize Russia, lived in Kharkov. Based on her experiences, she wrote eight articles for the *Post* and her best-seller, *Seeing Red.* She also authored twenty additional pieces on Russia for other large circulation magazines.

She covered the Harlan Mine War in Kentucky in 1931 for the *American Magazine* and did pieces for *Good Housekeeping, This Weekend* and *Today's Woman.* In 1936 Eve Garrette attended the Inter-American Peace Conference in Buenos Aires, one of the nine distinguished American women who were guests of South American governments and delegates of the Peoples Mandate Committee.

Eve Garrette's most successful work was *A Political Handbook for Women*, the first book of its kind when it was published in 1944. It became a college textbook for political science classes.

During the 1940s she was the personal secretary and literary consultant to former President Herbert Hoover and served as a member of the feeding program committee. President Hoover and Eve Garrette remained lifelong friends, and she was the only Pennsylvanian at the President's eightieth birthday party. She was a member of the board of directors of the Women's National Republican Club of New York as the Pennsylvania representative.

After moving to Huntingdon in 1948 she became active in many civic activities. In 1950 she was nominated by the Huntingdon Branch of the American Association of University Women as a "Pennsylvania Ambassador" in the field of journalism. In 1952 she was the president of the Friends of the Huntingdon County Library. In 1958 she wrote the book, *The Ladies Christian Union, 1858-1958*.

Eve Garrette had a keen interest in crossword puzzles. In 1949 she began editing and publishing a series of books called *The Expert's Crossword Puzzle Book*. She completed thirteen volumes prior to her death on January 27, 1969.

Huntingdon Branch
Researchers: Ruth V. Stewart and
Josephine B. McMeen
Writer: Nancy R. Taylor

8
WOMEN
AS
POLITICAL
ACTIVISTS

68
"Grandy" Miller
17-?–1865?

The women of the 1700s were taught to be courteous and retiring, deferring to the menfolk in all matters of politics and law. "Grandy" Miller did not adhere to these specifications of femininity. She emerges from county records as strong-minded and determined, confident enough to keep her first married name, "Miller," long after she was officially married to "Mr. Schaeffer," and to rebel openly against the unfair tax practices of her time.

Grandy, a resident of Millerstown, now Macungie, led the "Hot Water Rebellion" in 1799. Enraged by a new federal law which taxed houses according to their size and the number of windows they contained, Grandy and other Millerstown citizens proposed an extreme demonstration of their discontent.

On the day the tax was to be collected, they gathered in an upper room of Grandy's home. When the appraisers and soldiers reached the street below, the furious citizens doused them with buckets of steaming water.

The "Hot Water Rebellion" was just one of a series of insurrections that occurred during this time, but it was the only one led by a woman. It is said that the strong-willed Grandy rose from her childbed in order to accomplish the deed.

Allentown Branch
Researcher/Writer: Kae Tienstra

69

Hannah Wierman Gibbons

1787–1860 ————————————————————————————————

The home of Hannah Gibbons and her husband Daniel was a station on the Underground Railroad from the early 1800s to the time of the Civil War. Over 1000 slaves passed through their property of 1000 acres near the Bird-in-Hand station of the Pennsylvania Railroad. Both Hannah and her husband were well-to-do, devout Quakers, and the entire Gibbons family participated in helping fugitive slaves. Their sixteen-year-old son concealed slaves in a wagon at night and drove them to the next station.

On one occasion, while her husband was keeping a slave master occupied, Hannah spirited a young slave girl from the house and concealed her from her owner under an empty rain barrel. The ruse was successful, and the girl was not discovered.

In another instance in 1836, a very dirty, exhausted and visibly ill slave came for help. His physical condition quickly became more serious, and when a doctor was summoned, he declared him a victim of smallpox. Hannah Gibbons, at this time forty-nine years of age, closed herself in with the man for six weeks without concern for herself. She nursed him with great care and kindness until he recovered sufficiently to continue his journey.

To protect themselves, the Gibbons family built a special lane to their house, so that they could see strangers coming and be on guard for white spies seeking to kidnap runaways. For many years the family was under continuous strain to protect their own lives and property as well as the fleeing slaves they aided. Their son and daughter-in-law continued to help slaves until the Civil War.

Hannah Gibbons was described as a person of refined intelligence, great patience, self-denial and warm affection. Although she was breaking the laws of the time, she risked her life, safety and property to answer another call to free men from bondage. Hannah Wierman Gibbons, like others in the Underground Railroad, did not seek recognition, but her unselfish devotion to an ideal with its consequent risks has earned her a place in Pennsylvania history.

Lancaster Branch
Researchers: Frances Keller and
Betty Duncan
Writer: Leah Kresge

70

Lucretia Coffin Mott

1793–1880

Lucretia Coffin Mott represents one of the single most significant individuals working for two closely linked nineteenth century causes: the abolition of slavery and women's rights. She was born in 1793 on Nantucket Island, an area known for its strong Quaker heritage. The Quakers had escaped there when they were persecuted in Massachusetts. On the island of Nantucket, women had important roles because the men left for long periods of time, and the women were responsible for running the island.

By the age of fifteen, Lucretia was an assistant teacher. At eighteen, she married and moved to Philadelphia. About the time of the War of 1812, her husband turned to the cotton business, but believing that the slave system was unjust, Lucretia made up her mind to stay free of all activities which involved slave-gain products. When the family business faded, she opened a private school. Later, she turned to theology and the ministry of Friends until the Friends "separation" in 1827. The Quaker Meeting House was closed against her when she stood with the splinter group, the Hicksites.

Her distinguished appearance, beautiful face and nobility of expression brought her recognition, but her able mind made her a leader. At the convention in Philadelphia in 1833, at which the American Anti-Slavery Society was created, she was one of the few women in the United States who dared appear to be a friend of the slave. She became president of the Female Anti-Slavery Society, founded in Philadelphia that same year. At their meetings rioters threw insults, but she was not intimidated. She traveled thousands of miles preaching deliverance of the slaves. Her home became a famous station on the Underground Railway. Her wit and rare personality gradually led to her acceptance without the former riots.

In 1840 she was appointed a delegate to the Anti-Slavery Convention in London. However, she was refused admission as a delegate on the grounds that no woman could sit on the platform with male delegates. It was this incident that focused her attention on the "woman question." Her fight for women's rights was a repetition of her long battle against slavery. Now a more accomplished speaker, her gentleness and wit invariably turned the ridicule directed at her into victories for her cause. In this way, she was able to contend successfully with critics of women's rights. In 1848 Lucretia and her sister called the convention at Seneca Falls, New York, where she and Elizabeth Cady Stanton pushed through the "Declaration of Sentiments." Her struggles for the freeing of slaves, for women's rights and for peace continued until her death in 1880.

Philadelphia Branch
Researcher/Writer: Ellen H. Moore
Special Division Editor: Dr. Barbara Klaczynska

71

Anna Elizabeth Dickinson

1842–1932 ─────────────────────────────────────

An impassioned orator for many causes, but particularly for the equality of women and the abolition of slavery, Anna Elizabeth Dickinson was a powerful influence in the United States during and immediately after the Civil War.

Born in Philadelphia on October 28, 1842, she was the youngest of five children of John and Mary Edmondson Dickinson, both Quakers. As a young woman, her mother taught in a Quaker meeting house school near the present borough of New Brighton in Beaver County. After their marriage, her parents lived in Philadelphia, where her father was a dry goods merchant and active abolitionist. He died when Anna was only two.

In spite of the family's precarious financial state, Anna received good schooling, first from her mother, then at Friends' Select School of Philadelphia and finally at the Greenwood Institute in New Brighton.

At fifteen, Anna began working, first as a copyist, then as a school teacher and, in 1861, at the United States Mint in Philadelphia. In 1856 her first article on abolition was published in William Lloyd Garrison's *Liberator*. Four years later she spoke before the Pennsylvania Anti-Slavery Society.

The oppression and inequality of women was the other great theme she addressed. Well-known feminists such as Dr. Hannah Longshore, Lucretia Mott and Susan B. Anthony encouraged her and, abetted by them and by Republican politicians and abolitionists, she became a popular and effective lecturer on the national scene.

Her views, emotional intensity and eloquence were complemented by her youthful appearance. In her late teens, Anna became known as an American Joan of Arc; she was vivacious, slim and had short, curly, black hair. An 1862 photograph of her at age twenty shows her firm purpose and controlled power.

In that year she was invited to join the political campaigns in New Hampshire and Connecticut. She was a great success at the Cooper Institute in New York City where she spoke for the Unionist cause. In 1864 she spoke in the United States House of Representatives before a distinguished audience that included President Abraham Lincoln. After the Civil War Anna Dickinson moved to the lyceum lecture circuit and earned great sums for her appearances. She continued to champion Negro rights and the emancipation of women.

When her popularity as a speaker began to decline, she turned to writing. Her first book, *What Answer?* (1868), dealt with inter-racial marriage. *A Paying Investment* advanced the need for social reforms such as universal compulsory education, technical training for workmen, better treatment of prisoners and improved assistance to the poor.

In her later years she became a playwright and actress. Only one of her plays, *An American Girl*, achieved moderate success and toured the country in 1880.

In 1891 she was committed to the Danville State Hospital for the Insane. She had to struggle to be adjudged sane, and, although she won her court case, she was financially pressed to meet the legal costs of the action. Befriended by a New York couple after her release from Danville, she lived in quiet retirement until her death in 1932.

Aliquippa Branch
Researcher/Writer: Belle Adams

9

WOMEN AS COMMUNITY DEVELOPERS: LEADERS IN HUMANITARIAN, CULTURAL AND CIVIC SERVICE

72
Rebecca Gratz
1781–1869

Rebecca Gratz, called by many "the foremost American Jewess of her day," was born in Philadelphia on March 4, 1781, the fourth daughter and seventh child of twelve. Her father, Michael Gratz, and paternal uncle, Barnard, had emigrated from Upper Silesia in the 1750s and were prominent, successful merchants. Her mother, Miriam Simon, was descended from early settlers in Lancaster who were also merchants. Although the families had a German heritage they were active in the Sephardic (Spanish and Portuguese) Congregation Mikveh Israel in Philadelphia, the first synagogue in the city.

Showing an interest in charitable work from the age of twenty, Rebecca helped to organize and became the first secretary of the non-sectarian Female Association for the Relief of Women and Children in Reduced Circumstances. For over forty years she was the secretary of the Philadelphia Orphan Asylum which she helped to found in 1815. Four years later in 1819, she organized the Female Hebrew Benevolent Society. Her most significant achievement, however, was the creation of the Hebrew Sunday School Society of Philadelphia, the first of its kind in America. Organized on her birthday, March 4, 1838, it served girls as well as boys, free of charge. She was its president for the next twenty-six years.

The Gratz sisters were noted for their charm and great beauty. Rebecca's portrait was painted by the miniaturist, Edward Malbone, and by the even more eminent artist, Thomas Sully. The famed Gilbert Stuart painted the portrait of her younger sister, Rachel.

In 1798 Rebecca's brothers, Hyman and Simon, purchased the house in which Thomas Jefferson composed the Declaration of Independence, and the family lived there for a time.

Rebecca never married. It was said that she was in love with Samuel Ewing, son of the Reverend Dr. John Ewing, provost of the University of Pennsylvania, but that she refused to marry outside her faith. After her sister Rachel's early death in 1823, Rebecca raised her nine children.

In addition to her philanthropies and the social agencies, both Jewish and non-sectarian, she founded, tradition claims that Rebecca Gratz was the prototype for "Rebecca" in Sir Walter Scott's romantic novel, *Ivanhoe*. Washington Irving's fiancee, Matilda Hoffman, was a close friend of Rebecca's who nursed her during her final illness. After Matilda's death in 1809, Irving journeyed to Britain where he visited Scott at Abbotsford. Irving's description of the beautiful, remarkable Philadelphia Jewess, Rebecca Gratz, so impressed Scott that he put her into the novel he was then writing.

At the age of eighty-eight, on August 27, 1869, Rebecca died in Philadelphia and was buried in the old Jewish Cemetery of Congregation Mikveh Israel.

Philadelphia Branch
Researcher/Writer: Ellen H. Moore
Special Division Editor: Margaret D. Druse

73

Sarah Wilson

1795–1871 _____

Sarah Wilson was typical of the strong, devout rural women found among the Scotch-Irish farmers of South Central Pennsylvania. She was born in 1795 on a farm west of Chambersburg and never strayed from the path foreordained for her by her rural antecedents. She was the youngest of ten children and remained on the ancestral farm all her life, cooking meals over an open fireplace and keeping house for her seven brothers, who never married but spent their lives managing the twenty-four farms which the family had accumulated by 1860.

By 1867 however, only Sarah remained, and the management of these large holdings became her responsibility. She wisely chose her most competent tenants to manage her affairs, for she had only the education of a farm girl. She was able to read and write, but she was not a student nor did she read books, except her Bible to which she was devoted.

It was her strong religious feeling that led her to an important decision to contribute $10,000 to the Central Presbyterian congregation so they could build their church in Chambersburg. The very tall steeple planned for the church became a matter of much protest and was branded as "ostentatious sinfulness," but Sarah saw no reason to withdraw her money. "I gave it to them to erect a church," she said. "I made no restriction as to what kind of building it was to be. If they build a tall steeple such as you say they intend doing and the Lord does not want it there, he will knock it down." He never did.

The other important decision of Sarah Wilson's life presents a fascinating question about her deepest feelings about her life as a woman in nineteenth century rural America; she agreed to fund the creation of a college for women in Chambersburg. The fact that two Presbyterian clergymen applied to her for the necessary money certainly influenced her decision, since she had always been a faithful member of the church. But there was also an apparent understanding on her part of the value of higher education for women.

Since 1869 Wilson College, named for Sarah and her family, has prepared thousands of well-educated women who have made their mark out in the world Sarah never knew. But all of Wilson's graduates know "Aunt Sally," the benign spirit presiding over the academic halls of one of America's earliest colleges for women. Her portrait hangs in Norland Hall there—and even today, students can make the pilgrimage to the cemetery of the old Rocky Spring Church where Sarah Wilson lies buried alongside her parents and brothers.

Franklin County Branch
Researcher/Writer: Anne G. Vondra

74

Mary Johnson Ambler

1805–1868

Mary Ambler was a Quaker woman whose religious commitment guided her daily life and activities. Her place in community history was assured by her heroic action on July 17, 1856, the day of the famous "Terrible Train Wreck" of Ambler. Her actions that day demonstrated her intelligence, leadership and compassion, qualities she was known for throughout her life by her service to her family and community.

Mary Johnson, born in 1805, was wed to Andrew Ambler. They came to live in what is now Ambler, where Andrew operated a fulling mill. She was a tiny woman, never weighing more than 100 pounds. Yet she managed to raise seven sons and one daughter, while actively devoting herself to community service. She founded a Sunday School for children in the area and was known for her readiness to help her neighbors. She and her husband had the only well in Ambler, and, whenever necessary, she allowed neighbors to draw water from it.

Mary Ambler is best remembered for her relief efforts during the famous train wreck of 1856. On July 17 an excursion train left Philadelphia on the North Penn Railroad with 1,000 passengers aboard, most of them children, headed for a picnic near Fort Washington. Shortly before the scheduled arrival, the train collided head-on with another train. Fifty-nine people died instantly, and countless others were injured. Mary Ambler, hearing of the collision, walked several miles to the scene with medical supplies. She arrived before any doctors and began systematically organizing the rescue operations. She directed volunteers to carry the wounded to her home, using stretchers made from shutters torn off nearby buildings. She turned her home into a makeshift hospital, tearing up bed linens and petticoats for bandages and working tirelessly until the victims could be moved to their own homes.

After the tragedy, she resumed her everyday life. Her husband had died in 1850, and she and her sons managed the fulling mill. They did a thriving business, especially during the Civil War, supplying woolens and blankets to the Union Army. Mary died in 1868, a devout Quaker remembered for her selfless dedication and commitment to others.

Later in 1868, when the officials of the town decided to rename the railroad station, Mary Ambler's name was selected because of her direct connection with the history of the railroad. She never knew that the town had honored her in this way, but to Ambler residents her actions continue to serve as a model for community service.

Lansdale Branch
Researcher/Writer: Deborah O'Connell
Local Editor: Diane Brouillette

75

Sophia Georgiana Fisher Coxe

1841–1926

Sophia Georgianna Fisher, the "Angel of the Anthracite Region," was born in Philadelphia on November 26, 1841, the daughter of Joshua and Elizabeth Fisher. Her grandfather, Arthur Middleton, was one of the Signers of the Declaration of Independence.

Sophia obtained her education at private schools in Philadelphia and Switzerland. An excellent musician, she possessed an exceptional contralto voice. While studying abroad she was presented at the Court of Napoleon III of France.

On June 27, 1868, she married Eckley B. Coxe, and they settled in Drifton, Pennsylvania. It was there that she performed the labors of charity that earned her the title, "Angel of the Anthracite Region."

She began her charitable works by riding daily about the mining villages distributing food and medicine among the ill and injured. A hospital was established in Drifton and maintained by Coxe funds. When the Hazleton State Hospital was established, Sophia Coxe gave $50,000 to the state to erect a new addition. She was also a generous contributor to the Overbrook Institution for the Blind in Philadelphia, the Chapin Memorial Home for the Aged Blind in Philadelphia, the Seashore Children's Hospital in Atlantic City, the Laurytown Home and the White Haven Sanitorium.

Sophia Coxe organized a staff of nurses to visit the homes of the ill miners and their families. During 1889, while abroad, the Coxes investigated the cure for diphtheria and were instrumental in bringing it to the United States. They were the first to import the anti-toxin on a large scale, a move that virtually eliminated diphtheria in mining towns.

Sophia Coxe and her sisters-in-law founded the Drifton Sunday School and the St. James Episcopal Church at Drifton, and they also began an annual Christmas Tree observance in Drifton and other mining towns.

Lehigh University was another beneficiary of Sophia Coxe's generosity. She built and equipped the Eckley B. Coxe Memorial Mining Laboratory there. She and her husband also founded the Freeland Mining and Mechanical Institute. Sophia Coxe made her last public appearance on Thanksgiving Day in 1925, when she was present at the dedication of the new gymnasium at the Freeland Institute.

All of Sophia Coxe's philanthropy and services were carried on in a quiet manner. She lived simply and unostentatiously, was adverse to publicity and refrained from talking about her charities. There was nothing about her attire or demeanor to indicate her wealth.

Sophia Coxe died at her home in Drifton on March 1, 1926, in her eighty-fifth year. She was buried in Drifton. In her unassuming way she did much to improve the mining industry in Pennsylvania and to raise the quality of the lives of the miners.

Hazleton Branch
Researcher/Writer: Patricia Conahan

76

Sara Louisa Oberholtzer

1841–1930 ─────────────────────────────────

Sara Oberholtzer was a poet who influenced several generations of United States and Canadian school children by her promotion of the school savings bank movement. She learned of the movement while serving as a newspaper reporter at the 1888 meeting of the American Economic Association at the University of Pennsylvania. For the next forty years, she put all her efforts into the movement, speaking throughout the United States to teachers, superintendents of schools, women's clubs and bankers. She told how the savings plan would serve "to teach the children not to waste their pennies on candy, cigarettes and drink" and inspired others to become involved in this worthwhile enterprise. In 1892 she brought the plan, which had originated in Belgium, to West Chester and Norristown, Pennsylvania and Atlantic City, New Jersey. The school savings bank plan later spread as far as California, growing to over four million depositors. While on a visit to the Canadian province of New Brunswick, she explained the plan, and it was subsequently adopted there.

Sara was descended from a Quaker family that had followed William Penn to this country and had become well-known for the manufacture of superior earthenware. Their pottery, located in Uwchlan Township, Chester County, was a principal station on the Underground Railroad. Many slaves rested there en route from Maryland to Canada, aided by the conscientious Quakers. Sara was educated at Thomas' Boarding School in Lionville and at Millersville State Normal School. Because of illness, she was forced to abandon the study of medicine.

Sara discovered her talents as a rhymester early in life. At the age of fifteen, she sent her poetry to well-known poets for their criticism, thereby developing correspondence and friendships with John Greenleaf Whittier, William Cullen Bryant and Henry Wadsworth Longfellow. Whittier once said of her poetry, that it "sings," and she was a frequent visitor at his home. Her writings include several volumes of poetry, a novel about the Quaker people in southeastern Pennsylvania entitled *Hope's Heart Bells*, short stories and news articles.

In 1862 Sara married John Oberholtzer, a successful grain merchant and the originator of the Pickering Valley Railroad. She raised two sons who became distinguished, one as a lecturer on scientific subjects and the other as an historian and motion picture censor for Pennsylvania.

Sara Oberholtzer's decision to work as a newspaper reporter was not based on financial need, but represented her continued involvement in local, state, and national affairs. She headed the Woman's Christian Temperance Union (WCTU), addressed the World's Congress of Representative Women, served as the WCTU's state superintendent of narcotics, as well as speaking extensively to promote the school savings plan. She also published a periodical called *Thrift Tidings.* Her efforts introduced countless school children to the benefits of thrift through their participation in the school savings plan.

West Chester Branch
Researcher: Claire C. Etherton
Writer: Mary S. Pinkney

77

Mira Lloyd Dock

1853–1945 _____

Mira Lloyd Dock was born in 1853 into an old, financially comfortable family and lived the ninety-two years of her life to its fullest.

As a young woman, she, her sisters and several friends decided to change their "cooking club" to a music club. Thus, in her home in Harrisburg, on May 17, 1882, they founded the locally well-known Wednesday Club. Mira contributed to the programs as a pianist and later served a term as president from 1894 to 1895.

She was, however, first and foremost a naturalist who studied botany at the University of Michigan and became a noted horticulturist for the Pennsylvania Department of Forestry. The Pennsylvania Department of Agriculture sent her to England and the Continent to study forestry and urban arboriculture. She became a nationally acclaimed lecturer for the State Forestry Commission.

Mira Dock believed in saving rural environment and introducing it into urban areas. She could see that the two means available to leisured, middle-class women of her day for changing Harrisburg from a village to a more beautiful city were organization and publicity. In 1898 she became one of the founders of the Civic Club of Harrisburg formed to help clean up the city.

The following year she was sent to the International Congress of Women in London as a representative of the Federation of Pennsylvania Women and Parks Association of Philadelphia. Being a first-rate photographer, Mira returned with dozens of negative plates to complement the booklet she had written for the state. Focusing her early concern on the improvement and beautification of Harrisburg, she prepared a lantern–slide talk comparing lovely European parks and river banks with those of Harrisburg, pointing out the natural beauty hidden beneath the unkempt appearance of the Susquehanna River town.

According to a biographer, she compensated for her lack of physical beauty with an abundance of wit and charm, particularly enchanting the men she encountered. Using her myriad talents, she persuaded city councilmen and other influential male civic leaders, notably J. Horace McFarland and Vance C. McCormick, to aid her cause. They formed the League for Municipal Improvement and began a city-planning program that continued for forty years.

Victorian mores did not permit the participation of women in formal decision making, but men made use of Mira Dock's expertise and experience. Backing a bond issue to finance sewers and a water filtration system, she and the Civic Club led a campaign that brought about city garbage collection, river bank beautification and the transformation of Wetzel Swamp into Wildwood Park.

After helping to elect Vance McCormick mayor in 1902, Mira left Harrisburg, in 1903, to live in what she called her "forest country," Graeffenburg and Fayetteville. Several years later she donated one hundred pine seedlings for planting in Harrisburg's Reservoir Park.

In her later years her concerns broadened as she became an ardent feminist and suffragist. She was appointed a member of Pennsylvania's Forestry Reservation Commission, a post she held for twelve years. She also served as vice-chairman of the Conservation Department of the General Federation of Women's Clubs.

The Docks were a most remarkable family. Mira's only brother, George, studied medicine and moved west to practice. The five sisters remained together, residing in Harrisburg and then in Fayetteville. Lavinia, a nurse, wrote a textbook that was used in the nursing profession for years. She was also a pianist and a militant suffragist who embarrassed the family by being arrested and jailed several times. Emily was an accomplished violinist. Laura, an artist, was deaf which made her a difficult house guest according to those who remember her. Margaret was not known for displaying any particular talent other than being the housekeeper, but maintaining a happy home for such divergent people must surely have been an art in itself! Unfortunately not one of these six accomplished Dock children ever married, and so the line of a most talented family ended.

Mira Dock's success was based on a combination of her love of forestry and her desire to further urban improvement. Her contributions to Harrisburg's improvement and beautification were monumental.

Harrisburg Branch
Researcher/Writer: Ann Corby

78

Photograph courtesy of the Harrisburg Chapter of the American National Red Cross, Harrisburg, PA

Gabriella Cameron Gilbert

1864–1951

Gabriella Cameron, born in Petersburg, Virginia in 1864, came to Harrisburg in 1889 as the wife of Lyman D. Gilbert. She was exceedingly well-read, and, in a time when most women's lives were bounded by home and church, she took a lively and creative interest in her new community.

On January 21, 1898, she organized the Civic Club of Harrisburg and served as its president for twelve years. She encouraged its members to study the health and safety and educational problems of their city and to push for reforms where they were needed. The Club worked for clean streets (very important in the days of horses), for school libraries, for language classes for the foreign born, for Harrisburg's first sewer system and for the beautification of Front Street Park. Long before women's suffrage they found ways to have their proposals acted upon. One Harrisburg mayor even paid them a back-handed compliment: "The Club never asked City Council to do anything ill-considered. There was a complete absence of the 'nut' suggestions that so often characterize such appeals."

For a period of twenty-four years, from the beginning of the First World War until the beginning of the Second, Gabriella Gilbert was the chairman and guiding spirit of the Harrisburg Chapter of the Red Cross. In 1917 she presided over the reorganization of the Harrisburg Chapter after a request came from Washington that all war relief organizations merge with the Red Cross. New bylaws were adopted and committees were set up to deal primarily with the war effort. Women workers were organized to work on hospital linens, surgical dressings, hospital clothes and the knitting of socks and sweaters. A special canteen committee was organized to serve draftees and service people as they passed through Harrisburg. Money raised for the war funds exceeded the quota each time. In two years, membership of the Harrisburg Red Cross increased from 177 members to 33,000.

When the war was over the Red Cross, under the stewardship of Gabriella, organized the city for work during the influenza epidemic. Nurses were recruited to visit in homes as well as for service at home and abroad.

Gabriella continued to guide the local Chapter during the Depression years. In 1932 the Red Cross, with its nationwide outlets and organization, was asked to handle the colossal job of distributing flour and clothing. The Chapter was also called upon to organize relief activities during the greatest calamity to hit the Harrisburg area, the flood of 1936. Food, clothing and assistance were given to the victims of the flood, and, after the water subsided, nurses were busy giving typhoid inoculations. Gabriella resigned in 1941 when she felt the Chapter needed more youthful and vigorous leadership.

Robert C. Glenn in his history of the local Red Cross described her: "She brought the warmth and charm of old Virginia to Harrisburg. She was interested in civic affairs, welfare programs and cultural activities. While people and programs appealed to her more than administration, she had an unusual knack for getting people to do things."

George W. Reily, president of the Harrisburg National Bank and a member of the Federal Reserve Board, said of her, "In this part of Pennsylvania it is assumed that Mrs. Gilbert should have, and generally gets, everything that she wants."

Gabriella Gilbert was also convinced of the value of education and gave financial help to a long series of promising girls. These "scholarship girls" remained her lifelong friends. Another of her interests was the Art Association of Harrisburg. She was one of its incorporators in 1926 and served in various capacities, including president, until her death in 1951.

Harrisburg Branch
Researcher: Martha Dohner
Writer: Louise Eaton Walker

79

Laura Reider Muth

1872–1977 ─────────────────────────────────

Laura Reider was born on March 20, 1872. She was educated in the public schools of Hummelstown and graduated from the Hummelstown High School in 1888. She then enrolled as a student at Lebanon Valley College, Annville, receiving her Bachelor of Science degree in 1892. In 1893 she married Franklin Muth, a local jeweler, and they had ten children, two of whom died in infancy. When the youngest of the children was four years old, Franklin died. With the help of an elderly uncle, Laura Reider Muth reared the children, encouraging them to prepare for meaningful careers by earning college degrees.

As busy as she was with her home and family, Laura Muth still found time to lead a productive life outside her home by participating in the affairs of the community. During World War I, she was very active in the work of the Red Cross. On the enfranchisement of women in the early 1920s, she became a Republican committeewoman and canvassed the Hummelstown electorate, urging all women to register and to vote. She was a charter member of three Hummelstown organizations: the Community Club, which sponsored a well-baby clinic; the Parent-Teacher Association, of which she was an organizer and first president; and the Flower Club.

Laura Muth was also a charter member of the Natural History Society of Harrisburg. Always interested in the birds and the flora of the Central Pennsylvania area, she served as nature consultant to both the Boy Scouts and Girl Scouts, helping many scouts to qualify for nature badges.

Laura Muth was a lifelong member of the Hummelstown United Brethren Church, where for many years she served as president of the Dorcas Society. Throughout her life, she responded in various ways to those in need. Day after day during the Great Depression, she fed those who came to her door asking for food. She also helped in drives to collect and distribute clothing to the poor.

Endowed with great zest for life, Laura Muth communicated her enthusiasm to her children and her neighbors. She retained this remarkable quality to the very close of her life. She died on February 17, 1977, a month short of her 105th birthday.

Hershey Branch
Researcher: Nancy Curry Funk
Writer: Miriam Vanderwall

80
Eleanora "Nelle" Moyer Engle

1887–1963 _____

"Aunt Nelle" Engle, as she was affectionately called by a multitude of friends, had a concern for all whom she met. During her married life, her family never knew how many people would be staying in their home or what the color of their skins would be. She opened her home to students from Africa who were attending Lebanon Valley College in Annville, Pennsylvania. She made speaking engagements for them, drove them where they had to go, and helped them bank the money they earned. Members of her Sunday School class benefited greatly from her able instruction and her exemplary life. She was active in the missionary work of the United Brethren Church, holding offices in the Women's Missionary Society on both the local and national levels.

Nelle was involved in civic matters as well as church affairs. In 1919 she organized the first Girl Scout troop in Palmyra. She was president of the Palmyra Women's Club and served the organization in various ways. She was interested in government, and for a time she served as Committeewoman for the Lebanon County Republican Committee.

Following the death of her husband, Ray Engle, she offered her services to the Home Mission Board of the United Brethren Church, which, in 1942, sent her to New Mexico. There she spent a brief period in preparation for service as a field worker for the Board. She toured the country speaking about home missions and raising money for these missions in New Mexico, Kentucky and Florida. She was a dynamic speaker, and she thoroughly enjoyed all aspects of her work. In 1957 she was honored with the "Order of the Cross" for her fifty-one years of service to the Palmyra First United Brethren Chruch.

"Aunt Nelle" Engle lived to be seventy-six years old. Her career, her remarkable scope of activity and her deep social and religious concerns reflect the responses of one who was thoughtful and eager to contribute to the life of her time.

Hershey Branch
Researchers/Writers: Miriam Vanderwall
and Jean Bomgardner Gingrich

81

Eliza Ambler Foulke

b. 1893 ——————————————————————————————

Eliza Foulke is a woman whose life has been devoted to the service of others. Her grandmother was Mary Johnson Ambler, the heroine of the "Terrible Train Wreck" of 1856, for whom the town of Ambler is named. Eliza's father was killed in an accident when she was three years old, and her mother opened her home to boarders in order to support her three children. From her mother's strength and determination to keep a strong family unit, Eliza learned a deep sense of faith and commitment to others.

Eliza attended Plymouth Meeting Friends School, and the George School, a Friends boarding school in Newtown, Bucks County. She graduated in 1912 and took a teaching position at Gwynedd Friends School. At the age of nineteen, she had full responsibility for her own little school, teaching all eight grades in a single classroom.

Leaving the school in 1917, she accepted the post of executive secretary with the Young Friends Movement in Philadelphia. It was her responsibility to organize study groups, conferences and summer camps for young Quakers in the area. This marked the beginning of her lifelong commitment to the goals of brotherhood and understanding fostered by the Quaker religion.

Through the Young Friends Movement Eliza met her husband, Thomas Foulke, a young lawyer from Temple University. After their marriage, they moved to Ambler, where Eliza enthusiastically pursued community service. She helped found the Wissahickon Library of Ambler and was an active member of the Colony Club and the Needlework Guild, service organizations for the poor and needy. In 1919 she founded the North Penn Community Center, now known as the North Penn Visiting Nurse Association.

In 1949 Eliza and Thomas Foulke were asked by the American Friends Service Committee to travel to Japan to establish a neighborhood center in Tokyo. While in Japan, they also worked with the United States government programs, distributing food and clothing to the needy. The Foulkes established the International Students Seminar, which gathered young people of all nationalities together, following the Quaker belief that by learning of others' beliefs and ideas, we can create a united world community. In addition, Eliza began a nursery for the children of working mothers.

In 1960 she served as housemother for International House in Philadelphia. In 1963 after her husband's death, she returned to Tokyo for a year as acting director of the Friends Center. Throughout the 1950s and 1960s her American home was always open to Japanese friends who came to study or visit in this country. The Japanese government honored her, in 1971, with a citation for her service to the people of Japan.

Following her belief that documentation of the past helps us understand the community we live in today, Eliza Foulke has worked to chronicle local history, in which her ancestors played a major part. She wrote histories of the Foulke and Ambler families, dating back to their origins in Wales and England. She also wrote a history of the Gwynedd Friends Meeting, noting that there has always been a Foulke in the organization since its establishment in 1699. She also authored two volumes of *Devotional Readings for the Young in Years and the Young in Heart.*

Eliza's life and work reflect her faith that our future resides in bringing people together to share experiences and ideas. In the 1950s she helped organize the first World Day of Prayer, which eventually brought community churches together to share in worship. Typically modest about her contributions, she feels that every woman should do whatever is necessary to make this world a better place. The Quaker religion with its strong tradition of women taking active roles in service to God and community has enabled Eliza to bring help to those in need and to promote communication among all people.

Lansdale Branch
Researcher/Writer: Deborah O'Connell
Local Editor: Diane Brouillette

82

Lena Jane Kessler

b. 1901 _____

Lena Kessler represents the epitome of the unrecognized woman of modern history. Her dedication to her community and to the education of its youth throughout her life may be shared by thousands of other women across the state and the country. Her story is of interest because she is representative of the years of commitment women have given to their communities.

Lena Jane Kessler was born in Orbisonia, Pennsylvania, in 1901 and graduated from DuBois High School in 1920. With teaching credentials from Indiana Normal School, Pennsylvania State University and Columbia University, she taught elementary grades and secondary history and civics classes in the DuBois area for thirty-nine years. In 1962 she retired to dedicate herself to volunteer service.

Lena's life spans almost a century of history. When she was in her eighties, she could easily relay secondhand stories of the 1888 fire of DuBois, as told to her by her father and as remembered through a childhood oriented towards her family and closely-knit neighborhood. Although Lena was reaching the age of maturity at the time the Women's Suffrage Movement achieved the ratification of the Nineteenth Amendment, giving women the vote, the event made little impact on her family. Her mother wasn't interested in politics and never voted. Lena's mother's home orientation was passed on to her daughter. It wasn't until Lena began her teaching career in 1922 that her political awareness began to evolve. When asked her opinion of the women's movement of the 1980s, Lena Kessler replied emphatically, "I'm very much in favor of it."

Her life was relatively untouched by World War II, though she called it "the most interesting historical event" of her lifetime. Along with such important world events, she carefully noted the small but important changes occurring in her local area: the impact of the changes in the mining and railroading industries on the DuBois area, population migration, and the changing social scene as lifestyles adapted to each new decade.

Lena Kessler's entry into the world of education was almost accidental. Her high school preparation was in commercial courses, and her highest job goal was office work. She did work briefly in a local retail store and in the office of the Baltimore and Ohio Railroad. But then, Lena followed her grandmother's suggestions that she become a teacher because "we had never had a teacher in the family." She began teaching in the elementary school in 1922. By taking self-financed summer courses, she was able to earn a bachelor's degree from Pennsylvania State University and a master's degree in government from Columbia University.

In 1939 Lena Kessler joined the secondary school faculty as a teacher of history and Pennsylvania government. As the first "cooperative teacher" in the DuBois Junior High School, she guided eleven student teachers from Clarion State College. She also touched the lives of many Pennsylvania State students while teaching the history of education at the DuBois campus of the University and while serving as housemother at the Sigma Nu fraternity house on the State College campus after her retirement from teaching. According to the DuBois *Courier Express*, her effects on her students far exceeded the knowledge from the subjects she taught, for during those years, "Miss Kessler always expounded the ideals of patriotism, the American way of life, . . . loyalty to God and country, and living by Christian beliefs and attitudes."

Lena Kessler owns a number of firsts in her community. Besides being the first cooperating teacher in the DuBois area, she was the first woman to hold the position of clerk of sessions of the United Presbyterian Church of DuBois. This achievement was, she acknowledged, "quite an honor, back in those days, for a woman." In 1980 she was the first woman to be chosen Grand Marshal of the DuBois Christmas Parade because of her outstanding charitable accomplishments for many years." On May 21, 1981, she received the award of "Distinguished Volunteer Woman of the Year—Preserving the American Way of Life," earning state recognition from the General Federation of Women's Clubs for her documented 19,839 hours as a local volunteer.

Living world history was a necessity; teaching state history was an accident she said; but making local history was Lena Kessler's achievement. The fiber of history is woven of such women.

DuBois Branch
Researcher: AAUW PA Women in History
Committee, DuBois
Writer: Gail Anne Wasser

83

Frances Strong Helman

1903–1980 ——————————————————————————————

People throughout Indiana County remember her wit, dedication of purpose and untiring enthusiasm. Her correspondents from across the country knew her as a thorough researcher with a national reputation as a genealogist. In 1976 the Indiana County Commissioners declared her "Indiana County Historian", an appropriate title, since Frances Strong Helman had spent much of her life studying and researching the genealogy and history of the County and encouraging others to do the same.

Her interest in genealogy began in childhood, inspired by stories told by her mother. Born in Pitcairn, Pennsylvania on April 27, 1903, a daughter of Thomas and Jean Strong, Frances and her family moved to Rayne Township in Indiana County shortly after her birth. She was very proud of the Strong family name and always used it as part of her signature, even after her marriage. Her great-grandfather, James Strong, had been a founder of Strongstown in southern Indiana County, and Frances was a principal organizer of Strong family reunions and the annual Strongstown Homecoming.

In 1922 Frances married Daniel Blaine Helman. They had three children, one of whom died in infancy. A devoted wife and mother, Frances found time to pursue her love of history and genealogy. She expanded her research to include her husband's family, for whom she published *The Helman News* "as often as finances would permit." They had traced his family's lineage to Germany in 1725.

Frances continued researching her own family. She was contacted by relatives in Utah who wanted information about the family and, visiting them, was introduced to the work of the Mormon Genealogical Society in Salt Lake City. This inspired her to begin a similar organization. In 1938 she helped found the Genealogical Society of Indiana County "to receive, collect, record, and preserve the history and genealogical records of Indiana County and maintain a library and a museum."

For forty years Frances Strong Helman guided the Society through its many endeavors, which included both research and public relations activities. Her early contributions included an explanation of family record charts, the procedure for collecting genealogical data and many papers on Indiana County history. She organized the Society's library and actively sought new acquisitions. She wrote a pamphlet which explained how to obtain genealogical information. Both she and her husband served as curators in the Society's museum. In 1956 she organized the first Society-sponsored genealogical workshop. These workshops continue to attract people from throughout the United States. She worked with the Junior Historical Societies in the county schools, discussing local history and leading student tours of the museum. Through her writings and teaching, she assisted others in learning the techniques necessary to research their lineage.

Her interest in history and genealogy extended beyond Indiana County. She was a member of the National Genealogical Society, the Pennsylvania Folklore Society, the Daughters of the American Revolution (DAR) and the Children of American Colonists. She served as president and vice-president of the Federation of Pennsylvania Historical Societies.

As her reputation as a genealogist grew, she fulfilled requests for research from people throughout the United States. Her work frequently found her at the National Archives, the Library of Congress, the DAR Library and countless local county courthouses. In 1948 she founded and edited *Your Family Tree*, a magazine of Pennsylvania genealogy and history "dedicated to those hardy pioneer families of Western Pennsylvania who did so much toward the development of this country and had no writers to perpetuate their memory." She published many articles, including a series about Revolutionary soldiers from Indiana County which appeared in the *Indiana County Heritage*.

Frances was also involved in other community pursuits. In 1956 she founded the Armstrong-Kittanning Trail Society and was a founder of the Indiana County Tourist Bureau. From 1964 to 1972 she was the only woman director of Civil Defense in Pennsylvania. She was appointed executive director in 1974 and received the Richard S. Funck Memorial Award for excellence in civil preparedness.

Frances Strong Helman continued to be active in the Genealogical Society of Indiana County until her death in September 1980. In 1979 she received the Society's first Honorary Member Award. After her death, the Society established an endowment fund in her honor to serve as a permanent memorial to the woman whose name had become synonymous with Indiana County history.

Indiana Branch
Researcher/Writer: Evelyn D. Landon

84

Elizabeth Slafkosky Lipovsky

b. 1908 ───────────────────────────────

Elizabeth Slafkosky was born in Bethlehem, Pennsylvania, in 1908 of Slovak parents. Her father, George Slafkosky, had arrived in America in 1881 at the age of eighteen, one of the first settlers in South Bethlehem. Ten years after his arrival, he sent to his Slovakian homeland for Mary Sopko, who became his bride. In 1900 Mary was a founder of the eighty-ninth branch—Bethlehem's second—of the First Catholic Slovak Ladies Association (FCSLA).

Elizabeth, following family tradition, spent most of her life following the FCSLA creed: to love God and neighbor, to preserve Slovak ancestry, to cultivate the Slovak language and to aid those in need. (The FCSLA is a fraternal insurance and benefit organization which insures members of Slovak extraction from birth to age sixty-five. Headquartered in Beechwood, Ohio, the organization celebrated its ninetieth anniversary in 1982 and includes over 500 branches in the United States and Canada.)

Having joined the FCSLA as a child of six, Elizabeth eventually became a local branch officer in Bethlehem. In 1940 she became a national auditor and board member and, from 1960 to 1966, was editor of the FCSLA's monthly bilingual magazine with a circulation of approximately 39,000.

Elizabeth Lipovsky became national president of the FCSLA in 1964 and held that position until 1976. Highlights of her FCSLA activities were two invitations to the White House from President Lyndon Johnson and a papal audience with Pope Paul VI in 1979.

After the death of her husband in 1977, she remained busy with visits to her children and grandchildren in New Jersey, with baking traditional ethnic foods and with the activities of the Bethlehem branch of the FCSLA. She still serves on the Executive Committee of the Slovak Catholic Federation.

Bethlehem Branch
Researcher/Writer: Catherine D. Barrett

85

Photograph courtesy of Washington Crossing Foundation, Washington Crossing, PA

Ann Hawkes Hutton

b. 1909 ⎯⎯⎯⎯⎯⎯⎯⎯⎯⎯⎯⎯⎯⎯⎯⎯⎯⎯⎯⎯⎯⎯⎯

The history of the Delaware Valley, and especially the Revolutionary War era, lives, thanks in large measure to the efforts of Ann Hawkes Hutton. Combining her education in law, her career experience in public relations and advertising and her lifelong interest in history, Ann Hutton has devoted herself to bringing a part of this country's rich heritage into the public view.

Born in Philadelphia on February 16, 1909, Ann is the daughter of the late Thomas G. and Katharine (Gallagher) Hawkes. While she was a young girl, the family moved to Bristol, where she still resides. Ann attended the Friends Select School in Philadelphia. She received bachelor's degrees in education and in law and a Doctor of Laws degree from the University of Pennsylvania. Widow of Leon John Hutton, whom she married in 1939, Ann has one daughter and two granddaughters.

While attending the University of Pennsylvania, Ann did research for advertising projects and law school causes. At the time of her graduation in 1934, the law profession did not enthusiastically welcome women, and so she decided to take additional courses in visual education at Temple University. Later she held positions which required copywriting for radio programs, script writing and working on film productions for Caravel Films of New York, as well as on training films for business organizations. Ann wrote copy for some of the commercials used in the early days of television and served as advertising director for the Wetherill Paint Company of Philadelphia.

A member of many organizations, Ann Hutton was always an active volunteer. Her interest in American history, with special emphasis on the Revolutionary War period, is well-known. She is a past chairman and member of the board of Historic Fallsington, a non-profit corporation dedicated to the preservation of the colonial village where William Penn worshipped. In 1955 she was cited by the Commonwealth of Pennsylvania for her research and furnishing of the historic Thompson-Neely House.

But Ann Hawkes Hutton is, perhaps, most closely identified with Washington Crossing. She was first appointed to the Washington Crossing Park Commission in 1939 and has been reappointed by every Pennsylvania governor since. She was the first woman to become chairman of the Commission in 1963. As chairman of the board and chief executive officer of the Washington Crossing Foundation which was organized to promote the educational value of the historic event of George Washington's 1776 crossing of the Delaware River, she has become a distinguished authority on the life and leadership of the father of our country.

As early as her fourth birthday, Ann recalled, her interest in George Washington was sparked by stories told about him by her father. Using her past experience in advertising, she has worked both to promote Washington Crossing State Park and to revive interest in the life of George Washington through films, paintings, press releases and events, such as the annual re-enactment of the Christmas Eve crossing of the Delaware. She authored the award-winning color-sound documentary film, narrated by the late Chet Huntley, which is shown daily to Park visitors. She is an authority and speaker on the famous Emanuel Leutze painting of *Washington Crossing the Delaware*. Her efforts with the Washington Crossing Foundation have been directed toward making young people aware of our country's history and inspiring them to become active participants in government. The royalties from the several books she has written on Washington, along with monies from the Foundation's other functions, have provided scholarships given yearly to qualified high school graduates who aspire to careers in government service.

Not surprisingly, Ann Hutton was actively involved in the Bicentennial commemoration in 1976. Appointed to the American Revolution Bicentennial Commission in 1969 by President Richard Nixon, she was named Patriotic and Civic Organizations Chairman in 1972. She was later appointed to the American Revolution Bicentennial Administration and became its national vice-chairman. For her work, she was awarded the National Bicentennial Medal for service in 1976 and was cited by the Joint Committee on Arrangements of the United States House of Representatives for "Commemoration of the Bicentennial." Ann Hutton holds the distinction of being the first woman to receive the Freedom Leadership Award from the Freedoms Foundation at Valley Forge and, in 1976, on the 200th anniversary of Washington's Crossing of the Delaware, she was the first woman ever to participate in the re-enactment.

Ann Hutton's affiliations and honors include Distinguished Daughter of Pennsylvania (1958), president of the Daughters of Pennsylvania (1979–82), chairman and member of the Bucks County Historical Tourist Commission and president of the Historical Foundation of Pennsylvania (1982). For her tireless efforts at local, state and national levels to promote an appreciation of our history through education and preservation, Ann Hawkes Hutton received the Fame Award at the Forty-Fourth Friendship Fete of Philadelphia in April 1982.

Levittown-Lower Bucks County and Makefield Area Branches

Researcher/Writer: Mildred Ormond Ridolph
Researcher: Elizabeth Carfagno
Writer: Marie McGowan
Special Division Editor: Mary Ann Stangil

86

Ruth Scott

b. 1909

    "Ruth Scott, to put it plainly, is one of the most ardent and active conservationists in Western Pennsylvania history." So states the *Bulletin* of the Audubon Society of Western Pennsylvania in reporting its choice of Ruth to receive the W.C. Clyde Todd Award.

Rachel Carson, one of Ruth's friends and professional associates, would have agreed with the Audubon Society's choice. Rachel once stated:

> I can think of no individual more deserving of a conservation award. Here is no mere lip service to a cause—she lives it! Her efforts are intelligently planned and directed; her programs are executed with thoroughness and efficiency. Because of these qualities she is able to achieve tangible results to an extraordinary degree.

And, Ruth Jury Scott has received awards. In addition to the Todd award, she received the conservation award of the North Area Environmental Council in 1975 and was named "Conservationist of the Year" by the Allegheny County Conservation District in 1976.

To talk with Ruth Scott is to realize that this gentle, unassuming scientist is devoted to conservation efforts. She has worked tirelessly to further environmental education and to achieve the ecological goals she shared with Rachel Carson. She views herself as a "catalytic agent," developing ideas and programs to the point where others can take over and she can go on to the next project.

Ruth's educational background was in the fine arts. She attended Carnegie Institute of Technology, now Carnegie-Mellon University. With her husband, J. Lewis Scott, Ruth conducted environmental programs for children at Powder Mill, Carnegie Museum's nature reserve in Rector, Pennsylvania. She served as director of the Bioscience Center there from 1964 to 1971.

In 1976 Ruth was named an honorary research associate in the Museum's Section of Environmental Studies. She initiated the Fox Chapel School District's School–Park program in nature interpretation and outdoor environmental education.

Ruth Scott is also a founder of the Rachel Carson Homestead Association. This Association has preserved the Carson birthplace in Springdale, Pennsylvania, as a reminder of Miss Carson's work in ecology and as a center for study.

Ruth Scott's accomplishments are numerous. She has been the president of the American Nature Study Society, a representative to the National Council of State Garden Clubs, the founder of the Right of Way Resources of America, an organizer of the National Committee for a Department of Natural Resources and a member of the Pennsylvania State Air Pollution Commission. Her extremely high level of commitment to conservation has won her a respected place in Pennsylvania history.

Fox Chapel Area Branch
Researcher/Writer: Patricia Demase

87

Marion Deihner Brooks

1912–1973

In the southeastern corner of Elk County lies a peaceful wilderness area. A natural fieldstone monument marks the entrance. Acres of white birch rise majestically from the Pennsylvania soil. This place of quiet and magnificent beauty is named Marion Brooks Wilderness Area in honor of a woman whose life was devoted to conservation of just such natural wonders.

Born in Allegheny County, Pennsylvania, on September 25, 1912, Marion was the daughter of George and Mary Deihner. In 1945 Marion moved to Medix Run and purchased the residence which is a local landmark, situated at the foot of Haystack Mountain, near the banks of the popular native trout stream of Medix Run.

Marion was a person of strong convictions who became involved in the battle for the wise use and protection of natural resources long before it became a national issue and, certainly, before women were accepted in the field of conservation.

Her love of the outdoors led her in many directions of concern and activity. Her interest in hunter safety led her to help organize the Bennetts Valley Ambulance Association and to serve as a Civil Defense policewoman. When her community was threatened with water pollution from strip mining drainage, she became the force behind the founding of the Weedville Water Company and the Toby Valley Watershed Association. Marion was also a vocal member of the Elk County Soil and Water Conservation District, a director of the North Central Pennsylvania Economic Development District and a board member of the Pennsylvania Environmental Council.

Marion Brooks had the distinction of being the first woman to be elected to the Pennsylvania Federation of Sportsmen's Clubs and the first woman member of the Allegheny Chapter of Trout Unlimited. In 1972 she received the Conservationist Award from the Pennsylvania Forestry Council and was a recipient of the Pennsylvania Fish Commission's White Hat Award. (The White Hat Award is rarely given; it is a white felt hat bearing the insignia of the Fish Commission–white symbolizes the purity of the streams. This highly-prized award is given only to those who have been especially involved in the fight for clean waters.)

Following her death on April 1, 1973, the Pennsylvania Fish Commission, the Allegheny Trail Council of the Boy Scouts of America, Trout Unlimited, Explorer Scout Post 100 and the St. Mary's High School Outdoor Club collaborated to restore a portion of the Medix Run which had been damaged by Hurricane Agnes in 1972. This project was dedicated to Marion Brooks.

The Pennsylvania Department of Environmental Resources further honored her dedication to conservation in 1975 by setting aside the 975 acres near Quehanna, Pennsylvania, to be known as the Marion Brooks Wilderness Area. This stand of birch trees, through which marked nature trails meander, serves as a reminder of her concern for and her determination to improve the quality of life.

Elk County Branch
Researcher/Writer: Ruth A. Casaro

88

Patricia Kincaid Young

b. 1923 _____

She cannot remember a time when she was not interested in issues of national and international importance. In high school she had been on the debating team and later while attending Indiana State University in Terre Haute, Indiana, she helped organize a speakers bureau. Her global outlook, her organizational skills and her humanitarian instincts are Patricia Young's weapons in the battle against world hunger.

Pat was born September 21, 1923, to George and Louise Kinkaid in Monmouth, Illinois. She is married to a prominent Scranton architect and is the mother of four children. Her family has always been supportive of her varied outside commitments, even when they caused her to be away from home. Her concerns about household matters were kept to a minimum. "You see," she said, "my husband was the oldest of eight children. He knows how to cook and keep house and doesn't mind at all."

As coordinator of the National Committee of World Food Day, Pat Young works five days a week in Washington, D.C., as a dedicated volunteer. Her work days are usually twelve to fourteen hours long.

World Food Day is a day devoted to planning for the alleviation and eventual elimination of world-wide hunger, disease and poverty. It is a day when cities, towns and organizations take time to plan ways and means for generating aid throughout the coming year. It takes into account the need for immediate tangible aid as well as for methods of educating people to provide eventually for their own needs. The plans which are made on World Food Day are implemented throughout the remaining 364 days of the year.

Since World Food Day is not a singular national event when tons of food and supplies are gathered together and shipped out all at once, all needs are considered—tractors, training in irrigation methods and marketing know-how. Materials which cities, towns and organizations can use for this planning are inexpensive brochures, manuals, books, posters and audio-visuals provided by Pat Young's Committee. Individuals and organizations share materials and plans that have worked for them. Composers have contributed songs, artists have donated paintings and schools have given fund-raising guidelines. The number of organizations committed to World Food Day has grown from 170 in 1981 to a total of 300 on March 4, 1983.

The National Committee for World Food Day is building a constituency aimed at securing public awareness and action toward its goals. "The needs of five hundred million people who are seriously undernourished and of five hundred fifty million who do not get enough to eat are being recognized." commented Pat Young. In a brochure entitled "World Food Day," she wrote, "Our ultimate goal is not bigger and better World Food Days; our goal is food security for all people."

Pat Young is very excited about her work. She enjoys meeting people and sharing experiences. She never did stop to think how she was going to accomplish this monumental task because, if she had, she might have run in the opposite direction. One of her most frequently used methods for getting things done is to call on friends—those friends also have friends and are friends of friends.

Her interest and involvement in combatting world hunger and misery was precipitated by a nine-week ecumenical, fact-finding "mission" to Africa in 1966 and reinforced by a later trip in 1971. She believes the unrest in South Africa was, and is, potentially explosive. "The country is very, very beautiful, but the situation is very, very sad. Whites dominate and oppress eighty per cent of the population. Whites are not really living in freedom either when you consider the fear, dogs, guns, bars . . . ."

Patricia Young chaired a task force of the White House Conference on Food, Nutrition and Health in 1969. She attended, as a nongovernmental observer, the United Nations Food and Agriculture Organization (FAO) World Food Congress at the Hague in 1970, the FAO World Food Conference in Rome in 1974 and the FAO World Conference on Agrarian Reform and Rural Development in Rome in 1979. She was a delegate to the joint World Health Organization/UNICEF meeting on Infant and Young Child Feeding in Geneva in 1979. She believes that global need is so great that all governments must participate in the fight against hunger. She notes that, of all the governmental aid given, Canada contributes two-thirds of the total.

Patricia Young is reticent in talking about herself but her accomplishments speak for her. Her civic and church responsibilities have been impressive. She has served as the moderator of the United Presbyterian Church's Synod of the Trinity, which includes Pennsylvania, West Virginia and part of Ohio. She was the chairman of the Infant Formula Project of the Interfaith Center on Corporate Responsibility. She has written many magazine articles in support of the downtrodden of the world. She is a true humanitarian who does not tell others what to do unless she herself is doing one hundred percent more than anyone else. Her desire to help humanity overcomes her natural reticence when she feels compelled to speak out for those who cannot speak for themselves.

Scranton Branch
Researchers: Judith Evans and
Regina Petrauskas
Writer: Ethel De Virgilis

10
WOMEN
IN
RELIGION

89

Gertrud Rapp

1808–1889 ———————————————————————————

Gertrud Rapp, one of Pennsylvania's most fascinating nineteenth century women, was the granddaughter of George Rapp, the founder of the Harmony Society, an early commune. The only child of John Rapp and his wife, Jacobina, Gertrud was born in Butler County at Harmony, the first home of the German Pietists who followed her grandfather to the United States to lead a simple life away from the corruptions of Europe. When Gertrud's father died of influenza, she and her mother joined the grandfather's household.

Gertrud became fluent in English, French and German and was an accomplished vocal and instrumental musician. She studied painting and natural history and became skilled in needlecraft and in making wax fruit and artificial flowers. Among her achievements was the successful establishment of the silk industry within the Society. Some six thousand pounds of cocoons were produced yearly and the silk was woven into beautiful fabrics designed by Gertrud. In 1838 the Franklin Institute for the Promotion of Mechanical Arts recognized her for artistry in silk.

An educated and refined woman, Gertrud handled her grandfather's correspondence and traveled throughout the east to transact his business. She was also his hostess, entertaining the many visitors who came to observe Harmony. When Father Rapp died in 1847, she continued this function for forty-two years.

Although the group was devoutly religious, it was not a church but a social organization. As the Society grew wealthy, there were desertions, dissension, law suits and sometimes even violence, but Gertrud stayed on, loyal to the Harmonite ideals. Her modesty was striking; the 1880 census lists the mistress of the Great House and the industries that provided so much wealth, as "housekeeper, age 71." Celibacy had been adopted in 1807 by common consent of the members of the Society, and married couples lived as brothers and sisters. This practice led to the dissolution of the Society in 1905, when only three members were still alive.

Gertrud was welcomed into the social life of Pittsburgh and Philadelphia not only as a cultured representative of the Harmonites but because of her accomplishments as well. Contemporary reports indicate that she was admired, respected and loved.

Gertrud Rapp died of influenza in 1889 at the age of eighty-one and is buried among 500 other members of the Harmony Society in the common cemetery in Ambridge in an unmarked grave.

Aliquippa Branch
Researcher/Writer: JoAnne Walker

90

Deborah Norris Coleman Brock

1858–1932 ——————————————————————————————

Deborah Norris Coleman Brock, the first president of the State Federation of Pennsylvania Women, was born in Lebanon, Pennsylvania, on August 20, 1858, the eldest daughter and one of seven children of George Dawson and Deborah (Brown) Coleman. Her wealthy father owned a sizeable portion of the Cornwall Ore Banks and Mine Hills. The large estate where Deborah was born eventually became Lebanon's Coleman Park.

At fifteen, Deborah attended Miss Cleveland's School in Philadelphia. It was there that she was presented to Philadelphia Society, and where, in 1878, she married Horace Brock, a civil engineer with the Philadelphia and Reading Railroad Company. He was also treasurer of the New American Iron and Steel Company, had a large interest in the Pennsylvania Bolt and Nut Company and was associated with his brother and brothers-in-law in the management of the North Lebanon Furnaces. Deborah Brock was the organizer and first president of the Women's Club of Lebanon in 1897. She later made a sizeable donation towards the purchase of the Josiah Funck building, the club house and property of the Women's Club, which is listed on the National Register of Historic Places.

The Brocks were traveling in Europe when Deborah was elected the first president of the State Federation of Pennsylvania Women. She served four years. She was the originator and first president of the Lebanon Branch of the Needlework Guild of America. She also started several Bible study groups in Lebanon and Philadelphia.

In 1903 on the twenty-fifth anniversary of their marriage, the Brocks erected and equipped a commodious nurses' home on the Good Samaritan Hospital premises in Lebanon.

A devout Episcopalian, Deborah was the author of at least two religious books. While living in Philadelphia, she wrote *The Green Book* on church membership for the nation-wide campaign of the Episcopal Church. In this book she wrote, "The promise to obey in the marriage service has provoked a great deal of discussion. There cannot be two heads to a house. Woman under the Christian religion has been given a position she never had under any other civilization, and this is due to the fact our Lord exalted the virtues of humility, purity, patience, gentleness and spiritual force—virtues in which women could excel. As long as women stand for these things, men will reverence them, and woman's place of honor and power in society is assured; but if women belittle their spiritual power and influence, and sneer at this Christian virtue, their fall is certain."

Deborah Brock was critical of sermons which were lectures on social problems or current topics instead of being instructions in the Christian faith. She believed that a church should not seek political power but should be content to "render therefore unto Caesar the things which are Caesar's; and unto God the things that are God's."

In *The Green Book*, she gave this advice: "If we are to save our country from the evils that threaten us, we must go back to simpler living, we must revive family life and we must keep Sunday as the Lord's Day and in His Spirit."

On December 22, 1932, Deborah Brock died in her Lebanon, Pennsylvania, home at the age of seventy-four.

Annville Branch
Researcher/Writer: Mary Belle Weiss

91

Mother Mary Katharine Drexel (Katharine Mary Drexel)

1858–1955 _____

On a hill overlooking the Delaware River at Cornwells Heights, stands a large, Spanish-style structure reminiscent of the old missions of southern California. This is St. Elizabeth's Convent, the mother-house of the Congregation of the Sisters of the Blessed Sacrament, an order dedicated to the Christianization, education and elevation of American Indians and Blacks.

The woman who founded the order in 1891 was Mother Mary Katharine Drexel. She was born Katharine Mary Drexel in 1858, the second daughter of a prominent Philadelphia banker and one-time partner of J.P. Morgan, Francis Anthony Drexel, and his wife, Hannah Langstroth. Katharine and her two sisters had every advantage available to the children of the upper-class. They never attended school but obtained their education from private tutors, governesses and travel. Katharine made her debut into society in 1879 in a manner befitting a millionaire's daughter.

The Drexels gave generously of both their wealth and their time to the service of God and to benefit the less-fortunate. When Francis Drexel died in 1885, Katharine and her sisters became the beneficiaries during their lifetimes of the income from their father's estate. All three continued the charitable works of their parents and instituted several of their own.

As a girl, Katharine had helped care for the poor Black children of St. Peter Claver's parish in Philadelphia. As her attention was drawn to the hardships of Black people in the South and East, she extended her charity to them. Throughout her lifetime, through the Bureau of Colored and Indian Missions, she supported and encouraged missions in this country and abroad.

Katharine's own first special charity was directed toward the American Indians. Approached by two Catholic missionaries who were seeking financial aid to erect schools to educate Indians and to further the Catholic religion among them, she learned of the Indians' plight. With her two sisters, she visited the reservations and observed conditions firsthand. She began building schools on the reservations and supplied food, clothing, furnishings and salaries for teachers. She found priests to serve the spiritual needs of the people. While traveling in the West, she built schools and brought Franciscan Sisters to teach Indians in Washington, Oregon and Wyoming. Boarding schools were established for the Pueblo, Navajo, Winnebago and Omaha tribes and missions were set up for the Sioux of South Dakota and the Osage of Oklahoma.

In 1889, counseled by Bishop James O'Connor of Philadelphia, a family friend, Katharine entered religious life. She preferred a cloistered order, but Bishop O'Connor encouraged her to found an institute dedicated to the missions among American Indians and Blacks. Although she hesitated at the idea of founding a religious community, she came to accept this as her vocation and, on November 7, 1889, received the religious habit and the name Sister Mary Katharine. She pronounced her vows on February 12, 1891, and established the Congregation of the Sisters of the Blessed Sacrament.

With thirteen companions, she established residence at Saint Michel, the Drexel family's summer home in Torresdale, until the completion of St. Elizabeth's convent in Cornwells Heights in 1893. There, for the next forty-four years, Mother Katharine, as she was called, served as the dynamic administrator of the community. Sisters from the order went throughout the United States establishing missions and schools to serve, educate and inspire the poor among American Indians and Blacks. Over the years, boarding and day schools were opened in the East, the Midwest and in the rural and urban areas of the South. In 1917 a school to prepare teachers was established in New Orleans; it was chartered in 1925 as Xavier University. Eventually, the Sisters of the Blessed Sacrament numbered more than 600 at sixty-five different centers in twenty states. Mother Katharine's special apostolate was carried on in her native city of Philadelphia, in Germantown, on Broad and Lombard Streets and in West Philadelphia.

A severe heart attack, in 1935, forced Mother Katharine to relinquish her active role as Superior General. She spent the next twenty years in prayerful retirement at the motherhouse in Cornwells Heights, where she died on March 3, 1955 at the age of ninety-seven.

Mother Katharine was ahead of her time. In her concentration on the young and on training teachers for them, she anticipated Operation Headstart by many decades. She knew about "Third World, U.S.A." not from books and newspapers but from personal contact with the poor and miserable. She sought to help others spiritually, as well as materially and intellectually. In the opinion of her contemporaries, she was truly saintly. Accordingly, the cause of her beatification was formally opened in 1964 by John Cardinal Krol. Her writings were approved by the Congregation of the Causes of the Saints in 1973 and her elevation to sainthood awaits further evaluation by the Roman Catholic Church.

Levittown-Lower Bucks County and Makefield Area Branches
Researcher/Writer: Margaret Mahoney
Researcher/Writer: Beatrice Donini
Special Division Editor: Mary Ann Stangil

92

Hanna Clemmer Rittenhouse Clemens

1880–1977

Hanna Rittenhouse was a deeply religious woman with a strong commitment to her Mennonite heritage. Her first dream had been to become a teacher, a goal encouraged by her father, who had been a school director. But a chance event altered the course of Hanna's life and, curiously, allowed her to pursue her love of learning in another way.

At the age of nineteen, Hanna married Jacob Clemens, a teacher and banker. She later confided that "the biggest attraction about him was that he was a schoolteacher." Jacob was also a devout Mennonite, and six years later he was chosen to become minister of the Plains Meetinghouse. The selection had been made by lot, following Mennonite custom and based on ancient Biblical tradition. Neither Jacob nor Hanna had any choice in the matter. Forfeiture of church membership was the penalty for refusing the pastoral call. Recalling that day years later, Hanna said, "I didn't want to be a preacher's wife. I knew that a preacher was a public servant, and I shrank from publicity. I loved seclusion."

Jacob Clemens was no more prepared for his new role than Hanna. But Hanna was determined not only to accept her new life but to throw herself completely into her husband's new calling. She actively assisted Jacob in his Bible studies and helped research and prepare his sermons.

As the wife of a Mennonite minister, Hanna spent a great deal of time alone. Jacob was gone on church matters for one and two weeks at a time, leaving Hanna in charge of a twenty-seven acre farm and six children. As the minister's wife, she had a responsibility to the Mennonite community as well. Sometimes this meant preparing Sunday dinners for as many as three other families.

She continued in her love of education, however, even studying with her children as they advanced through school. Her determination to see her children through high school was itself remarkable, for, in the early decades of the century, the Mennonite church was firmly opposed to secondary education and the Clemens faced severe criticism.

In her later years, Hanna eagerly supported the movement within the church to preserve Mennonite heritage. She willingly related her reminiscences on videotape for the Mennonite Heritage Center and for various church publications. She particularly loved to recount her experiences to children, and she was the primary source for countless high school term papers and Sunday School discussions about the Mennonite past. Perhaps her dream of being a teacher was realized after all.

Lansdale Branch
Researcher/Writer: Karen Methlie
Local Editor: Diane Brouillette

93

The Reverend Bessie S. Wheeler

1902–1981 _____

Photograph courtesy of *Bucks County Courier Times,* Levittown, PA

Bessie Wheeler once said that she came to Bucks County with her husband in 1935 with three strikes against her: she was black, a woman, and a preacher. But she was undaunted by traditional barriers. In her forty-five years as pastor of the Linconia United Pentecostal Church in

Trevose (northeast of Philadelphia) which she and her husband, Deacon Lincoln Wheeler, helped to found, she won the respect and admiration of her parishioners and of the community.

Born in Philadelphia in 1902, Bessie Wheeler joined the Mount Pisgah African Methodist Episcopal Church at age eleven. She eventually left the Methodist Church to join the Pentecostal Church, the only church that would ordain women at that time, because she felt a calling to the ministry "so strong you can't refuse it . . . I tried a long time before I submitted." She never saw gender as an issue; it was the "calling" that mattered.

A 1931 graduate of the Philadelphia College of the Bible, Bessie Wheeler and her husband held prayer meetings in their home and the surrounding Bensalem community. During the Depression, Bessie Wheeler also made clothes for unfortunate children and organized a sewing group and a soup kitchen for them. She was ordained in 1936 and, shortly thereafter, helped found the church in Trevose, then called the Linconia Tabernacle United Holiness Church. The beginnings of the church were far from smooth. The Ku Klux Klan burned a cross on the highway near her then-new church and the Jewish cemetery. "The cross was meant to scare both us and the Jews away," she recalled. "Neither of us moved, though."

In 1976 she organized the Delaware Valley branch of the Evangelistic Missionary Conference of which she was president. She was known as a good friend to people in other churches and was the first female member of the Bensalem Interfaith Ministerium.

Christian charity and personal courage were among her outstanding characteristics. Rev. Wheeler often said she was committed to God and the love of her fellow man. "My main desire is to help the young people; let them know that there are people who love them," she said. "I see so many children who aren't loved, so how can they be expected to love when they don't know what love is?" Her philosophy was borne out by her actions. One member of her church recalled that she wrote to him every week for the four years he was in the Air Force. "What I try to do is let the people know that God loves them," she said. Those whose lives she touched know how well she succeeded.

Makefield Area Branch
Researcher/Writer: Marie McGowan
Special Division Editor: Catherine Barrett

11
WOMEN IN THE HEALTH AND SOCIAL SERVICES

94

Mother Francis Warde

1810–1884 _____

Generations have passed since the April morning in 1845 when Mother Francis Warde, the major superior of the Sisters of Mercy, came to Saint Vincent's Parish, Latrobe, to open Mount Saint Vincent's Young Ladies Academy. (The school later became Saint Xavier Academy.) The success of the school was due primarily to the spirit of Mother Francis Warde, a pioneer, educator, and bearer of the message of the Christian Gospel.

She was the leader of the first seven Sisters of Mercy who came from Ireland to Pittsburgh in 1843 to establish the first permanent religious congregation of women in the Diocese of Pittsburgh. Mother Francis Warde opened the first Mercy Academy on Penn Street, later known as Our Lady of Mercy Academy.

When calls came for help from distant parts of the country, Mother Francis Warde did not hesitate to launch into the unknown with practically no reserves and limited personnel. In addition to those in Pittsburgh, she established convents and schools from Maine to California. Each had its unique story of difficulties and hardships and each presented challenges. In Providence, Rhode Island, the Sisters experienced flagrant bigotry. Repeatedly their convent was stoned and the Sisters insulted on the streets. In Omaha, the Sisters met extreme poverty. In 1864 Nebraska was not yet a state and Omaha was described as "a ragged cluster of houses springing out of the mud."

Mother Francis Warde was always keenly aware of the importance of education to the nation and to the Roman Catholic Church. In addition to schools and academies, she also established a House of Mercy, a residence for working girls, where they could be taught skills that would enable them to find suitable work.

She was also a pioneer in health care, establishing Mercy Hospital when there was no other hospital in western Pennsylvania. In the hospital, every effort was made to bring to patients consolation through their faith. As an example of Christian love and dedication the entire staff of Nursing Sisters at Mercy Hospital once sacrificed their lives in serving the victims of a cholera epidemic.

As a proclaimer of the Gospel, Mother Francis Warde is said to have traveled more than Saint Paul of Tarsus. In addition to being a dynamic teacher of the Christian doctrine, she established novitiates throughout the nation where the young teachers learned how to present and live the Gospel message of love.

Mother Francis Warde was truly a pioneering leader in both education and health care. The scope of her contributions bears testimony to her outstanding leadership and dedication.

Greensburg Area Branch
Researcher: Pat Sivak
Writer: Sr. Adele Caslin

95

Mother Mary Agnes Spencer

1823–1882

The founder of the first hospital in Meadville, Pennsylvania was "a woman of strong personality, great tact and ability" and with great compassion for the sick and injured: Mother Mary Agnes Spencer, of the Sisters of St. Joseph. Mother Agnes was also a leading force in establishing St. Vincent's Hospital in Erie, but her abilities were not limited to hospital administration. She was also unusually skillful in ministering to ailments of the eye and is said to have prevented permanent eye damage in many cases which she treated.

Mother Agnes was born Mary Agnes Spencer in Brindle, Lancashire, England, on August 15, 1823. When she was still a child, her family emigrated to the United States. She entered the novitiate of the Sisters of St. Joseph at Carondelet, Missouri in 1846. Because of her natural talent for leadership, she was able to gain a great deal of administrative experience at a young age, operating various schools, orphanages and hospitals. In 1860 she arrived in the Diocese of Erie to establish a foundation of the Sisters of St. Joseph. Devoted to the education of children, she opened many select schools (comparable to private academies of today.)

With seven Sisters, Mother Agnes started a settlement in the community of Meadville in 1863. From a personal inheritance, she purchased the property for a new convent and the Sisters busied themselves in teaching and caring for orphans and aged women. In those early days Meadville had no hospital, so the Sisters opened their doors to receive the sick as well, especially when epidemics during the fall of 1866 and the spring of 1867 made such charity a necessity.

In 1868 all the orphans were moved from Meadville to an orphanage Mother Agnes had opened in Erie. This was a fortunate step, as it turned out, for the following year a train wreck on the Atlantic and Great Western Railroad near Meadville resulted in a number of deaths and serious injuries. When the railroad surgeon appealed to the Sisters to help care for the injured and dying, the convent was converted into a temporary hospital to provide a central place to care for the injured. From that time, Mother Agnes began to formulate plans for a hospital. St. Joseph's Hospital was incorporated in 1870 as a charitable institution for the sick and disabled. By 1875 the increased number of patients required the addition of five Sisters to the nursing staff.

In her community Mother Agnes was recognized as a woman of deep spirituality, diverse talents and indomitable will. As Superior, she required of the Sisters a strict regard for carrying out their duties, but at recreation times she enjoyed participating and often provided entertainment as an accomplished pianist. She involved herself personally in the medical as well as the administrative tasks of the hospital. As a leader, she showed clear judgment and decisive action. She was rather slight in appearance, but radiated great vitality. She was well-known all over the Diocese for her unflagging efforts on behalf of the orphaned, the hungry and the sick.

Her last years were spent as Superior General of the Sisters of St. Joseph in Erie. As ill health overtook her, she was forced to confine her labors to the care of the patients at St. Vincent's Hospital there. It was at St. Vincent's, as a patient herself, that Mother Agnes died on March 22, 1882, in the fortieth year of her religious life. In a quaintly touching tribute, the Erie *Morning Dispatch* reported on her funeral that "all the Sisters of the Order accompanied the remains to Trinity Cemetery, bedewing the hallowed dust with their tears" in mourning for "this eminently humane woman." In 1888 the name of St. Joseph's Hospital was changed to The Spencer Hospital in honor of its founder.

Meadville Area Branch
Researcher/Writer: Rebecca Borthwick

96

Sarah Ann Reed

1838–1934 ——————————————————————

Sarah Ann Reed was dedicated to the service of the Erie County community throughout her ninety-six years of life. She helped found and maintain the first social welfare agency in the county. She organized literary and travel study classes and started the first business women's club in Erie. She was committed to improving the quality of life for others and was involved in twenty-five different social and service organizations, reflecting her wide range of interests and contributions to her community.

Sarah Ann Reed was the great-granddaughter of Erie's first woman settler, Hannah Harwood Reed. Her commitment to service began during the Civil War. As a member of the Ladies' Aid Society, she assisted in "furnishing relief to the sick and wounded soldiers in the field." She aided local families in need of assistance while their men served as soldiers, and she boarded the hospital trains which passed through Erie to provide food and nursing care for the wounded and dying. She was twenty-seven years old at the end of the war and was a leader in the efforts to build a memorial sculpture honoring Erie's Civil War dead, which was finally erected at Perry Square in 1872.

In 1871 along with twenty-nine other women, Sarah Ann Reed helped form the first welfare agency in Erie: "The Erie Association for Improving the Conditions of the Poor and a Home for the Friendless." She was actively involved in the operation of the Home during its early days, when it was supported by donations of food and goods from local citizens. She served as the Home's president for forty-four consecutive years, overseeing its growth from one building to two and the establishment of separate living quarters for children and older women. She derived great satisfaction from her work with residents of the Home and devoted her Sunday afternoons to her "little flock," as she called them, by conducting Sunday school classes.

During the 1870s Sarah, along with most other women of social standing, supported the Woman's Christian Temperance Union and joined the Erie chapter when it was formed in 1876. In the following years she was involved in a variety of organizations, including the Needlework Guild, the League of Women Voters, the Erie County Council of Republican Women, the Erie Art Club, the Young Women's Christian Association and the Women's Auxiliary of St. Paul's Episcopal Church. As a regent of the Presque Isle Chapter of the Daughters of the American Revolution, she participated in the 1910 dedication of a bronze memorial to Revolutionary War soldiers at the Erie Public Library, the 1913 relaunching of the *Brig Niagara* in Lake Erie harbor and the 1922 unveiling of a statue of George Washington in Waterford.

An avid reader and world traveler, she was well-qualified to conduct literary and travel study classes. She organized the classes in her home and, during the course of fifty years, attracted as many as 1,000 members. In the late 1800s she began an evening class for secretaries, the first business women's club in Erie. She also wrote many children's books, dedicating them to her Sunday school class.

Sarah Ann Reed played an active role at the Home for the Friendless until her death in 1934. During her lifetime, she would not allow the name of the home to be changed in her honor, but, in 1936, it was renamed the Sarah A. Reed Home. Almost thirty years after her death, the Erie *Times News* reported, "Her years of dedication to the community, which still benefits from her wisdom, foresight, and confidence in the future, were recognized by her friends, neighbors, and beneficiaries, and all paid tribute." Her long life of service to others demonstrated her belief that ". . . life is not years but achievement."

Erie Branch
Researcher: Helen Spencer
Writer: Sabina Shields Freeman

97

Sister Mary Carmelita (Anna Regina Barrett)

1869–1964

On the wall of an upper corridor of the large, modern DuBois Hospital hangs an oil painting of Sister Mary Carmelita, known as "The White Lady." The portrait depicts a Sister of Mercy wearing a spotless white nun's habit gracefully pleated at the waist. The delicate attire contrasts with the large, strong hands firmly grasping a pen and open ledger. Thus, the portrait encompasses Sister Carmelita's qualities of religious commitment coupled with an understanding of the practical details of providing medical care to the community of DuBois.

Sister Mary Carmelita was born Anna Regina Barrett in Franklin, Pennsylvania, October 24, 1869. Her life was to span ninety-five years. She entered the Order of the Sisters of Mercy in 1899 working as a teacher and social worker.

In 1910 the Sisters of Mercy assumed responsibility for the struggling DuBois Hospital, and Sister Carmelita was asked by her order to become a nurse. She was one of a group of seven nuns who pioneered modern health care facilities in DuBois. During her fifty-four years of service, she was head of the DuBois Hospital's School of Nursing from 1913 until its closing in 1935 and was hospital superintendent from 1926 until her retirement in February, 1964. Under her direction, the institution grew from a small twenty-five bed hospital to one of ninety-seven beds in 1953. With her progressive leadership, the hospital achieved full recognition by the American Hospital Association and the Joint Commission on Accreditation of Hospitals.

Sister Carmelita's accomplishments were all the more remarkable considering that the hospital received no state or federal aid and was supported entirely by donations. Above all, her faith was essential to the hospital's survival. A notable example of this powerful faith occurred in 1930, when there was not enough money to cover a particular month's payroll expenses. Sister Carmelita began to pray. Soon a call came from the bank that the needed amount—ninety-two dollars—which she had not known existed was in the hospital's account. Thereafter, she continued to pray for enough money to operate the hospital, and, somehow, her prayers were always answered.

Throughout the World Wars and the Great Depression, Sister Carmelita never waivered from her goal of continually improving the hospital's facilities and services. In recognition of her abilities, she was named Woman of the Year in 1948 by the DuBois Business and Professional Women's Club. In 1960 she received the Benjamin Rush Award from the Pennsylvania Medical Society and the Jefferson County Medical Society for outstanding health service. Also, she was a charter member of the Pennsylvania Association of Hospital Administrators.

Sister Carmelita was small in physical stature; yet her attention to detail, her steadfastness of purpose and her dedication to humanity made her a giant in the history of DuBois. In 1982, nearly twenty years after her death, the DuBois Hospital completed yet another addition to its structure. Still under the direction of the Sisters of Mercy, the hospital continues to provide excellent and compassionate health care to the community. And Sister Carmelita's portrait hangs there as a reminder of what one small "White Lady" could do.

DuBois Branch
Researcher/Writer: Judy Furlow

98

Mary Belle
Harris, Ph.D.

1874–1957

Very much against early indications and certainly contrary to tradition, Mary Belle Harris became the outstanding woman penologist of
her times.

She grew up in Lewisburg, Pennsylvania, the daughter of the president of Bucknell University, where she received a bachelor's degree in
music and a master's degree in Latin. She continued her studies at the
University of Chicago and, in 1900, earned a doctorate in Sanskrit and
Indo-European comparative philology. While in Chicago, she became
interested in settlement work during a brief association with Hull
House. There she met Jane Addams and Katherine Bement Davis, who
were later to influence the direction of Mary Harris' life from classical
studies to prison work.

First, Mary embarked on a teaching career in Latin and also did
scientific work in archaeology and numismatics at Johns Hopkins University in Baltimore. She spent two years from 1912 to 1914 in Rome
and Berlin pursuing her work in these areas.

On her return, with no prospect of a teaching job, she accepted
from Katherine Davis, who was then Commissioner of Corrections in
New York, the newly created post of superintendent of women at the
Workhouse on Blackwell's Island. With no previous experience in prison
work, Mary Harris rose to the challenge presented by the dire human
needs of women in prison. Continuing her career, she became a most

successful prison administrator, the first female superintendent of a federal penal institution and one of the great experts on women's prison reform in the world.

At Blackwell's Island, it did not take her long to see the futility of the old penal methods in outmoded, overcrowded prison conditions. Her outstanding success as a prison administrator was based mainly on common sense. She began by creating a library, allowing card-playing and knitting in cells and encouraging daily outdoor exercise. When, in 1919, she became the superintendent of the New Jersey State Home for Girls at Trenton and, soon after, of the New Jersey State Reformatory for Women at Clinton, she instituted a policy of providing inmates with some freedom and responsibility for institutional management, a policy that was to become her trademark. She taught the women what it meant to be on their honor and gave them new faith in themselves and the world. She also taught them practical skills and ways to improve their minds, so that many could find jobs in clerical professions or domestic work and lead useful lives after their release.

Her methods were nothing short of revolutionary for their time and soon attracted attention. In 1925 when the federal government planned its first penal institution for women, Mary Harris' services were called upon from the planning stage onward. She was named the first superintendent of the Alderson, West Virginia, facility, where she had the unique opportunity to create an institution that incorporated her ideals and utilized her methods of correction and rehabilitation. At Alderson there were no cells, no bars, no walls—nothing but the honor system stood guard. The inmates were housed in residential cottages with a matron and a democratic system of self-government. The educational system allowed each inmate to acquire the education that had so far eluded her and instruction was also given in practical skills. There were recreational clubs, library contests and Bible study. Each fall a country fair was held, complete with parades and prizes, booths and side shows, to stimulate the inmates' interests in all aspects of agricultural work.

Alderson was described as "a large and hard-working place that carries on many forms of activity, both outdoors and in, and each inmate takes her share of these duties in accordance with her strength, abilities and fitness. The superintendent's aim is to make the entire scheme of life rehabilitating both physically and psychologically, an inspiration and an aid to the women to rebuild themselves from within. She believes that there is always something in the individual that will respond to good manners, to clean, tidy, pleasant conditions, to beauty and harmony in surroundings."

Mary Harris' long, successful career confirmed her belief that "women's criminality was largely due to economic or psychological dependency, particularly upon men." It was her life's work to teach the women in her care to "build within themselves a wall of self-respect" and to learn marketable skills which would free them from dependence on a man or on the community. She created a community of women working together under the guidance of other women. *I Knew Them in Prison*, published in 1936, tells the story of her work at Alderson.

In retirement, from 1941 until her death in 1957, she lived in Lewisburg, where she was active in the community and served for many years as a trustee of her alma mater, Bucknell University. She traveled and lectured extensively here and in Europe picking up again on her original interests in archaeology and numismatics during her travels. Being musically gifted, she kept up her training in voice and piano and even published music of her own composition. An unusual hobby she had was collecting cowbells; her collection is considered one of the most unusual and interesting in the country.

Susquehanna Valley Branch
Researcher: Lois Kalp
Researcher/Writer: Elsbeth S. Steffensen

99

Jessie Barclay

1874–1965

Jessie Barclay's family were early settlers in Bedford County. Her great-grandfather was Colonel Hugh Barclay, who had served at Valley Forge with his commission signed by General George Washington. He was the first postmaster in Bedford and entertained Alexander Hamilton during the Whiskey Rebellion. Her father was John Jacob Barclay, a lieutenant in the Civil War, who was wounded at Reams Station, Virginia and imprisoned in Libby Prison. He returned to Bedford, where he practiced law and reared five children; Jessie was the eldest. After her mother's death when Jessie was fourteen, she managed her father's household. She attended Wheaton Academy, now Wheaton College. A world traveler, she spent the summer of 1910 in Europe and visited Alaska in 1920.

Because of a childhood illness, Jessie was only four feet nine inches tall, but she was a bundle of energy with a great sense of civic duty. In the early 1920s she organized a public library without benefit of government aid and somehow managed to keep it stocked with current literature and keep all the books in good repair with the help of volunteers. The library continued until the Bedford County Library was established in 1944.

Jessie Barclay organized a woman's club known as the Civic Club, which was dedicated to improving Bedford cultural opportunities. She was also very active in the Bedford County Federation of Women's Clubs and was a member of a group that studied all forms of art in depth. She was instrumental in starting the first children's aid society in Pennsylvania. About 1925 she managed to obtain some state funds and a social worker to find foster homes for many abandoned and neglected children.

A dinner was held in her honor April 14, 1955. At that time the director of the Bureau of Children's Services of the Pennsylvania State Department of Welfare commended Jessie Barclay's lasting contributions to the child welfare movement on both the county and state level.

Bedford County Branch
Researcher/Writer: Mary Sue Whisker

100

Kate Hillis Boyd

1885-1976 ───

"Quietness" was the characteristic chosen by her classmates for Kate Boyd in the college yearbook, but Kate conquered her shy nature and went on to speak for a world-wide organization before gatherings of notables both here and abroad.

Her life work was with the Young Women's Christian Association (YWCA) where she began as a young graduate of Wilson College, class of 1905. Kate was born in Chambersburg, the daughter of Joseph Fulton Boyd and Kate Gordon Boyd, on May 14, 1885, and died there on February 26, 1976, but during her career with the "Y" she went as far afield as Europe and the Far East.

During World War I, Kate was sent to France to serve as hostess to American nurses at "Y" rest and recreation facilities in Dijon, Tours and Paris. She stayed on after the war to assist in the organization of the YWCA in war-torn Belgium; this was finally accomplished by 1921.

When she returned to New York, she continued her work with foreign women students in conjunction with the Inter-collegiate Cosmopolitan Club. The result was the establishment of an International House for students of all countries attending colleges in New York.

Kate served as general secretary of the Germantown, Pennsylvania, YWCA for seven years before returning to the Foreign Division in the early 1930s. She was assigned to Manila, where Filipino women were seeking to establish the "Y." Kate Boyd's task was "to promote, encourage and train women for leadership." In letters and articles, she gave vivid descriptions of life in the Philippines before they were given commonwealth status. Her work in the Far East took her to such large cities as Tokyo, Shanghai and Singapore, where the "Y" was already established.

When her mission in the Philippines was completed, Kate returned to the United States and retirement, although she took a job as social dean at Penn Hall, a private school in Chambersburg, and devoted her summers, for three years, to the "Y's" Foreign Students Division. She worked for the Children's Aid Society and the local effort to save the Georgian-style jail, which is now the headquarters of Chambersburg's historical societies.

Kate Boyd had learned to speak up when she had to, promoting the YWCA and raising funds here and aboard, addressing the appropriate political and diplomatic leaders in every city in which she served. She was awarded an honorary degree in 1955 by Wilson College. She lived to celebrate her ninetieth birthday at a family party in 1975 and died eight months later.

Franklin County Branch
Researcher/Writer: Anne G. Vondra

101

Adena Miller Rich

1888–1967 ─────────────────────────────────────

Immigration to the United States reached its all-time high in the years from the turn of the century until the beginning of World War I in 1914. Some thirteen million Europeans arrived during those years to be assimilated into the American way of life—and not always smoothly. Care and concern for the foreign-born became the life focus of Adena Miller Rich. Her work at Hull House in Chicago and with the Immigrants' Protective League helped many newcomers to this country to find their way.

The daughter of a lawyer, Adena Miller was born in Erie on October 12, 1888. She was educated in Erie schools and earned a bachelor's degree from Oberlin College in 1911. She received a Certificate of Graduation from the Chicago School of Civics and Philanthropy and also did work at the New York School of Social Work and at the University of Chicago.

In 1912 she became supervisor of visitors for the Immigrants' Protective League, whose purpose was "to apply civic, social and philanthropic resources of the city to the needs of foreigners in Chicago . . . and to protect the right of asylum in all proper cases." From this position, Adena moved on to several other social work situations.

In 1917 she married Kenneth F. Rich, a Chicago broker, and they became residents of Jane Addams' Hull House. The Richs were among a group of relatively well-off people who chose to "settle" among the poor. Jane Addams described the rationale of such a choice: "He who lives near the poor, he who knows the devastating effects of disease and vice, has at least an unrivaled opportunity to make a genuine contribution to their understanding."

During World War I, Adena Rich served as director of the Girls' Protective Bureau, a wartime agency for the protection of young girls living in the environs of training camps. In the years after the war, she achieved a degree prominence for her involvement with the League of Women Voters. According to *Survey* magazine, "All Illinois knew her as the perfect vice-president of the League of Women Voters, with her power to meet people competently and agreeably."

In 1926 Adena again took up the problems of immigrants when she became the director of the Immigrants' Protective League, a post she held until 1954. Drastic changes in United States immigration laws in the early 1920s had created problems both for the newly arrived immigrants and for their relatives who had come to this country earlier. Of Adena Rich's efforts on their behalf, Jane Addams wrote: "Hundreds of distracted relatives have come to Hull House begging for information as to this new government regulation, and the stream has scarcely ceased since. This is largely because the Immigrants' Protective League occupies a Hull House building, and the fine superintendent, Mrs. Kenneth Rich, and her staff, are constantly ministering to their wants." In addition to helping immigrants with their legal problems, Adena Rich encouraged them to make use of such Hull House programs as naturalization classes, English language courses, employment counseling and child care facilities.

When Jane Addams died in 1935, Adena Rich became head resident of Hull House, fulfilling a promise she had given to Jane, whom she had served as secretary. The new head resident was congratulated by the mayor of Erie and interviewed by several national magazines. The *Literary Digest* described her as "tall and alert with kindly blue eyes and a sympathetic address that denotes years of close association with the homeless and friendless." By this time, Hull House had grown into a complex covering two full blocks with thirteen buildings and with an average of 1500 people entering daily.

Unfortunately, Adena Rich and Louise Bowen, an extremely influential member of the Hull House Board of Directors, clashed repeatedly and Adena finally resigned in 1937. According to a niece, Adena Rich did not feel that the new policies being put into effect at Hull House were in keeping with the tradition established by Jane Addams.

Although, the Richs left Hull House, Adena continued her work with the Immigrants' Protective League, establishing many lasting friendships with the families she served. She often lectured on college campuses such as Northwestern and the University of Chicago, sharing her knowledge of immigrants.

After her death on March 15, 1967, her remains were cremated and the ashes buried in Erie County next to her husband. Both headstones bear the inscription "Hull House, Chicago."

Erie Branch
Researcher/Writer: Margaret L. Tenpas

102

Laura "Nan" Campbell Rossiter

1892–1977 ─────────────────────────────

Imagine being a mother to forty children! Laura Campbell Rossiter, fondly known as "Nan," an Erie County woman with a boundless love and concern for others, became a foster mother to thirty-eight children over a period of twenty-five years. Moreover, she began taking in her foster children as a fifty-nine-year-old widow, who had already raised two children of her own.

Laura's record of unselfish service began early. When just a bride of eighteen, she helped organize "The Tracy Helping Hand." This was a group of rural women who joined together to aid the unfortunate. They made quilts and raised money in various ways, continuing their association for nearly fifty years.

Laura and her husband, Earl, raised two children of their own, a boy and a girl, at their home in Conneaut Township, where from 1934 to 1937 Laura served as a school director. When two of the one-room schools in the district closed in 1940, Earl used his own car to drive the local children to a consolidated school. He bought a bus to provide better service, but, because of poor health, often needed a substitute. Laura filled in, becoming the first woman bus driver in the area. She took over the route as the regular driver from 1942 to 1946.

Earl died two years later and Laura, at fifty-six, found herself alone in her large home. With her children grown, her usefulness in life seemed ended. She searched for something to fill the void, working first as a cook at the Ashtabula County Home in Ohio for a year. Then, in 1951 she contacted the Children's Services of Erie County to explore the possibilities of becoming a foster parent. However, because Laura was now fifty-nine and there was no man in her household to provide a father image, her request was denied. But her name was not forgotten, and a year later, when there was a shortage of foster homes, Laura's offer was accepted.

In July, 1952, Laura received her first child, an eighteen-month-old boy name Henry Hayes. Two months later she received four children from the Dewey family, ages five through ten, and two years later four more of the Dewey children came to live with her. Her own grandchildren called her "Nan" and her foster children followed suit. Nan kept and loved as many as twelve children at a time. Only once, in her twenty-five years as a foster mother, did she find a child she could not control, and he was later placed in a boys' home.

Henry Hayes remained with Nan until he graduated from the Albion Area High School and could be officially released from her care. He remained in the Erie area, marrying and raising his own family and "checking in" on Nan as regularly as her natural children.

Nearly all of Nan's foster children graduated from high school. Only one was placed for adoption, an experience that was both sad and happy for Nan. The numbers of children increased considerably when Nan began taking children in the community for day care. A handicapped girl named Peggy, who was placed with her about that time, remained for more than eighteen years, helping with the day care children and the others as she grew older.

One of Nan's foster boys became a patrolman for the borough of Albion and then was promoted to police chief. Later, he studied for the priesthood at Aquinas Institute, Graduate School of Theology in St. Louis. Although Nan was a lifelong Methodist, she encouraged him and all the others in their choices for life.

In 1973, the Albion Area Lions Club named Nan Rossiter their "Citizen of the Year" for her outstanding contribution to humanity. At the testimonial, her first foster son, Henry Hayes recalled, "We were the luckiest kids who ever lived." Over 250 well-wishers attended the banquet in her honor on October 22, 1973. She was lauded as being a "builder and a molder, not with bricks or mortar, but of character in young lives, and the basic ingredients necessary are love and understanding."

Part of Nan's ability to keep children at her advanced age was her good health. That, plus her natural instinct for raising children and her honest expressions of love for each, made her a success. At the time of her death at age eighty-five, three foster children were still living with Nan Rossiter.

Erie Branch
Researcher/Writer: Sabina Shields
Freeman

103

Ella Frazier

190?–197? _____

Ella Frazier, the executive secretary of the Phyllis Wheatley Branch of the Harrisburg Young Women's Christian Association (YWCA) for thirty-two years, from 1923 until 1955, was not only a director of an agency but a presence in the community. She brightened the scene, both directly and indirectly, throughout her years in Pennsylvania's capital city.

This dynamic woman was born in the Pittsburgh area, the youngest of nine children of parents "who gave their children a Christian upbringing." She attended public schools and eventually worked for the Freedman's Bureau of the Presbyterian Church. She received her YWCA training at the Germantown Training Center. Before moving to Harrisburg, she was employed for three years as assistant secretary of the Phyllis Wheatley Branch of the Youngstown, Ohio, YWCA.

The Phyllis Wheatley Branch of the YWCA served young Black women, since, at that period in the history of the organization, its services were segregated, as were most other organizations in America in 1923. At the time of Ella's arrival in Harrisburg, the Branch, which had been organized in 1920, was housed in one large room.

The goal of providing opportunities for growth and development for girls and women through clubs, classes and community organizations was a broad one, but Ella set about this task in an efficient manner by talking with volunteers, explaining purposes and searching out needs and aspirations. From initial reluctance there gradually came wholehearted cooperation from girls and women from all walks of life. The one room became a center of activity. By 1938 the space of a whole building was required, and the membership numbered more than 1200. The house next door was bought for a dormitory for girls working away from home.

Sewing classes, typing classes, gymnastics, choral groups and food preparation training courses were typical activities carried on by the Branch. A camping program was organized as a summertime activity. An employment agency of sorts was set up, as well as a registry of rooms, whereby more girls could find suitable homes away from home.

A Mothers' Club was formed, later becoming a scholarship club which earned money to provide $100 scholarships for girls who wanted to continue their formal education after high school. During the 1920s the teenage program of the YWCA was called the Girl Reserve Movement. Locally, hundreds of girls were organized into groups which met after school and provided encouragement, training and inspiration.

The Branch building was used as a community center at times of crisis, such as the flood of 1936, at which time food and clothing were distributed from it by welfare groups, and it also provided shelter for those left homeless. During the Second World War the Phyllis Wheatley Branch cooperated in activities run by the United Service Organizations (USO) for servicemen and women stationed in the area, carrying out such services as serving Sunday breakfast for hundreds of people.

Ella Frazier's influence upon the lives of the young women of Harrisburg was far-reaching and is impossible to chronicle in its entirety. In 1955 in keeping with the intention of the National Association of the YWCA, the Phyllis Wheatley Branch was integrated into the Harrisburg YWCA. It was said that Ella Frazier was a powerful influence in bridging the color barrier and bringing about joint efforts between white and Black community groups.

As a tribute to her unusual involvement in the total community, a recognition dinner was given for her when she retired in 1955. The dinner was attended by people representing all sectors of the community, who came to honor her for her long years of service.

Ella Fraizer returned to Pittsburgh in 1969 and lived there until her death.

Harrisburg Branch
Researcher/Writer: Louise M. Vastine

104

Susan Brownell Anthony II, Ph.D.

b. 1916 _____

Susan Brownell Anthony II has devoted her life to helping women. Her life and work "involve both words and actions to serve the poor, to serve alcoholics, and, above all, to serve God." Susan currently lives and works in Florida, where she is a counselor of alcoholics and their families, a lecturer and writer.

Susan B. Anthony II was born in Easton, Pennsylvania, on July 26, 1916. Her parents were Charlotte Sutherland and Luther B. Anthony, a nephew of suffragist Susan B. Anthony. Susan's strong family ties with parents, sisters and aunts influenced her goals and ambition. Their interest in feminism, the suffrage movement, writing, drama and public speaking provided enduring models for a life of active public service.

The Anthony family lived on College Hill in Easton and summered at Raubsville, until Susan finished college. She attended the public schools of Easton and graduated from the University of Rochester as a Susan B. Anthony scholar in 1938, receiving a bachelor's degree, *magna cum laude*, in political science. She later earned master's degrees in both political science and theology and received a doctorate in theology in 1965 from St. Mary's Graduate School of Theology, Notre Dame, Indiana. In 1980 St. Mary's-of-the-Woods, Terre Haute, Indiana, awarded her an honorary degree.

Susan has written seven books and many articles for both professional and popular publications. She was a college correspondent for *The New York Times* and a reporter for the *Washington Star* and the Associated Press. She hosted and appeared on many radio and television programs and has lectured in over 100 American cities and in Africa. She has been a professor of theology and of women's studies and continues to be interested in these areas.

While at the University of Rochester in the 1930s, Susan became interested in the peace movement. She has been active in local, national and international peace organizations.

In 1976 a United States Senate Committee on Alcohol and Drugs honored Susan for her work with alcoholics and asked for her testimony on the problems of female alcoholics. She feels that women drinkers face different problems than men drinkers and that different therapies must be developed for women. Women alcoholics find it difficult to admit their need for treatment, and their road to recovery is often long, lonely and difficult. Susan's counseling approach is holistic, stressing the psychological, social, economic, political and theological aspects of the disease.

Susan B. Anthony II has definitely been influenced by her Great-aunt Susan B. Anthony, whom she calls "the ghost in my life." When she was quite young, a well-known phrenologist examined her skull and concluded: "Her mind is already attuned to public work. She is like her great-aunt. She will want to do all the good she can in the largest possible way for the largest number of people. She will feel at home when standing in front of an audience." This seems to have been quite an accurate forecast of the life of service that has followed.

Easton Branch
Researcher: Margaret D. Druse
Writer: Nancy Catanach

12
WOMEN
AS
EDUCATORS

105

Margaret Kerr
Bell Miller

1826–1874

Margaret Bell Miller was an outstanding founding administrator at Waynesburg College who helped bring about co-educational higher education in western Pennsylvania.

Margaret was born on October 2, 1826, in Washington, Pennsylvania, and graduated with honors from Washington Female Seminary before coming to Waynesburg. The Cumberland Presbyterian Church employed her as principal of the Female Seminary at Waynesburg in 1850. When the Waynesburg College building was completed in November 1851, she joined the college and founded the Female Department of the college. The first class to graduate from the Female Department boasted three members: Martha Bayard, Elizabeth Crawford and Caroline Hook.

Margaret Bell was a well-educated woman and her constant regard for the rights and feelings of others made her a favorite with young and old alike. In 1854 she married mathematics professor Dr. A. B. Miller, who became president of Waynesburg College in 1859.

From the time the college was opened in the "new" building (now Hanna Hall), all students attended co-educational classes. Margaret Bell Miller was a pioneer in education who believed in co-education and worked hard to achieve it. When the college was chartered, the new president, J. P. Wethee, insisted that the college be conducted without reference to the sex of the students. After several stormy sessions, a decision was finally reached that the institution would be regarded as "one college with male and female departments." By-laws prescribed the duties and privileges of the president and of the principal of the Female Department. The college was certainly one of the first to admit both sexes. It is likely that only one—Oberlin—preceded it in this respect. As time passed, the entire college family became increasingly convinced that co-education was desirable. The 1871–72 catalogue proudly states:

> Waynesburg College was one of the first to admit both sexes. Many more colleges are adopting this practice. Association of sexes is good. Association of sexes is *encouraged*. In this institution the two sexes associate under proper restriction. . . . Ladies are permitted to receive the company of gentlemen only one day a week, and never at a late hour of night. They are allowed outdoor recreation during each day but must repair to their rooms on the ringing of the evening bell.

Margaret Bell Miller taught six hours a day, maintained a home for her husband and eight children and entertained many friends. Her death on April 27, 1874, at the age of forty-seven was attributed to a stroke caused by overwork. To the young people under her she was teacher, counselor and sympathizing friend, and teaching was the great mission of her life. One of her students overheard her say, "I would rather lose my right hand than give up teaching."

After her death, the college's alumni erected a monument in her memory. More than half a century after her death she was still remembered with the greatest esteem. A new high school built in Waynesburg in 1928 was named in her honor.

Margaret Bell Miller was, in actuality, the first dean of women at Waynesburg College. Her inspirational character and the superb quality of her work singled her out as a pioneer in higher education.

Waynesburg Branch
Researchers/Writers: Anna Meighen and
Sarah Olmstead

106

Fanny Marion Jackson Coppin

1837–1913 ——————————————————————————

Fanny Marion Jackson Coppin was born a slave in 1837. She owed her liberation to a self-sacrificing aunt, Sara Orr Clark, who purchased Fanny's freedom for $125—Fanny herself earned only six dollars a month. Fanny was sent to relatives in New England when she was fourteen years old, where she worked for the George H. Calvert family in Newport, Rhode Island. Mrs. Calvert took an interest in training the young girl. Fanny worked, studied and saved her earnings so she could enroll in the state normal school at Bristol, and, with the generous aid of her aunt Sara, she entered Oberlin College in 1860. She spent over five years studying Greek, mathematics and French.

When the freedmen poured into Ohio at the close of the Civil War, Fanny formed a class for them. Teaching adult men and women to read and write convinced her she had chosen the most worthwhile way to serve her people.

When a request came from the Institute for Colored Youth in Philadelphia for a teacher of Greek, Latin and higher mathematics, Fanny Jackson was highly recommended. She began her work at the Institute in 1865 as principal of the girls' high school department. Four years later she became head of the school, and, during her thirty-seven years there, she trained many leaders of her race. An educational innovator, Fanny introduced normal school training in 1871. (That same year she married the Reverend Coppin, an African Methodist Episcopal minister from Washington, D.C.)

Aware of the needs of young Blacks for industrial training, she worked during the 1880s to enlarge the curriculum. She was the key organizer and fund-raiser for the Institute's industrial skill department which opened in 1889, making it the only school in the city offering such training to Blacks.

In 1900 her husband became a bishop and was assigned to Africa. Fanny joined him and assisted in the missionary work, spending a decade in South Africa as a missionary. She, then, returned to Philadelphia, where she died in 1913.

Philadelphia Branch
Researcher/Writer: Ellen H. Moore
Special Division Editor: Dr. Barbara Klaczynska

107

Martha Schofield

1839–1916

Adventure and peril pervaded the life of Pennsylvania-born Quaker, Martha Schofield. Her years of struggle and sacrifice to educate the Southern freedmen testified unequivocally to the depth of her religious beliefs and her dedication as a teacher. At the Civil War's end, "only a few went forward to answer the agonized cry of the liberated, homeless blacks" and Martha Schofield was among them.

Martha was born in 1839 on the farm of her parents, Oliver and Mary Jackson Schofield, and was taught early the concept of the brotherhood of man. She witnessed firsthand the plight of the runaway Negro slave, for her parents, who were Hicksite Quakers and abolitionists, often sheltered Canada-bound runaway slaves at their farm near Newton, Bucks County, Pennsylvania, until 1852 when Oliver Schofield died.

Martha's mother's remarriage to John Child, a widower, brought the Schofield family of four daughters and a son to Darby. There, Martha continued her education under the guidance of her maternal uncle, John Jackson, a private school headmaster. Completing her education, Martha taught first in a Friends' school in New York State, and later in a Philadelphia school for Negroes. During the Civil War Martha worked as a visiting nurse at Summit Hospital in Darby.

After the War, the northern abolitionists called for an "intensive wartime educational effort" to prepare the freedmen for productive citizenship. As a volunteer with the Pennsylvania Freedmen's Relief Association, Martha Schofield accepted an assignment to the Sea Islands of South Carolina in 1865. Martha taught school on Wadmalaw Island. The teachers there struggled to feed and clothe the helpless Negroes who were their students. An 1865 entry in Martha's diary speaks clearly of some of the hardships: "This morning I took my bread to school to watch; when light enough I made it up and sent it half-mile away to be baked in the only stove in the village. We distributed clothing for 102 today."

In 1868 Martha contracted malarial fever which necessitated bed rest for two months. Unselfishly, she conducted small bedside classes for Negroes even while she recuperated. In 1870 Martha moved one hundred miles inland to Aiken, South Carolina, and a more healthful climate, where she taught in a two-year-old Freedmen's Bureau School. Finding the school facility inadequate after a time, Martha successfully persuaded the Freedmen's Bureau to erect a new building on land she personally donated.

The fledgling school became the influential and reputable Schofield Normal and Industrial School, a vocational boarding school for Negroes. Despite the cessation of Freedmen's Bureau support for her school, Martha Schofield appealed to a sympathetic group of Friends in Germantown, Pennsylvania, to support her financially floundering institution. Aid also came from the John F. Slater Fund for Negro education and from wealthy Philadelphia area Quakers and philanthropists.

Martha Schofield's leadership ability was based on an unfaltering courage in facing all opposition in her path towards achieving justice. When the robbery and murder of both Negroes and white sympathizers became commonplace during Reconstruction, Martha offered her home and school as shelter, especially during "Red Shirt" raids described by Dr. Matilda Evans, a former student:

> . . . large bodies of white men on horses dressed in white uniforms decorated in red, with crosses and skeleton heads approached and rode through the town. The leader riding in front carried a huge banner made of a shirt large enough for Goliath. It was spotted all over with large red spots indicative of pistol wounds. On either side was placed a Negro dough-face ornamented at the top by chignons. This banner turned high in the air . . . in the swift ride through Aiken from every side that the Negro looked, all that they could see was a bleeding, grinning, dying Negro.

In bravely aiding the blacks, Martha jeopardized her own safety; however, her moral courage sustained her throughout many violent incidents that occurred in Aiken during the Reconstruction years. As a result of her lifelong devotion to the cause of the freedmen's education, the Schofield School acquired an outstanding reputation as a model school in the South. Among its graduates were counted pastors, teachers, dentists, contractors and physicians; notable among them was Matilda Evans, one of the first Black women in the United States to receive a medical degree from the Woman's Medical College of Pennsylvania. Retiring as principal of the Schofield School in 1881, Martha maintained the position of business manager until her death in 1916.

The year 1916 was the fiftieth anniversary of the Schofield School, which then encompassed two city blocks and a farm of four hundred acres and boasted an enrollment of three hundred pupils. Dr. Matilda Evans explains, "The operation of the school, including the farm, the store, and the boarding house dormitories, became a part of the curriculum; and each student was provided with practical, concrete examples of everyday business life with a solution for each worked out before the eyes of the whole school."

A far cry from the Sea Islands village schools of the Reconstruction years, Martha Schofield's school was a tribute to the efficiency of her administrative abilities and her dauntless courage and untiring zeal in living a Christian life of brotherhood toward all men.

Martha Schofield is buried in the Friends' Burying Grounds in Darby. She worked tirelessly for fifty years so "that the tremendous sacrifices of the Civil War might not have been in vain."

Levittown-Lower Bucks County Branch
Researcher: Jean Green
Researcher/Writer: Karen Anne Capie

108

Elizabeth Lloyd

1848–1917 ─────────────────────────────────

Elizabeth Lloyd was a lifelong resident of Pennsylvania who taught for thirty years in Bucks County schools. An esteemed Quaker educator in the area, her presence was felt both inside and outside the classroom. For Elizabeth, education and cultural enrichment did not stop at the schoolhouse door. A love and talent for writing manifested itself in many forms during her lifetime. She was a reporter and, for many years, associate editor for the *Friends Intelligencer*, a weekly newspaper. She wrote articles for a variety of magazines, sometimes under the pen name Ruth Craydock. She also enjoyed writing in verse, and one of her most widely known poems, "The Song of The Twentieth Century," received special praise from President Benjamin Harrison.

As a member of the Woman's Christian Temperance Union, Elizabeth Lloyd used her special writing talent to express her thoughts on the value of Friends' principles and temperance. Her book for children, *The Old Red Schoolhouse*, told a story "about some boys who enticed their companions to drink hard cider, and had come, of course, to a bad end."

In her personal and religious life, her teachings and presence as a role model served her community well. As a cousin fondly remembers, ". . . Cousin Lizzie . . . was a beloved relative . . ., a spinster, a homely little lady who nevertheless commanded great respect. Elizabeth Lloyd was one of the really gifted preachers and spiritual leaders in the Society of Friends, much sought after at marriages for her wise counsel and at funerals for sympathetic messages."

Attempting always to improve the quality of schools and educational programs, Elizabeth Lloyd wrote a paper entitled "The Schools of Buckingham" read at the Buckingham town meeting, October 23, 1883. Her ideas on education convey a feeling for her strengths as an educator.

> The real glory of the schools of a township is not found in the number of great men which they produce; genius can take care of itself always; it is mediocrity that needs to be encouraged. It should be the aim of our schools to make of all their pupils, not celebrities, but honest, industrious, intelligent

citizens; . . . But all experience proves that the mastery of a few things is better than a smattering of many things; and that the motto of every school should be, "Not how much but how well."

This approach to education, expressed so clearly one hundred years ago, seems to be returning to many school programs, even today in our complex society.

Southampton Area
Researchers: Edna Pullinger and
Elizabeth Harrison
Writer: Joan Frame

109

Ella M. Boyce

186?–19?

In 1886 Bradford, Pennsylvania, was finally beginning to gain some respectability after the uproarious oil rush of the 1870s. In that year Ella Boyce came to town to teach in the high school. A year later Miss Boyce was elected city superintendent of schools by the school controllers, the first woman in the United States to hold such a position. The announcement of her election received a one-paragraph notice on the back page of *The Era*, Bradford's daily newspaper.

Competition for the superintendent's post had been keen. Sixty-seven applications had been received from places as far away as Iowa, Illinois, Rhode Island, Massachusetts and New York City. Ella Boyce, however, was well-qualified, both intellectually and professionally, for the job. As an added endorsement, fifty-three high school students wrote to the school board in support of her.

When Ella Boyce assumed the superintendency, Bradford had five public school buildings with a total of thirty-two rooms. The district had thirty-three teachers, including Miss Boyce, who continued to teach classes in addition to her administrative duties. All the teachers were women. Pupil registration numbered 1905, divided almost equally between boys and girls. The high school, unlike many schools at that time, boasted a library, a chemistry laboratory and manual training and commercial departments.

During her term as superintendent, all communications between Miss Boyce and the all-male school board were required to be in writing. She could only make recommendations which were sent to the board for final approval. Handwritten records of school board meetings for the three years Ella Boyce served as Bradford's superintendent reveal that much of her official correspondence was concerned with finances, pleas for more classroom space and additional teachers and requests for textbooks and supplies. There was a continual battle for higher salaries for the teachers.

In one instance in 1888, Miss Boyce asked for a five-dollar-a-month raise for a high school teacher who also served as a principal. When her request was rejected by the board, she threatened to resign at the end of her two-year term. Recognizing her outstanding abilities, the board made concessions at contract time to retain her; they relieved her of her teaching duties so she could concentrate on administration and granted her a pay raise to $1600 a year. When the board approved five-dollar-a-month raises to only a few of the teachers, Miss Boyce was furious and spoke out strongly in the community about such unfairness. She was assailed in the newspapers for her protest and accused of disloyalty to the district for encouraging teachers to seek jobs with higher salaries elsewhere in an effort to force the Bradford school board to raise teacher salaries. Miss Boyce asked to be released from her contract, but the board refused.

In 1890 when she was still getting nowhere with the school board in her fight for higher salaries and better working conditions for teachers, she submitted her resignation. The board accepted but with the following commendation: "As a teacher, principal and superintendent, you have made a lasting impression on the schools, and won a high degree of popular esteem."

Soon after her resignation, Ella Boyce married David Kirk, a prominent Bradford oil producer and moved to Pittsburgh. After her husband's death, she lived in New York City until her death.

Bradford Branch
Researcher: Madeline Miles
Writer: Mary Keller

110

Sarah McCune Gallaher

1864–19-? ———————————————————————————————

A well-known Pennsylvania educator and one of the first women representatives elected to the Pennsylvania Legislature, Sarah McCune Gallaher was born in New Washington, on June 8, 1864. She was the daughter of George Washington Gallaher and Elizabeth Hallesen Gallaher.

Sarah Gallaher attended the village school until she was sixteen, then briefly taught school in Coal Run, Patchinville, and LaJose. She attended Indiana Normal School (now Indiana University of Pennsylvania) where she received her Bachelor of Education degree in 1884 and her Master of Science degree in 1888. In 1895 she obtained a Bachelor of Philosophy degree from Cornell University. She continued her education at Oxford University in England, Berlin University in Germany and the University of Pennsylvania, where she was awarded a fellowship in American history, with a Master of Arts degree in 1902.

In her career as an educator, she served as an instructor at Indiana State Normal School from 1888 until 1893. From 1896 to 1900 she was an associate principal at the College Preparatory School in Birmingham, Pennsylvania. She held a position on the editorial staff of the University Publishing Company in New York from 1902 until 1904.

In 1904 Sarah Gallaher realized her life-long ambition when she established her own boarding school, Hallesen Place, the Ebensburg Elementary School for Younger Pupils. She managed the school until 1942 when she retired from active teaching. During that time, she inspired thousands of young students who attended the school. She also established a school in Puerto Rico.

Before opening Hallesen Place, Sarah Gallaher, a professional reader, was in demand as an entertainer. She performed at institutes and in some of the wealthiest homes in New York and Philadelphia. Large-boned and dignified, with large gray eyes which were not easily forgotten, she made a striking appearance in her dress of black chiffon over satin, with a deep yoke of Irish lace.

She was an unquestioned authority on George Washington, Benjamin Franklin and William Penn. During her studies in England, she had been admitted to the room at the Library of London which held the historical records of William Penn, the first American to have the privilege of doing research there.

Locally, she remained active throughout her lifetime in Ebensburg civic and political clubs. She was a spiritual lay leader of the local Methodist church. She was a founder of the Ebensburg Free Public Library and was named "Member *Emerita*" of the library's board of directors.

Her political career, although brief, was noteworthy. Sarah Gallaher was the first Cambria County woman to serve in the state legislature during the first term women became eligible to hold legislative positions under the nineteenth Amendment. Her legislative aims differed from most others of her sex. She was especially interested in good road legislation and scoffed at the idea that a "woman's bloc" might exist among the eight female colleagues in the assembly.

Sarah chose not to be a candidate for re-election. "I remember it as a very pleasant and instructive experience but not one that I care to repeat. I did not care to devote my time to the legislature. I ran only the first time because women were given the right to sit and most of them were timid about running. I did it to give them an example."

Johnstown Branch
Researcher/Writer: Anne McDonald

111

Mary Hunter Mayer

1864–1946 ─────────────────────────────────

When Mary Hunter Mayer walked the halls of the Reading Girls' High School, pupils displayed their best behavior. The giggling and chattering, typical of young school girls, promptly ceased. Any girl who may have lined her lips with color, powdered her nose or pinched her cheeks for a blush, quickly tried to hide her face from the "grand matriarch of learning."

Miss Mayer, who was principal of the Girls' High School in Reading, detested any ostentatious trace of make-up. In fact, there were no mirrors in the girls' lavatory, and only one student at a time was allowed a rest room pass. She tolerated no misbehavior and had no second thoughts about informing parents of their daughters' "unladylike" conduct.

Although she was known as a fair and capable administrator, Miss Mayer's stern expression and austere attire—usually a long black dress adorned only by a gold pendant watch—held her charges in awe. Many were frightened by this tall, slender lady who controlled the high school education of young ladies in Reading for more than a quarter of a century from 1897 to 1928. But it was during Miss Mayer's tenure that the school became recognized as one of the finest in the state.

Under her leadership enrollment grew so that by 1929 a total of 8,754 students had attended the school and 3,147 were graduated. Soon after her appointment as principal, Miss Mayer added a post-graduate "normal course" which continued until 1908, when it was transfered to a separate unit of education under the Berks County superintendent of schools.

Miss Mayer was the first Reading educator to implement the passing of classes from one room to another and to initiate separate courses of study including Latin, history, mathematics, foreign languages, science and commercial arts. Under her supervision the department of domestic science was created, and a household arts department was added. Both evolved into what is known today as home economics. At the beginning of the 1913 school term, a class in the care of infants was organized, the first of its kind in Pennsylvania. Sewing was added in 1914.

Miss Mayer, who was born in Reading and graduated from the high school herself in 1881, was often annoyed at having to handle such "trifling crises" as the invasion of knickers in the school and the first teacher to bob her hair. She considered herself, first and foremost, an educator. Meting out discipline was a necessary distraction that went with the job. But, despite her stern exterior, Miss Mayer loved young people and worked hard to see they got a good education. If being known as a "harsh disciplinarian" was the price she had to pay, so be it.

After her own high school graduation, she prepared for her teaching career at St. Agnes' School, Albany, New York. She and another Reading woman, Jennie Cooper, operated the Miss Cooper and Miss Mayer School for Young Ladies and Children in Reading until Miss Mayer was hired by the high school to teach mathematics. She was named principal in 1897 and held that position for thirty-one years, until the Girls' High School became a part of the new co-educational high school, Reading Senior High School. Her retirement came in 1929, just one year after the founding of the senior high school, where she also served one year as co-principal with John Eisenhauer.

Before the end of her career, Miss Mayer had taught two generations of pupils. In recognition of her contributions to the city school system, a scholarship was created in her honor in 1927. When Miss Mayer died May 11, 1946, at the age of eighty-two, Reading lost one of its most dedicated pioneers in education, beloved and feared, but always respected.

Reading Branch
Researcher/Writer: Carole Simpson

112

Ruth Sprague Downs

1878–1962 _____

Ruth Sprague Downs, born in Nova Scotia, on March 16, 1878, was brought by her family to the town of Lewisburg, Pennsylvania. She was educated in Lewisburg schools and at Bucknell University which, in those days, had two college preparatory schools, a Female Institute and an Academy for Boys in addition to its University.

An example of the new free spirit of women determined to be useful in a work world prejudiced in favor of men, Ruth Sprague diligently pursued her work in seldom-studied languages, graduating with honors from Bucknell University in 1898. She then tackled the tedious task of translating arithmetical and classical texts from English into Amharic, the language of Ethiopia, and, then, into braille because the incidence of blindness was greater among Ethiopians than among any other people in the world. This work was interrupted in 1905 by the marriage of Ruth Sprague to Edgar Downs of Ardmore, Pennsylvania.

After raising her family, Ruth Downs returned to her work in Amharic and Braille translations, winning the acclaim of the educational world. In 1952 she was honored by the Commonwealth of Pennsylvania with the Distinguished Daughter of Pennsylvania Award. She died in Ardmore, Pennslyvania, on December 24, 1962.

Susquehanna Valley Branch
Researcher/Writer: Lois Kalp

113

Photograph courtesy of The Woods School and Residential Treatment Center, Langhorne, PA

Mollie Woods Hare

1881–1956 ——————————————————————

Mollie Woods Hare, educator and founder of The Woods School for Special Children, was the oldest of eight children. She lived in Duncannon, Pennsylvania, with her family until she was a teenager, then went to Philadelphia to live with her two maiden aunts. In 1901 she graduated from Philadelphia Normal School.

She was one of only six graduates to earn a certificate which qualified her to become a principal as well as a teacher in the Philadelphia school system.

Mollie, a young girl filled with patience and understanding, took a special liking to the slower children in her classes. She found them interesting—a challenge. She enjoyed working with children whom other people felt were a "waste of time." After only five years of teaching, Mollie, at the age of twenty-five, became one of the youngest principals in the Philadelphia school system. She became principal of Special School Number Six, a school for retarded and delinquent children.

With only $175 and the help of her sister who was a trained nurse, Mollie Woods decided to start a school of her own. Combining her unending energy and drive with her unique and forward-looking ideas about educating special children, Mollie opened her own school in a farmhouse in Roslyn, Pennsylvania. She had a single pupil. To gain more students, Mollie went to Philadelphia General Hospital and enrolled five retarded children. The hospital paid weekly for each child. At the end of the year the school's enrollment had jumped to twenty-five children. During the first year of her school, Mollie taught and, when necessary, bathed the children, visited parents and shopped for needed supplies. She also kept her job in the Philadelphia school system.

In 1919 Mollie married John Ridgeway Hare. John joined Mollie in what became a combined lifetime project for them both, The Woods School. Two years later the school moved to Langhorne where Mollie and her husband purchased a home they called Greenwood. The home is still in use today as part of The Woods School and Residential Treatment Center. In 1982 the school had grown to house over 500 residential special children, fulfilling Mollie Woods Hare's lifelong dream.

Levittown-Lower Bucks County Branch
Researcher: Jean M. Green
Writer: Grace Jones

114

Sister Doloretta
Thorn, Ph.D.

1883–1977

In 1941 Sister Doloretta Thorn of the Sisters of St. Joseph at Villa Maria College was the only nun to hold a national office in the American Chemical Society. She became one of only three women representatives to the organization's national council. In 1942 in recognition of her standing as a scientist, she was unanimously voted a fellowship in the American Association for the Advancement of Science.

Sister Doloretta was born in Kylertown, Pennsylvania, on October 16, 1883. She was the daughter of Dr. and Mrs. A. I. Thorn. She entered the order of the Sisters of St. Joseph on August 14, 1901, earning her Bachelor of Science degree at Canisius College in 1926. She continued the study of science and earned her master's degree, *magna cum laude*, in 1931, and her doctorate, *cum laude*, in 1936, from Notre Dame University. She also pursued additional post graduate studies at Catholic University of America. She was a professor and the first head of the Department of Chemistry at Villa Maria College and later became dean of the college, a position she held for nearly twenty-five years.

Sister Doloretta was active in many organizations relating to science and education. In addition to her memberships in the American Chemical Society and the American Academy for the Advancement of Science, she belonged to the Catholic Round Table of Sciences, the New York Academy of Science and the American Museum of Natural History. She was also a member of the American Association for Student Teaching, the American Conference of Academic Deans, the National Catholic Education Association, the Pennsylvania Association for Student Teaching and the National Education Association.

The published research of Sister Doloretta Thorn appeared in the *Journal of the American Chemical Society.* Her contributions have been listed in *World Biography, Who's Who of American Women,* and *Men of Science.* In 1967 she was awarded the Doctor of Laws, *honoris causa,* by Gannon University.

Sister Doloretta was also a dedicated patron of the arts. She served on the board of directors of the Erie Philharmonic Society and was responsible for arranging the first chamber music series and the first "pops" concert in Erie. As director of the cultural series at Villa Maria College, she introduced Shakespearean theater and brought singers and musicians from New York to the college community. She considered attendance at cultural events an important part of a student's development at college.

As dean of Villa Maria College, Sister Doloretta introduced special educational programs which included certification in home economics in 1942, the elementary education program, and the first collegiate school of nursing in northwestern Pennsylvania in 1950. Under her direction, Villa Maria College grew from its first home on Liberty and Eighth Streets in Erie to the establishment of the college campus on West Lake Road in 1961.

This gentle nun was often seen walking on the campus, checking the rose bushes and young pine trees. The landscape planning on the new campus is evidence of Sister Doloretta Thorn's sensitivity to beauty in the world of academia. Following her retirement in 1966, she served as a consultant for academic cultural affairs, continuing her involvement with the college until her death on April 6, 1977.

Erie Branch
Researcher: Sister Eunice Carlos, S.S.J.,
Archivist
Villa Maria College
Writer: Peggy Krider

115

Victoria M. Lyles, Ph.D.

1889–1966 ──

Dr. Victoria Lyles, a native of Wagoner, Oklahoma, was a pioneer in the field of education. She was the state supervisor for Oklahoma schools before moving to York, Pennsylvania, in the early 1930s. Dr. Lyles served the city of York as director of elementary and kindergarten education and, during her twenty-five-year tenure, experimented with many new ideas and programs that are generally accepted today.

Dr. Lyles foresaw a plan for injecting international understanding into public education that resulted in the development of a foreign language program. The York bilingual program was instituted in 1952 and within two years was expanded in several schools. The success of this venture led to York's being chosen as a "twin" city with Arles, France, in 1954. In 1979 a school in Arles was named in Dr. Lyles' honor.

A great innovator, as early as 1940 she developed case studies to show how the psychological factors of background and home life could affect a child's ability to learn. These studies helped the schools to deal with emotionally disturbed children and to establish special courses so that they could obtain a proper education.

Dr. Lyles also recognized the damaging effects of racial discrimination on a child. For many years she was an outspoken advocate of integration in the elementary schools of York. Dr. Lyles wrote and distributed bulletins that gave information on various races and creeds. Students were encouraged to study one another's backgrounds in hopes that prejudices would eventually dissolve. In 1947 Dr. Lyles' plan for school integration resulted in the opening of the first interracial kindergarten in York. The success of this experiment led to the integration of eighteen more schools which used the plan designed by Dr. Lyles.

In 1949 Dr. Lyles was named a Distinguished Daughter of Pennsylvania. She is listed in *Who's Who in American Education,* and has received many other honors. In York she is known as an educational reformer who cared for people and practiced and promoted the spirit of brotherhood.

Dr. Lyles retired to Oklahoma in 1954 and continued her work in the field of education until her death in 1966.

York Branch
Researcher/Writer: Dorothy Baker

116

Ruth Crawford Mitchell

b. 1890 _____

An appreciation for cultural differences played a prominent role in the life of Ruth Crawford Mitchell. Her father was president of a large department store in St. Louis and found it necessary to make many trips abroad, so he took his wife and daughter along. As a child of nine, she rode her bicycle over the cobblestoned streets of an old French village. Every summer vacation she traveled to Europe with her parents, gaining a knowledge of Europeans, rich and poor, and of their culture. It is not surprising that Ruth acquired a world view, with a knowledge of foreign places, people and their cultures. This contact with far away places whetted her appetite for travel and helped determine the course of her adult life. While a student at Vassar, her parents gave her a trip that would round out her world experience: together with a classmate, she went to Finland, Norway, Russia and Japan by way of the Trans-Siberian Railroad. She never lost her interest in people and their cultures.

Ruth graduated from Vassar and went on to Washington University in St. Louis where she received a master's degree in social work. Her first job was with the national board of the Young Women's Christian Association, and her knowledge of other cultures was put to good use, since her work was helping immigrants adjust to the American way of life. After World War I, she was sent to Czechoslovakia to do a social survey in Prague for Dr. Alice Masaryk, president of the Czechoslovakian Red Cross and the daughter of the President of Czechoslovakia.

When she returned to the United States in 1922, she married LeRoy Bradley Mitchell, a mining engineer. His work took him to Pittsburgh, so Ruth came to that city as a new bride. The marriage lasted for ten years, after which she was on her own for the rest of her very active life.

The University of Pittsburgh appointed Ruth Mitchell a lecturer on immigration and the problems of assimilation, and she became intrigued by the great number of nationalities represented in her classes. At the same time she was appalled at the students' lack of knowledge of the homeland and culture of their parents. She was instrumental in having admission forms at the University of Pittsburgh include data on the country of origin of the students and their parents. A four-year study of this information revealed that the heritage of students at the University of Pittsburgh encompassed the entire world.

Ruth Mitchell came to the attention of the university chancellor when discussions began about an appropriate interior decor for the University's "Cathedral of Learning," so-called because of its exterior gothic architecture. Working together, they came up with the idea of "Nationality Rooms" that would reflect the diverse backgrounds of the student body. Ruth was relieved of her classroom duties and asked to bring the concept of Nationality Rooms to fruition. She asked people of immigrant backgrounds to help interpret their culture through the rooms. Committees were organized in 1925 which still function today. Mrs. Mitchell was special advisor to each committee, going abroad to consult with architects and to give orders for the authentic adornments. The first rooms were dedicated in 1938, and by 1957 all of the classrooms on the first floor of the Cathedral of Learning were completed. They are a visual record of the heritage of students at the University of Pittsburgh.

Many honors have come to Ruth Crawford Mitchell who has been variously described as dynamic, intelligent, loquacious and headstrong. She was awarded the Chancellor's Gold Medal in 1972 and received an honorary Doctor of Humanities degree from the University of Pittsburgh. She has been decorated by Czechoslovakia, Yugoslavia, Poland, France and Italy and is the only woman to receive the David Glick Award from the World Affairs Council of Pittsburgh. The state of Pennsylvania added her to its list of Distinguished Daughters.

She retired officially in 1956 but continued as a consultant to the Office of Cultural Education which she had instituted at the university. It was largely through her efforts that the 300th anniversary of the first academic degree awarded to a woman was celebrated in 1978. The Center for International Studies published Mrs. Mitchell's book, *Alice Garregue Masaryk*.

The University of Pittsburgh saluted Ruth Crawford Mitchell on her ninetieth birthday in 1980. Chancellor Wesley W. Posvar said of her:

> Her dynamism, imagination, and creativity have combined with her love of people to enable her to establish an outstanding record of unequaled programs in her some thirty years of official affiliation with this University.

Pittsburgh Branch
Researcher/Writer: Dr. Ann Quattrocchi

117

Althea Kratz Hottel, Ph.D.

b. 1907 ————————————————————————————————

"How Fare American Women?" is the title of a landmark report produced by Althea Hottel during her tenure as director of the Commission on the Education of Women. The title perfectly summarizes her lifelong commitment to studying and elevating the status of women in American education. As a professor of sociology and the dean of Women at the University of Pennsylvania, she was a constant advocate for the advancement of women. She also served for six years as President Dwight D. Eisenhower's delegate to the United Nations Social and Economic Council. As past president of the American Association of University Women (AAUW), she shepherded the organization through one of the most controversial periods in its national history.

Althea Kratz was born in Lansdale in 1907. After graduation from high school in 1925, she enrolled at the University of Pennsylvania, where she wanted to "try her wings." She majored in history, but after a year as a high school teacher, she decided to pursue a graduate degree. She won a graduate fellowship and returned to the University of Pennsylvania.

She was no stranger to the subtle forms of discrimination women traditionally faced in education. As an undergraduate, her desire to study medicine or law had been firmly discouraged by her professors. As a graduate student, her ambition was to do doctoral work in political science, but she was told there would be no opportunities for women in this field. Since she was interested in social issues, she decided to take her Ph.D. with a concentration in sociology. After completing her degree, she joined the University of Pennsylvania faculty in sociology and was also appointed dean of women. At the time she was the only woman on the university's administrative council. Her position as dean of women gave her ample opportunity to evaluate the ways in which the university could meet the educational needs of its women students. She strongly encouraged women not to impose restrictions on their own advancement.

Althea Hottel served as president of the Philadelphia Branch of the American Association of University Women (AAUW). In 1947 she became national president of the association and was involved in the controversy over racial and religious prejudice in one of the organization's branches. Determined to eliminate discrimination based on race or creed, she presented the resolution ending restrictive membership to AAUW's National Convention in Seattle in 1949. The resolution was passed and the only requirement for membership in AAUW became a college or university degree.

After her retirement, Althea Hottel moved to Bryn Mawr, where she continues her involvement in education as a trustee of the Philadelphia Commission of Higher Education, the State Board of Education, and the Council of Higher Education and a board member of several local educational organizations. Her contributions have been widely recognized and she is the recipient of twelve honorary degrees. As a state and national leader in higher education, she has spent over forty years evaluating and promoting educational opportunities for American women.

Lansdale Branch
Researcher/Writer: Marilyn Solvay
Local Editors: Diane Brouillette
Kathie Sachs

118

Helen
Hulick Beebe
b. 1908

Helen Hulick Beebe, executive director of the Helen H. Beebe Speech and Hearing Center of Easton, Pennsylvania, is an internationally known speech pathologist. Helen Beebe is a pioneer in the use of the "unisensory" method in training profoundly deaf children to listen through amplified hearing and to speak normally. Families come to Easton from all over the world to bring their hearing-impaired children to the Center for therapy.

Helen Hulick Beebe was born in Hellertown, Pennsylvania, on December 27, 1908. She was the third of five children born to Charles Hulick and Helen Chidsey Hulick. Helen received her early education in Hokendaqua, Pennsylvania, and later, her family moved to Easton, Pennsylvania, where she graduated from Easton High School. Following studies at Wellesley College, Helen trained and taught at the Clarke School for the Deaf in Northampton, Massachusetts, and in oral schools for the deaf in California and Oregon. In 1942 she began studying in New York City with Dr. Emil Froeschels, a noted Austrian speech pathologist, from whom she learned the unisensory method of training deaf children. During this time she also studied speech pathology at Columbia University. Over the next twenty years she continued to commute to New York City from Easton several days each week to work with Dr. Froeschels.

The unisensory method was developed during the 1940s and is based on the surprising evidence that ninety-five per cent of all the hearing-impaired, even the profoundly deaf, have some remnant of trainable hearing. The unisensory method concentrates on developing the hearing that exists. Therapy begins as soon as the handicap is detected, ideally as early as two or three months of age. The child is carefully fitted with binaural hearing aids to bathe his consciousness in sound during all his waking hours.

The therapist institutes a program of intensive listening for the child. The program includes the training of parents as well as biweekly individual sessions with the child. The parents must continue the training in the home on a daily basis. Sign language and lip reading, both visual skills, are not permitted, so that the child can concentrate entirely on the development of hearing. As the parents increase the child's normal desire to listen and to talk, the child gradually learns to distinguish words from other sounds, to form words into patterns, to use hearing to modulate his/her own voice and to achieve natural speech and voice quality.

Instead of being isolated in the protected and limited world with other "special" children, the child is able to attend a regular nursery school where he/she can hear and repeat normal speech patterns throughout the day. At school age, nine out of ten children taught the unisensory method can take their places in a standard classroom.

The unisensory method requires patient, hard work by the child, the therapists and the family. It is worth the effort because it allows a deaf child to live a normal rather than an isolated life. "Graduates" of the unisensory method have entered school programs for the gifted, becoming lawyers, medical technicians and secretaries.

In 1944 Helen Beebe established a small private practice in her home in Easton. As her practice grew she moved several times to larger quarters. In 1972 the Larry Jarret Memorial Foundation was incorporated to "promote the Helen Beebe philosophy of unisensory training and to make this training available to all hearing-impaired children." In 1978 the Foundation and Helen Beebe's practice joined to become the Helen Beebe Speech and Hearing Center, a charitable, nonprofit organization.

The Center recently moved to a newly-renovated building in Easton. The building houses the clinic and the Larry Jarret House, a demonstration home for visiting families of clients, where parents are taught how to apply the unisensory method in a normal home setting. Many families come from as far away as Europe and South America to receive this special and vital instruction.

The clinic employs four full-time therapists and has a case load of forty-two clients. About seventy-five professionals in the field of teacher-in-training visit the clinic each year to observe the treatment program.

Helen Beebe has lectured both nationally and internationally. Specialists from Canada, Europe and South America have sought her guidance in establishing clinics in their countries. She has written numerous articles for professional journals which have appeared in the United States and in foreign publications. She authored the book *Guide to Help the Severely Hard of Hearing Child.*

Mrs. Beebe is a life member of the American Speech and Hearing Association and holds a Certificate of Clinical Competence in Speech Pathology. She is a member of the Pennsylvania Speech and Hearing Association the Northeast Pennsylvania Speech and Hearing Association, the Alexander Graham Bell Association for the Deaf and the International Association for Logopedics and Phoniatrics. She serves on the honorary board of the International Foundation for Children's Hearing, Education, and Research and is Coordinator of the International Committee on Auditory Verbal Communication.

Helen Hulick Beebe has developed and promoted a proven technique for teaching the profoundly deaf to hear and speak. Her energy in lecturing, writing and training of specialists has enabled many severely handicapped individuals to live richer and fuller lives.

Easton Branch
Researcher: Margaret D. Druse
Writer: Nancy Catanach

119

Anna Lucille Carter

1912–1979 ─────────────────────────────

Born in Harrisburg on November 16, 1912, Anna Carter's childhood was secure and happy in the love of her adoptive parents, Walter and Mary Elizabeth Carter. Anna was industrious, talented in many areas, and precocious. She enrolled at Shippensburg State College at the age of sixteen.

After graduation Anna worked with the Works Progress Administration (WPA) as a health and home instructor where she taught others how to can and preserve foods and how to have clean, organized homes.

In 1936 Anna started teaching at the Glenwood School in the Edgemont Community of Susquehanna Township. She initiated a "hot lunch" program for the needy children and an outgrowth of it was the formation of a Mothers' Club. Along with Anna Carter this group started a cafeteria and raised $500 for equipment.

In the 1940s Glenwood was renovated and combined with the B. J. Crouse School. Anna became the head teacher and in 1951 was appointed principal. She worked at various jobs during summer vacations and managed to take graduate courses in supervision and administration at Columbia and Temple Universities.

Anna's efforts were responsible for establishing the Edgemont Recreation Program and swimming pool. In 1962 she received an award from the Pennsylvania Department of Public Instruction in recognition of outstanding service to the children and community of Edgemont. The road leading from Locust Lane up to the Glenwood School was named "Carter Drive" by the township.

Upon her retirement in 1978, after forty-two years of service, she was given the honor of having the Glenwood School renamed the Anna L. Carter School. In late 1978 she received the "Teacher of the Year" award from the Pennsylvania Principals' Association. She was nominated for the American Educators' Medal Award from the Freedoms Foundation of Valley Forge and received numerous other honors and awards during her lifetime. On November 29, 1979, an unfortunate accident claimed the life of Anna L. Carter.

February 24, 1980, was declared "Anna L. Carter Day" by Governor Dick Thornburgh, Harrisburg Mayor Paul E. Doutrich, Jr. and the Susquehanna Township Commissioners. This was the first time in the Commonwealth of Pennsylvania that a Black school administrator was so honored.

Harrisburg Branch
Researcher/Writer: Peggy Davenport

120

Lois Teal
Hartley, Ph.D.

1923–1968

Lois Teal Hartley was a demanding teacher of literature and Asian studies. As a professor and writer, her contribution can probably best be recognized in her leadership in the Modern Language Association and as editor of *Literature East and West*. Many outstanding Pennsylvania women have distinguished themselves in academia. The story of Lois Hartley is an example of what one determined woman from a small town in Pennsylvania was able to achieve in the academic world during her short lifetime and the pride that her community took in her accomplishments.

Lois was born in Rices Landing, Pennsylvania, on July 31, 1923. She was the elder of two daughters of Thomas T. and Hazel Price Hartley. In Greene County, a farming and coal mining area of rolling hills along the Monongahela River, she had an idyllic childhood. Perpetually observant, joyfully seeking experience, constantly trying what was new and an avid reader, Lois Hartley was a superior student. She received scholarships for her education at Waynesburg College where she was graduated *summa cum laude* in 1944, as well as for her graduate degrees from Pennsylvania State University in 1945 and the University of Illinois in 1950. She was elected to Phi Beta Phi and Phi Beta Kappa.

Whatever Lois Hartley undertook, whatever friendship she formed, whatever work she did, she remained faithful to it and made it fruitful. She readily acknowledged her indebtedness to her teachers and relatives for making her what she was. Although her work took her to many states and foreign countries, nothing pleased her more than to return to the simple pleasures and beauty of her childhood home.

Because she valued her American heritage, Lois chose American literature as her field. She wrote her master's thesis on the popular plays about Pocahontas written between 1805 and 1865 and her doctoral dissertation on Edgar Lee Masters. Following extensive visits with Masters and his family, she published a monograph, "Spoon River Revisited," which contained a series of articles on Masters' prose, and Masters and the Chinese. Her literary interests also included the early Puritan tradition and the Transcendentalists, especially Henry David Thoreau. Once she conveyed his principles so vitally to her class that a student left college to live them. She also published significant essays on Thomas Wolfe and Henry James.

Lois Hartley was a demanding teacher, intolerant of slipshod standards and imprecision, yet dedicated beyond classroom work to the student as a person, whom she wanted to meet, know and encourage. She began teaching in 1945 as a graduate student at the University of Illinois. After a year at the Library of Congress, she taught at Ohio State University and at Ball State University. From 1962 until her death, she was at Boston College, where she was made a full professor.

In 1959 on leave from Ball State, she served as teacher, dean and administrative assistant for the International School of America, a school where students learned by traveling around the world. She had always had a passion for travel and had already explored the United States, Nova Scotia, Mexico, South America and twenty countries in Europe and the Near East. This position provided her with an opportunity to visit India for the first time.

In the summer of 1964, with a Fulbright grant and another from the Asia Society, she returned to India. She made friendships with Indian authors and scholars whom she often entertained in her home. She built a large collection of Indian literature and in 1967 introduced a course on the Indian novel, thought and culture at Boston College.

Lois became a member of the Conference on Oriental-Western Literary Relations at the Modern Language Association, serving on several literary panels. In April 1965 she read a paper at the University of Kentucky Foreign Language Conference on Ruth Prawer Jhabvala, whom she had known personally. She wrote many reviews for a number of journals, including *Literature East and West*. In 1966 she became the editor of this journal and produced its first all-India issue. She edited twelve issues before illness claimed her life on August 6, 1968.

As a woman from the little town of Rices Landing, Lois Teal Hartley found many challenging opportunities in her forty-five year life. Although her last year was filled with devastating illness and surgery, she met every commitment. Her influence through her friendships and teaching has been felt both in the United States and abroad.

Rices Landing Branch
Researcher: Ina Price Vance
Writer: Sarah Appleton Weber

13
WOMEN AS WRITERS

121

Margaret Junkin Preston

1820–1897 ───────────────────────

A poet and prose writer who attained national distinction in the world of "belles lettres," Margaret Junkin, eldest of the eight children of the Rev. George Junkin and his wife Julia, was born in Milton, Pennsylvania. The family were descendants of Scottish Covenanters. Dr. Junkin, a Presbyterian minister, moved to Easton in 1832, where he became the first president of the nascent Lafayette College.

A diminutive child with blue eyes and masses of auburn hair, Margaret was educated privately, like most upper-class young ladies of that time. Her instruction was undertaken by her father and professors and tutors of the College. Along with studying Latin, Greek and Hebrew before she was twelve, she still carried a full domestic load; embroidery was required of young ladies, and all clothing for the large family was hand sewn. Margaret showed great promise in painting and watercolor, her first love as she said later, until poor eyesight caused her to seek other artistic expression.

During her sixteen years in Easton, Margaret wrote verses which were graceful and devotional that appeared often in the Easton newspapers. She was influenced by the beautiful, romantic scenery surrounding her home on the college campus on Mount Lafayette (now called College Hill) which overlooks the town and its two rivers.

The path of Margaret's life turned sharply in 1848 when her father accepted the presidency of Washington College (later Washington and Lee University) in Lexington, Virginia. There, in 1857, she married Major John T. L. Preston, professor of Latin at Virginia Military Institute, a widower with seven children. During the next four years she had two sons of her own, and her literary career was temporarily halted by the immense volume of work which fell to the mistress of a "fine home" in the South of that period.

The coming of the Civil War was especially tragic for Margaret Preston and her family. Her father, an ardent abolitionist, left the South with a widowed daughter. Her brother William became a captain in the Confederate army, while her brother John served as a surgeon in the Federal army. Her sister Eleanor was the wife of Thomas J. Jackson, a military genius better known as "Stonewall" Jackson. Margaret's husband, although past military age, served General Jackson with the rank of colonel.

Dutiful wife that she was, Margaret fervently supported the Confederate cause. The journal that she kept from 1861 to 1866 paints a vivid and valuable picture of the trials of a southern woman of this period. Parts of it are printed in *The Life and Letters of Margaret Junkin Preston*, written by her step-daughter Elizabeth Preston Allen. Margaret's strongest lyrics are found in *Beechenbrook*, which contains her anguished poems about the sorrow and patriotism of the South: "Stonewall Jackson's Grave" and "Slain in Battle." After the war, in addition to her own writing, she reviewed books for various publications. After her husband died in 1890, she spent the last years of her life with a son in Baltimore.

Margaret Junkin Preston, sensitive, shy, conscientious and deeply religious, represents the literary flowering of well-educated women of both the North and the South in the decades before and after the Civil War. She was called "Poetess-Laureate of the South." The New York *Evening Post* characterized her poetry as belonging "to the school of Mrs. Browning" (Elizabeth Barrett Browning). Some of those who wrote letters complimenting her writing were Henry Wadsworth Longfellow, Oliver Wendell Holmes, John Greenleaf Whittier, Paul Hayne, and John Burroughs.

Among her works are: a translation of the Latin hymn "Dies Irae," 1855; *Silverwood,* a novel, 1856; *Beechenbrook, A Rhyme of the War,* 1866; *Cartoons,* 1875; *Old Songs and New,* her best known work, 1870; *For Love's Sake,* 1886; *A Handful of Monographs, Continental and English,* 1887; *Semi-Centennial Ode for the Virginia Military Institute, Lexington, Virginia 1839-1889; Aunt Dorothy, An Old Virginia Plantation Story,* 1890.

Easton Branch
Researcher: Margaret D. Druse
Writer: Cynthia Gordon

122

Helen Reimensnyder Martin

1868–1939 ───────────────────────────────────────

During her lifetime Helen Reimensnyder Martin was known to many as a novelist who wrote comical portrayals of the Pennsylvania Germans. Her novels, however, were not written as literature, but as a means to express her lifelong crusade for feminism and socialism.

Helen Reimensnyder Martin was born in Lancaster, Pennsylvania, on October 18, 1868, to immigrant German parents. Educated at Swarthmore and Radcliffe, she taught school for a time in New York City. After her marriage in 1899, she lived in Harrisburg but spent much of her time traveling. Throughout her life she defended the rights of women, working actively for suffrage. She was also a socialist, attacking the capitalistic establishment in much of her writing. Although such ideas ran counter to those of most of the novel readers of her time, her books gained wide acceptance. Between 1896 and 1939 she published thirty-five novels and many short stories. The popularity of her novels led to the dramatization of her 1914 novel *Barnabetta* into a stage play and movie under the title *Erstwhile Susan*. The feminism in her first novels of high society, which symbolized the shallow values of society in its treatment of women, did not find popular acceptance. Her successes were achieved when she disguised her material through the use of the Pennsylvania German milieu.

Long before the twentieth century the Pennsylvania Germans were a nationally recognized regional minority. With other ethnic minorities, they were often the subjects of ridicule. It was in Helen Martin's novels that they were most unfavorably portrayed. From the publication of her popular *Tillie: A Mennonite Maid* in 1904 until her death in 1939, she wrote and rewrote the story of Pennsylvania German women as repressed victims of a harsh, male-dominated, illiterate social group, often in terms of pure melodrama.

The initial impetus in Helen Martin's choice of the simple and usually rural background was given by a Philadelphia magazine which requested a friend of hers to write the history of his Pennsylvania Dutch ancestry. He turned the research over to her with the result that she realized she had struck a rich source for her own fiction. Reviewers of her ensuing works complimented her on the skilled use of the Pennsylvania Dutch dialect. There is no better way to disarm defenders of the established order than humor. Her readers, in finding her characters comical, usually missed the satire based on her strong convictions. Her novels underline the materialism of the Pennsylvania Germans, using it as a dramatic device to represent the economic bondage of all women. Accustomed as they were to stereotyped ethnic portrayals, her readers found her villains and situations comically amusing.

The simple old-fashioned home life of the Amish Germans, with their stable values, their gentleness, their closeness to the elemental things of life, did not influence or soften Helen Martin's views. For a woman with a deep belief in the wrongs of the male-female relationship in American society, the Pennsylvania German attitude toward women was outrageous. However, her melodramatic exaggeration, sometimes viewed as "caricature," served to make her portrayals comically ridiculous.

In reply to criticisms of the dismal picture she presented of the Pennsylvania German culture, she claimed she was not biased but knowledgeable. Considering her theme of the advancement of human rights, her practice of extreme ethnic stereotyping seems rather ironic.

Lancaster Branch
Researcher/Writer: Mary Krogman

123

Mary Roberts Rinehart

1876–1958 ─────────────────────────────────

Mary Roberts Rinehart was born in 1876 in Old Allegheny, now part of the city of Pittsburgh, and lived there until she and her family moved to Sewickley in 1912. Educated in the public schools of Pittsburgh, she graduated from the Public Training School for Nurses (later known as the Shadyside Hospital School of Nursing). She entered the nursing profession when there were only 400 graduate nurses in the whole country.

While in nursing school, Mary met and married Dr. Stanley N. Rinehart, a young intern just beginning practice. She served as secretary and nurse for her husband while raising three sons, Stanley, Alan and Frederick. She had often suppressed a desire to write, but it took a financial panic and stock market collapse to free the impulse. Finding the family with a debt of $12,000, she wrote down a story that her husband related to her about a patient and sent it to *Munsey's Magazine*. Back came a check for $34 and a request for more stories. This was a modest beginning, but that year she sold forty-five short stories and novelettes, earning $1,800.

Mary continued to write short stories, timidly avoiding long ones. After much encouragement, she wrote her first serial, *The Man in Lower Ten*. Her first book, *The Circular Staircase*, was published in 1908 and sold 800,000 copies. Intended as a satire on the usual pompous, self-important crime story, it was taken seriously and reviewed favorably by *The New York Times*. By the end of 1911, Mary Roberts Rinehart had published five successful books and produced two plays.

In 1911 she purchased "Casella," a long, white, two-story house in Glen Osborne, near Sewickley. Shortly after moving into this mansion, she published a mystery novel, *The Case of Jennie Brice*. It was set in Pittsburgh's North Side during a spring flood. *Jennie Brice* was soon followed by *The After House* in 1913, a book of very funny Tish stories, and two plays, *The Rejuvenation of Aunt Mary* and *Cheer Up*.

When World War I broke out in Europe, the *Saturday Evening Post* sent Mary to Belgium as a war correspondent. She visited and wrote of the battlefields and trenches and sent back reports on the desperate conditions among the civilian populations in England and France.

Because of her efforts to help the victims of the war, she received numerous commendations and honors, including the *Medaille de la Reine Elizabeth*.

In 1920 she was nominated as a candidate-at-large to the Republican National Convention because of her stands on conservation, the registration of aliens, adequate child labor laws and opposition to the water power bill which would have placed a vast fortune in the hands of a few. She was also an advocate of equal rights for women. On this last point she was particularly outspoken, having participated actively in the women's suffrage movement, but she notes, "I was no feminist. I wanted men and women to walk shoulder to shoulder, and not the successful woman ahead."

The Rinehart family moved from Sewickley in early 1922 so that Stanley Rinehart could work on important tuberculosis research for the Veterans Administration in Washington. After his death Mary Roberts Rinehart moved to New York but noted that she and her family considered "The Bluff" in Glen Osborne as home.

Her three sons were active in the publishing field as Rinehart and Company, and, when Mrs. Rinehart died in 1958, they gave her literary effects, books, papers and the furniture from her study to the University of Pittsburgh.

In *Improbable Fictions: A Life of Mary Roberts Rinehart,* Jan Cohn states:

> Mrs. Rinehart's claim to fame was that she was an important, respected American in an era when few women achieved national influence. Even though she was ahead of her time as a successful professional writer, she reflected middle-class American values and rarely challenged them.

Pittsburgh Branch
Researcher/Writer: Ellen M. Panetta

124

Elsie Singmaster

1879–1958 —————————————————————————————————

The literary career of Elsie Singmaster spanned forty-seven years, during which time she wrote thirty-eight books and published more than 300 articles in the country's leading periodicals. Her interest in local, state and national history was expressed in her writings. Many of her stories featured Pennsylvania Germans and Adams County backgrounds, and she often dealt with historical subjects, such as the Battle of Gettysburg. *Rifles for Washington,* published in 1938, chronicled the experiences of the Adams County Company in the American Revolution. Other notable works were *Ellen Levis,* a 1921 novel about life in the Ephrata Cloisters, and *I Speak for Thaddeus Stevens,* a 1947 biography of the famous United States Representative from Pennsylvania. In 1909 she published her first children's book, *When Sarah Saved the Day.* Her many other works for children include: *A Boy at Gettysburg* as well as books about Martin Luther, United States history, and the United States Constitution.

Elsie Singmaster was regarded by her contemporaries as one of the outstanding literary figures of her time. Her writings were regularly reviewed in major publications, and a sampling of the critics' comments reveals the magnitude of her subjects and her talents. In 1909 one reviewer found in her work "the first time that the Pennsylvania German people have been treated in a decent way and in a manner that does them justice." H. C. Long wrote that she was "intensely interested in Pennsylvania history, especially the period of the Civil War, and she ranges from historical narratives peopled by local characters to pure local color stories and is successful in both." Dayton Kohler concluded that "from the very outset of her career she belonged to that small group of writers who find in a faithful portrayal of human nature the only sound and abiding literary values."

Elsie Singmaster was born in Schuylkill Haven, Pennsylvania, and spent her early life in the Allentown area. She was one of five children of Dr. John Alden Singmaster and Caroline Hoopes Singmaster and their only daughter. She moved to Gettysburg in 1901, when her father, a Lutheran minister, joined the faculty of the Lutheran Theological Seminary, where he later served as president for twenty years. She attended Cornell University and published her first short story in 1903, four years before she received her Bachelor of Arts degree from Radcliffe College. In 1912 she married Harold Steck Lewars, a musician and professor of English at Gettysburg College. They moved to Harrisburg, where her husband taught music and served as an organist for a Lutheran church. Following the death of her husband in 1915, Elsie Singmaster returned to her parents' home in Gettysburg. She continued to write under her maiden name and became well-known for her descriptions of rural and small-town life.

Although Elsie Singmaster's love of the past was represented in her writings, her commitment to the present was evident in her work as a community activist. She was one of the organizers and the first secretary of the Adams County Chapter of the American Red Cross and served as chapter chairman from just after World War I until 1946. The National Red Cross awarded her a Citation of Merit in honor of her many years of service.

Education was one of her lifetime concerns. In 1944 she helped organize the Adams County Free Library and became a member of the first board of directors. She later served as president of the board and, after her retirement, was made an honorary director for her lifetime. She was an active supporter of the Adams County Historical Society and the Pennsylvania Historical Association. She led in the successful movement to make Gettysburg College coeducational. She was also a member of the board of directors of the Gettysburg Civic Nursing Association and was affiliated with the American Association of University Women and the Pennsylvania German Association.

Elsie Singmaster was quite small, standing only five feet tall, and of a gentle nature. However, she had definite opinions concerning personal behavior and was an advocate of women's suffrage and prohibition. Neither alcohol nor cards were allowed in her home. She was a member of Christ Lutheran Church in Gettysburg and was active in seminary affairs. She loved music and, for a time, played the organ for daily chapel service. She also taught brief courses in the history of the church.

The literary and civic contributions of Elsie Singmaster earned her numerous awards and honors. She was elected to Phi Beta Kappa at Radcliffe. In 1916 she became the first woman to receive an honorary degree, Doctor of Literature, from Gettysburg College. In 1928 she was awarded an honorary Doctor of Literature degree from Muhlenberg

College in Allentown. For more than forty years, Elsie Singmaster was listed in *Who's Who in America* and was the first woman from Adams County to achieve that recognition. Her final honor came in 1950, when the state of Pennsylvania named her a Distinguished Daughter of Pennsylvania.

Gettysburg Branch
Researchers: Marilyn Culp Bollingner,
Christine Ritter and
Aileen Sechler
Writer: Donna Schaefer

125

Hilda "H. D." Doolittle Aldington

1886–1961 ————————————————————————————

Hilda Doolittle, who over her long lifetime achieved an international reputation as one of the twentieth century's most distinguished poets, was born and is buried in Bethlehem, Pennsylvania. According to The Reverend Henry L. Williams:

> Hilda Doolittle is a poet for Bethlehem. She was born September 10, 1886, in a house on East Church Street, where the City Center now stands. . . . The poetry of H. D., as she always signed her writing, is not as accessible as, let us say, Robert Frost. She was part of the Imagist movement of which Ezra Pound was the leading member, yet her poetry and prose still fascinate other poets and students of literature. Scholars have come from Europe to see the town where she was born and about which she wrote in her later years. The family roots of H. D. go back to the early years of the community and through the generations gather in the names of its ministers and bishops, its teachers and headmasters, its silversmith, clockmaker, gunmaker and its musicians.

H. D.'s father was Charles L. Doolittle, professor of mathematics and astronomy at Lehigh University. Her mother, Helen Wolle, his second wife, was the sister of Fred J. Wolle, founder of the Bethlehem Bach Choir. Hilda was baptized and educated as a Moravian. She was always proud of her heritage and allowed it strongly to influence her poetry and prose.

She attended Moravian Academy until she was nine, when her family moved to Philadelphia. There she attended Miss Gordon's and the Friends Central Schools. She began her undergraduate work at Bryn Mawr College, but she was obliged to leave in her sophomore year because of ill health. Her first published work consisted of stories for children which appeared in a Presbyterian paper.

In 1911 she went to Europe for the summer and, discovering the exciting literary life of London, decided not to return to the United States. She renewed her acquaintance with Ezra Pound (to whom she had once been engaged) and was drawn into the flourishing Imagist movement, of which she became a principal figure. The Imagist movement was a literary movement which tried to convey direct impressions to the reader through the choice of words. Her first poems, sent by Pound to Harriet Monroe's *Poetry* magazine, were published in 1913. Pound persuaded her to sign the poems "H. D. Imagiste." The initials "H. D." became her professional name.

In 1913 Hilda married Richard Aldington, then an Imagist poet, and later a well-known English novelist. With him, she began a translation of Greek poets. When he joined the British Army during World War I, she took over his editorship of the magazine, *The Egoist*. The couple had one daughter, Perdita, born in 1919. They separated shortly after the war and were divorced in 1938. Following the divorce, she regained her United States citizenship.

These years had been difficult for Hilda. Besides marital difficulties, she suffered from poor health; her favorite brother was killed during the war in France, and her father died shortly thereafter. About this time, she became a close friend of Winifred Ellerman, a wealthy novelist who wrote under the name Bryher. The two women traveled together in Greece, Egypt and America.

In 1920 H. D. settled in Switzerland with her daughter and spent most of the rest of her years writing from her residence near Zurich. She published many volumes of poetry as well as essays, translations and novels. She was analyzed by Sigmund Freud and wrote of him in "A Tribute to Freud," 1956. During World War II she lived in London; and out of her experience came her great trilogy, "The Walls Do Not Fall," one of this century's most important poems about war.

In the last years of her life, two other major works were published: *Bid Me To Live* in 1960, considered her best novel, and the epic poem "Helen in Egypt" in 1961. A number of her manuscripts still remain unpublished. She died in Zurich on September 28, 1961; her ashes are buried in Nisky Hill Cemetery in Bethlehem in the family plot.

The Commonwealth of Pennsylvania and the Bethlehem City Council authorized placement of a marker on the site of Hilda Doolittle's birthplace which was dedicated on September 10, 1982. On that date the Friends of "H. D." arranged a gathering to read from her works and to insure that a writer of international reputation would not be forgotten in the town she had remembered with such fondness.

Hilda Doolittle and her work are described in *Twentieth Century Authors* in these words:

> It has been said of H. D. that among American women poets only Emily Dickinson ranks as her superior. Early in her career she became interested in the civilization and literature of ancient Greece. This love of all things Greek

pervades most of her writing. In work after work she explores her perennial themes of nature, art, love and war. Although she has never achieved a broad popularity, many regard her as one of the most significant voices in modern poetry. She is remembered by her friends as being tall, graceful and shining with an inner beauty. H. D. looked like a poet with deep-set gray eyes and delicately aquiline features. Richard P. Blackmur spoke of her "clarity of sound, economy of words, direct appeal to the visual imagination." Harriet Monroe said that she and other Imagists "shook the Victorian tradition and discarded its excesses."

Bethlehem Branch
Researcher: Catherine D. Barrett
Writer: Mary Archer Bean Eppes

126

Photograph by Richards' Studio, South Orange, N.J.

Agnes Sligh Turnbull

1888–1982

The rolling hills of western Pennsylvania provided a rich source of material for the works of one of America's best-loved woman novelists, Agnes Sligh Turnbull. Characters, settings, language and mores from her childhood years in New Alexandria can be found throughout the novels and short stories she produced during her long writing career.

Agnes, a daughter of devout Scottish Presbyterian stonemason, Alexander Sligh, and Lucinda McConnell, was born in New Alexandria on October 14, 1888. Both parents had a love of good literature and music. No restrictions were placed on the books Agnes was allowed to read, and she was encouraged to write poems and stories even as a child. She attended the village school, then Washington Seminary, graduating in 1910 from Indiana Pennsylvania State Normal School. After a year's study in English at the University of Chicago, Agnes taught high school English in western Pennsylvania until her marriage in 1918 to James L. Turnbull of Hebburn-on-Tyne, England. After the marriage the Turnbulls resided in Maplewood, New Jersey, for the rest of their lives, however, Agnes kept close ties with her New Alexandria friends and often visited there.

Religion was an important part of the Sligh's family life. When Agnes was fifteen, one of her poems was published in the *Presbyterian Banner*, a religious weekly. She sold her first short story to the *American Magazine* in 1920. For ten years she wrote only short stories, most of them with a religious background.

In 1936 she became a nationally known author with the publication of a novel, *The Rolling Years*, about three generations of Scotch-Irish women in rural western Pennsylvania. The story was based on the history of her mother's family. The book has passed its thirty-sixth printing.

As a young girl, Agnes was fascinated by the story of the burning of Hanna's Town by Indians in 1782. Her parents pointed out the site of the colonial county seat as they drove by on their way to Greensburg. *The Day Must Dawn*, published in 1942, tells of that exciting period in history and its hardships from a woman's point of view. Pittsburgh's early years were brought to life in *The King's Orchard*, a novel about General James O'Hara. Agnes Turnbull's historical novels brought about a renewed interest in the history of western Pennsylvania, and especially Hanna's Town which has now been restored.

The Bishop's Mantle, a national best-seller which sold nearly one million copies in 1948, proved that inspirational writing about decent people could be very successful. Agnes Turnbull found it most satisfying to tell an absorbing story about normal people in language that was always in good taste.

Agnes wrote every day, starting with vague characters and letting the stories and language evolve as she wrote. She developed fondnesses for her characters and was careful to have them speak and react to situations as they would have in real life. Her stories are so convincing because of her scrupulous attention to detail. Her characters are "just folks" who live in the small mining towns of Westmoreland County. Although some of her early works are now considered "quaint" and even a little "campy," critics are quick to point out that each of her books has enjoyed wide readership for many years. They have appeared in foreign translations and have all been reprinted in paperback.

Agnes Sligh Turnbull received the honorary degree of Doctor of Letters from Westminster College, New Wilmington, in 1945 and from her alma mater, now Indiana University of Pennsylvania, in 1974. Even after her ninetieth birthday she continued to write. On January 31, 1982, at the age of ninety-three, Agnes Sligh Turnbull died. She is buried in the family plot in the Union Cemetery overlooking her beloved New Alexandria.

Greensburg Area and Murrysville Branches
Researcher: Pat Hitcho
Writer: Trish Smithson
Researcher/Writer: Carolyn Glick
Special Division Editor: Mary Ann Stangil

127

Katharine Haviland Taylor

1891–1941

Katharine Haviland Taylor was born in 1891 in Mankato, Minnesota. Her father was an Episcopalian minister. Because of a heart condition, she was educated at home and at private schools, a fact she is known to have regretted, since she told friends she "missed meeting all the nice young people who go to public schools."

Katharine began to write at age seventeen. Her first story, "Cecelia of the Pink Roses," was published in a magazine, then in book form. Marian Davies appeared in the screen version of the story. At that time Katharine was living with her parents in Bethlehem, Pennsylvania, and saw the movie in Allentown.

The family spent many years living abroad, first in Florence, Italy, then in London. An adopted brother was an accomplished artist and archaeologist who has been cited for his work in the detection of spurious Egyptian specimens.

When the family moved to York, Katharine was content to cook and do housework. The simple life appealed to her; however, she continued to write. She said that she wrote of things she knew best. Although she admitted using local environment in her books, she claimed that her characters were not intentionally biographical. Of her more than twenty books of light fiction, two, *Yellow Soap* and *The Nine-Hundred Block* were set in York.

One of her many short stories, "The Failure," was made into a movie in 1933 entitled *One Man's Journey*. It starred Lionel Barrymore and May Robson. It was produced again in 1938 as *A Man to Remember* and was again an immediate success.

In addition to her novels, she wrote and illustrated numerous poems, and several children's books, including stories, plays and games with an international appeal. She felt language was very important and saw her work translated into Spanish, Swedish, French, Danish and Dutch.

After several years decline, Katharine Taylor died of bacterial endocarditis in November 1941 at her winter home in Clearwater, Florida. Two of her children's stories were published posthumously.

York Branch
Researcher/Writer: Dorothy Baker

128

Pearl S. Buck

1892–1973 ────────────────────────────────

Pearl Sydenstricker Buck, author and humanitarian, belonged to the whole world, but she called Bucks County home. Known primarily for her novels which contributed to a broader understanding of Oriental culture, she was also widely recognized for her work with Amerasian children.

She was born in Hillsboro, West Virginia. At the age of four months, she was taken by her missionary parents to China where she spent her childhood and some of her young adult life. In Chinkiang she learned the language and became so familiar with Chinese culture and attitudes that Lin Yutang, the famous writer, once said to her, "You are Chinese." She was, in fact, a proud American who revered the similarities which she saw in the American and Asian people.

Pearl Buck returned to the United States in 1910 to enroll in Randolph-Macon Woman's College. Her mother, an ardent feminist, helped her select the school, assuring her that her education would be exactly the same as that offered to a man. Among her schoolmates, she was an object of curiosity because of her conservative Oriental upbringing, but, with effort, she won the respect and admiration of her peers to become president of the senior class. She was graduated in 1914, thoroughly schooled in science, mathematics and Latin.

She felt that she could not become a missionary because she had met too many good non-Christians to feel that she should try to convert anyone. After a brief assistantship in psychology at her alma mater, the illness of her mother prompted her to return to China as a teacher under the auspices of the Presbyterian Board of Foreign Missions. She also managed the home and cared for her mother. In 1917 she became the wife of an agriculturalist with the Mission Board to whom she was married for seventeen years. John Lossing Buck gave her the name she was to use professionally except when she wrote on American life under the pseudonym of John Sedges.

While still a young girl, at the urging of her mother, Pearl Buck began to write. Her first American article appeared in *Atlantic Monthly* in 1923. Her first book, *East Wind: West Wind*, was published in 1930. She was awarded the Pulitzer Prize in 1932 for *The Good Earth*, her first widely-read novel, which unlocked the secrets of the interior of China for the rest of the world. It was on the American list of best sellers for twenty-one months and has been translated into more than thirty languages.

In 1938 Pearl Buck became the first American woman to receive the Nobel Prize for Literature. In her Nobel lecture, she said that she adhered to the tradition of the Chinese novel which teaches that the main object of the novelist should be to entertain. Her style was simple and unaffected. Some critics characterize it as "Biblical," repeating the stately rhythms of the King James version and expressing passionate moral concern with human values. She expressed liberal views on interracial matters in her many volumes on China, which helped Western readers understand the Chinese. As a motherly woman, she often wrote about problems of women. She was the first popular novelist to dare to discuss the intimate details of sex, childbirth and menstruation.

Pearl Buck's only natural child was retarded, but with her second husband, Richard J. Walsh, president of the John Day Company, a New York publishing firm, she adopted nine children of different nationalities. Her private delight in home and family centered in her comfortable, rambling, old farmhouse on the edge of Doylestown, Bucks County, Pennsylvania, which she purchased in 1934. She referred to this house as the root of her American life. In *My Several Worlds* she wrote of this acreage which once belonged to William Penn's brother, "I looked out over the land that is to me the fairest I know."

Pearl Buck held great respect for the family unit and the need for family, real or adopted, to be an individual's stronghold. Although she claimed no truly crusading spirit, with the help of Doylestown residents, Lois and David Burpee and Dorothy and Oscar Hammerstein, she founded Welcome House in 1949. This is an agency which brings children of Amerasian heritage to this country for adoption. She considered Welcome House a fitting demonstration that no child is unadoptable.

Her missionary training instilled in her a feeling of responsibility to do something about a situation in need of mending. Thus, after twenty-five years of experience in the field of lost and needy children, she gave her name to a foundation dedicated to the education and general welfare of the displaced children of the world. The Pearl S. Buck Foundation endeavors to eliminate injustice and prejudice suffered by children of American fathers and Asian mothers who, because of the Asian culture, are not accepted into society in the land of their birth. Originally established in Philadelphia, which Pearl Buck called the most cultivated of cities, the foundation moved to Bucks County in 1977.

Pearl Buck authored more than sixty-five books and hundreds of short stories and essays. Her writings set a tone of morality, caring, and human dignity; her life echoed these virtues. She died in 1973 and is buried on her beloved Green Hills Farm in Bucks County where someone places fresh flowers on her grave each day.

Doylestown Branch
Researcher/Writer: Mary McCaw

129

Nora Waln

1895–1964

Living as a daughter of a Chinese family, experiencing life in Germany during Hitler's rise to power, covering the Korean War from the front line—these are experiences upon which Nora Waln based her books and newspaper articles. Nora ranged far from her small birthplace of Grampian, Pennsylvania, to become a reporter, author and world traveler.

The circumstances of her birth in 1895 determined the beginning of her career. She was one of seven children of a Swedish mother and Quaker father, and family financial need brought about the first writing that she sold. This was a publication about her love of birds and flowers which brought her the friendship of naturalist John Burroughs. Nature was a continuing interest for Nora.

Her interest in China began with a hole in her rubber boot when she was visiting her grandparents at the age of nine. Forbidden to go out into the rain, she disobeyed and was banished to her room for punishment. She climbed to the attic instead. Rummaging in an old chest, she found copies of the *United States Gazette;* many of them were dated 1805. The Waln name was prominent among the shipping notices from Philadelphia to Canton in South China. These notices piqued her interest, and Nora began collecting Chinese histories and dictionaries.

In China, meanwhile, a similar interest was developing in the House of Lin, traders with the Walns. As a result, Nora was summoned to the telephone one day while she was an undergraduate at Swarthmore College. The caller was a woman of the Lin family who had found Nora Waln's name by looking through school catalogues because she wished to meet one of the Walns.

The Lins and Nora Waln spent a week together. When they parted, the woman told her, "You must come to me." Five years had passed when in December 1920, she went to China and lived with the Lin family. During that time Nora kept journals and some ten years later asked permission of the Lin family council to publish the manuscript written from her experiences. After deliberating, the Elder said, "There is no untruth in what she has put down." Thus, she was allowed to submit her story, *The House of Exile*, for publication. The book was one of her most important writings and brought her international attention.

Two years after she went to China, Nora planned to marry an English diplomat, Edward Osland-Hill. The Church of England service was to be used for the wedding, but arrangements almost collapsed when it was discovered that Quakers are not baptized. It was decided, however, that "all water from heaven is holy, and words said over it won't change it." Consequently, Nora was baptized, her husband-to-be was named as her godfather, and they were married.

In the late 1920s China seethed in a sort of combined civil war–revolution–invasion. The Communists set Chinese against Chinese, and Japan forced its way into Manchuria. The China Nora and her husband were living in had become a very different country from the one she had met and loved ten years before. They left the country in the early 1930s.

Ironically, as they fled the turmoil of China, the Osland-Hills went to live in Germany in 1934. Hitler was rising in power, and World War II was brewing. Nora's book on China had made her a popular figure—so much so that even Hitler had ordered thirty-five copies for friends—and she was allowed to see almost anything she wished. Her second book, *Reaching for the Stars*, covers this period.

During World War II Nora was a war correspondent. When the Korean conflict broke out, she was already in Japan for the *Saturday Evening Post* and was quickly assigned to the front line. An injury to herself and the death of her husband brought her back to the United States.

In 1960 she was in Clearfield to address the County Historical Society and, at that time, visited *The Progress* newspaper, her one-time employer. She proposed that during her next trip abroad, during which she expected to collect material for a book as well as write articles for the *Atlantic Monthly*, *National Geographic* and *Saturday Evening Post*, she write some exclusive articles for *The Progress*. "Watch out for my spelling and grammar," she humbly cautioned George Scott, the editor, in a letter at this time. "The more I use foreign languages in which, as with English, I am fluent without being a scholar, the less grammatical I get with American."

Five stories from East Berlin and many photographs appeared in *The Progress* under her byline. Illness leading to her death in 1964 prevented her finishing all she had intended to do. Nevertheless, Nora Waln had forged a place for herself in the literary world. Her writing is witness to the life and the times she lived.

Clearfield Area Branch
Researcher/Writer: Jane Hess

130

Catherine Drinker Bowen

1897–1973 _____

Catherine Drinker Bowen was a well-known and highly admired author and musician with many ties to the Lehigh Valley of Pennsylvania.

Born in Haverford on January 1, 1897, Catherine Drinker was the youngest of six children, most of whom were to become famous in a variety of fields. Her mother, Aimée Ernesta Beaux, was a sister of the portrait painter, Cecilia Beaux. Her father, Henry Sturgis Drinker, became president of Lehigh University in Bethlehem in 1905. Catherine was raised in Bethlehem and attended Moravian Academy and St. Timothy's in Catonsville, Maryland. Raised in a musically-oriented family, Catherine continued her studies at the Peabody Conservatory of Music in Baltimore and later at the Institute of Musical Art in New York. She was an accomplished violin and viola player but decided not to pursue a professional career in music. Instead, in 1919 she married Ezra Bowen, who in 1920 became head of the economics department at Lafayette College. The couple lived in Easton, where their two children were born.

Catherine's writing career began when she won ten dollars in a writing contest sponsored by *The Easton Express*. She wrote a daily column for the paper until 1924. Many articles followed, the themes of which were music or yachting. These were published in *Current History, Pictorial Review* and the *Woman's Home Companion.*

Her first books, *The Story of the Oak Tree* and *A History of Lehigh University,* appeared in 1924. Her only novel, *Rufus Starbuck's Wife,* was published in 1932; it was followed in 1935 by *Friends and Fiddlers,* an essay on music and musicians.

One of the early biographies for which Catherine Drinker Bowen was to become famous was *Beloved Friend: The Story of Tchaikowsky and Nadejda von Meck,* in 1937. This work was translated into Swedish, French and German and was chosen as a Book-of-the-Month selection, the first of five of her books to be so honored. It was followed in 1939 by *Free Artist: The Story of Anton and Nicholas Rubenstein,* the teachers of Tchaikowsky.

Catherine then began a series of biographies of men who were involved in forming and interpreting the constitutional government of the United States. The first of these was *Yankee from Olympus: Justice Holmes and his Family* (1944); next was *John Adams and the American Revolution* (1950). The third, which is thought by many to be her greatest work, was *The Lion and the Throne: The Life and Times of Sir Edward Coke, 1552-1634,* published in 1957. For this book she received the Henry M. Phillips Prize from the American Philosophical Society for an "outstanding book on the science and philosophy of jurisprudence" and in 1958 a National Book Award. Her fourth book on the development of constitutional thought was *Francis Bacon: The Temper of a Man* (1963), and the last in the series was *Miracle at Philadelphia: The Story of the Constitutional Convention* (1966).

Three collections of essays on the writing of biographies were written by Catherine Drinker Bowen. They were: *The Writing of Biography* (1951), *Adventures of a Biographer* (1959) and *Biography: The Craft and the Calling* (1969). She also wrote a biography of her own family in 1970, entitled *Family Portrait.*

Catherine Drinker Bowen's last book, *The Most Dangerous Man in America: Scenes from the Life of Benjamin Franklin,* was published posthumously. She died in 1973 in Haverford, Pennsylvania, near where she had been born.

Easton Branch
Researcher: Margaret D. Druse
Writer: Susan Berkowitz

131

Mildred Jordan Bausher

1900–1982 _____

Mildred Jordan Bausher was born and raised in Chicago and, perhaps, when she moved to this comparatively quiet area of the country in Berks County, Pennsylvania, there may have been some misgivings about life in a small city. But as she lived and worked in the area, she became an advocate of the prevailing life-style. Some of her books, including *The Distelfink Country of the Pennsylvania Dutch*, which took four years of research and writing, reflect her interest and concern for the area.

Mildred Bausher had the opportunity to visit many of the places about which she eventually wrote. The inspiration for her first novel, *One Red Rose Forever*, came from a trip to Mannheim, Germany, to see where "Baron" Stiegel lived and to learn about his glass. *The New York Times* called this "a novel written with the care and dignity of a first-rate biography, . . . by any standard an extraordinary first novel." The manuscript sold for $5,000 at a books-for-bonds rally held in Allentown in 1943. Another novel, *Miracle in Brittany*, was the result of a trip to that area. Others of her better-known works include *Asylum for the Queen*, *Echo of the Flute* and *Apple in the Attic*, which was on *The New York Times* best-seller list for seven weeks.

In addition to being an author, Mildred was also an active community leader. She founded and, for a time, totally funded Camp Meo for young mothers; later a group of her friends helped provide funds. Today Camp Meo is located on the site of the Young Women's Christian Association Blue Mountain Camp near Hamburg. It provides a week's free holiday without husband and children to forty young mothers at a time. Among Mildred Bausher's honors was being named a Distinguished Daughter of Pennsylvania in 1970.

Mildred Bausher was a transplanted Berks Countian, but her involvement in the community showed a caring and sharing affection for this Pennsylvania Dutch county.

Reading Branch
Researcher/Writer: M. Susan Johns

132

Hildegarde Dolson
(Hildegarde Dolson Lockridge)

1908–1981

It was Black Tuesday, October 29, 1929, the beginning of the Great Depression, when a young woman from Franklin, Pennsylvania, arrived in New York City. She was twenty-one-year-old Hildegarde Dolson, later to become a writer well-known for her humorous articles and books. Meanwhile, she and her cousin, Betty Dunn, shared a twelve-dollar-a-week room on Broadway and waited for their chance in the big town.

Hildegarde's fascination with journalism had come early. As a child, the daughter of Clifford and Katherine Dolson, she begged to be allowed to sell newspapers along with the neighborhood boys. "Maybe you can sell papers the day the war ends" her father said, thinking that she would forget such an urge. But when she learned that the armistice had been declared, she ran to line up with the boys for papers. The distributor told her that it was against regulations for girls to sell them. But the boys took her part, and one even showed her where to stand for good sales. By the time her father happened along, her allotment was gone, and she was helping the boys to sell theirs.

An avid reader, she also exhibited an active imagination. As a sixth grader, she was involved in a debate "Should the United States Keep Prohibition?" Determined that her affirmative team would win, Hildegarde described so convincingly what it was like to live with a drunken father that she received unusual solicitude from her teacher. But the explaining she had to do at home was another matter.

In high school she wrote for the school newspaper and subsequently studied journalism at Allegheny College in Meadville, Pennsylvania, but she left before graduation to pursue her career in New York.

While her cousin, Betty, studied dancing and singing, Hildegarde watched from the sidelines until the piano player for the class said that he needed someone to write song lyrics for a show. The resulting performance at a burlesque hall–to the horror of Hildegarde's Allegheny College boy friend–featured Betty in the dance line-up, while Hildegarde's lyrics were being sung.

Hildegarde, the writer, by now accustomed to a long line of rejection slips, accepted any job: work in a department store and a fifteen-dollar-a-week office job in a dingy picture frame company, among others. Meanwhile she submitted a series of weekly columns to her home town paper, *The News-Herald*, entitled "Here and There in Gotham."

She sent a story to the *New Yorker* and forgot about it until six weeks later when a check for $50 arrived. A bank teller, sensing her regret at parting with this precious paper, shoved a piece of it back for her to frame as her first New York success. Gradually, other achievements followed: writing advertising copy for Saks Fifth Avenue and Macy's, short pieces for *Good Housekeeping, Mademoiselle, Reader's Digest* and the *Ladies' Home Journal.*

Hildegarde Dolson's first book, *We Shook the Family Tree*, describes her childhood growing up with a brother and a sister in Franklin. Its humorous appeal led to its being reprinted in paperback and dramatized as a play. A second book, *Sorry to Be So Cheerful*, follows the same theme.

In the late 1950s Hildegarde returned to Franklin to research the history of oil in Venango County. The result was the publication of *The Great Oildorado* in time for the 1959 centennial of the world's first drilled oil well near Titusville. Her book is a lively and reliable account of the excitement surrounding the discovery of oil in northwestern Pennsylvania.

In 1957 she received an honorary degree of Doctor of Letters from Allegheny College, where a few years later she lectured for a week to journalism classes.

In 1965 she married Richard Lockridge, a journalist, author, critic and originator of the *Mr. and Mrs. North* series.

Other literary endeavors include two Landmark Books for Random House: one about the Johnstown flood and the other about William Penn. She collaborated with Elizabeth Stevenson Ives on *My Brother Adlai*, a biography written to promote Stevenson's candidacy for president. To produce a screen version of her book, *The Form Divine*, she spent some time in Hollywood. Hedda Hopper commented, "She's just about the wittiest ninety-pound female around these parts."

Hildegarde Dolson died on January 15, 1981, in Tryon, North Carolina, which had become her home in later years.

Oil City-Franklin Branch
Researchers/Writers: Margaret D. Reid and
Judy Reynolds

133

Gladys Schmitt
(Gladys Lenore Schmitt Goldfield)

1909–1972 ——————————————————————————

Gladys Schmitt is known as a writer of historical fiction; however, there was much more to be said about her by friends, colleagues and biographers. With an unusual talent for artistic writing, she taught creative writing for thirty years and was an inspiration to others. It would seem that she has only begun to be appreciated, though she has been a literary personality for three decades. Possibly the greatest tributes to this remarkable woman are in the minds and hearts of the legions of students who left her classes with a new image of life and literature which she provided.

Gladys Lenore Schmitt was a Pittsburgher, born May 31, 1909, to Henry and Lenore Elizabeth Link Schmitt. She attended local schools and graduated, *magna cum laude,* from the University of Pittsburgh. In 1937 she married Simon Goldfield whom she had met while a student at Schenley High School.

While still in grammar school, she wrote four plays in verse, and her first novel was written when she was fifteen. *Story* magazine published her first short story; the *Atlantic Monthly,* her next. Those that followed appeared primarily in "slick" magazines, with "an agent's efforts to tap the money market." Gladys worked for *Scholastic Magazine* in both the Pittsburgh and New York offices. In 1942 she returned to Pittsburgh to teach at Carnegie Institute of Technology (now Carnegie-Mellon University), where she remained for thirty years as a professor and a loyal friend to many in the Pittsburgh community.

Obsessed with her art, Gladys Schmitt once said, "I have to write." Her historical novels include *Gates of Aulis, David the King, Alexander, Confessors of the Name, The Persistent Image* and *A Small Fire.*

The University of Pittsburgh, her alma mater, granted her an honorary degree in 1961, and she was named a Distinguished Daughter of Pennsylvania. Three of her novels were Literary Guild selections, and she also won a Dial Press Award. In 1972 she received the Ryan Award for Meritorious Teaching from Carnegie-Mellon University.

Her admirers feel that she has not been given sufficient recognition as a writer and novelist of historic fiction. Anita Brostoff of Carnegie-Mellon University edited *I Could Be Mute,* a collection of writings about

Gladys Schmitt by friends, relatives and colleagues, designed to give recognition to her artistic genius. It is "the only work of book length proportions devoted to the author, while scattered articles have frequently been too pedantic in tone."

Stanley Mayer states in *Carnegie Magazine*, "Of all the writers who have touched or been touched by Pittsburgh in some rite of passage, whether accident of birth, years of apprenticeship, journalistic stint, university poet, or whatever, it is difficult to think of one who was born here and elected to produce a life's creative work here. Gladys Schmitt is the exception." Sylvia Sachs of *The Pittsburgh Press* described her as "the literary personality of Pittsburgh for three decades." Mary O'Hara emphasized her influence on creative writing and on the many students she inspired. Gladys Schmitt was one of western Pennsylvania's finest authors and teachers.

Pittsburgh Branch
Researcher: Anne Skoog
Writer: Nellie Marie Oliver

134

Margaret Maze Craig

1911–1964 ──

When little Peggy Maze was in the fourth grade, she wrote a novel and dreamed of herself as a rival of Laura Lee Hope, author of the *Bobbsey Twins* books. For many of us, girlhood dreams remain dreams but Peggy's would come true. In 1950 Margaret Maze Craig published her first novel *Trish* which was reviewed favorably in *The New York Times*. The reviewer said, "Mrs. Craig joins humor with sensitivity in this story of a girl's entry into social life."

Margaret Maze was born January 16, 1911, in Ridgway, Pennsylvania, and graduated from high school there. She received a Bachelor of Science degree in home economics from Indiana State College (now Indiana University of Pennsylvania). After graduation she was a home economist for West Penn Power Company in Kittanning, Pennsylvania.

Peggy married Roy Craig and moved to Moundsville, West Virginia. While her husband was in the service, she began to write greetings for cards and sold verses to ten different companies. Her first check was for two dollars. She wrote to her husband, "Today I am a writer."

In 1946 the Craigs moved to Oil City, Pennsylvania. Peggy was the busy mother of two girls. She began to write articles based on her personal experiences, which were published in women's magazines. Her first short story, "And Never Been Kissed," appeared in *Woman's Day*. The story attracted the attention of Elizabeth Riley, secretary of the board of Thomas Y. Crowell Publishing Company and director of the juvenile department. Miss Riley encouraged Peggy to attempt her first novel. The successful *Trish* was published in 1950. *Julie* followed in 1951. Other novels published were *Marsha, Three Who Met, Now That I'm Sixteen* and *It Could Happen to Anyone,* all from Peggy's attic writing room.

Several of these novels were selected as Teen Age Books-of-the-Month when they were reprinted in paperback. They have been translated into Swedish, German and Japanese.

Peggy Craig also continued her home economics career. She taught at the South Side Junior High School in Oil City. So successful was she that in 1962 *Seventeen* magazine selected her as one of the ten homemaking teachers of the year. In citing her, *Seventeen* stated, "Mrs. Craig has developed an approach to teaching based on her belief that homemaking is a creative profession that 'can be and ought to be fun.' Her ideas include recognizing outstanding work via a Hall of Fame display; developing special study sheets to present textbook information selectively; grading each girl according to her own ability rather than comparatively with others; encouraging the application of individual ideas to basic learnings; organizing special clubs, contests, trips, scrapbook collections to give girls the pleasure of accomplishment."

Peggy's dual success was apparent in her activities. She was a member of the Tri-County Economics Group of Venango, Mercer and Butler Counties; American Pen Women; and Delta Kappa Gamma, National Honorary Society of Educators.

In 1963 cancer struck Margaret Craig and she died in Allegheny Hospital, Pittsburgh, Pennsylvania, December 5, 1964. She left behind a legacy of books whose moral themes were presented "in a realistic manner without any hint of a 'sugar-coated sermon'."

Oil City-Franklin Branch
Researcher/Writer: Lois E. Follstaedt

135

Martha
McKeen Welch

b. 1914 _____

Martha McKeen Welch has spent various periods of her life as a teacher, artist, inventor, photographer and writer. She also received the Meritorious Service Award in 1945 from the United States Air Force for her service with the American Red Cross during World War II.

Born in Easton, Pennsylvania, Martha attended school in France and the American School of Design in New York. She developed an early interest in animals and nature which she has held throughout her life.

Martha began working as an art teacher in her own studio and at Moravian Academy in Bethlehem. Her creativity was evident in the line of greeting cards she designed and the patent she received for the unique packaging of these cards. Her invention was a transparent-backed envelope which showed her designs called "Peeks and Scoops."

During World War II Martha served as Director of the Hamilton, Bermuda United Service Organizations (USO), our country's first overseas club to entertain servicemen. Later she became a director with the American Red Cross, working in England, France, Germany and Luxembourg.

During this time in her life, her interest in another art form developed: photography. Martha attended New York's School of Modern Photography and began another career as a photographer of animals and children. Eventually this interest led her into writing children's books and illustrating all of them, except the first, *Saucy*, with her own photographs. Two of her books, *Sunflowers!* and *Close Looks in a Spring Woods*, have been selected by the Children's Book Council of the National Science Teachers Association as outstanding science books for the years 1980 and 1982, respectively. These and her other books, *Pudding and Pie, Just Like Puppies, Nibbit*, and *Will That Wake Mother?*, all clearly show her continuing interest and understanding of nature, animals and children.

Easton Branch
Researcher: Margaret D. Druse
Writer: JoAnn Harak

136

Ruth
Nulton Moore

b. 1923 ——————————————————————————

A deep interest in her country's past is one of the many elements in the writings of children's author, Ruth Nulton Moore. In her books she combines history with an exciting story involving children as the main characters. Her works for children include historical fiction, mysteries and a book about social problems.

Ruth Nulton Moore was born in Easton, Pennsylvania, the daughter of Jacob Wesley and Stella Houck Nulton. She received her Bachelor of Arts degree in 1944 from Bucknell University, where she specialized in English literature. In 1945 she received a master's degree from Columbia University and did postgraduate work in education at the University of Pittsburgh. In 1946 she married Carl L. Moore, a professor of accounting and a writer. She taught English and social studies at Wilson Borough High School and in the secondary schools of Detroit, Michigan.

As a child, Ruth Nulton Moore developed an interest in writing. She began to write poetry in the fifth grade and continued writing poems throughout junior and senior high school. When she was fifteen, one of her poems was published in *The Messenger*, a church magazine. During her teaching years, she "discontinued writing," but she began again in the 1960s. A postgraduate course in Children's Literature made her aware of a "vacuum" in this field and inspired her to direct her works toward children.

The poetry and short stories of Ruth Nulton Moore have appeared in *Children's Activities* magazine and *Jack and Jill*. Her first book, *Frisky, The Playful Pony,* was published in 1966. In the following twelve years, she wrote nine other juvenile novels. Many of her books have been translated into foreign languages.

Each of her books takes approximately one year to complete. She enjoys her extensive research, calling it "fun and fascinating," and often travels to the places where her stories are set. The Lehigh Valley area, in eastern Pennsylvania, has served as a setting for some of her books. *Hiding the Bell,* is based on the history of the Liberty Bell's removal from Philadelphia to Allentown during the American Revolution. *Ghost Bird Mountain* is also based on a local site, the Hawk Mountain Sanctuary in Kempton.

Ruth Nulton Moore maintains a daily regimen of writing. She also lectures to students from local schools and colleges on the art of writing and the publishing process. Her hobbies center around historical activities, canoeing and helping with the family farm in the Endless Mountains of Pennsylvania. She believes it is "important for youngsters to read about the past . . . to have a tie-in with the past in order to live the present more fully." This belief is reflected in her writings.

Easton Branch
Researcher: Margaret D. Druse
Writer: Suzanne Gallagher

137

Photograph by Bachrach, Scranton, PA

Jean Collins Kerr

b. 1924 _____

A tall, pretty girl with long 1940s-style hair and memorable blue eyes, Jean Collins, was chosen to be Queen of the May at Marywood College because she was the only girl student tall enough to crown an enormous statue of the Virgin. At Marywood she dabbled in dramatics and played the Mother Superior in *The Kingdom of God.*

A native Scrantonian, daughter of Thomas J. and Kitty O'Neill Collins, Jean, was the oldest of four children. Kitty Collins was the second cousin of playwright Eugene O'Neill; she is better known to readers as "My Wild Irish Mother." Even as a youngster, Jean was articulate. Her father once burst out at her: "The only damn thing in this world you're good at is talking," and to that moment of encouragement she pollyannaishly traces her bent for writing dialogue.

Jean met Walter F. Kerr while she was working as stage manager for *Romeo and Juliet* at Marywood. She graduated from Marywood College in May 1943, and in August she married Professor Kerr, who later became a drama critic with the *New York Herald-Tribune.*

Jean Kerr is considered by many to be the closest thing to a humorist since Robert Benchley. "By humorist, I mean she writes of common things—of husbands and houses and children, with great humanity and tremendous perception," writes John Crosby. In *Please Don't Eat the Daisies*, she utilizes common family situations with children to display her sharp and hilarious wit.

Jean has been known to do some of her writing in her car. She writes "to make people laugh and to make money." She was reportedly paid $75,000 by Metro-Goldwyn-Mayer for the rights to *Please Don't East the Daisies*, and Warner Brothers paid $500,000 for screen rights for the *Poor Richard* comedy. In addition, she was paid ten per cent of the film's gross after production costs were recovered.

Jean and Walter Kerr were among the twenty-four most influential couples, who were selected for their individual impact upon the civilization of the 1970s, according to a *Ladies' Home Journal* article. Jean is the mother of five sons, including twins, and a daughter, Kitty, who is also a Marywood College graduate.

It is amusing to note that the Kerr home, Larchmont Manor, is known throughout Larchmont for its unusual musical chimes. The bells were cast in France. Electrically controlled, they play several arias from "Carmen," and can also be manually operated. At noon, after the hour is struck, the duet from "Carmen" is played, and at 8:00 p.m., the "Westminster Chimes."

The works of Jean Kerr include: *The Song of Bernadette* by F. Werfel (dramatization by Kerr, 1944); *Our Hearts Were Young and Gay* by C. O. Skinner and E. Kimbrough (dramatization by Kerr, 1946); *Touch and Go* (with W. Kerr and J. Gorney, 1949); *King of Hearts* (with E. Brooke, 1954; film version, "That Certain Feeling," 1956); *Please Don't Eat the Daisies* (1957; film version, 1960; television series, 1965–67); *Goldilocks* (with W. Kerr and L. Anderson, 1958); *The Snake Has All the Lines* (1960); *Mary, Mary* (1961; film version, 1963); *Poor Richard* (1964); *Penny Candy* (1970); *Finishing Touches* (1973) and *How I Got to Be Perfect* (1978).

Scranton Branch
Researchers/Writers: Ethel DeVirgilis,
Judith Evans,
Ann Costello,
Georgianna
Cherinchak Cole and
Brenda Williams

14
WOMEN AS ARTISTS

138

Blanche Nevin

1841–1925

Anyone who tours the Hall of Fame, located in the Capitol in Washington, D.C., remembers the statues. They stand, larger than life, part of our heritage and national pride, representing the states of the Union. General Peter Muhlenberg is one of the two Pennsylvanians whose statues stand in the Capitol's Hall of Fame. Blanche Nevin, a Lancaster artist, was selected to do the sculpture. She is recognized as one of the first women sculptors in America. Other pieces of Blanche Nevin's art still admired in Lancaster are a lion in Reservoir Park, sculpted in 1905, and the *Horse Fountain* at West Orange Street and Columbia Avenue.

Blanche Nevin was born in Mercersburg, Franklin County, Pennsylvania, on September 25, 1841. Her father, a theologian known here and abroad, became president of Franklin and Marshall College in 1855. As a child Blanche was educated by tutors and later studied art in Philadelphia, Rome, Venice and Florence. Such formal education was unusual in an age when most women were taught the basics. Her father's interest in education and his academic position probably played an important role in the extensive education she received.

Blanche Nevin also painted and wrote short verse; however, she is mainly known for sculpting busts and full statues. Marble statues of *Maud Muller* (1875), *Eve* and *Cinderella* (1876), and the previously mentioned *General Muhlenberg* statue demonstrate her artistic ability. The statues of Blanche Nevin serve not only as a lasting testament to those who inspired them but also to the artist who created them.

Lancaster Branch
Researcher: Frances Keller
Writer: Gail White

139

Mary Cassatt

1845–1926 _____

Impressionist paintings of a mother and child, of young women in pastel dresses and perky hats at the opera or at the seashore are characteristic of the work of artist Mary Cassatt. Although she was an expatriate who lived abroad most of her life, her roots were in America, particularly in Pennsylvania where she was born and where she received her early art training. And, although Mary Cassatt followed the French Impressionist school of painting, she lent her own American flavor to it.

Born in Allegheny City, which is now a part of Pittsburgh, in 1845, Mary spent several years of her childhood in Paris. There she was introduced to the great works of art in museums all over Europe. When her family returned to the United States, they settled in Philadelphia, where Mary studied at the Pennsylvania Academy of the Fine Arts from 1861 to 1865. She then traveled in Europe for several years, studying the works of such masters as Correggio in Italy and Rubens in Antwerp, before taking up permanent residence in Paris.

Mary became acquainted with Whistler, Degas, Manet, Monet, and Courbet and was greatly influenced by the Impressionist school of painting. Although clearly Impressionistic, her own works were more precise than the Europeans' works. This can be attributed to her American background and training which emphasized illustration to a greater degree. Where the European Impressionists used quick brush strokes to suggest, Mary Cassatt's paintings were always carefully drawn. Her Impressionistic bent is evident, however, in the bright colors, thick paint, foreshortened figures and lack of perspective which characterize her paintings.

Her best Impressionistic works were produced in the years 1879 and 1880. They include *The Cup of Tea* (Metropolitan Museum of Art, New York), *La Loge* (William Coxe Wright Collection, St. David's, Pennsylvania), and *Woman and Child Driving* (Philadelphia Museum of Art, Philadelphia). These paintings convey an individualistic style, sensitive and gentle, with more emphasis on pleasing color than on form.

Her later paintings exhibit broad, fluid brush strokes and a more stylistic approach, as seen in the portrait of her mother, *Reading "Le Figaro"* (Mrs. Eric de Spoelberch Collection, Haverford, Pennsylvania),

The Lady at the Tea Table (Metropolitan Museum of Art) and *Girl Arranging Her Hair* (National Gallery of Art, Washington, D.C.).

Mary Cassatt exhibited with the artists of the Impressionist school from 1879 to 1886, having her first independent showing in 1893. She worked in oils and pastels and is also known for her etchings and prints. One of her most important contributions, however, was that she encouraged wealthy Americans to purchase Impressionist art which has resulted in an excellent collection of works of that period being in this country.

After 1900 failing eyesight caused by cataracts forced Mary Cassatt to adopt a coarse and relatively formless style, and after 1914 she was unable to paint at all. Her blindness and a sadness about World War I darkened her remaining years both spiritually and physically. She died at her country home near Paris on June 14, 1926.

Pittsburgh and Valley Forge Branches
Researcher/Writer: Marie Iwanczyk
Researcher/Writer: Anne Odenweller
Special Division Editor: Mary Ann Stangil

140

Jennie Brownscombe

1850–1936 _____

Jennie Brownscombe, an artist of national and international fame, was born in Honesdale, Pennsylvania, on December 10, 1850, to William Brownscombe, a native of Devonshire, England, and Elvira Kennedy from Mount Pleasant, Pennsylvania. Her maternal ancestors came to this country in 1630, settling in Massachusetts. During the Revolutionary War her great-grandfather served as a soldier, and in 1794 her grandfather, David Kennedy, settled in northeastern Pennsylvania.

An only child, Jennie Brownscombe had a love for art and literature and was apparently gifted in both. When the time came for her to choose her life's work, it was a difficult choice. Her father died while she was attending school, and in order to continue her education, she taught for two terms. Encouraged by her mother, who was a gifted author, she selected art as a career and spent her first year at the Cooper Union in New York City where she received a medal for her work. The next six years she spent at the National Academy of Design and then went to France and Italy to continue her studies. Her first oil painting was exhibited in 1876 and was sold at the Academy.

She established a studio on Fifth Avenue in New York City and a summer studio in Pleasantville, New York. Never without commissions, she painted figure subjects in oil and watercolor representing the late eighteenth and early nineteenth centuries as well as medieval and ancient Greek times. Her portraits, including a self-portrait, are noteworthy. However, her distinguished representations of historical incidents and characters brought her most esteem.

Included among her works are: The *First American Thanksgiving* (Pilgrim Hall, Plymouth, Massachusetts) which depicts the solemn feast held in December 1621; *Mrs. Murray Receiving the British Officers* which shows a lady entertaining British officers so that the American detachment they were harassing could escape; and *Carry On*, a World War I scene which was used in Liberty Loan Drives.

Many of her works show scenes from her background. In *On Main Street*, for example, some of the stores and people are recognizable as being from Honesdale.

Jennie Brownscombe returned to her Honesdale home as often as possible up to the time of her death. She died at the age of eighty-six on August 5, 1936, at her cousin's home in Bayside, Long Island, New York, and she is buried near Honesdale. Her work preserves some of the flavor of incidents in American history.

Hawley-Honesdale Area Branch
Researchers: Mary Todd and Anne Baschon
Writer: Marie Casper

141

Ann Dorris Chisolm

1863–1918

   Ann Dorris was born December 5, 1863, to a prominent Huntingdon family. After her graduation with high honors from Birmingham Seminary, she studied art in Dresden, Germany. Although she sketched and painted very well, her special field of interest was stained glass. She became renowned and was widely recognized as the pioneer woman in that field of art. For a large, stained glass window exhibited in the Women's Building at the Chicago World's Fair in 1893, she received both premiums and medals. John La Farge, of New York, the most gifted man in the profession at that time, sought the talent of the Huntingdon girl for his studios, but she decided to work at home with her father who was also a stained glass artist. Some of the works of father and daughter are found in church windows in the Huntingdon area.
   At the age of forty-nine, Ann married a local lawyer, William Wallace Chisolm. He apparently encouraged her early interest in politics. She became a suffragist and was active in the National Woman's Party. It is known that she participated in a demonstration in Washington, D.C., for which she was jailed. William went to Washington to bail her out, but she insisted on staying with the others in jail.

Ann Dorris Chisolm was greatly devoted to helping with local efforts during World War I. This involvement lead to her death. It is believed that she died either from exhaustion or influenza which struck the area at that time. Her husband's will recounts her sacrifice: "Her life was one of sacrifice, of love and service. Had she been content to have paused, even for the day in her labor of love for the soldier boys she would not have died. Her life was given to her country—the country which has not yet become enough enlightened to permit women to aid in its government—as certainly as though she had fallen on the field of battle."

As part of her legacy to the Huntingdon community and to show her love for children, her husband established the "Ann Dorris Chisolm Christmas Fund" which each year provides a Christmas party and gifts for the underprivileged youngsters of the area.

Huntingdon Branch
Researchers: Ruth V. Stewart and
Jean P. Harshbarger
Writer: Nancy R. Taylor

142

Ida Jones

1874–1959

The paintings of Ida Jones earned her a reputation as Chester County's Grandma Moses. Some of her works can still be seen in the Chester County area. Her subjects were drawn principally from nature, and she especially enjoyed painting various types of trees. She said that everything she saw gave her ideas for compositions, and she used photographs, post cards and even little cards enclosed in baking powder packages as the basis for some of her works. Of particular interest is a painting of her small home and the shed formerly used for smuggling slaves on the Underground Railroad.

Ida Jones was born in Chatham, Chester County, the daughter of a slave who had been freed after the Civil War. Her education ended at the fourth grade. She worked for a Quaker woman, Lucretia Haines, who noticed the girl's intense interest in sketching and gave Ida a brief lesson in oil painting. Despite long hours of work, Ida's love of painting inspired her to paint late at night after she had "fetched" the jugs of hot water for the family members' baths.

She married a blacksmith, William Jones, and raised at least ten children. Her family responsibilities left her no time for her art work. She was an active member of the Church of Christ until her death and conducted and sang in the church choir.

At the age of 72, Ida Jones found herself dependent upon a daughter for a home and subsistence. Her situation made her moody and depressed, and she turned once again to art as a means of gaining independence. She resumed painting, and her work began to attract attention. Dr. Horace Bond, president of Lincoln University in Chester County, and Mrs. Walter Townsend of Cheney, Pennsylvania, sponsored art shows which furthered the interest in Ida's work.

Initially, her pictures were primitive and flat, with straight lines and no perspective. Yet they possessed a freshness and an innocence that people found charming and imaginative. She later produced more balanced compositions with bright colors and sure brush work. Her medium was oil until her small grandson showed her how to mix watercolors.

Ida Jones's paintings were exhibited at the Art Alliance in Philadelphia, where they came to the attention of a New York art dealer,

Allan Wolf. He purchased fifteen of her works and was so impressed with her talent that he visited her in Ercildoun, Pennsylvania. He later showed her work to Fleur Cowles, co-publisher of *Look* magazine, who purchased one of the snow scenes.

Ida Jones was proud of her work and the independence that their sale provided her. She once said, "I've never had an old age pension yet." Despite her lack of formal training and opportunities, she strove to develop her talents as an artist and achieved remarkable success.

West Chester Branch
Researchers/Writers: Claire C. Etherton
and Mary S. Pinkney

143

Ruth Eleanor Newton

1884–1972 _____

Ruth Newton was an internationally known illustrator of children's books and designer of dolls. From 1925 to 1945 she illustrated forty books for the Whitman Publishing Company. In 1949 she created the "Amosandra" doll for the Columbia Broadcasting Company in conjunction with the popular Amos and Andy show.

Ruth Newton was born on March 6, 1884, in Erie, Pennsylvania. She began taking art courses in high school and on Saturdays at the Catlin School of Art. In 1902 her instructor, Louisa Card-Catlin, helped her obtain a scholarship to the Pennsylvania Academy of the Fine Arts in Philadelphia. While studying there, she entered her drawings in a contest for the best illustrations for the book *The Old Schloss*. The book's author, Margaret L. Corlies, selected Ruth Newton's drawings to be published.

After completing art school, she went to Boston to continue her work as a free-lance artist. Among her clients were the Rust-Craft Corporation and Ivory Soap (Proctor & Gamble). She later moved to New York City and spent the next thirty-eight years in Greenwich Village, working as an illustrator and designer.

An avid traveler, she made many trips in the United States, Mexico and Europe, often using the people and sites she saw as the basis of her illustrations. Her success as an illustrator was recognized both here and abroad, where her books were translated into five languages. Among the books she illustrated were *Mother Goose, Peter Rabbit, The Night Before Christmas* and *Kittens and Puppies*.

In 1949 her interest turned to designing dolls, perhaps the most famous of which was the popular Black baby doll, "Amosandra." This doll was designed for the Sun Rubber Company of Barberton, Ohio, and was the idea of the company's general manager, Tom Smith. He presented to Freeman F. Gosden and Charles J. Correll, of the famous radio team of Amos and Andy, the proposal to create a Black rubber doll for the toy market. From the many artists who submitted sketches for the doll, Ruth Newton's drawings, made from studies of photographs of Harlem children, were chosen. The "Amosandra" doll was an instant success and was followed by more than twenty-five other creative dolls.

Ruth Newton often returned to Erie, residing at an apartment on West Sixth Street. On her Erie visits, her pastime of outdoor landscape painting took her to one of her favorite places, Harborcreek, where her father's family had lived on a farm. She retired in 1968 to live permanently in Erie. A fall resulted in her move to the Rondal Nursing Home, where she resided until her death on May 27, 1972.

Erie Branch
Researchers: Dorothy Corboy
and Becky Knapp
Writer: Peggy Krider

144

Rachel McClelland Sutton

1887–1982

A native Pittsburgh artist, Rachel McClelland Sutton painted many scenes of western Pennsylvania during her long career. She captured in her genre paintings the still fresh essence of a familiar Pittsburgh– views of houses clinging to hillsides, clusters of rooftops with mill chimneys in the background, the verdant foliage of early summer, the clouds blowing in over the western hilltops. Her paintings serve as a reminder of the charm and beauty, the all-American homeyness of Pittsburgh in the 1920s, '30s and '40s, of the qualities which existed alongside the heavy industrial, smoky recitations of the Renaissance legend.

Rachel Pears McClelland was born in 1887 in Pittsburgh's Shadyside area, the daughter of Dr. James H. McClelland, a founder of the Homeopathic Hospital (now Shadyside Hospital) and Rachel May Pears of the Bakewell-Pears glass family. She and her older sister, Sarah, were raised at Sunnyledge, a house built by their parents in 1888 in accord with a design by Henry Hobson Richardson and completed after his death by Frank E. Alden and associates. With the exception of a period of time during her marriage, she lived most of her life in the family home. As an artist, she made use of the house when she set up her subjects; she painted views from windows—across the street to the little dress shop, down through the tree limbs to snowy rooftops and lawns—and she used the windows as a background for still life arrangements and a source of daylight. Sunnyledge was also home, replete with all the details of daily domestic life which likewise became subjects of her paintings. Her earliest childhood efforts were directed to the apples and nuts, onions and turnips of her mother's kitchen. As a mature painter, she experimented with the vases of flowers from her own garden, the lemonade tray on the porch, a Christmas morning view of the parlor.

Her experiences, however, were not limited to her home and Pittsburgh. As a two-year-old child she made the first of her sixteen trips abroad. As an adult she traveled extensively in the United States and Canada. Although she did not paint while traveling, she did store away memories and impressions which later found expression as she explored the media of egg tempera and watercolor.

Education was highly valued by Dr. and Mrs. McClelland; they employed a German governess for their daughters until, at the age of eight, Rachel was enrolled in Miss Ward's School. It was at this time that Rachel began her art lessons with Miss Stoney. She continued her education in the preparatory division of the Pennsylvania College for Women (now Chatham College) and the Masters School at Dobbs Ferry, and graduated from Carnegie Institute of Technology with a degree in fine arts in 1916.

As a young woman she became seriously committed to the development of her skills as an artist. She attended the Art Students Leagues in Pittsburgh and New York and was an active member of the Cordova Club and several other working groups of artists. She joined the Associated Artists of Pittsburgh in 1919, frequently exhibited with them, and was awarded several prizes throughout the sixty-one years of her membership. In 1945 when her interest shifted to watercolor development, she joined the Watercolor Society, of which she was made an honorary member in 1974. She had exhibitions at Carnegie Institute Museum of Art, Pittsburgh History and Landmark Foundation, Carnegie-Mellon University, Chatham College, Harmarville Rehabilitation Center (of which she was one of the founders), Bird-in-Hand Gallery, East-West Gallery, Winchester-Thurston School and the Westmoreland County Club.

Rachel McClelland Sutton's sensitive paintings of western Pennsylvania, and especially twentieth century Pittsburgh, earn for her a lasting place among Pennsylvania women artists.

Mt. Lebanon-South Hills Branch
Researcher/Writer: Martha L. Hunter

145

Wealtha Vann Ausdall

1900–1969 ───────────────────────────────────────

Wealtha Vann Ausdall was absorbed in her craft from childhood on. Following graduation from Oil City High School, she enrolled in the Philadelphia School of Design for Women. Completing her courses there, she accepted the recommendation of a prominent local physician, Dr. Ada McKee, that she study dissection at the Woman's Medical College of Pennsylvania. She furthered her art education at various schools and studios such as the Balano Studio in Philadelphia, Temple University and the Wagner Institute of Science; among her many outstanding teachers were George Harding, Howard Pyle, N. C. Wyeth and P. H. Balano. She studied stained glass technique and sculpting, the latter under Samuel Murray.

Her works were widely displayed in various cities: lithographs at the Art Institute of Chicago, Pasadena, and Seattle; six paintings in a four-artist show in New York; others at the New York World's Fair. An article about her appeared in *Art News* and in *The New York Times*. She is believed to have been the first woman lithographer in the United States. In her search for a technique that would best express her artistic images, she discovered that the paint suited her best when applied with the stubs of burnt matches of the type found in match folders.

Several of her works are in the permanent collection at the Philadelphia Graphic. Two of her works are on display at the Drake Museum in Titusville and two in the Franklin Library. Christ Episcopal Church in Oil City, of which she was a member, prizes *The Patriarch*, a charcoal sketch of an ancient, gnarled tree, and numerous friends and admiring pupils in the area own her works.

She was sought after as a teacher of both children and adults because she strove to bring out what was in the pupil. "You must make youth use their imagination," she believed, "inspire them, help them to become creative." She frequently arranged art shows in Oil City featuring works from such institutions as the Philadelphia Society of Etchings, as well as her pupils' efforts and her own.

Though she attained success, and her pictures were sold nation-wide, she suffered the all-too-frequent fate of an artist. She lived her later life in abject circumstances, too proud to accept adequate help from her admirers and too poor to live in any degree of comfort. But to the end she retained her principles and the love of her students.

Oil City-Franklin Branch
Researcher/Writer: Margaret D. Reid

146

Maya Matsuura Schock

1928–1975

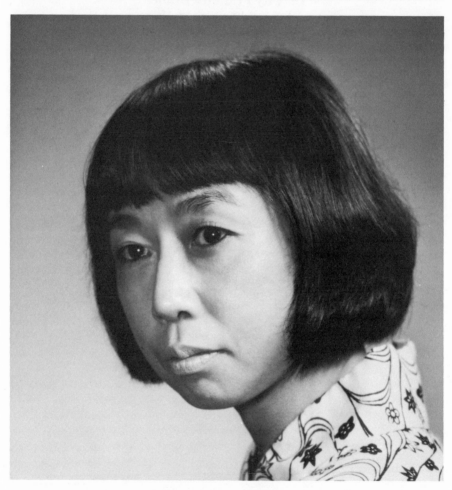

Maya Matsuura Schock, actress and painter, was born in Osaka, Japan, August 7, 1928, to a publisher father and a mother who was a poet. Beginning at the age of ten, she studied Kabuki and Noh drama. In 1949 she received a Bachelor of Arts degree from Baika Women's College in Osaka where she majored in English literature and appeared in many student theater productions, including Shakespearean plays.

Both her parents had died by the time Maya reached twenty-one, and she moved to Tokyo to become a classical ballet dancer, actress, and part-time interpreter in English and Japanese at the United States Army Ordnance Depot where she met Floyd Schock. After Floyd was discharged from the Army, he returned to Tokyo as a civilian where he and Maya were married in 1956.

Maya and Floyd came to live in the Schock home, a little north of Dauphin at Speeceville, Pennsylvania. After attending Thompson Institute in Harrisburg, where she studied typing and shorthand, Maya became a secretary in the city. She joined the Harrisburg Community Theater working with her husband behind the scenes as a set and costume designer. In the summer of 1957 Maya had the opportunity to act, playing the lead in the Allenberry Playhouse production of the *Teahouse of the August Moon.*

In February 1963 Maya enrolled in the York Academy of Art. In her own words, she was the oldest freshman in the history of the school. At her graduation in June 1965, she received the first among her many recognitions, the A. I. Watts Award, named for the founder and first director of the York Academy of Art. As the years progressed, Maya's work was becoming popular in the local art circles, and in 1968 she won a place in the finals of the Benedictine Art Awards, a national competition.

In September 1968 after three years of teaching, she left the York Academy to enroll in the Pennsylvania Academy of the Fine Arts in Philadelphia to study advanced painting. She thus launched the most productive period of her life. After her exhibit in September 1970 at the Camp Hill Gallery (which later became the William Ris Gallery), Maya's following in Harrisburg grew.

Maya returned to teaching until 1971 when she gave full attention to the affairs of Gallery Doshi. Doshi, meaning in Japanese, "comradeship or brotherhood, people who are united by the same ideal," was the name Maya and Floyd gave to their dream. With great courage they purchased a building at Second and Reilly Streets to house a new gallery and school where Maya could expose the public to the art of the present: fine quality regardless of style, traditional art as well as avant-garde. Opening on May 21, 1972, Gallery Doshi became the center for contemporary art in Harrisburg.

Maya's painting talents continued to develop. Her series *Journey Within* attracted attention in exhibits in national and regional shows in New York, New Jersey, Delaware, Maryland, Virginia and Pennsylvania. Besides being in numerous private collections, her work may be found at the William Penn Memorial Museum, Harrisburg; Lebanon Valley College, Annville; Harrisburg Public Library; and the Philadelphia Museum of Art. In addition to Doshi and the Philadelphia Chapter of Artists Equity, Maya worked on the boards of directors of the

Fellowship of the Pennsylvania Academy of the Fine Arts and the Art Alliance of Philadelphia.

She painted intermittently in 1974, although her work was definitely improving. The *Yin Yang* series and the new *Journey Within* paintings were smaller in size than predecessors but more accomplished.

Her appearances at Doshi board meetings grew infrequent. In the spring of 1975 Maya announced her intentions of resigning from active and strenuous participation in the administration of Doshi, remaining only as a teacher.

In 1975 she began a new direction of small works, mostly pastel and acrylic on paper. She called them *Ode to Summer,* and completed the last just before her death. They are undoubtedly the most beautiful, colorful, lyric and poetic works she produced, blending artistic techniques with rich textures and style. After an agonizing search through the *Journey Within* series, Maya found herself in these last works, combining mature self-assurance with control and purpose.

On September 17, 1975 Maya Schock, just forty-seven years old, died. Her achievements were those of an artist twice her age.

Harrisburg Branch
Researcher/Writer: Marilee K. Pellegrini

15
WOMEN AS PERFORMERS: BALLET, MUSIC, THEATER AND ATHLETICS

147

Belle Archer
(Arabella Mingle)
(Belle Mackenzie)

1858–1900

> By her brilliant accomplishments and rare graces of mind
> and person she gave distinction in the histrionic arts to the
> name of Belle Archer.

These words are part of the inscription found on the tombstone of
Belle Archer, a most versatile actress of the 1800s.

Born Arabella Mingle in Easton, Pennsylvania, on September 5,
1858, Belle Archer was the daughter of James L. Mingle, a superintendent for the telegraph company in Easton, and his wife, Mary Elizabeth
Tomer Mingle. Belle was one of seven very talented daughters. The
Mingles lived in Easton in a brick home on Spring Garden Street until
the 1870s when the family moved to Philadelphia.

When Belle was sixteen, she left Easton hoping to become an actress.
She first appeared at the National Theatre in Washington, D.C., in *The
Mighty Dollar*. She had only one line in this play, but this part was
followed by her appearance in *H.M.S. Pinafore* as cousin Heve.

Another step in her acting career was playing the role of Meenie
in *Rip Van Winkle*. She appeared with veteran comedian Joseph

Jefferson. Jefferson, interested in aiding young players, took her under his tutelage.

Early in her career, Arabella Mingle changed her name to Belle Mackenzie. In the late 1870s she joined a stock company formed by John T. Ford which toured Washington, Baltimore, Richmond and many other Southern cities. During this time she appeared in several different roles. Some of these included "ingenue" parts in plays by Bartley Campbell. Other characters portrayed were Lucius in *Julius Caesar*, Mrs. St. Clair and Topsy in *Uncle Tom's Cabin*, Maggie Mitchell in *Fanchon and the Cricket* and an Indian girl in *Pocahontas*, a famous burlesque show.

In 1880 she married Captain Herbert Marshall, an actor from London. She then became Belle Archer. The marriage, however, ended in divorce in 1889.

In 1882 Belle starred in her first major role in the play, *Hazel Kirke*, which was staged at the Madison Square Theatre in New York City. After this she had several other leading parts. One of her most popular was that of a waif, Tom Chickweed, in *Alone in London*.

Her versatility as an actress was evident in the variety of roles she played. She starred in melodramas, comedies and farces.

The Mingle family knew many persons prominent in the arts at that time, including Walt Whitman and Joaquin Miller, "the poet of the Sierras." Belle was personally acquainted with many of her contemporaries, some of whom were Mary Anderson, Lilly Langtry, Lillian Russell, Edwin Booth and Lawrence Barrett.

It was said that Belle Archer was one of the most photographed stage personalities of the 1890s. In 1899 she commissioned a playwright from Syracuse to write a play for her. It was while she was on tour with this play, which was called *Jess at the Bar Z*, that she fell on a railway platform and died on September 19, 1900, in Warren, Pennsylvania.

Easton Branch
Researcher: Margaret D. Druse
Writer: Suzanne Gallagher

148

Madeline Stokes (Amanda Bertha Straw Snyder)

1875–1972 ─────────────────────────────────────

The face and figure, if not the name, of Madeline Stokes were known to millions of Americans at the turn of the century. As a favorite model for the most celebrated artists, sculptors and illustrators of her day, she was depicted on magazine covers, calendars, commercial advertisements and in statuary.

Madeline Stokes was born Amanda Bertha Straw (a name anglicized from the German "Stroh") in Fishing Creek Valley, south of Harrisburg, on June 2, 1875. She later chose her professional name because the initials were the same as "Mandy" Straw.

She attended local one-room schools until the age of eighteen when she went to the Pierce Business College in Philadelphia. Before graduating, she left to appear on the vaudeville stage in "living pictures" which were tableaux or still scenes set on a revolving stage.

It was there that she was discovered by illustrators George Gibbs and Lazir Raditz. With Madeline as a model, Raditz's illustrations eventually won him three art scholarships. She quickly became the favorite model of George Gibbs and appeared on menus, resort brochures, calendars and in numerous advertisements for Oldsmobiles, corsets, toiletries, Rogers Brothers' silverware, wireless electric batteries, Cream of Wheat, mattresses, bicycles, wedding gowns and dress patterns. She also appeared in magazine story and exercise illustrations. She was the cover girl for the *Ladies' Home Journal,* the *Ideal American Beauties Series,* the *Saturday Evening Post,* the *Delineator* and the *Metropolitan* magazine. For top illustrator J. L. G. Ferris, she was the model for Nellie Custis in "George Washington's Last Springtime at Mount Vernon" (*Ladies' Home Journal,* May 1918) and for an Indian maiden in "Henry Hudson" (*Ladies' Home Journal,* August 1917). N. C. Wyeth, Robert Henri and John Sloan painted her portrait. Violet Oakley used her as a model for her murals in the Governor's Reception Room, the Senate Chamber and the Supreme Court Room in Harrisburg. J. F. Copeland painted her into his mural for Trenton High School in October 1909.

Between 1907 and 1914 she worked at such leading art schools as the Industrial Art School of Pennsylvania in Philadelphia, the Cleveland Art School, the Art Institute of Chicago, Syracuse University College of Fine Arts, Normal School Museum and Art Gallery in Toronto and for anatomy classes at the University of Buffalo. One of the most famous artists' models of the day, she was five feet, four inches tall with a perfect figure, and she remained a topflight model until she reached the age of thirty-eight.

She was the model for several well-known sculptures as well. In 1904 Alexander Stirling Calder used her as the symbol for the State of Missouri and also for the *Sun Dial* in Fairmount Park in Philadelphia. She told of being cast in plaster for nine hours at a time, fainting, then resuming her position—all for ten dollars. In 1909 she was the model for Giuseppe Donato's figure of *Philadelphia.* Charles Grafly used her for the *Pioneer Mother Monument* for the Panama-Pacific Exposition in San Francisco in 1915.

The most controversial statue for which she posed, the *Dance of Eternal Spring* depicting three nude dancing bacchantes, *Spring,*

Summer, and *Autumn,* was also sculpted by Donato in 1909. It was commissioned by Milton S. Hershey, who, on a verbal agreement, paid $2,000 toward a $3,100 down-payment. When Hershey refused to pay the final bill of $30,000, Donato sued him in Dauphin County Court where the jury awarded Donato $23,931.25. In 1920 the sculpture was given to the city of Harrisburg and eventually erected in Reservoir Park, hidden by shrubbery. It was moved to the J. Horace McFarland Rose Garden in the Polyclinic Hospital grounds in 1938.

In the meantime, Madeline had given up modeling, at the age of thirty-eight, shortly after marrying artist Albert Snyder in 1914. They retired to a ten-acre farm near Clinton, outside of Utica, New York, which they named "Snyd-Brook Farm." After Albert's death in 1939, Madeline returned to the Fishing Creek Valley and, in 1955, became a resident of Homeland, a nursing-retirement home in Harrisburg.

In March of 1971 she asked Harrisburg City Council to move the fountain statue to Italian Lake Park. The Council agreed to do so, and, with Madeline present, it was erected in Italian Lake on July 16, 1971.

She died at Homeland on October 29, 1972, at the age of ninety-seven.

Harrisburg Branch
Researcher/Writer: Ann Corby
Special Division Editor: Margaret D. Druse

149
Evelyn Nesbit
(Florence Evelyn Nesbit Thaw Montani)
1884–1967

It was called "the crime of the century," the tragic aftermath of a love triangle involving Evelyn Nesbit, the beautiful chorus girl, of whom author Irvin S. Cobb wrote, "the most exquisitely lovely human being I ever looked at;" her disreputable, insanely jealous husband, Harry K. Thaw, a spoiled playboy worth over $40,000,000, and the unfortunate victim, Stanford White. At fifty-two White was not only the most famous architect in America and a founding member of the prestigious firm of McKim, Mead and White, but he was also the social arbiter for high society in New York City, and hence the country, at the beginning of the twentieth century.

Florence Evelyn Nesbit was born on December 25, 1884, in Tarentum, Pennsylvania. Her family lived there and in Pittsburgh until 1896 when, after her father's death, they moved to New York City where her mother was employed as a seamstress. Within two years the strikingly beautiful fourteen-year-old Evelyn was working regularly as a model for artists of the period, including one of the most famous, Charles Dana Gibson, who penned her perfect profile as "The Eternal Question."

Among her numerous admirers as a member of the cast of "Floradora" was Stanford White, a charming, energetic, gregarious man-about-town who was the architect of magnificent mansions for the super-rich, the Washington Arch, the Century and Manhattan Clubs and the original Madison Square Garden. At sixteen Evelyn Nesbit became his mistress. He delighted in pushing her, naked, in a red velvet swing suspended from the ceiling of his Manhattan apartment—far from his wife and family on Long Island.

Another admirer, one who it was said, "threw roses wrapped in fifty dollar bills at her feet," was Harry K. Thaw, an heir to the Pennsylvania Railroad fortune. After two pre-marital tours of Europe with Thaw, Evelyn, at the age of twenty, married him in 1905. Thaw, sadistic and emotionally unstable from childhood, became increasingly obsessed with Evelyn's previous liaison with Stanford White, repeatedly pressuring Evelyn for details of the affair. On June 25, 1906, in the roof theater restaurant of Madison Square Garden, Harry Thaw shot Stanford White.

Twice Thaw was brought to trial, creating international sensations, and in 1908 was found not guilty by reason of insanity, the judge declaring him to be a manic-depressive. He was in and out of mental hospitals until 1924. He died of a heart attack in 1947 at the age of seventy-six.

Evelyn gave birth to a son in 1910, whom Thaw denied was his, and he divorced her in 1913. Although she was recognized on both sides of the Atlantic as "the woman in the case," most of Evelyn's remaining years were downhill with an incompatible marriage to her dancing partner, Jack Clifford (whose real name was Vergil James Montani), money troubles and law suits, heroin addiction, arrests, tawdry affairs, burlesque and nightclub appearances and suicide attempts.

In 1955 Joan Collins starred in *The Girl in the Red Velvet Swing* purporting to be Evelyn's "true" life story, although through the years she had given differing versions of the "truth."

Evelyn became an amateur sculptor in Los Angeles in her later years. In the early 1960s she went into a convalescent home where she died of a stroke on January 18, 1967. Thirty people attended her funeral.

Fox Chapel Area Branch
Researcher/Writer: Patricia Demase
Special Division Editor: Margaret D. Druse

150

Ardelle Cleaves Ford

1890–1969 ─────────────────────────────────

Ardelle Cleaves was born in Franklin, Pennsylvania, on October 14, 1890, to Catherine Heffner Cleaves, a wig maker and hair dresser, and Stephen Cleaves, who had oil interests. Ardelle soon moved with her family to nearby Oil City where by age four she was learning to play the violin. At six she played in *Uncle Tom's Cabin* at the Oil City Opera House. By sixteen she conducted a dancing school, a year before she graduated as valedictorian from Oil City High School.

For professional training she enrolled in the Sargent School of New York, now the American Academy of Performing Arts. There her class-mates included such incipient stars as Edward G. Robinson, William Powell and Joseph Schildkraut. It was with Powell that she played her first professional performance. Early in her career she had an oppor-tunity to be an entertainer on a three-month cruise to South America aboard the *Victoria Louise*; on the cruise she met the Prince of Wales, then a shy teen-ager.

Sometimes called "the brunette Mary Pickford," she later traveled throughout the country acting with various members of the Barrymore family, with Sarah Bernhardt and with Douglas Fairbanks, Sr. She met Mary Pickford, whom she regarded as more beautiful than her pictures. By 1917 her name was in lights at the Palace Theater in New York.

It was Oscar Hammerstein who discovered her ability to sing and dance. She appeared in such shows as *Somebody's Sweetheart, Rose Marie, Song of Love* and *The Poor Little Rich Girl*, which was Richard Rodgers' first comedy. One, *The Cat and the Fiddle*, she described as a costly extravaganza, which featured a tree of feathers and one lace table-cloth costing $1,000. Arthur Treacher played in *The Cat and the Fiddle* with Ardelle.

Sigmund Romberg wrote the song "Since I Found You" for her. For a stint of sixty weeks, she played in vaudeville with Fred Allen as master of ceremonies. Producers discovered her ability as a violinist and encouraged such talents as Jerome Kern, Rudolph Friml and Oskar Straus to include "Ardelle Cleaves and Her Magic Violin" in their works.

In the midst of her busy career, she found time to study philosophy and to marry Harold L. Ford of St. Marys, Ontario. In 1935 she retired from the stage, but not from activity. During World War II she taught Christian philosophy and dramatics in Detroit and Cleveland.

In her later years Ardelle returned to live in Oil City where she participated in various civic endeavors. Often in fine weather she would sit on a bench in front of the library, willing to take an interest in any passerby who stopped to talk. Very few were aware of the distinguished career of this elegant but modest woman.

Oil City–Franklin Branch
Researcher/Writer: Margaret D. Reid

151

Alvina Krause

1893–1981 ─────────────────────────────────

"The core of Alvina Krause . . . is that she is an experience that changes your life." This statement in the program notes of the Pacific Conservatory of Performing Arts, 1970, summarizes the feelings of all who came into contact with this legend of the theatre. For more than a third of a century, Alvina Krause taught and trained students for careers in the theatre. Included in her roster of students are Charlton Heston, Richard Benjamin, Robert Reed, Patricia Neal, Inga Swenson, Walter Kerr, Paula Prentiss and many more. But to count only the famous overlooks the hundreds of students she affected in her classes at Northwestern University, where she taught acting for thirty-three years; at her own Eagles Mere Playhouse in the mountains of north central Pennsylvania, where she was director during the summers for twenty years; in Bloomsburg, Pennsylvania, where she served as artistic director of the Bloomsburg Theatre Ensemble and in acting workshops and lectures all over the country. All who came into contact with her were impressed at her vitality, her drive, her vision, her concern for others. Those who worked directly with her "were never quite the same" after the experience.

Alvina Krause was characterized as a worker, an optimist, someone who never gave up on a dream. This is evident in the fact that she began her teaching career at Northwestern University at age thirty-five. (Until then younger women were barred from teaching at most colleges.) In addition to a Bachelor of Science and Master of Science in speech from Northwestern University, she held an honorary doctorate from Doane University. As an associate professor of the theatre department, she designed the reputable and extensive four-year acting program still in use there. Along with her professional work at Northwestern, she was invited to serve as guest director for numerous other universities. In 1974 at the American College Theatre Festival, Alvina Krause was presented with an Award of Excellence.

Her summers were spent at Eagles Mere Playhouse fulfilling another dream—building her own repertory theatre. Alvina felt strongly that repertory theatre was the only hope for American theatre. In an interview with the *Los Angeles Times* in 1970, she stated, ". . . the hope lies in repertory, because it provides the only constant opportunity for playwrights, actors and directors." Eagles Mere Playhouse served as the training ground for many of Alvina's students who were to distinguish themselves in the professional world of theatre and film. Alvina Krause gave equal time and energy to all students—not only the ones who became commercial successes. Her work with actors was not concerned with producing virtuoso performers, but rather in having the actor perform as part of a group to create a theatrical experience for the audience. On her seventy-fifth birthday, she commented to former student Neal Weaver, "We're saddled with a star system that creates personalities, not actors. The play should be the star, together with the whole company, not an individual." To further these aims, she founded in Chicago, in 1966, the Eagles Mere Associates, a professional repertory theatre to complement her beloved playhouse in Eagles Mere, Pennsylvania.

In 1978 at age eighty-five, Alvina Krause "came out of retirement" when she agreed to serve as the artistic director for the Bloomsburg Theatre Ensemble (BTE), northeastern and central Pennsylvania's only resident professional theatre company. Under her direction, BTE grew into an established regional theatre company providing quality entertainment through the development and maintenance of a permanent acting ensemble and continual training of individual artists. In addition to providing over-all artistic guidance, Alvina Krause directed some memorable productions, chief among which were Chekhov's *The Seagull* (1979) and *Lady Audley's Secret* (1981).

One of Alvina Krause's greatest satisfactions was to see her students grow as actors, but others recognized her achievements. Among her awards were the Presidential Award presented by Northwestern University in 1979, the Hazlett Memorial Award for Excellence in the Art of Theatre presented for the first time in 1980 by Pennsylvania Governor Richard Thornburgh and the naming of the Alvina Krause Theatre (West 38th Street, New York City) in 1981.

Alvina Krause's teaching talent has been captured in *Acting: A Study of Life*, a series of six films showing her in workshops with students at the University of South Dakota, and also, in *Alvina Krause: Class Notes 1976-1977*, a full-length film of classes held in her home in Bloomsburg. In an interview she stated that she wanted her students to "learn to observe, perceive, understand the astonishment of living, which is the core, the source of drama."

Although she rarely wrote for publication, Alvina Krause was the subject of many articles in prominent newspapers and professional journals. A former student, William H. Wegner, says, ". . . she has published little. This is largely due to the nature of her teaching which is improvisational and based upon the interaction of teacher and student and does not lend itself to expression in formula . . . hers was an art, not a system."

Before her death in December 1981, Alvina Krause was honored by the Educational Foundation of the American Association of University Women, when she received the Centennial Award for outstanding achievement in cultural interests and for contributions that have made a lasting impact in her field.

Bloomsburg Branch
Researcher: Florence Thompson
Special Division Researcher/Writer:
Marilou L. Gary

152

Marjorie
Berlin Fink

b. 1900 _____

Marjorie Berlin Fink has been called the "First Lady of Ballet in the Lehigh Valley." In her fifty years as ballet teacher, she brought dance to the Lehigh Valley. In her twenty-two summers as a playground director, she enriched the lives of countless children living in public housing.

Of Moravian heritage, Marjorie Fink was born in Bethlehem in 1900 and has been a lifelong resident. She saw her first ballet and became "hooked" at age eight. The discipline, however, was not taught in the United States until about 1913. Thus, her weekly train trips to Philadelphia for dance lessons, beginning at age eleven, did not include ballet until she was sixteen years old. She was determined that future children would be able to receive ballet lessons and see ballet performances locally.

Shortly after graduation from Moravian Preparatory School in 1919, Marjorie established the Marjorie Berlin Fink School of Dance in September 1922. She married in 1926, had one son and was divorced in 1933 returning to the use of her maiden name. The school continued under her direction for fifty years, most of them in the Brodhead Building adjacent to the historic Sun Inn in Bethlehem.

In 1957 Marjorie was instrumental in organizing the Ballet Guild of the Lehigh Valley, bringing top ballet teachers and fine cultural performances to the area. Annual free performances for schoolchildren of Tchaikowsky's *Nutcracker* were begun in 1966.

Another aspect of her concern for children and community was her work with underprivileged children. For twenty-two years she supervised the summer recreation program of the Bethlehem Housing Association's Pembroke Village playground.

Her recognition and awards included being named "Woman of the Year" by the Bethlehem Chapter of the American Business Women's Association. In 1972 she was honored by the Bethlehem Fine Arts Commission and by the City of Bethlehem for "unselfish service." In 1982 the Bethlehem Housing Authority (BHA) dedicated a new "Marjorie Berlin Fink Recreational Building" for the Pembroke-Fairmount communities. At that dedication, a BHA administrator remarked: "She was a sort of surrogate mother to many of the kids who used that playground, to many who remember her fondly. It seemed fitting that we name the building after her. She'll be eighty-two shortly, and she's just a delight to be around."

In 1981 Marjorie Fink was "awarded" a great-granddaughter by one of her two granddaughters. Now in retirement, she teaches weekly exercise classes for tenants of the Monocacy Tower residence in Bethlehem.

Bethlehem Branch
Researcher/Writer: Catherine D. Barrett

153

Marian Anderson

b. 1902 _____

Easter Sunday, April 9, 1939, dawned cold and cloudy. At the Lincoln Memorial a temporary stage had been set up on the wide terrace from which steps led up to the marble colonnade and down to the mall lawn and reflecting pond. As the morning gray gave way to sunshine, the crowds began to gather. By noon traffic was snarled around the mall, and hundreds of extra Park Service and regular city police were on duty. Filling the spectator stands were many Washington notables, including the Chief Justice of the Supreme Court, members of President Franklin D. Roosevelt's Cabinet, a host of senators and congressmen, labor federation leaders and a seemingly endless list of the "Who's Who" in Washington society. Newspaper and magazine reporters and photographers jammed every available space near the stage.

While the crowd was still cheering the introduction by Harold Ickes, Secretary of the Interior, two figures appeared from the colonnade and started down the wide steps: a tall black woman and a white man. She wore a brown fur coat under which a green and gold brocade dress fanned out like a train. Everyone could see her stop and look out at the huge crowd. She bowed her head, as if in acknowledgement of the applause, and continued down the stairs. Regally she took her place at the rostrum behind the microphones, waiting for quiet. Her accompanist took his seat at the baby grand piano on the platform. He struck the first chord.

For one terrible moment Marian Anderson could not think of the first words of the anthem she knew as well as her name. She was very nervous. She forced herself to breathe naturally, regularly, not too fast, not too deeply. She called on everything she had learned during her years of vocal training and concert singing. The pounding of her heart began to lessen and her throat relaxed. The words came into her mind, and her beautiful contralto voice began singing, "My country, 'tis of thee, sweet land of liberty, of thee I sing." Across the country people listened by radio. History was being made and an injustice was being turned into a triumph.

Marian Anderson, world-famous Negro concert singer, who had been denied the right to sing in Constitution Hall in Washington D.C. and in a Washington high school auditorium because of her color, chose to give her concert outdoors, and the huge audience loved her.

The brief concert included an aria, which she had previously sung at the New York Philharmonic concert at Lewisohn Stadium in New York City, and Schubert's "Ave Maria." Marian ended with three favorite spirituals she had learned as a young girl growing up on Philadelphia's South Martin Street and taking voice lessons with scholarship money she earned from small town concert competitions.

Now Marian Anderson was in the Nation's Capital and thrilling her audience once again. No one at the Lincoln Memorial that Easter Sunday cared about the color of her skin. They were listening to a remarkable artist who had been given the ultimate compliment by Arturo Toscanini. The world-renowned maestro had said hers was a voice that "comes along once in a century."

It seemed only fitting that Marian appear at the "Great Emancipator's" memorial. People were ashamed that the officers of the Daughters of the American Revolution (DAR) had refused to allow Marian to sing in Constitution Hall because of a "Jim Crow" policy forbidding Black performers. When Eleanor Roosevelt heard about the incident, she withdrew her membership in the DAR in protest. The ensuing outcry from other protest groups brought Marian Anderson to the Lincoln Memorial to show the world, once and for all, that this courageous Black woman refused to be silenced by discrimination.

Marian's earlier career was often marred by ugly prejudice. She was forced to travel in dirty, segregated railroad cars and was refused taxi service at airports because of her color. More than once she had a concert registration booth window slammed in her face. But Marian recalled her Baptist mother's words, "Marian, there will be many times in life when you're pulled up short by disappointment. Don't despair. God will find a way for you."

Marian, her two sisters and their widowed mother, who had been a schoolteacher in Virginia before moving to Philadelphia to marry their father, were alike in the way they reacted to injustice. They went quietly "into the well of our faith to find peace of mind and understanding." Marian was not a fighting crusader. She simply wanted to sing. But all that her countrymen could see was her color.

It wasn't until she went abroad to study voice and sing in London, Berlin and the Scandinavian capitals that she was finally recognized as a brilliant vocalist. In Paris the popular manager Sol Hurok discovered her and brought her back to the states. She packed Town Hall in New York City despite a broken foot which she tried to conceal. Appearing as Ulrica, the sorceress, in Verdi's *The Masked Ball*, she became the first Black to sing with the New York Metropolitan Opera.

In 1957 the U.S. government sent her on a trip to Asia. She had become the symbol of the American dream—that hard work and perseverance can pay off. She had achieved world-wide fame as a concert artist. That had been her dream, and it came true.

Reading Branch
Researcher/Writer: Carole Simpson

154

Elizabeth Wysor

b. 1908

Three careers appealed to the unusual talents of Elizabeth Wysor, daughter of a professor of metallurgy at Lafayette College, Easton, Pennsylvania. Elizabeth realized she had an outstanding musical gift when James Beam, head of the music department of Easton High School, auditioned her for the senior class musical. He found that the young lady's rich contralto voice had a range of three octaves, compared with the average of one and a half. He urged the young student to consider a singing career; she had expected to study sculpture. Her wise parents, knowing that only she could decide in which direction her abilities should take her, gave her a year of study in both voice and art.

Under the tutelage of the Rome Fentons of Easton, music took possession of Elizabeth. She won a scholarship to the Juilliard School of Music in New York City, graduating with high honors in 1932. A year in Munich followed, where she studied voice and also German, French and Italian at the *Akademie der Tonkunst*. She next worked intensively under Metropolitan contralto Madame Margaret Matzenauer. She continued to study in Europe and performed in Munich, London, Paris, Vienna, Rome and in Sweden.

Elizabeth Wysor's operatic debut in 1936 was in the role of Fricka in Wagner's *Die Walkure* in Cincinnati. Since that time she has sung to large audiences in America as well as in Europe. The extraordinary range and intense color of her voice have brought her high acclaim, particularly in Germany, in Wagnerian opera.

Her second career began when she was asked to be visiting professor of voice at Mary Washington College in Fredericksburg, Virginia, a part-time teaching post which she held for four years. In 1955 she joined the faculty of Northwestern University in Chicago, where she held a professorship until her retirement in 1973. To her graduate students, she has taught special techniques, including the art of proper breathing. Ann Ayer, internationally known soprano, has also studied with Miss Wysor.

During a sabbatical leave in 1962, Elizabeth spent several months in Greece doing research in ancient Greek music and photographing Greek art treasures. These studies enriched her lectures and performances at the University and elsewhere.

In yet a third way, Elizabeth Wysor added to her artistic dimensions. After her retirement from Northwestern University, she published a volume of poetry, *Moments of Radiance,* in which she expressed her deep, quiet appreciation of the beauty of nature and of the human soul.

Elizabeth Wysor's farewell performance as a concert artist was, most fittingly, given in 1981 at the First Presbyterian Church of Easton where she had belonged as a young girl.

Easton Branch
Researcher: Margaret D. Druse
Writer: Cynthia Gordon

155

Photograph courtesy of Singing City, Philadelphia, PA

Elaine
Isaacson Brown

b. 1910 _____

All eyes in the audience watched as Elaine Brown crossed the stage and mounted the podium to conduct the Singing City of Philadelphia, a choral group comprised of 150 voices. Singing City was founded as a true community chorus by its director Elaine Isaacson Brown.

Music had been a part of Elaine's life from youth. She was born in Ridgway, Pennsylvania, March 10, 1910. Her father, J. R. Isaacson, a prominent building contractor, sang bass in the Evangelical Covenant Church choir. Her mother, Anna, served as organist. Thus, it was not surprising when their child became an accomplished contralto and pianist.

After graduating from Ridgway High School at the age of fifteen, Elaine attended the Bush Conservatory of Music (now Roosevelt University) in Chicago where she was graduated with the degree of Bachelor of Music Education in 1929. In 1934 she received a Bachelor of Music degree from Westminster Choir College, Princeton, New Jersey; and in 1945 Temple University, Philadelphia, granted her a Master of Science in education degree.

In 1948 Elaine Brown began her most notable work, the organization of the Singing City of Philadelphia. The singers came from all walks of life, races and age groups and, after thirty years, some of the members of the original group were still singing.

The goals of Singing City are to perform music as excellently as possible and to reach as many people as possible by performing in local neighborhoods as well as concert halls. The chorus's active schedule includes concerts with the Philadelphia Symphony Orchestra with which it has made recordings, numerous appearances throughout the city, joint recitals with school choirs and tours. Singing City has an international reputation. In 1982 the group traveled to Israel and Egypt and performed with Maestro Zubin Mehta and the Israel Philharmonic Orchestra, and the Cairo Symphony.

Elaine Brown was the first American woman to conduct the Philadelphia Symphony Orchestra. She often conducts orchestras in connection with her principal work, that of leading Singing City. In addition, she is in demand as a lecturer and guest conductor in colleges and universities. She has served on the faculties of such schools as the Julliard School of Music, Westminster Choir School and Temple University College of Music where she holds the position of professor *emerita.*

Elaine has been recognized throughout the world for both her artistic and humanitarian endeavors. Among the awards she has received are the French government's *Prix d'Excellence* for conducting, the National Conference of Christians and Jews Tribute and the Philadelphia Gimbel Award. She was selected a Distinguished Daughter of Pennsylvania by Governor John S. Fine in 1953. She has also served on the panel of choral advisers to the National Endowment for the Arts. In 1957 she was honored with an honorary Doctorate of Music from the Philadelphia Conservatory of Music, and in 1981 Villanova University presented her with an honorary Doctor of Fine Arts.

Elaine Brown has made full use of her talents and abilities. Her choral art has created good will and a sense of community among diverse audiences not only in the United States but also throughout the world. Her lasting contribution has improved the aesthetic quality of life for her fellow man.

Elk County Branch
Researcher/Writer: Joan Donovan

156

Ruth McGinnis

1911–1974

Ruth McGinnis, a Honesdale, Pennsylvania native, was the Women's Pocket Billiard Champion of the World for approximately twenty-five years.

Ruth's first introduction to billiards was at seven years of age in her father's pool parlor. Ralph Greenleaf, the World's Pocket Billiard Champion when Ruth was ten years old, thought her to be one of the greatest performers he had ever seen. At fourteen she played Henry Adams, another well-known player in New York City and won fifty-six to twelve in three innings with a high of twenty-eight. Seventeen years after she first met Ralph Greenleaf, Ruth defeated him as well.

In high school Ruth excelled in sports; she was involved in basketball, softball and track. She was a member of the amateur team that won the state basketball championship in 1919. While she attended East Stroudsburg State Teachers College, Ruth established a new world's record for the women's basketball throw (212 feet).

Before graduation from college, Ruth McGinnis competed in the Philadelphia Billiards Tournament and was named officially "Women's Pocket Billiard Champion of the World." One of the highlights of her career came in the 1932–33 season: a match with the Olympic Champion, Mildred "Babe" Didrikson, better known as "Babe" Zaharias, possibly the best all-around woman athlete who ever lived. In this match, which lasted six days, Ruth McGinnis defeated "Babe" 600–12. It should be noted that "Babe" was not a billiard champion; however, it is significant that Ruth had defeated the top woman athlete in the world. The following year the National Billiard Association acclaimed Ruth McGinnis as Queen Billiard Player of the World.

Throughout her career she toured the United States in exhibition matches. During a two-year period she played 240 matches and lost only eight to her male competitors. At one time she had a high run of 128 balls on a 4.5' x 9' table and many other runs of over one hundred balls. The record for a 5' x 10' table was 126.

During the 1930s Ruth appeared in Hollywood movies, her most notable film being *Behind the Eight Ball* with Paul Douglas.

At the New York State Pocket Billiard Championship Match in 1942, Ruth McGinnis was defeated by Lenny Nonn of Brooklyn, New York and by Joe Procibo of Gloversville, New York. Upon returning to her home in Honesdale in 1950, she devoted her time to managing her father's pool hall, barber shop and newsstand. Later, about 1960, she worked as a physical education teacher in a Philadelphia school for underprivileged and mentally retarded children.

Ruth McGinnis devoted her lift to sports and physical education. She was the first woman named to the National Women's Billiard Hall of Fame. After she died in 1974, the Honesdale High School made an award to the most outstanding girl athlete in each graduation class in her honor. Some of the memorabilia of her career is on display in the Smithsonian Institution in Washington, D.C.

Hawley-Honesdale Area Branch
Researcher: Anne Baschon
Writer: Marie Casper

157

Lizabeth Virginia Scott (Emma Matzo)

b. 1922 _____

Photograph by Hal Wallis Productions, Inc., Hollywood, CA

"Sultry American leading lady of the forties, a box office concoction of blonde hair, defiant expression and immobile upper lip," is an apt description given to motion picture star, Lizabeth Scott, in an article written by Leslie Halliwell in *The Filmgoer's Companion.* A witty vignette by *Collier's* writer, Jim Marshall, called her "a tawny blonde with hazel-green eyes." Marshall noted that "Scotty," as he called her, enjoyed her work, was a down-to-earth, friendly, easy-to-know person who had not been spoiled by success and even did her own cooking and housework.

Lizabeth (christened Emma) was one of four girls and two boys born to John and Mary Pennock Matzo of Scranton, Pennsylvania. Although she had always been interested in drama and even performed in several plays while a student at Central High School, her parents demurred when she pleaded with them to allow her to go to New York to be on the stage. She attended Marywood College in Scranton for a time before her mother relented and allowed her to take a course at the New York Alviene School of Drama. She did fashion modeling, played in *Hellzapoppin* for a road company and played leads in the *Subway Circuit*. She was in W. Somerset Maugham's *Rain* as Sadie Thompson when she received the opportunity to understudy for Tallulah Bankhead in *The Skin of Our Teeth*, the play for which the author, Thornton Wilder, won the Pulitzer Prize for Drama in 1943.

When Paramount producer Hall Wallis saw a picture of her in a fashion magazine, he persuaded her to take a screen test, then in 1946 directed her in her first picture, *You Came Along*. Her screen debut was followed by over fifteen motion pictures for Paramount, RKO and Columbia Studios in Hollywood. In 1952 she starred in *Stolen Face* in the United Kingdom, and in 1970 she made *Pulp* with Michael Caine.

In addition to her work in motion pictures, she also appeared in the theater, summer stock and on television, notably the *Lux Television Theatre* series, formerly the *Lux Radio Theatre*.

In the years following her active involvement in the theater, she has traveled extensively, attended classes at University of California at Los Angeles and has been involved with fund-raising for Project Hope and other charities. She has also been an active participant in the Ancient Arts Council of the Los Angeles Museum.

Besides being a beautiful and talented actress, Lizabeth Scott had a lovely singing voice and was an accomplished pianist. Above all she had a philosophy that would be applicable to women of any period of time. "I believe primarily," she said in an interview for *Who's Who in America*, "that one must be enveloped and bound by God's laws. One must have unwavering faith in one's talent and proceed toward one's goals with idealism, fervent desire, abundant tenacity, overwhelming love, and extraordinary enthusiasm."

Scranton Branch
Researchers: Margaret D. Druse and
Brenda Williams
Writers: Ethel DeVirgilis, Margaret Akerly
and Judith Evans

158
Grace Kelly

1929–1982

"Grace Patricia, Her Serene Highness, Princess of Monaco" is the current heading in the biographical material for the woman also known as "Philadelphia's Grace Kelly." Both expressions seem appropriate in describing her.

Grace Patricia Kelly was born November 12, 1929, in Philadelphia, a daughter of John B. and Margaret Majer Kelly of the East Falls section of the city. Grace's father began his career as a bricklayer and amateur oarsman; her mother was a former physical education teacher and the first woman athletic coach at the University of Pennsylvania.

Grace grew up as an introspective and imaginative child, often sick with colds and asthma and not as athletically inclined as her two sisters, Margaret and Lizanne, and her brother, John B., Jr., later an Olympic oarsman. She attended the convent school, Academy of the Sisters of the Assumption (Ravenhill) in Germantown and Stevens School in Philadelphia from which she graduated in 1947. She went on to attend the American Academy of Dramatic Arts in New York, taking modeling jobs to support herself, as she insisted on doing.

In addition to its athletes, the Kelly family was known to have a background in the theatre. An uncle, George Kelly, won the Pulitzer Prize for dramatic writing in 1925, and another uncle, Walter Kelly, was a famous vaudevillian. In July 1949 Grace made her professional debut at the Bucks County Playhouse in New Hope in a revival of her uncle's play *The Torchbearers.* On November 16, 1949, she made her Broadway debut in August Strindberg's *The Father* which ran for several months. She appeared in a number of television productions: the *Philco Television Playhouse* for the National Broadcasting Company (NBC), *Studio One* for Columbia Broadcasting System, the *Hallmark's Hall of Fame* (NBC) and others.

In 1951 she appeared in a small part in a film, made for Twentieth Century Fox in New York, called *Fourteen Hours* and in the summer of 1951 she performed in the Ellitch Gardens Theatre in Denver. In the fall of 1951 she was cast in the supporting role of the Quaker wife in *High Noon* opposite Gary Cooper for United Artists. Signing a seven-year contract with Metro-Goldwyn-Mayer (MGM), Grace appeared in *Mogambo* with Clark Gable in 1959. She was nominated as the Best Supporting Actress by the Academy for that role.

On loan to other studios for most of the seven years, Grace Kelly made *Dial M for Murder* with Ray Milland for Warner Brothers. This was directed by Alfred Hitchcock, as was *Rear Window* with James Stewart for Paramount, both in 1954; Hitchcock took credit for much of her movie success. She then made *Bridges of Toko-Ri* with William Holden (1955) for Paramount.

Paramount was also the studio featuring the film that won for Grace Kelly not only the New York Film Critics Award, but also the "Oscar" of the Academy of Motion Picture Arts and Sciences for Best Actress: *Country Girl* with Bing Crosby. Crosby was also a co-star later in the musical version of *The Philadelphia Story* made for MGM called *High Society.*

Grace Kelly was suspended by MGM after turning down two bad scripts following the release of a unsuccessful film called *Green Fire*. Largely through the efforts of Alfred Hitchcock, she was again loaned to Paramount for *To Catch a Thief* with Cary Grant. This film, made on the Riviera, radically changed her future. While on location, she met Prince Rainier III of Monaco at the Cannes Film Festival in the spring of 1955. In the fall of 1955 she made another film for MGM called *The Swan*, the story of a girl who marries a prince. At Christmas time that year Prince Rainier came to Philadelphia to meet the parents of Grace Kelly, and on January 5, 1956, they became engaged.

There was a "story book" wedding on April 18, 1956, and Grace became a member of the Royal House of Grimaldi in Monte Carlo and assumed the responsibilities of consort to Prince Rainier, primary among these being a wife and mother. Her first child, Caroline, was born on January 23, 1957, followed by Albert, some fourteen months later, and Stephanie in 1965. As the wife of the reigning monarch of Monaco, Princess Grace was president of many organizations, including the Monagasque Red Cross, the Garden Club of Monaco, Princess Grace Foundation for Artists and Craftsmen, Girl Guides and the Irish-American Cultural Institute. She was also a member of the Board of Directors of Twentieth Century Fox Film Corporation.

As her children grew older, Princess Grace took responsibility for more public concerns, chiefly the promotion of Monaco tourism. She began the International Arts Festival there in 1966. Of the many awards and decorations given to her were the Ceres Medal in 1977 given by the United Nations Food and Agriculture Organization, an honorary degree from Duquesne University in Pittsburgh and the designation as a Distinguished Daughter of Pennsylvania in 1954.

During the late 1970s, Princess Grace returned to the performing arts, presenting poetry readings at the Edinburgh Film Festival and participating in other film and television specials. In the spring of 1982, Princess Grace returned to visit her family and help her native Philadelphia celebrate its three hundred years of history. Her friends from all phases of her life attended a gala at the Annenberg Center of the University of Pennsylvania where the first Award of Merit was presented to "Philadelphia's Grace Kelly." A few months later the world was stunned to learn that Princess Grace was fatally injured in a car crash in the south of France. She died September 14, 1982, at the age 52.

Levittown-Lower Bucks Branch
Researcher/Writer: Jean M. Green

16
WOMEN IN THE NATURAL AND SOCIAL SCIENCES

159

Florence Barbara Seibert, Ph.D.

b. 1897 ————————————————

Although the cause of tuberculosis, the *tubercle bacillus*, was identified early in the twentieth century, accurate testing for the disease was not possible because of the varying degree of impurity in Koch's "old tuberculin." It was the ten-year work, begun in 1924, of Florence Seibert that made possible the isolation of the active substance of pure tuberculin.

For the scientific community of the 1930s that was a prodigious accomplishment. The tuberculin molecule is protein, and purification of protein was one of the most difficult tasks in the chemical world. Through a process of filtration and precipitation, Florence Seibert succeeded in isolating PPD, as it is known today: Purified Protein Derivative. A special batch of PPD made by her and an assistant was used to establish our national standards. It was adopted by the World Health Organization and is now the international standard for tuberculin made in any laboratory in the world.

Florence Barbara Seibert was born in Easton, Pennsylvania, the second of three children of George and Barbara Memmert Seibert. When she was three years old, she and her older brother contracted polio in the epidemic of 1900. The resulting severe lameness affected her life scarcely at all, she says. Although slight in build, she had boundless determination and dealt creatively with her physical limitations.

After graduating from Easton High School, she entered Goucher College in Baltimore on a scholarship. It was there that her imagination was captured, first by biology, then by chemistry. In 1918, the spring of her graduation, she was appointed to work at the laboratories of the Hammersley Paper Mills in Garfield, New Jersey, with a Goucher faculty member. This opportunity, unusual for a woman, occurred because the First World War had created a shortage of scientifically trained men. During her two years at Hammersley she collaborated on three papers which were published in technical journals. She was awarded a scholarship at Yale, then two fellowships, which allowed her to complete her doctorate there in 1923.

That fall she went to the University of Chicago as instructor in pathology and assistant at Sprague Memorial Institute. There she met Dr. Esmond Long who encouraged her in research and became her friend and mentor. While she was still under thirty years of age, she was awarded the Ricketts Prize by the University of Chicago for solving a problem that had plagued the medical world. Intravenous therapy was in its infancy, and although distilled water should have been safe for injection into veins, it sometimes produced a brief severe fever. Elimination of pyrogens (fever-producing chemicals) that remained after the usual distillation, and even after sterilization, was perfected by Dr. Seibert in a new distillation process.

In 1932 Dr. Seibert went to the Henry Phipps Institute of the University of Pennsylvania where she did most of her tuberculin work. She was awarded a Guggenheim Fellowship in 1937 to study and work in Sweden with Professor Theodor Svedberg, Nobel Prize winner. She retired from Phipps in 1958 and went to live in Florida. There she volunteered for two years in the St. Petersburg Hospital and for eleven years in Bay Pines Veterans Administration Research Laboratories in the bacteriological etiology of cancer.

More than one hundred scientific publications attest to Dr. Seibert's accomplishments. Her autobiography, *Pebbles on the Hill of a Scientist*, is a manual of encouragement for young women interested in entering the world of scientific research. Dr. Seibert has received many honorary degrees and other honors; among them are the Achievement Award in the White House, conferred by Eleanor Roosevelt (1944), the Gimbel Award (1945), the Trudeau Medal (1938) and the First Achievement Award of the American Association of University Women (of which she is a member) (1943). In 1964 an endowed fellowship was established in her name by the AAUW.

Dr. Seibert, in several ways, has made contributions to the health of people the world over. Her most critical data has been placed in the National Medical Library in Bethesda, Maryland, and all other scientific data has been given to the American Philosophical Society in Philadelphia.

Easton Branch
Researcher: Margaret D. Druse
Writer: Cynthia Gordon

160

Sophie
Reiter Gordon

1899-1979

Studying the effects of smoking on the body's vascular system; patenting Provasin, a prescription drug to lower serum cholesterol in the blood; establishing a wheat germ and pharmaceutical company—these were the main achievements of Sophie Reiter Gordon. Because of the nature of Sophie's research and accomplishments, her life has affected the health of millions of her fellow human beings.

Sophie Gordon was born in Pittsburgh, Pennsylvania, May 11, 1899. She was the daughter of Cadmus Zaccheus and Katherine Acheson Gordon and lived in Brookville. After graduation from Brookville High School, Sophie attended Smith College and received a Bachelor of Arts degree in biology in 1922. She went on to earn her Master of Arts degree from Brown University in 1924.

Sophie was appointed a graduate assistant in biology at Women's College of Brown University in 1922-23 and worked as an assistant in the serology laboratory in Columbia College of Physicians and Surgeons in 1925. From 1925 to 1948 she supervised a clinical laboratory in New York City for Dr. Walter Timme, a pioneer in endocrinology, and did research related to the treatment of vascular disease, particularly in smokers.

In 1939 Sophie Gordon established the Gordon Wheat Germ Company in New York City. In 1946 the Gordon Pharmaceutical Division was added. The company distributed, among other items, Provasin, a drug patented by Sophie Gordon.

The author of many articles and monographs for the medical profession, she was also a member of the New York Academy of Science and a member of the Business and Professional Women's Club, which she served as president from 1946 to 1948. She belonged to Sigma Delta Epsilon and served as treasurer from 1968 to 1971. A member of the Club Altrusa of New York City, she was the group's recording secretary from 1954 to 1956, served on the board of directors from 1964 to 1966 and from 1968 to 1970 and edited the newsletter from 1959 to 1969.

Sophie Gordon's biography appeared in the *International Biographical Dictionary* and *Who's Who of American Women, 1974-75.* She was also named "Woman of the Day" by Eleanor Roosevelt and given coverage by Mrs. Roosevelt in her column "My Day."

Sophie was a "rugged individualist who was very sure of herself," according to some of her friends. She was a very confident woman, viewed by some as being outspoken and spicy when women were expected to be quiet and docile. She showed a great deal of enthusiasm and support for other women working in the field of scientific research. She was described as a jolly person with a keen sense of humor. Some of her favorite pastimes were working anagrams and crossword puzzles, sometimes in French to confound her friends.

In 1959 Sophie Gordon was recognized by the first Brookville Laurel Board as the "Outstanding Citizen of the Year." Her life, much as a stone cast into the water causes ever larger concentric circles, touched the lives of many others.

She died August 30, 1979, at Toms River, New Jersey, and is buried in Brookville.

Brookville Area Branch
Researcher/Writer: Patricia McCoy Gill

161

Mildred M.
Hicks-Bruun, Ph.D.

b. 1900 _____

"We don't take women chemists" were the words heard repeatedly by Mildred Hicks-Bruun when she applied for positions with corporations during the 1920s. Her professors asked, "Why don't you teach?" Mildred's aim, however, was to work in industrial research which required not only a better than average record—she was a member of Phi Beta Kappa and Sigma Xi—but also much initiative, ingenuity, and energy. In time she became an assistant director of research for a major oil company. "As I look back," she said, "I realize that I was one of the few early pioneer women research chemists in the chemical industry."

Mildred was born in 1900 and grew up on an ancestral farm in Virginia before beginning her career in the chemical world which took her to many states and finally to Pennsylvania. After graduation from Randolph-Macon Woman's College, Mildred began her career as instructor of chemistry and physics at Columbia College, South Carolina. Two years later she moved to Minnesota and became the head of the science department at Biwabik High School. While working on her doctorate, Mildred stepped into the industrial world as the head of the Analytical

Department at American Aniline Products, Inc. After a year she moved on to become a research chemist with the National Bureau of Standards in Washington, D. C.

At this time women chemists were almost unheard of in the industrial world. Little was known about petroleum, and many scientists thought it was too complex to be separated. Mildred initiated a research project to isolate, separate and identify the compounds in petroleum. New methods had to be developed and new apparatus designed to achieve the results. She determined the composition of petroleum by first separating and identifying the components of the gasoline fraction. Later the heavier hydro-carbons, fuel oils, lubrication oils and paraffins were also studied. The project was financed by the petroleum industry through the American Petroleum Institute and conducted at the National Bureau of Standards.

Mildred remained in the position of consultant with the Bureau of Standards for some time after receiving her doctorate from the University of Iowa in 1930. In 1932 she became the assistant director of research for the Sun Oil Company. Here, for the next ten years, she helped to start and develop a research department. Her achievements resulted in her being granted patents for catalytic reactions and lubricating oils. Because she suffered from severe anemia caused by mercury poisoning, her career as an industrial research chemist ended prematurely in 1942.

In 1943 she accepted a position as a research chemist for the Sloan-Kettering Cancer Center. While there she was involved in steroid research. During these years Mildred published over twenty papers concerning the various aspects of her work which appeared in such respected publications as the *Journal of Physical Chemistry, Bureau of Standards Journal of Research, Journal of American Chemical Society, Industrial and Engineering Chemistry* and the *Chemical Encyclopedia.*

Mildred continued her career as a technical writer. She married a Norwegian, Dr. Johannes Bruun, and together they have traveled extensively throughout the world. Mildred has chaired committee meetings of several national organizations and served on the boards of many civic organizations and political committees.

Aside from her interest in science, Mildred has a deep affection and interest in her roots and recently published a two-volume historical narrative entitled *Polly's Journal,* in which she shares with readers the joys and sorrows of her ancestors' lives in a small Virginia community.

Easton Branch
Researcher: Margaret D. Druse
Writer: JoAnn Harak

162

Margaret Mead, Ph.D.

1901-1978

Margaret Mead was one of the world's foremost anthropologists. She was adjunct professor of anthropology at Columbia University, president of the American Anthropological Association (1959-1960), curator *emerita* of the American Museum of Natural History and the author of hundreds of articles and many books.

Margaret was born in Philadelphia, the daughter of Emily Fogg and Edward Sherwood Mead. She grew up in the Doylestown area of Bucks County, Pennsylvania, where she began her formal education in the local schools and was graduated from Doylestown High School in 1918.

Margaret was always a leader. In her own writings, she admits that she was "different." Referred to as a "legend, a certified household word," it has been said, "There's no one like Margaret." In moving from one house to another, even at an early age, Margaret assumed the initiative in settling the entire household.

Throughout all the work and writings of Margaret Mead, her love and care for little children shows clearly. Through her studies of children of various cultures, she hoped to improve the understanding of all children everywhere, thus making a better world for them. By understanding the children better, she hoped for a better understanding of adults also. She believed that too many opinions were drawn simply from reading and studying various printed reports, and most of these reports had been written by men. Margaret Mead felt that more studies should be made by women since they were usually closest to the children. This was her main reason for traveling to faraway places like Samoa, New Guinea and Bali to study children in their natural home environment.

Being very observant, Margaret compared every phase of the life of these children with that of children in the Western cultures. For example, she noted how differently the Balinese mothers held their infants, thus making the child more relaxed and less pugnacious than children reared in the Western culture. Such comparative studies of cultures by anthropologists have played a significant part in giving a sort of balance to the attempts to revise our own methods of child care.

The books on her experiences in these distant cultures were well received both in scientific and public circles.

Her first book in 1928, *Coming of Age in Samoa*, was the best-selling anthropology book of all time. *Growing Up in New Guinea* (1930) helped to establish her reputation as the world's most famous anthropologist.

It was Margaret Mead's belief that anthropology enlarged our knowledge of the meaning of religion. She stressed the utilization of technology, especially that of radio, television and telestar in the service of Christian principles. She hoped for the initiation of a common planetary faith which would show a compassionate concern for each living being, tradition and community.

She had deep religious convictions and early in life became a member of Trinity Episcopal Church in Buckingham, Pennsylvania. It was the burial ground of this church which she chose for her final resting place.

Honest and forthright in defending her beliefs, Margaret Mead was trained to become a woman who could live responsibly in the contemporary world. By going to some of the most remote areas of the world and studying the customs of the inhabitants, she believed that she could learn ways that would help her fellow Americans better understand themselves.

Doylestown Branch
Researchers/Writers: Anna E. Shaddinger
and Mary McCaw

163

Rachel Louise Carson

1907-1964

Photograph courtesy of the *Valley News Dispatch*, Tarentum, PA

Rachel Carson was born in Springdale, Pennsylvania, in 1907. She was the youngest of three children born to Robert Warden and Maria Carson. Rachel began her college education as an English major but switched to biology. Graduating from Chatham College, *magna cum laude*, she received a Master of Arts in zoology from Johns Hopkins

University. She joined the Zoology Department at the University of Maryland and spent her summers working at the Marine Biological Laboratory in Woods Hole, Massachusetts.

With the deaths of her father in 1935 and her married sister in 1936, Rachel became the sole support of her mother and her two young nieces. She began working for the United States Bureau of Fisheries as a junior aqua-biologist. Rachel's first book, *Under the Sea Wind,* was published in 1941, just before Pearl Harbor, selling only a few copies at the time. During World War II, Rachel wrote conservation bulletins and was manager of publications of the United States Fish and Wildlife Service.

Family obligations left Rachel little time for writing, but she did manage to supplement her income by doing some magazine articles on natural history. *The Sea Around Us* was written over a long period of time during Rachel's evenings and brief leaves of absence from the Service. The book became an immediate best-seller and catapulted Rachel Carson into national prominence. It was eventually published in thirty-two languages.

Financial independence followed Rachel's national recognition, and in 1952 she was able to devote her full time to writing. In 1955 Rachel finished *The Edge of the Sea.* Family obligations took precedence once again when Rachel adopted her orphaned nephew, Roger. Roger inspired the magazine article "Help Your Child to Wonder," published in *Woman's Home Companion* in 1956.

Silent Spring, Rachel Carson's most influential book, was published in 1962. The book focused on pesticide poisoning. It was vehemently attacked by special interest groups and the agricultural chemical industry which launched a public relations campaign against Rachel, but to no avail. The direct effect of *Silent Spring* was the formation of a special panel of the President's Science Advisory Committee to study the environmental effects of pesticides. Rachel testified before Congress and was an important influence in gaining legislative action. Rachel Carson, often characterized as shy and "self effacing," had become a tenacious scientist.

Upon finishing *Silent Spring,* knowing that her health was failing fast, Rachel was hopeful that the unsavory facts laid out in the book would not overshadow her message of life: "The beauty of the living world I was trying to save has always been uppermost in my mind." Rachel Carson died April 14, 1964.

Fox Chapel Area Branch
Researcher/Writer: Patricia Demase

164

Photograph courtesy of the Public Relations Office, Bucknell University, Lewisburg, PA

Hulda
Magalhaes, Ph.D.

b. 1914 _____

When young Dr. Magalhaes began her Bucknell University career as assistant professor of biology in 1946, it was necessary for her to find a research project which could be approached without reliance on certain pieces of glassware which were in short supply in her new laboratory. Recognizing that research in animal nutrition would fit such circumstances, she ordered a supply of rats and, almost as an after-thought, a few hamsters. Little could she have guessed that her love for these golden hamsters would determine the future course of her professional career and would result in her position among the out-standing authorities in hamster research. Known to generations of Bucknell students as an outwardly gruff but personally warm, caring and brilliant professor, Hulda Magalhaes was a mentor to many students, an admired colleague to many faculty members and an expert of enviable reputation among biologists throughout the world.

Hulda, a direct descendant of the Portuguese navigator Ferdinand Magellan, was born in Brooklyn, New York, on April 9, 1914. After receiving a Bachelor of Science degree from New Jersey College for Women (now Douglass College) in New Brunswick, New Jersey, in 1935, she served as a graduate assistant at Mount Holyoke College while completing study for her Master of Arts degree in physiology, granted in 1937. This degree led to positions as instructor in physiology at Woman's Medical College in Philadelphia from 1937 to 1940 and instructor in zoology at Duke University from 1943 to 1946. Her Ph.D. in zoology, begun at Duke University in 1940, was awarded by that institution in 1944. Among her academic honors were membership in Phi Beta Kappa, Phi Sigma and Sigma Xi.

The detailed breeding of and research with hamsters not only provided Hulda's Bucknell students with invaluable training in the study of animal nutrition, genetics and management, but resulted in benefits to many scientists who dealt with hamsters and other laboratory animals. She was asked by the National Institutes of Health to develop a pure strain of hamsters and, thus, contribute to the progress of cancer research; at one time Bucknell was the only place in the world able to provide the National Institutes with the strain of hamsters specifically suited to their needs. During the 1953-54 academic year she was awarded a Ford Foundation Fellowship which made possible the development of new courses in embryology, histology and genetics at Bucknell. She also secured valuable background for future publications on the care, use and management of the golden hamster as a laboratory animal. She visited research laboratories and commercial animal facilities in the United States and Great Britain, and while in England, presented a paper at the Seventh Animals Bureau Conference at the University of Sheffield.

A sabbatical leave from Bucknell for the 1963-64 year, plus a contract with the National Library of Medicine in Bethesda, Maryland, enabled Dr. Magalhaes to prepare for the library a hamster bibliography for the period 1931-1963. During that year she also completed much of the work for one of her most important scientific contributions, the preparation of two chapters and the master bibliography for *The Golden Hamster: Its Biology and Use in Medical Research* published in 1968 by the Iowa State University Press. Many other articles and reports by Dr. Magalhaes alone or with others appeared through the years in such periodicals as the *Journal of Animal Technology*, the *American Zoologist* and the *Anatomical Record* and in the publications of the National Academy of Science, the Bucknell University Press and, in Great Britain, the Universities Federation for Animal Welfare. Additional honors included the Lindback Award for Distinguished Teaching in 1968, listing in the 1972 edition of *Outstanding Educators of America* and citations in a number of editions between 1946 and 1980 of *American Men and Women of Science*.

Always interested in a broad spectrum of the biological sciences, over the years Hulda conducted research in such diverse fields as ecology, marine biology, genetics, reproduction and nutrition. It was a short step from research in nutrition to a 1981 summer Fellowship in American History from the National Endowment for the Humanities. Her research was in the history of diet and nutrition, comparing the nutritional values of modern and colonial diets.

When Hulda became professor *emerita* in 1982, a delightful article about her was written by Marsha Scott Gori for the *Bucknell World*. A few lines from that article describe her: "From a distance she looks fierce. . . . Close in on Hulda Magalhaes and the image softens. Her face, framed by a helmet of close-cropped white hair, crinkles into a smile. . . . 'I was blessed or cursed with a sense of humor,' she laughs. 'Because of the twinkle in my eye, most folks won't believe what I tell them.'"

But over the years Hulda's students, friends and colleagues *have* believed what she told them and have reflected in their lives and their work her twinkle, her keen sense of humor and her fine mind.

Susquehanna Valley Branch
Researchers: Lois Kalp
and Martha Zeller
Writer: Mary Jane Stevenson

165

Sarah Kleiger Schenck, Ph.D.

b. 1915 ――――――――――――――――――――――――――

Sarah Kleiger Schenck was born in Brooklyn, New York, but was a Pennsylvania resident most of her life. She made significant contributions to the field of chemistry. While working on her doctoral dissertation in organic chemistry at the University of Chicago, Sarah developed the metal halide catalysis in the Grignard reaction. The Grignard reaction is one of the most useful and versatile reactions known to the organic chemist in synthesizing specific compounds.

Upon receiving her doctorate, Sarah went to work at the Bob Roberts Memorial Hospital in Chicago. There she did research on vitamin levels, primarily vitamin B, in pregnant women and newborn infants. In 1943 she accepted a position as research chemist with the Veisicol Corporation. While there she helped to isolate the structure of chlordane, which was then widely used as a base for a powerful insecticide. She was chosen to supervise the first pilot plant for production of that compound.

In 1945 Sarah left Veisicol to become Senior Research Chemist for the Ansco Corporation, a division of General Aniline and Film Corporation. At this time Ansco was in the process of improving the color quality of its film through the development of new color-formers and sensitizers. Sarah was awarded a number of patents for her work in this field.

In 1952 she accepted a position as Director of Research for J. W. Neff Laboratories. Here she was involved in still another area of chemistry, that of plastics and plastic formulation. The company made a material from which phonograph records were pressed. The process involved recycling old records and adding vinyl for strength and durability. In addition, Sarah was also involved in the development of a vinyl that could be used for traffic markers. These permanent markers are used in various parts of the country instead of painted lines and are laid down on the roadbed while the blacktop is still soft.

Because of her broad experience in the field of research chemistry, Sarah's writing was published in many science journals. Sarah married Remsen Schenck, also a chemist. In addition to her distinguished work in chemistry, Sarah Schenck was also active in her community, especially with the Girl Scouts where she served on the board of directors and as a professional executive director of a council in Maryland.

Easton Branch
Researcher: Margaret D. Druse
Writer: JoAnn Harak

APPENDICES

APPENDICES

APPENDIX A

Selected Bibliography

Beard, Mary R., ed., *America Through Women's Eyes* (New York: Macmillan Company, 1933)

Biddle, Gertrude B. and **Sarah D. Lowrie,** eds., *Notable Women of Pennsylvania* (Philadelphia: University of Pennsylvania Press, 1942)

Bodnar, John E., ed., *The Ethnic Experience in Pennsylvania* (Lewisburg, PA: Bucknell University Press, 1973)

Carroll, Bernice A., ed., "Mary Beard's Woman as Force in History: Critique," *Liberating Women's History* (Chicago: University of Illinois Press, 1976)

Ehrenreich, Barbara and **Deirdre English,** "Witches, Midwives, and Nurses: A History of Women Healers" (Old Westbury, NY: The Feminist Press, 1973)

Gordon, Ann D., Mari Jo Buhle and **Nancy Shrom Dye,** "The Problem of Women's History," Bernice A. Carroll, ed., *Liberating Women's History* (Chicago: University of Illinois Press, 1976)

James, Edward T., Janet Wilson James and **Paul S. Boyer,** eds., *Notable American Women 1607–1950*, 3 Vols. (Cambridge, MA: Belknap Press of Harvard University Press, 1971)

Kessler-Harris, Alice, *Out to Work* (New York: Oxford University Press, 1982)

Klein, Philip S. and **A. A. Hoogenboom,** *A History of Pennsylvania* (New York: McGraw-Hill Book Company, 1973)

Lerner, Gerda, "The Lady and the Mill Girl: Changes in the Status of Women in the Age of Jackson," Jean E. Friedman and William G. Shade, eds., *Our American Sisters* (Boston: Allyn and Bacon, Inc., 1976)

Sicherman, Barbara and **Carol Hurd Green,** eds., *Notable American Women: The Modern Period* (Cambridge, MA: Belknap Press of Harvard University Press, 1980)

Wallace, Paul A. A., *Indians in Pennsylvania* (Harrisburg, PA: Historical and Museum Commission, 1970)

APPENDIX B

References and Notes

Aldington, Hilda "H. D." Doolittle (125)
1. The Rev. Henry L. Williams, "A Poet for Bethlehem," *Reeves Library Book Notes* (Bethlehem, PA: Moravian College, 1982)
2. Stanley J. Kunitz and Howard Haycraft, *Twentieth Century Authors* (New York: H. W. Wilson Co., 1942) p. 391.
3. *The Globe-Times*, Bethlehem, PA, September 10, 1982.

Alliquippa, Queen (1)
1. Paul A. W. Wallace, *Indians in Pennsylvania* (Harrisburg: Pennsylvania Historical and Museum Commission, 1961) p. 87.
2. George Thornton Fleming, *History of Pittsburgh and Environs*, vol. 1, (American History Society, Inc., 1922) pp. 71, 224.
3. C. A. Hanna, *The Wilderness Trail*, vol. 1, 1911, pp. 79–82.
4. George Washington, *Journals*.
5. George Washington, *Letters*.
6. Kay Ryall, "Aliquippa Borough Named After Indian Queen Famous in Colonial Days," *The Pittsburgh Press*, Pittsburgh, March 19, 1933.

Allison, Marjorie (30)
1. *The Morning Call*, Allentown, PA, October 31, 1951, November 4, 1953, February 4, 1955, October 6, 1959, March 14, 1964.
2. Dr. Esther Swain, headmistress *emerita*, The Swain School, interview by Camille S. Bucci, Allentown, PA, September 1982.

Alpern, Anne X., Judge (56)
1. *Post-Gazette*, Pittsburgh, PA, February 3, 1981, June 14, 1937, September 7, 1961, March 3, 1973.

Ambler, Mary Johnson (74)
1. M. P. H. Hough, *Early History of Ambler* (Ambler, PA: 1936)
2. *Bicentennial Perspective for Women: Prominent Women of the Wissahickon Valley Area* (Ambler, PA: Ambler Business and Professional Women's Club, 1976)
3. "Fifty-Nine Met Death in Crash of Two Engines," *Ambler Gazette*, Ambler, PA, July 19, 1856.
4. "Ambler Was Officially Named in 1869," *Ambler Gazette*, Ambler, PA, June 13, 1938.

Anderson, Marian (153)
1. Carole Simpson, "Anderson Broke Color Barrier," *Reading Eagle*, Reading, PA, March 12, 1982. Article reprinted courtesy of the *Reading Eagle*.

Anthony, Susan Brownell II, Ph.D. (104)
1. Susan B. Anthony II, personal communications on file at the Henry F. Marx Historical Room in the Easton Area Public Library, Easton, PA.
2. Susan B. Anthony, *The Ghost in My Life* (New York: Chosen Books, 1971)
3. *The Plain Dealer*, Cleveland, OH, February 1, 1982.

Archer, Belle (147)
1. Harold D. Smith, "Memories of Belle Archer," pp. 1–4. On file in the Easton Area Public Library, Easton, PA.
2. *Who Was Who in America*, vol. 1, 1897–1942 (Chicago: A. N. Marquis Co., 1942)

Barclay, Jessie (99)
1. Bedford County Library Records.
2. *Bedford Gazette*, Bedford, PA, April 15, 1955.
3. Mrs. H. S. Blayman, letter to Mary Sue Whisker, Tenafly, NJ, May 14, 1982.
4. Mrs. Robert M. Henninger S. Kolb, letter to Mary Sue Whisker, Tucson, AZ, April 30, 1982.

Bausher, Mildred Jordan (131)
1. *Reading Eagle*, Reading, PA, October 24, 1982.
2. Richard Kepler Brunner, *The County Magazine*, September 1978, pp. 34, 36, 46, 47.

Beebe, Helen Hulick (118)
1. Helen Hulick Beebe, *A Guide to Help the Severely Hard of Hearing Child* (New York: S. Karger, 1953).
2. *The Express*, Easton, PA, November 6, 1981.
3. *The Globe-Times*, Bethlehem, PA, October 1, 1981.
4. Helen Hulick Beebe, personal communications on file at the Henry F. Marx Historical Room in the Easton Area Public Library, Easton, PA.
5. Service to Mankind Award of the Sertoma Club of Easton, March 18, 1980, on file at the Henry F. Marx Historical Room in the Easton Area Public Library, Easton, PA.

Beecher, Katharine (32)
1. Henry Beecher, son, interviewed by Betty K. Hooker, September 19, 1982.
2. David Beecher, son, interviewed by Betty K. Hooker, September 20, 1982.
3. *The York Dispatch*, York, PA, February 2, 1981.
4. *Five Star News*, Manchester, PA, February 18, 1981.

Benjamin, Sarah Matthews (34)
1. *The News Eagle*, Hawley, PA, July 21, 1978.
2. Reverend Samuel Whaley, *A History of the Township of Mount Pleasant, Wayne County, Pennsylvania* (New York: W. W. Dodd, 1856) pp. 75–81.
3. Application of Jeanne Crisp Schroder, descendant of Sarah Matthews Benjamin, to the Daughters of the American Revolution, Washington, DC, October 24, 1978.

Bentley, Alice Marie (11)
1. *The Edinboro Independent,* Edinboro, PA, May 1, 1974.
2. *The Tribune Republican,* Meadville, PA, August 8, 1949.
3. *The Philadelphia Record,* Philadelphia, November 8, 1925.
4. Scrapbook owned by Mrs. H. B. Patterson, niece, Saegertown, PA.

Blatt, Genevieve, Judge (57)
1. *The Pennsylvania Manual,* vol. 104, 1928–29, p. 481.
2. Sylvester K. Stevens, *Pennsylvania: The Heritage of a Commonwealth* (West Palm Beach, FL: American Historical Company, Inc., 1968) vol. 4, p. 20.
3. *Who's Who in America,* 40th ed. (Chicago: A. N. Marquis Company, 1978–79) vol. 1, p. 300.

Blissell, Elisabeth Surowski (33)
1. *Biography of Elisabeth S. Blissell* (New Kensington, PA: New Kensington Chamber of Commerce, 1982)

Bly, Nellie (63)
1. Mignon Rittenhouse, *The Amazing Nellie Bly* (New York: E. P. Dutton and Co.) pp. 11, 19, 51, 112, 207, 245, 250, 253.
2. *Encyclopaedia Britannica,* 1978 edition, vol. 2, p. 104.
3. Allen Johnson and Dumas Malone, eds., *Dictionary of American Biography XV* (New York: Charles Scribner's Sons, 1946) pp. 533, 534.
4. *Pittsburgh Women* (Pittsburgh: Western Pennsylvania Historical Society, 1976)
5. Mrs. Don Bush, telephone interview by Debbie Popp Gilbert, September 1982.
6. Lynwood Mark Rhodes, *The American Legion Magazine,* June 1967.
7. *Good Housekeeping Magazine,* February 1955.
8. Muriel Nussbaum, "Bylined Nellie Bly," (play), presented in Pittsburgh, PA, October 20, 1982.
9. News files of *The Pittsburgh Press,* Pittsburgh, PA.
10. News files of the *Post-Gazette,* Pittsburgh, PA.
11. *Encyclopedia Americana,* 1978 edition, vol. 4, p. 115.

Bowen, Catherine Drinker (130)
1. Barbara Sicherman and Carol Hurd Green, eds., *Notable American Women: The Modern Period* (Cambridge, MA: Belknap Press of Harvard University Press, 1980) pp. 97–99.
2. *Current Biography* (New York: H. W. Wilson, 1944) p. 62.
3. Claire Walter, *Winners: The Blue Ribbon Encyclopedia of Awards* (New York: Facts on File, 1978) pp. 39, 47.

Boyce, Ella M. (109)
1. *NRTA Journal,* May-June, 1980, pp. 12–14.
2. Information from the Administrative Office of Bradford Area Schools, Bradford, PA.

Boyd, Kate Hillis (100)
1. "Alumnae profile—Kate Boyd," *Wilson College Alumnae Quarterly,* vol. 52:3, May 1976, p. 7.

2. Dorothy Hollar Miller, "Kate Hillis Boyd, YWCA Secretary," *Wilson College Alumnae Quarterly*, vol. 6:3, May 1930, pp. 8, 9.
3. Kate H. Boyd, "An intimate view of life in the Philippines," *Wilson College Alumnae Quarterly*, vol. 13:1, November 1936, pp. 6–11.
4. Kate Hillis Boyd, "Centers of friendship: the YWCA in the East," *Wilson College Alumnae Quarterly*, vol. 10:3, May 1934, pp.12–14.
5. Cornelia Cree, niece, interview by Anne G. Vondra, Chambersburg, PA, October 20, 1982.

Brock, Deborah Norris Coleman (90)
1. Mrs. Horace Brock, *The Green Book*, deposited with the Women's Club of Lebanon, PA, historical records.
2. *A Visit to Aunt Agnes, Floral Album, In Memoriam New Testament* and *Lyric Gem Book*, all previously owned by Mrs. Brock but now the property of the Women's Club of Lebanon.
3. Public records in the office of the Register of Wills, in the Orphans' Court of the City-County Building in Lebanon, PA, and in the Lebanon County Historical Society.
4. Mary Belle Weiss, *Historian's Report*, (Lebanon, PA: Women's Club of Lebanon, 1978) Printed by the *Lebanon Daily News* and on file at the Lebanon County Historical Society.
5. Horace Brock, Alexander Biddle Brock, Deborah Norris Rush and Horace Brock Bent, grandchildren of Deborah Brock, correspondence and interviews by Mary Belle Weiss. Correspondence on file at Women's Club of Lebanon.

Brooks, Marion Deihner (87)
1. *The Bennetts Valley News*, Weedville, PA, April 5 and April 12, 1973.
2. Paul Swanson, *Pennsylvania Angler*, March 1975, p. 16.
3. *The Daily Press*, St. Marys, PA, October 6, 1975.

Brown, Elaine Isaacson (155)
1. Alice L. Wessman and Harriet Faust, *A Sesquicentennial History of Ridgway* (Ridgway, PA: Ridgway Publishing Company, June 1974) p. 193.

Brownscombe, Jennie (140)
1. *Illustrated Wayne County*, 1900–1902 ed.
2. Jeannette Birdsall Brownell, *The Wayne Independent*, Honesdale, PA.
3. *The Wayne Independent*, Honesdale, PA, April 12, 1899, August 6, 1936.

Buck, Pearl S. (128)
1. P. C. Mendelson and D. Bryforski, eds., *Contemporary Literary Criticism* (Detroit: Gale Research Company, 1977) vol. 7, pp. 32–34, 140.
2. Pearl S. Buck, *My Several Worlds* (New York: John Day Co., 1954) pp. 3, 89–93, 96, 97, 129, 366.
3. Pearl S. Buck, *Children for Adoption* (New York: Random House, 1964) pp. 229, 230.
4. Carolyn Taylor, friend of Pearl Buck and member of Welcome House and the Pearl S. Buck Foundation, interview by Mary McCaw, Doylestown, PA, January 1982.
5. Pearl S. Buck with Theodore F. Harris, *For Spacious Skies* (New York: John Day Co., 1966) pp. 97–100.

6. William Major, Director of Development Resources, Pearl S. Buck Foundation, interview by Mary McCaw, Perkasie, PA, January 1983.

Carmelita, Sister Mary (97)
1. Sisters of Mercy Archives, Mother House, Erie, PA.
2. *Courier Express*, DuBois, PA, November 22, 1964 and October 7, 1982.
3. *The Pittsburgh Press*, Pittsburgh, PA, December 25, 1960.
4. Norma Hiller, R.N., interview by Judy Furlow, DuBois, PA, October 19, 1982.

Carson, Rachel Louise (163)
1. Barbara Secherman and Carol Hurd Green, eds., *Notable American Women: The Modern Period* (Cambridge, MA: Belknap Press of Harvard University Press, 1980) p. 138, 139.
2. Paul Brooks, *The House of Life: Rachel Carson at Work* (Boston: Houghton Mifflin Co., 1972) pp. 13, 201.

Carter, Anna Lucille (119)
1. Personal file located in the district office of Susquehanna School District, Harrisburg, PA.
2. Obituary, *The Patriot-Evening News*, Harrisburg, PA, November 30, 1979.

Cassatt, Mary (139)
1. News files of the *The Pittsburgh Press*, Pittsburgh, PA.
2. Alexander Eliot, *Three Hundred Years of American Painting* (New York: Time Incorporated, 1957) pp. 124–127, 188.
3. *The Golden Encyclopedia of Art* (New York: Golden Press, 1961)

Chisolm, Ann Dorris (141)
1. *The Semi-Weekly News*, Huntingdon, PA, January 10, 1918.
2. Huntingdon County Recorder's Office, Will Book, 26, p. 541.

Clemens, Hanna Clemmer Rittenhouse (92)
1. P. Delp, "Hanna C. Clemens," *Franconia Conference News*, 1975.
2. Hanna Clemens, tape recording of a speech on the occasion of her husband's fiftieth ordination anniversary, owned by Ernest Clemens, son, Lansdale, PA.
3. M. Clemens, "Her Lifestyle Reflected Her Values," *Voice*, 1977.
4. Four videotapes on file at the Mennonite Heritage Center, 1974.
5. Ernest Clemens, son, taped interview by Karen Methlie, on deposit at the Montgomery County Federation of Historical Societies, Peter Wentz Homestead, Worcester, PA, March 1981.

Coble, Frances J., Lieutenant Colonel (40)
1. Department of the Army, Office of the Surgeon General, Washington, DC.
2. Gilbert H. Coble, brother, supplied documents, papers and information on her military record to Miriam Cokel, Punxsutawney, PA, 1982.

Coppin, Fanny Marion Jackson (106)
1. *Historical Negro Biographies*, International Library of Negro Life and History, (New York: Wilhelmina S. Robinson, Publisher's Company, Inc., 1967)
2. Edward T. James, ed. et al., *Notable American Women, 1607-1950* (Cambridge, MA: The Belknap Press of Harvard University Press, 1971)

Corbin, Margaret Cochran (35)
1. Edward Hagman Hall, *Margaret Corbin, Heroine of the Battle of Fort Washington, 16 November 1776* (New York: American Scenic and Historic Preservation Society, 1932)
2. Edward T. James, ed. et al., *Notable American Women, 1607-1950* (Cambridge, MA: The Belknap Press of Harvard University Press, 1971)
3. Sara Rohr, "Margaret Cochran Corbin, Revolutionary Heroine," *Papers Read Before The Society,* vol. 15 (Chambersburg, PA: Kittochtinny Historical Society, 1970) pp. 28-31.

Coxe, Sophia Georgiana Fisher (75)
1. *The Standard Sentinal,* Hazleton, PA, December 3 and December 5, 1955.

Craig, Margaret Maze (134)
1. *The News-Herald,* Franklin, PA, December 7, 1964.
2. *Notable Women of Venango County,* Alpha Tau Chapter, Delta Kappa Gamma, Oil City, PA, 1979, p. 7.
3. *Seventeen-at-school,* May 1962, p. 6.
4. Resource materials of Roy Craig, husband, and Anabel Samonsky, Oil City, PA.

Darlington, Isabel (54)
1. Clipping files of the Chester County Historical Society, West Chester, PA.
2. *Philadelphia Record,* Philadelphia, PA, January 19, 1941.
3. *Evening Bulletin,* Philadelphia, PA, January 16, 1941.

de Schweinitz, Dorothea (31)
1. *The Globe-Times,* Bethlehem, PA, May 11, 1937.
2. Dorothea de Schweinitz, *A Summary History of the Schweinitz Family, 1350 to 1975* (Washington, DC, 1974)
3. Central Moravian Church Office, Bethlehem, PA.

Dickinson, Anna Elizabeth (71)
1. Joseph Bausman, *History of Beaver County,* 1904, p. 723.
2. *Famous Women of Pennsylvania,* 1899.
3. Stanley J. Kunitz and Howard Haycraft, eds., *American Authors, 1600-1900, Biographical Dictionary,* pp. 475, 476.
4. James R. Warren, letter in *News Tribune,* Beaver Falls, PA, July 28, 1976.

Dock, Mira Lloyd (77)
1. Paul B. Beers, *Profiles from the Susquehanna Valley* (Harrisburg, PA: Stackpole Books, 1973) p. 119.
2. Marcella Thorp Emerick, *Hi-Notes—A Century of Music with the Wednesday Club of Harrisburg, Pennsylvania,* 1981, pp. 2-63.
3. William H. Wilson, "More Almost Than the Men: Mira Lloyd Dock and the Beautification of Harrisburg," *The Pennsylvania Magazine of History and Biography,* October 1975, pp. 490-499.
4. Louise Walker, personal recollections, interview by Ann Corby, Harrisburg, PA, 1982.
5. Dock Family Papers, MG 43, Box 3, William Penn Archives, Harrisburg, PA.

Dolson, Hildegarde (132)
1. Hildegarde Dolson, *We Shook the Family Tree* (New York: Random House, 1946) pp. 28, 49, 147.
2. *The News-Herald*, Franklin and Oil City, PA, January 16, 1981.

Downs, Ruth Sprague (112)
1. *The Main Line Times*, Philadelphia, July 1956.
2. Articles and interview material in possession of Lois Kalp, Lewisburg, PA.

Drexel, Mother Mary Katharine (91)
1. Sister Consuela Marie Duffy, S.B.S., *Katharine Drexel, A Biography* (Cornwells Heights, PA: Sisters of the Blessed Sacrament, 1966)
2. *Mother Katharine Drexel* (Cornwells Heights, PA: Mother Katharine Dre xel Guild)
3. Bishop Joseph McShea, homily delivered at the Mass of Prayers for the Beatification of Mother Katharine Drexel, Cathedral of SS. Peter and Paul, Philadelphia, March 7, 1982.

Engle, Eleanora "Nelle" Moyer (80)
1. Personal knowledge of the subject by the writers Miriam Vanderwall and Jean Bomgardner Ginrich, Hershey, PA.
2. Article in possession of Miriam Vanderwall, dated November 1963.

Ferree, Mary Warenbauer (2)
1. *Note:* There is considerable confusion about her name. It is generally agreed it was Mary Warenbauer Ferree, but in the records one finds Fierre, Fiere, Feree, and Ferree; her maiden name as Weimar, Warenbier, and Warenbur; her first name as Maria, Marie, and Mary.
2. Marion Wallace Reninger, *Famous Women of Lancaster County Pennsylvania* (Lancaster, PA: Lancaster County Historical Society) pp. 146, 147.
3. Gertrude B. Biddle and Sarah D. Lowrie, eds., *Notable Women of Pennsylvania* (Philadelphia: University of Pennsylvania Press, 1942) p. 18.
4. John W. W. Loose, "Madam Marie Warenbauer Ferree," *Lancaster County Observes Pennsylvania's Tercentenary* (Lancaster, PA: 300th Anniversary Committee, Lancaster County, 1982) p. 33.

Fink, Marjorie Berlin (152)
1. *The Globe-Times*, Bethlehem, PA, December 10 and 12, 1972, August 22, 1973, March 10, 1975, May 10, 1979, November 27, 1981, June 21, 1982.
2. Marjorie Berlin Fink, interview by Catherine D. Barrett, Bethlehem, PA, March 27, 1982.

Finney, Sarah (22)
1. Susan Brubaker, interview by Carole Simpson, Reading, PA, March 1982.
2. Carole Simpson, "Widow Finney was a 'Gutsy Lady'," *Reading Eagle*, Reading, PA, March 11, 1982. Permission to reprint sections granted by the *Reading Eagle.*

Ford, Ardelle Cleaves (150)
1. *The News-Herald*, Franklin and Oil City, PA, July 28, 1969.

Foulke, Eliza Ambler (81)
1. Eliza Ambler Foulke, taped interview by Deborah O'Connell on deposit at the Montgomery County Federation of Historical Societies, Peter Wentz Homestead, Worcester, PA., 1980.

Frazier, Ella (103)
1. Brochure prepared for the Testimonial Banquet honoring Ella Frazier, September 16, 1955, Harrisburg, PA.

Frazier, Jane Ball (4)
1. Ruby Frazier Frey, *Red Morning* (Terre Haute: Popular Library Edition, 1945)
2. Maryland historical marker erected close to the spot of her kidnapping near Oldtown, MD.
3. Pennsylvania historical marker near Schellsburg, PA noting burial place of William Frazier, first white child born in Bedford County.
4. Pennsylvania historical marker on Greystone Hotel, formerly Frazier's Tavern.
5. Bedford County Courthouse records, *Will Book*, p. 5.

Gallaher, Sarah McCune (110)
1. Materials on file at the Cambria County Historical Society Museum, Ebensburg, PA.

Garrette, Eve (67)
1. Eve Garrette, ed., *The Experts' Cross Word Puzzle Book No. 13* (New York: Doubleday & Company, Inc., 1967)
2. *The Daily News*, Huntingdon, PA, September 16, 1946, November 15, 1949, July 11, 1950, August 24, 1954, January 29, 1969.

Gibbons, Hannah Wierman (69)
1. Marion Wallace Reninger, *Famous Women of Lancaster County Pennsylvania* (Lancaster, PA: Lancaster County Historical Society, 1961–64) p. 30.
2. *Journal* (Lancaster, PA: Lancaster County Historical Society) vol. 15, p. 115.

Gilbert, Gabriella Cameron (78)
1. Robert C. Glenn, *1917-1967, Fifty Years of Red Cross in Harrisburg.*
2. Minutes of the Harrisburg Red Cross Chapter annual meetings.
3. Richard H. Steinmetz and Robert D. Hoffsommer, *This Was Harrisburg* (Harrisburg, PA: Stackpole Books, 1976)

Gilmore, Dorothea McClure, M.D. (51)
1. *Detroit Free Press*, Detroit, MI, August 18, 1961.
2. *The Progress*, Clearfield, PA, May 13, 1969, May 19, 1976, April 30, 1980.
3. Dorothea McClure Gilmore, interview by E. Jane Kinkead, Clearfield, PA, October 14, 1982.

Gordon, Sophie Reiter (160)
1. *The Jeffersonian Democrat*, Brookville, PA, October 18, 1979.
2. Agnes Means, friend, personal communication, "Christmas, 1975", newsletter on file at Rebecca M. Arthurs Memorial Library, Brookville, PA.
3. *Who's Who of American Women*, 8th ed. (Chicago: A. N. Marquis Company, Inc., 1974) p. 352.

4. Clyde Shaffer, nephew, personal communication letter on file at Rebecca M. Arthurs Memorial Library, Brookville, PA.
5. Margaret Johnson, family friend, interview, Brookville, PA, May 29, 1980.

Granahan, Kathryn O'Hay (15)

1. June Nordahl, "When You Pass the Buck It Will Bear the Name: Kathryn O'Hay Granahan," *The Express,* Easton, PA, September 28, 1962.
2. "Mrs. Granahan, 82, Was U.S. Treasurer," *The Express,* Easton, PA, July 2, 1979.
3. "Mrs. Granahan, Treasurer of United States, To Be Honored at Annual EHS Day," *The Express,* Easton, PA, March 9, 1963.
4. Katherine Dunlap, "City '1st': Woman In Congress," *Inquirer,* Philadelphia, November 9, 1956.
5. "Rep. Kathryn Granahan, Native of Easton, Is Named Treasurer of U.S.," *The Express,* Easton, PA, September 29, 1962.
6. *Who's Who in American Politics,* 2nd ed. 1969–1970 (New York: R. R. Bowker Co., 1969)

Gratz, Rebecca (72)

1. Gertrude B. Biddle and Sarah D. Lowrie, eds., *Notable Women of Pennsylvania* (Philadelphia: University of Pennsylvania Press, 1942).
2. Allen Johnson and Dumas Malone, eds., *Dictionary of American Biography* (New York: Charles Scribner's Sons, 1931) vol. 7, pp. 505, 506.
3. *Encyclopedia Americana* (New York: Americana Corporation, 1956 ed.) vol. 13, p. 162.
4. Joseph Franklin Ambrose Jackson, *Literary Landmarks of Philadelphia* (Philadelphia: David McKay Company, 1939) pp. 151–153.
5. Tina Levitan, *The Firsts of American Jewish History* (Brooklyn: The Charuth Press, 1952 and 1957) pp. 77–80.
6. *National Cyclopedia of American Biography* (New York: James T. White and Company, 1900) vol. 10, p. 130.
7. Edward T. James, ed. et al., *Notable American Women 1607–1950,* A Biographical Dictionary (Cambridge, PA: The Belknap Press of Harvard University Press, 1971), vol. 2, pp. 75, 76.
8. *Women's Historical Philadelphia, A Walking Tour* (Philadelphia, PA: The Philadelphia Area Cultural Consortium, 1982)

Greenwood, Grace (61)

1. *The New York Times,* April 21, 1904.
2. *The News Tribune,* Beaver Falls, PA, August 1967.
3. Grace Greenwood, *Haps and Mishaps of a Tour in Europe* (Boston: Ticknor, Reed and Fields, 1854) pp. 1, 37–39, 47–49, 435.
4. John G. Whittier, "The Barefoot Boy," *The Little Pilgrim,* vol. 2, no. 1, January 1855.
5. Grace Greenwood, *Record Of Five Years* (Boston: Ticknor and Fields, 1867)
6. Grace Greenwood, *New Life In New Lands* (Cambridge: Welsh, Bigelow and Co., 1872)
7. Grace Greenwood, *Life Of Queen Victoria* (New York: John R. Andrews and Henry Allen, 1883)

8. Grace Greenwood, *History Of My Pets* (Boston: Ticknor, Reed and Fields, 1851)
9. Grace Greenwood, *Greenwood Leaves* (Boston: Ticknor, Reed and Fields, 1851) p. 362.
10. Joseph B. Lyman, "Grace Greenwood–Mrs. Lippincott," *Eminent Women Of The Age* (Hartford: S. M. Betts and Co., 1869) p. 147.
11. Joseph H. Bausman, *History Of Beaver County* (New York: Knickerbocker Press, 1904) vol. 2, p. 723.
12. A. Warner, *History Of Beaver County* (Warner and Co., 1888, reproduced by Unigraphic, Evansville, IN)
13. *Pennsylvania Women*, 1899.

Groth, Geneva E., D.D.S. (50)
1. Geneva E. Groth and Alma Groth, taped interview by Margrett Beckett on deposit at the Montgomery County Federation of Historical Societies, Peter Wentz Homestead, Worcester, PA, 1980.

Hale, Sarah Josepha Buell (60)
1. Gertrude B. Biddle and Sarah D. Lowrie, eds., *Notable Women of Pennsylvania* (Philadelphia: University of Pennsylvania Press, 1942)
2. Edward T. James, ed. et al., *Notable American Women, 1607-1950* (Cambridge, MA: The Belknap Press of Harvard University Press, 1971)
3. *Women's Historical Philadelphia, A Walking Tour* (Philadelphia: Philadelphia Area Cultural Consortium, 1982)

Harbison, Massa White (5)
1. Hale Sipe, *History of Butler County, PA* (Historical Publishing Co.) pp. 181, 182, 185, 186, 188, 191, 192, 195.
2. Gertrude B. Biddle and Sarah D. Lowrie, eds., *Notable Women of Pennsylvania* (Philadelphia: University of Pennsylvania Press, 1942) pp. 98–99.
3. "Journey of Massie Harbison in 1792," privately published account of M. Harbison's capture and escape. On file at the Western Pennsylvania Historical Society, Pittsburgh.
4. "Pittsburgh Women," (Pittsburgh: Western Pennsylvania Historical Society, 1976).
5. Carol Jo Lee, *Merry Old Middlesex* (privately published by Carol Lee, 1976) pp. 24, 43.

Hare, Mollie Woods (113)
1. Mary Dock, associate at The Woods School, interview by Jean Green, Langhorne, PA.
2. "Mollie Woods Hare" pamphlet from The Woods School.

Harris, Mary Belle, Ph.D. (98)
1. *American Women* (Los Angeles: American Publications, Inc., 1939) vol. 3.
2. Edward T. James, ed. et al., *Notable American Women* (Cambridge, MA: The Belknap Press of Harvard University Press, 1971)
3. Charles M. Snyder, *Union County, Pennsylvania; A Bicentennial History*, Lewisburg, PA, 1976.
4. File on Mary Belle Harris at the Bucknell University Archives, Lewisburg, PA.

5. *The New York Times Book Review*, March 1, 1936.
6. *The Trenton News*, Trenton, NJ, July 31, 1941.

Harrison, Mary Scott Lord Dimmick (10)
1. The Wayne County Historical Society, Honesdale, PA.
2. *United States Encyclopedia of History* (Philadelphia: Curtis Books, 1970) vol. 9, p. 1548.
3. *The Presidents and Their Wives From George Washington to James Earl Carter, Jr.* (The National Souvenir Center, Inc., 1975) p. 32.
4. Conrad F. Weitzel, reference librarian, Ohio State Museum, Columbus, Ohio, letter to Nellie Kimble, November 25, 1960. Copy on file in the Honesdale Public Library.
5. *The Wayne Independent*, Honesdale, PA, January 8, 1948.

Hartley, Lois Teal, Ph.D. (120)
1. Lois Teal Hartley, personal correspondence to Ina Price Vance on file in Waynesburg College Library.
2. Ball State University, Monograph Number One (Muncie, IN, 1963)
3. Testimonies of friends and Professor Carol Green, Dean at Boston College and co-editor of the *Dictionary of Notable American Women* from Schlesinger Library, on file at Waynesburg College Library.
4. "Vita" and "Bibliography" by Lois Teal Hartley on file at Boston College.
5. Professor Alfred H. Marks, taped interview, State University of New York, New Platz, NY.

Harvey, Maria A. (24)
1. *The Women's Centennial Paper*, August 26 and 27, 1896, p. 15. On file in the Eva K. Bowlby Library, Waynesburg, PA.

Hayes, Nelle Sweeney (27)
1. Mrs. Edward Hayes, step-daughter-in-law, interview by Gretchen Hiller, Houtzdale, PA, 1982.
2. *Houtzdale Citizen*, Houtzdale, PA, June 1953.
3. *100 Years in Brisbin, Houtzdale and Woodward Township* (Clearfield, PA: Clearfield County Historical Society, 1976)
4. Mr. Raymond Hayes, step-grandson, reared by Nelle Hayes, interview by Gretchen Hiller, Houtzdale, PA, August 1982.

Helman, Frances Strong (83)
1. William Delahan, "Cultivating a Family Tree," *The Pittsburgh Press*, Pittsburgh, PA, May 2, 1965.
2. Jean Helman Newton, daughter, telephone interview, Falls Church, VA, October 1, 1982.
3. Clarence Stephenson, "F. S. Helman", *Indiana County Heritage*, Fall/Winter 1982, pp. 1–3.
4. Frances Strong Helman, "The Helman News," on file in the Historical and Genealogical Society of Indiana County, Indiana, PA.
5. Frances Strong Helman, *Your Family Tree*, 1948–1968, on file in the Historical and Genealogical Society of Indiana County, Indiana, PA.

6. The minutes and charter of the Historical and Genealogical Society of Indiana County and periodicals and pamphlets on file in the Society's library, Indiana, PA.

Henry, Ann Wood (8)
1. Marion Wallace Reninger, *Famous Women of Lancaster County Pennsylvania* (Lancaster, PA: Lancaster County Historical Society) p. 23.
2. Gertrude B. Biddle and Sarah D. Lowrie, eds., *Notable Women of Pennsylvania* (Philadelphia: University of Pennsylvania Press, 1942) p. 42.

Hicks-Bruun, Mildred M., Ph.D. (161)
1. Mildred Hicks-Bruun, personal correspondence with JoAnn Harak and Margaret Druse on file in the Easton Area Public Library, Easton, PA.
2. *Who's Who of American Women*, 12th ed. (Chicago: A. N. Marquis Company, Inc., 1981–82)
3. *American Men and Women of Science*, 14th ed. (New York: Jacques Cattell Press, 1979)

Horting, Ruth Grigg (16)
1. *Who's Who of American Women* (Chicago: A. N. Marquis Company, 1958–1959) p. 607.
2. *Lancaster County Historical Society Journal* (Lancaster, PA: Lancaster Historical Society) vol. 64, p. 53; vol. 83, p. 131.
3. John Ward Willson Loose, *The Heritage of Lancaster* (Woodland Hills, CA: Windsor Publications, 1978) p. 165.
4. *Intelligencer Journal*, Lancaster, PA. References beginning in 1937 and continuing to March 6, 1982; June 28, 1966, May 22, 1954.
5. *New Era*, Lancaster, PA. References beginning in 1937; February 17, 1959, March 16, 1967.
6. Ruth Grigg Horting, interview by Frances K. Keller, Lancaster, PA, January 22, 1982.

Hottel, Althea Kratz, Ph.D. (117)
1. Althea Kratz Hottell, taped interview by Marilyn Solvay, on deposit at the Montgomery County Federation of Historical Societies, Peter Wentz Homestead, Worcester, PA.

Hutton, Ann Hawkes (85)
1. Ann Hawkes Hutton, personal interview by Mildred O. Ridolph, June 2, 1982.
2. *Who's Who In America*, 42nd ed. (Chicago: A. N. Marquis Company, 1982) vol. 1, p. 1623.
3. Program of the Forty-Fourth Friendship Fete at the Bellevue–Stratford Hotel, Philadelphia, April 3, 1982.
4. Program of the Thirteenth Annual National Scholarship Awards Ceremony, Washington Crossing Foundation, 1982.

Johnson, Eleanor Murdoch (66)
1. Eleanor M. Johnson, interview by Betty K. Hooker, Gaithersburg, MD, May 29, 1982. Tape on deposit at the Historical Society of York County, York, PA.

2. Biographical sheet prepared by Eleanor M. Johnson.
3. *Who's Who in American Education,* First Volume 1967–68 (Hattiesburg, MS: Who's Who in American Education, Inc.)

Johnston, Harriet Lane (9)
1. Philip Auchampaugh, "James Buchanan, Squire in the White House," *The Pennsylvania Magazine Of History And Biography,* vol. 58, 1934, pp. 270–285.
2. James Buchanan, *The Works of James Buchanan,* ed. John Bassett Moore (Philadelphia: J. B. Lippincott Co., 1908)
3. George Ticknor Curtis, *Life of James Buchanan* (New York: Harper and Brothers, 1883)
4. Edward T. James, ed. et al., *Notable American Women, 1607-1950* (Cambridge, MA: The Belknap Press of Harvard University Press, 1971)
5. Homer T. Rosenberger, "The Education and Training of Harriet Lane, a Franklin County Girl Who Became an International Figure," *Papers Read Before The Society, 1963-1970* (Chambersburg, PA: Kittochtinny Historical Society, 1970) vol. 15, pp. 259–325.
6. Mary Virginia Shelley and Sandra Harrison Munro, *Harriet Lane* (Lititz: Sutter House, 1980) pp. 3, 47, 48.
7. Marion Wallace Reninger, *Famous Women Of Lancaster County Pennsylvania* (Lancaster, PA: Lancaster County Historical Society) pp. 31, 33, 35.
8. Gertrude B. Biddle and Sarah D. Lowrie, eds., *Notable Women Of Pennsylvania* (Philadelphia: University of Pennsylvania Press, 1942) pp. 184, 185.
9. Philip S. Klein, *President James Buchanan* (University Park: Penn State University Press, 1962) p. 246.
10. Amy LaFollette Jensen, *The White House And Its Thirty-Two Families* (New York: McGraw-Hill Book Co., Inc., 1958) p. 79.

Jones, Ida (142)
1. *Coatesville Record,* Coatesville, PA, February 12, 1954, September 23, 1958.
2. *Daily Local News,* West Chester, PA, October 31, 1890, February 2, 1959.
3. Clipping files of the Chester County Historical Society, West Chester, PA.

Kelly, Grace (158)
1. *International Who's Who* (Detroit: Gale Research Books, 1980–1981) p. 466.
2. Charles Moritz, ed., *Current Biography* (New York: H. W. Winston, 1977) pp. 172–174.
3. *Newsweek,* September 2, 1982, p. 36.
4. Russel F. Weigley, ed., *Philadelphia: 300 Year History* (New York: Norton, 1982) pp. 592, 621, 697, 698, 750.
5. *Who's Who in America,* 42nd ed. (Chicago: A. N. Marquis Company, 1982–83) p. 1274.

Kerr, Jean Collins (137)
1. Jack Taver, UPI Drama Editor, *The Scranton Tribune,* Scranton, PA, December 3, 1964.
2. *Who's Who of American Women,* 12th ed. (Chicago: A. N. Marquis Company, 1981–82) p. 222.

3. John Crosby, "Jean Kerr's Book is Included on Crosby's Yuletide Gift List," *The Scranton Times*, Scranton, PA, November 15, 1957.
4. *The Scranton Tribune*, October 24, 1964, August 18, 1972.
5. Géné Brislin, *The Scranton Tribune*, May 31, 1955.
6. Lena Marniero, ed., *American Women Writers* (New York: Frederick Unger Publishing Co., 1980) vol. 2, p. 449.

Kessler, Lena Jane (82)
1. *Courier Express*, DuBois, PA, June 1, 1981.
2. Lena Kessler, interview AAUW PA Women in History Committee, DuBois, PA, January 7, 1982.
3. "The G.F.W.C. Free Enterprise Program/1981, G.F.W.C. Distinguished Volunteer Awards Program," DuBois Women's Club, February 6, 1981, p. 2.
4. *Courier Express*, DuBois, PA, November 24, 1980.

Krause, Alvina (151)
1. William H. Wegner, "Alvina Krause Revisited," *Educational Theatre Journal*, May 1977, pp. 221, 222, 229.

Letort, Ann (21)
1. Evelyn A. Benson, *The Letort Family: First Christian Family on the Conestoga* (Carlisle, PA: Huguenot Publishing Co., 1961)
2. *Journal* (Lancaster, PA: Lancaster County Historical Society) vols. 9, 12, 19 20, 37, 57, 64.

Lewis, Elizabeth Fair, M.D. (49)
1. Margaret Boles, ed., *The History of Punxsutawney*, 1949.
2. Alice Lewis, sister, personal article, March 1975, on file with Punxsutawney Branch AAUW records.

Lipovsky, Elizabeth Slafkosky (84)
1. *Men of Bethlehem* (Bethlehem: F. L. Shankweiler, Publisher, 1918) p. 106.
2. Elizabeth Lipovsky, "Nine Blessed Decades," *1982 Good Shepherd*, Dobry Pastier, ed. (Slovak Catholic Federation)
3. *Fraternally Yours*, First Catholic Slovak Ladies Association, vol. 67, no. 8, May 1982, p. 2.
4. Elizabeth Lipovsky, interview by Catherine D. Barrett, Bethlehem, PA; May 19 and July 1, 1982.

Lloyd, Elizabeth (108)
1. Gertrude B. Biddle and Sarah D. Lowrie, eds., *Notable Women of Pennsylvania* (Philadelphia: University of Pennsylvania Press, 1942) pp. 236, 237.
2. Dr. Arthur Bye, *Bucks County Tales 1685-1931* (Cornell Press, 1970) pp. 165, 166.
3. B. F. Fackenthal, Jr., *A Collection of Papers read before the Bucks County Historical Society* (Press of the Chemical Publishing Co., 1908) vol. 1, pp. 142, 143.

Longshore, Hannah E. Myers, M.D. (43)
1. Lucretia L. Blankenburg, *The Blankenburgs of Philadelphia* (Philadelphia: John C. Winston Company, 1928)

2. Edward T. James, ed. et. al., *Notable American Women, 1607-1950* (Cambridge, MA: The Belknap Press of Harvard University Press, 1971)
3. *Who Was Who in America* (Chicago: A. N. Marquis Company, 1942) vol. 1, pp. 386–388.

Lukens, Rebecca Pennock (25)
1. Clara Huston Miller, *Reminiscences: The Lukens Family,* a private publication in Eleutherian Mills Historical Library, Wilmington, DE, p. 31.
2. Madeline B. Stern, *We, the Women: Career Firsts of Nineteenth Century America* (New York: Schulte Publishing Co., 1963) pp. 236–248.
3. Robert Wilson Wolcott, *A Woman in Steel,* A Newcomen Address, December 12, 1940, The Newcomen Society of England, American Branch, New York, 1948.
4. Gertrude B. Biddle and Sarah D. Lowrie, eds., *Notable Women of Pennsylvania* (Philadelphia: University of Pennsylvania Press, 1942) p. 123.
5. *Rebecca Lukens: Woman of Steel* (Cassette tape), American History Cassettes, Hollywood, CA.
6. J. Smith Futhey and Gilbert Cope, *History of Chester County Pennsylvania* (Philadelphia, 1881)
7. Lukens Iron & Steel Co. Ledgers, Ledger No. 68 February 1825–April 1828.
8. *Remarkable American Women Who Influenced Our Lives* (Film strip and kit), Eye Gate House, Jamaica, NY, 1977.
9. Clipping files of the Chester County Historical Society, West Chester, PA.

Lyles, Victoria M., Ph.D. (115)
1. Personal recollections of subject by her friend, Dorothy Baker, York, PA.

Magalhaes, Hulda, Ph.D. (164)
1. Department of Public Relations, Bucknell University, Lewisburg, PA.
2. Marsha Scott Gori, "Mixing the Flavor and the Authority: A Visit With Hulda Magalhaes," *Bucknell World,* vol. 10, no. 5, May/June 1982, pp. 10, 11.

Marbourg, Esther, M.D. (45)
1. Margaret Truman, *Women of Courage* (New York: Wm. Morrow & Co., Inc., 1976) p. 130.
2. *Biographical and Portrait Cyclopedia of Cambria County, Pennsylvania* (Philadelphia: The Union Publishing Co., 1869) pp. 141, 142.

Marsh, Mary Montgomery, M.D. (47)
1. Dr. William E. Marsh, son, interview by Susan Steinbrenner. Record on file with Greensburg Area Branch.
2. Sara Ruth, interview. Record on file with Greensburg Area Branch.
3. *A Town That Grew at the Crossroad—Borough of Mt. Pleasant, Pennsylvania, 1978*—The Sesquicentenial Edition (Laurel Group Press, 1978) pp. 82–84.
4. "Cornerstone of New Hospital Laid," *Mt. Pleasant Journal,* Mt. Pleasant, PA, September 11, 1964.
5. Jean Marsh Brownfield, daughter, interview. Record on file with Greensburg Area Branch.
6. Information from the Hospital Aid Society, Fricke Hospital, Greensburg.

Marshall, Elizabeth Nath (19)
1. Elizabeth N. Marshall, interview by Joan R. Schumacher, York, PA, September 20, 1982.

Martin, Helen Reimensnyder (122)
1. Gertrude B. Biddle and Sarah D. Lowrie, eds., *Notable Women of Pennsylvania* (Philadelphia: University of Pennsylvania Press, 1942) pp. 289, 290.
2. Beverly Seaton, "Helen Reimensnyder Martin's 'Caricatures' of the Pennsylvania Germans," *Pennsylvania Magazine of History and Biography,* vol. 104, January 1980, pp. 86–95.

Mayer, Mary Hunter (111)
1. Carole Simpson, "Miss Mayer was a Marvel," *Reading Eagle,* Reading, PA, May 10, 1946. Portions reproduced with the permission of the *Reading Eagle.*
2. Mable K. McClellan, *From Academy to Castle,* pp. 24, 41, 74, 75, 93, 98.
3. Daniel K. Hoch, *Historical Review,* March 1955, vol. 20, no. 2.

McGinnis, Ruth (156)
1. Keith Sutton, *Wayne County Sports History (1871-1972)* (Honesdale, PA: *Wayne Independent*) pp. 17–18.
2. *The Wayne Independent,* Honesdale, PA.

McLaughry, Elizabeth, M.D. (46)
1. Elizabeth McLaughry, M.D., *Letters to my Nieces and Nephews Written as Pleasant Memories,* 1935, 1961, 1962, unedited, unpublished, pp. 5–24.
2. Alma D. Morani, M.D. "Elizabeth McLaughry, M.D.," *Medical Women's Journal,* January 1946.
3. Elizabeth Veach, M.D., "Dr. Elizabeth McLaughry–Her Philosophy of Psychotherapy," read before the Lawrence County Medical Society, May 1953, and subsequently printed in their *Bulletin,* pp. 2–5.
4. Elizabeth Veach, M.D., interview by Mary Beth McLaughry, Lawrence County, PA, 1982.

Mead, Margaret, Ph.D. (162)
1. *Collier's Encyclopedia* (New York: Macmillan Educational Corp.) vol. 15.
2. Margaret Mead, *Blackberry Winter: Earlier Years* (New York: William Morrow & Co., Inc., 1972)
3. Margaret Mead, *Twentieth Century Faith* (New York: Harper & Row, 1972)
4. Margaret Mead and Martha Wolfenstein, eds., *Childhood in Contemporary Culture* (Chicago: University of Chicago Press, 1955)
5. Personal recollections of Anna E. Shaddinger who attended Doylestown High School 1917–1921, graduating with Margaret Mead's brother, Richard Ramsey Mead.

Miller, Emma Guffey (12)
1. Paul B. Beers, *Pennsylvania Politics Today and Yesterday* (University Park: Pennsylvania State University Press, 1980) pp. 147–149.
2. Materials on file at the Slippery Rock State College Archives, Maltby Library, Slippery Rock, PA.

Miller, Frieda Segelke (29)

1. Barbara Sicherman and Carol Hurd Green, eds., *Notable American Women, The Modern Period* (Cambridge, MA: Harvard University Press, 1980) pp. 478, 479.
2. *Current Biography, 1945* (New York: H. W. Wilson, 1945) p. 405.
3. *Survey Midmonthly,* vol. 79:5, May 1943, p. 154.
4. *The Express,* Easton, PA, October 15 and 17, 1956; July 23, 1973.
5. "Who Was Who," *The New York Times,* July 22, 1973.

Miller, "Grandy" (68)

1. Charles Rhoads Roberts, et. al., *History of Lehigh County, Pennsylvania* (Allentown: Lehigh Valley Publishing Co., Ltd., 1914) vol. 1, p. 660.

Miller, Margaret Kerr Bell (105)

1. Dr. William Howard Dusenberry, *Waynesburg College Story, 1848-1974* (Kent State University Press, 1975) pp. 23-103.
2. "Woman's Centennial Paper," Waynesburg, PA, vol. 1, no. 1, August 26-27, 1896, p. 1.
3. Samuel P. Bates, *History of Greene County, Pennsylvania* (Nelson Publishing Company, 1888) pp. 331-334.
4. L. K. Evans, "History of Greene County, Pennsylvania", *Waynesburg Republican,* Waynesburg, PA, April 3, 1941.
5. Anna Meighen, "Margaret Bell Miller, First Dean of Women," 1940. Pamphlet available from Anna Meighen, Wayneburg, PA.

Mitchell, Ruth Crawford (116)

1. *The Pittsburgh Press,* Pittsburgh, PA, November 20, 1966, June 25, 1978.
2. *Pitt,* University of Pittsburgh, Pittsburgh, PA, February 1981.
3. *Post-Gazette,* Pittsburgh, PA, March 2, 1951.
4. *Carnegie Magazine,* June 1975, pp. 253-254.
5. *A Birthday Salute to Ruth Crawford Mitchell,* June 2, 1980, University of Pittsburgh.

Moore, Ruth Nulton (136)

1. Frances Carol Locher, ed., *Contemporary Authors* (Detroit: Gale Research Co., 1979)
2. Ruth Nulton Moore, oral interview by Suzanne Gallagher, tape no. 1, Easton, PA., August 18, 1982.
3. "Ruth Nulton Moore," *Lehigh Valley Monthly,* August 1977, p. 38.

Morgan, Elizabeth "Mammy" Bell (53)

1. *Easton Daily Argus,* "The Story of Mammy Morgan," October 30, 1906, p. 74, 75, from *The Book Shelf Scrap Book of Easton and Northampton County,* Easton Area Public Library.
2. *The Express,* Easton, PA. Article by Eileen Kenna; interview with Ethel Hineline Helms, a descendant of Mammy Morgan, August 2, 1981.
3. *Genealogy of Edelman and Allied Families of Northampton County,* compiled by Forest Edelman. Philadelphia, PA, 1936.
4. *Northampton County Historical Society Guidebook,* pp. 16, 17.

5. Michael C. Schrader, "Bench & Bar," *Two Hundred Years of Life in North-ampton County, Pennsylvania, A Bicentennial Review,* Northampton County Bicentennial Commission, vol. 5, 1976.

Mott, Lucretia Coffin (70)
1. Gertrude B. Biddle and Sarah D. Lowrie, eds., *Notable Women of Pennsylvania* (Philadelphia: University of Pennsylvania Press, Philadelphia, 1942)
2. Edward T. James, ed. et al., *Notable American Women, 1607-1950* (Cambridge, MA: The Belknap Press of Harvard University Press, 1971)
3. *Women's Historical Philadelphia, A Walking Tour* (Philadelphia Area Cultural Consortium, 1982)

Mountz, Ella J. (26)
1. Bernice Lindgren, niece, interview by Gretchen Hiller, Smithmill, PA, 1982.
2. *The Daily Journal,* Philipsburg, PA, March 14, 1924.
3. *The Houtzdale Citizen Standard,* Houtzdale, PA, political advertisement, not dated.
4. Dedication Program of Mountz Memorial Community Park, September 6, 1971.
5. Miss Eleanor Close, childhood friend of daughter Viola, interview, Ginter, PA.
6. Mrs. Andrew Close, teacher in Guelich Township when Ella was on the school board and whose husband, a carpenter, worked on the Mountz's home and store, interview, Smithmill, PA.
7. Miss Mary Korman, teacher in Guelich Township when Ella was on the school board, interview, Smithmill, PA.
8. Mr. Robert Williams, coal operator, interview, Ramey, PA.

Muth, Laura Reider (79)
1. Personal knowledge of her by the writer, Miriam Vanderwall.
2. James V. Bowman, "Laura Reider Muth, '92, What of the *Next* Century?" *The Review,* Lebanon Valley College, vol. 6, no. 2, March 1972.
3. Ann K. Monteith, "'Visionary' to Mark 100th Milestone," *Sunday Patriot-News,* Harrisburg, PA, March 19, 1972.
4. Obituary, *Harrisburg Evening News,* Harrisburg, PA, February 18, 1977.

Myers, Caroline Clark (65)
1. *Who's Who of American Women,* 1970-1971 and 1979-1980 (Chicago: Marquis Who's Who, Inc.)
2. *The Wayne Independent,* Honesdale, PA, February 17, 1976.

Nesbit, Evelyn (149)
1. Larry G. McKee, "Evelyn Nesbit: The Gibson Girl Ghost," *Pennsylvania Illustrated,* February 1978, p. 47.
2. John B. Gibson, "Evelyn Nesbit Left Tarentum to Find Fame," *Valley News Dispatch,* July 1, 1981.
3. Michael Mooney, *Evelyn Nesbit and Stanford White: Love and Death in the Gilded Age* (New York: William Morrow and Company, Inc., 1976)
4. Cleveland Amory, *Who Killed Society?* (New York: Harper and Brothers, Publishers, 1960) pp. 366, 367.

5. Richard M. Ketchum, "Faces from the Past-XXIII," *American Heritage*, June 1969, p. 65.
6. "Lovely Girl, Lurid Crime," *Life*, September 12, 1955, pp. 70–76.

Nevin, Blanche (138)
1. James G. Wilson, ed., *Appleton's Cyclopedia of American Biography* (D. Appleton and Co., 1888–1889) p. 500.
2. *Intelligencer Journal*, Lancaster, PA, October 22, 1982.
3. Gertrude B. Biddle and Sarah D. Lowrie, eds., *Notable Women of Pennsylvania* (Philadelphia: University of Pennsylvania Press, 1942) pp. 209, 210.

Newton, Ruth Eleanor (143)
1. *The Times-News*, Erie, PA, June 13, 1969, July 18, 1969 and May 22, 1980.

Oberholtzer, Sara Louisa (76)
1. Clipping files of the Chester County Historical Society, West Chester, PA.
2. *Daily Local News*, West Chester, PA, February 17, 1889 and February 12, 1911.
3. Gertrude B. Biddle and Sarah D. Lowrie, eds., *Notable Women of Pennsylvania* (Philadelphia: University of Pennsylvania Press, 1942) p. 210.
4. Charles Francis Jenkins, *Quaker Poems: A Collection of Verse Relating to the Society of Friends* (Philadelphia: J. C. Winston, 1893).

Olewiler, Kathryn Fourhman (20)
1. Kathryn Fourhman Olewiler, interview by Joan Schumacher, York, PA, September 9, 1982.

Palladino, Madaline, Judge (58)
1. *The Morning Call*, Allentown, PA, October 26, 1981 and September 1, 1982.
2. Judge Madaline Palladino, interview by Margaret G. Smart, October 17, 1982 and February 27, 1983.

Parry, Florence Fisher (64)
1. Personal family records in the possession of Florence Parry Heide, daughter of Florence Parry, of Kenosha, WI.

Passavant, Fredericka Wilhelmina Basse (6)
1. Gertrude Ziegler, president, Zelienople Historical Society, interview by Jane Davis. Interview based on family documents on file with the Zelienople Historical Society.

Penn, Hannah Callowhill (7)
1. William J. Buck, *William Penn in America* (Philadelphia: Special Edition, 1888)
2. Bonamy Dobrie, *William Penn, Quaker and Pioneer*, Folcroft Library Edition (Boston: Houghton Mifflin, 1932)
3. Hildegarde Dolson, *William Penn* (New York: Random House, 1961)
4. Sophie Hutchinson Drinker, *Hannah Penn and the Proprietorship of Pennsylvania* (Philadelphia: International Printing Company, 1958)
5. *Papers of William Penn, Volume One 1644-1679.* (Philadelphia: University of Pennsylvania Press, 1981)
6. Allen Tully, *William Penn's Legacy* (Baltimore: Johns Hopkins University Press, 1977)

7. Paul A. W. Wallace, *The Vision of William Penn*, (Harrisburg, PA: Pennsylvania Historical and Museum Commission, 1965)
8. Harry Emerson Wildes, *William Penn* (New York: Macmillan Publishing Company, Inc., 1974)

Pitcher, Molly (36)
1. Elizabeth Cometti, "McCauley, Mary Ludwig Hays," *Notable American Women, 1607-1950*, Edward T. James, ed., et al. (Cambridge, MA: The Belknap Press of Harvard University Press, 1971) vol. 2, pp. 448, 449.
2. Henry Steele Commager and Richard B. Morris, *The Spirit of 'Seventy-Six: The Story of the American Revolution as Told by the Participants*, (New York: Bobbs-Merrill, 1958) vol. 2, pp. 710, 714, 715.
3. Joseph Plumb Martin, *A Narrative of Some of the Adventures, Dangers and Sufferings of a Revolutionary Soldier, Interspersed with Anecdotes of Incidents that Occurred Within His Own Observation*, 1830. Republished as *Private Yankee Doodle*, George F. Scheer, ed. (Boston: Little, Brown and Co., 1962)
4. Joseph B. Mitchell, *Decisive Battles of the American Revolution* (New York: G. P. Putnam's Sons, 1962) pp. 134–147.
5. Page Smith, *A New Age Now Begins: A People's History of the American Revolution* (New York: McGraw-Hill, 1976) vol. 2, pp. 1097, 1098.

Platt, Lois Irene, M.D. (52)
1. *Bulletin of Goucher College*, Series 3, vol. 39, no. 5, December 1973.
2. *The Derrick*, Oil City, PA, January 3, 1979.

Preston, Anne, M.D. (42)
1. Gertrude B. Biddle and Sarah D. Lowrie, eds., *Notable Women of Pennsylvania* (Philadelphia: University of Pennsylvania Press, 1942) p. 143.
2. Joyce Fullard, "Anne Preston Pioneer of Medical Education and Women's Rights," *Pennsylvania Heritage*, vol. 8, no. 1, Winter 1982, p. 4.
3. Clipping files of the Chester County Historical Society, West Chester, PA.

Preston, Margaret Junkin (121)
1. William J. Heller, *History of Northampton County, Pennsylvania* (Boston: American Historical Society, 1920) vol. 1, pp. 265, 266.
2. Ethan Allen Weaver, *Poets and Poetry of the Forks of the Delaware* (Germantown, PA, 1906) pp. 245, 246, 253.
3. Fred Lewis Pattee, *A History of American Literature* (New York: Silver, Burdett & Co., 1897) p. 410.
4. John Bartlett, *Familiar Quotations* (Boston: Little, Brown & Co., 1938) 11th ed., p. 541.
5. *Encyclopedia Americana* (New York: Americana, 1956) vol. 22, p. 559.
6. Ethan Allen Weaver, *Margaret Junkin Preston, an Easton Lass of Long Ago*, memoir read at the Northampton County, PA, Historical and Genealogical Society, September 20, 1921, pp. 1, 3–6.
7. Allen Johnson and Dumas Malone, eds., *Dictionary of American Biography* (New York: Charles Scribner's Sons, 1935) vol. 15, p. 204.
8. *National Cyclopedia of American Biography* (New York: James T. White Co., 1897) vol. 7, p. 147.

Rapp, Gertrud (89)
1. J. R. Arndt, *George Rapp's Harmony Society 1785-1847* (Philadelphia: University of Pennsylvania Press, 1965)
2. J. H. Bausman, *History of Beaver County*, (New York: Knickerbocker Press, 1904) vol. 2.
3. Publications of the Harmony Society (Ambridge: George Hays, Printer, 1959)

Reed, Sarah Ann (96)
1. S. P. Bates, B. Whitman, N. W. Russell, et al., *History of Erie County* (Warner, Beers, 1884) p. 469.
2. Laura G. Sanford, *History of Erie County, Pennsylvania*, (Philadelphia: J. B. Lippincott Co., 1894) pp. 332–334, 419.
3. John Miller, *A Twentieth Century History of Erie County, Pennsylvania* (Chicago: The Lewis Publishing Co., 1909) vol. 1, pp. 370, 674–679, 771.
4. Records and scrapbooks of the Home for the Friendless on file at the Sarah A. Reed Home, Erie, PA.
5. *Nelson's Biographical Dictionary and Historical Reference Book of Erie County, Pennsylvania* (Erie: S. B. Nelson, 1896) pp. 432, 433.
6. Helen Spencer, historian for the Sarah A. Reed Home, letter on file in Mercyhurst College Archives.
7. Erie County Biography Scrapbook C., Erie Main Library, pp. 167, 167a.
8. League of Women Voters records and papers, Acc. 247, on file at the Mercyhurst College Archives.
9. *The Dispatch*, Erie, PA, November 10, 1936.
10. *The Times News*, Erie, PA, December 3, 1961.

Reibman, Jeanette, Senator (18)
1. Senator Jeanette Reibman, interview by Margaret D. Druse and Ann Peaslee, Easton, PA, 1982.
2. Re-election literature and biographical information, 1978.
3. Biographical sketch of Senator Reibman from her senate office.
4. *Who's Who in American Politics*, 7th edition 1979–1980, (New York: Jacques Cattell Press)
5. Andrew Ratner, "Reibman's vote a Shocker," *The Express*, Easton, PA, January 23, 1982.
6. "Reibman to Run for 5th Pa. Senate Term," *The Express*, Easton, PA, February 5, 1982.
7. "Mrs. Reibman Gets Award As Distinguished Daughter, *The Express*, Easton, PA, September 19, 1968.
8. "Jeanette Reibman-Eastonian Facing An Uphill Struggle Against Green," *Call-Chronicle*, Allentown, PA, April 11, 1976.

Rich, Adena Miller (101)
1. Jane Addams, *The Second Twenty Years of Hull House* (New York: Macmillan Company, 1930) pp. 143, 268, 406.
2. Lucy Miller Davies, niece of Adena Miller Rich, interview by Margaret L. Tenpas, June 20, 1982. Notes on file in Mercyhurst College Archives.
3. "Fifty Years At Hull House," *Newsweek*, May 27, 1940, p. 38.
4. "Former Erie Woman Succeeds Jane Addams at Hull House," *The Times*, Erie, PA, August 16, 1935.

5. "Head Resident," *Survey,* September 1935, p. 272.
6. "In Jane Addams Post: A. M. Rich Elected Head of Noted Hull House," *Literary Digest,* August 24, 1935, p. 18.
7. Obituary, Adena Miller Rich, *The Times,* Erie, PA, March 15, 1967.
8. *Who's Who* (London, 1950) p. 2348.
9. *Who's Who In America* (Chicago: A. N. Marquis Company, 1950–51) p. 2294.
10. Judith Anne Trolander, *Settlement Houses and the Great Depression* (Detroit: Wayne State University Press, 1975)

Rinehart, Mary Roberts (123)
1. Mary Roberts Rinehart, *My Story: A New Edition and Seventeen New Years* (New York: Rinehart & Company, Inc., 1948)
2. Mary Roberts Rinehart, "At Home in Glen Osborne," *Sewickley Herald,* Sewickley, PA, January 14, 1976.
3. Jan Cohn, *Improbable Fictions: A Life of Mary Roberts Rinehart* (Pittsburgh: University of Pittsburgh Press, 1980)
4. *The Pittsburgh Press,* Pittsburgh, PA, April 26, 1959.

Ross, Betsy (23)
1. Gertrude B. Biddle and Sarah D. Lowrie, eds., *Notable Women of Pennsylvania* (Philadelphia: University of Pennsylvania Press, 1942) p. 71.
2. Edward T. James, ed., et al. *Notable American Women, 1607–1950* (Cambridge, MA: The Belknap Press of Harvard University Press, 1971)
3. *Women's Historical Philadelphia, A Walking Tour* (Philadelphia Area Cultural Consortium, 1982)

Rossiter, Laura "Nan" Campbell (102)
1. Erie County Department of Children's Services, Mr. Merritt, director, interview, Erie, PA.
2. Albion Area Lions Club Citizen of the Year Award program, Albion, PA, October 22, 1973.
3. *The Albion News,* Albion, PA, October 24, 1973.
4. *The Daily Times,* Erie, PA, November 7, 1973.
5. Marion Rossiter Grate, daughter, telephone interview.
6. Obituary, *The Daily Times,* Erie, PA, October 18, 1977.

Royall, Anne Newport (59)
1. Edward T. James, ed. et al., *Notable American Women 1607–1950,* (Cambridge, MA: The Belknap Press of Harvard University Press, 1971) pp. 204–205.
2. Allen Johnson and Dumas Malone, eds., *Dictionary of American Biography, (New York: Charles Scribner's Sons, 1933) vol. 16, pp. 204–205.*

Sachs, Mary (28)
1. *Patriot-Evening News,* Harrisburg, PA, March 8, 1982.
2. Hannah Sachs Cantor, oral history, February 24, 1982.
3. Michael Coleman, *The Jews of Harrisburg* (Bates and Co., 1978)
4. Rabbi David L. Silver, oral history, February 16, 1982.
5. Albert Hirsh, oral history, February 16, 1982.
6. Paul B. Beers, *Profiles from the Susquehanna Valley* (Harrisburg: Stackpole Books, 1973) pp. 57, 58.

Schenck, Sarah Kleiger, Ph.D. (165)
1. Sarah Kleiger Schenck, personal interviews, correspondence and telephone conversations with JoAnn Harak and Margaret D. Druse; information on file in the Easton Area Public Library.
2. *Who's Who of American Women*, 3rd ed. (Chicago: A. N. Marquis Company, Inc., 1964–65)

Schluraff, Helen Stone (14)
1. John G. Carney, *High-Lights of Erie Politics* (Erie, PA: self-published, 1960) pp. 63, 64.
2. League of Women Voters, records and papers, Acc. 247, Mercyhurst College Archives.
3. Ft. LeBoeuf Chapter, Daughters of the American Revolution, records and papers, Erie, PA.
4. *The Times News*, Erie, PA, October 16, 1946, December 9, 1964, October 17, 1982.
5. Zonta International of Erie, records and papers.
6. Robert Schluraff, son, correspondence in Mercyhurst College Archives.
7. Jean Caldwell, historian for Business and Professional Women's Club, interview by Sabrina Freeman.
8. Rose Lewis, historian for Zonta International of Erie, telephone interview by Sabrina Freeman.

Schmitt, Gladys (133)
1. Mary O'Hara, "Associates Pay Tribute to Gladys Schmitt," *The Pittsburgh Press*, Pittsburgh, PA, October 4, 1972.
2. Stanley D. Mayer, "Gladys Schmitt," *Carnegie Magazine*, October, 1980, pp. 31–33.
3. Sylvia Sachs, "Friends Recall Gladys Schmitt," Western Pennsylvania Historical Society, Pittsburgh.

Schock, Maya Matsuura (146)
1. *Retrospective Catalogue*, Gallery Doshi, December 1975.
2. Paul B. Beers, *Profiles from the Susquehanna Valley* (Harrisburg: Stackpole Books, 1973) p. 104.

Schofield, Martha (107)
1. Richard Hanser and Donald B. Hyatt, *Meet Mr. Lincoln* (New York: Golden Press, Inc., 1960) p. 79.
2. Gertrude B. Biddle and Sarah D. Lowrie, eds., *Notable Women of Pennsylvania* (Philadelphia: University of Pennsylvania Press, 1942) pp. 199–201.
3. Matilda A. Evans, M.D., *Martha Schofield, Pioneer Negro Educator* (Columbia, South Carolina: DuPre, 1916) pp. 4–7, 13, 15, 18, 51 and 119.
4. Dr. Edward H. Magill, "When Men Were Sold; Reminiscences of the Underground Railroad in Bucks County and Its Managers," B. F. Fackenthal, Jr., *Papers Read Before the Bucks County Historical Society*, Doylestown, PA, 1909, vol. 2, p. 500.
5. Edward T. James, ed. et al., *Notable American Women, 1607–1950* (Cambridge, MA: The Belknap Press of Harvard University Press, 1971) vol. 3, p. 239.

6. Last Will and Testament of Anna Mary Williamson, Register of Wills, #16997, Doylestown, PA.

Scott, Kate M. (38)
1. *The Brookville Republican*, 1911, on file at the Jefferson County Historical and Genealogical Society, Brookville, PA.
2. Brookville Hospital Auxiliary business minutes, September 17, 1931, on file at Brookville Hospital.

Scott, Lizabeth (157)
1. Leslie Hallowell, *The Filmgoer's Companion*, 4th ed. (New York: Hill and Wang, 1974) p. 683.
2. Jim Marshall, *Collier's*, August 18, 1945, pp. 59, 60.
3. John M. Smith and Tim Cawkwell, eds., *The World Encyclopedia of Film* (New York: Galahad Books, 1972) p. 249.
4. Richard Gertner, ed., *1982 International Motion Picture Almanac* (New York: Quigley Publishing Company, 1982) p. 237.
5. Margaret Akerley, former guidance counselor at Central High School, interview by Ethel DeVirgilis, Scranton, PA, 1983.
6. Lizabeth Scott, personal correspondence with Ethel DeVirgilis, 1983.
7. William P. Lewis, executive director, Lackawanna Historical Society, interview by Ethel DeVirgilis, Scranton, PA, March 1983.
8. Maureen Garcia-Pons, "Spotlight Local Achievers for Women's History Week," *The Scrantonian*, Scranton, PA, March 14, 1982.
9. News files of *The Scranton Tribune*, Scranton, PA.
10. *Who's Who In America*, 42nd ed. (Chicago: A. N. Marquis Company, Inc., 1982) p. 2993.

Scott, Ruth (86)
1. *Bulletin*, Audubon Society of Western Pennsylvania, vol. 43, no. 10, June 1979, p. 1, 2.
2. *The Herald*, Sharpsburg, PA, August 21, 1974 and September 22, 1976.

Scranton, Marion Margery Warren (13)
1. William P. Lewis, executive director of Lackawanna Historical Society, interview by Ethel DeVirgilis, Scranton, PA, 1983.
2. Oil painting, second floor, Scranton Historical Society Building.
3. Maureen Garcia-Pons, "Spotlight Local Achievers for Women's History Week," *The Scrantonian*, Scranton, PA, March 14, 1982.

Seibert, Florence Barbara, Ph.D. (159)
1. Edna Yost, *American Women of Science* (Philadelphia: J. B. Lippincott Co., 1955) pp. 178–184.
2. Florence B. Seibert, *Pebbles on the Hill of a Scientist* (St. Petersburg, FL: St. Petersburg Printing Co., 1968) pp. 8–145.
3. Florence Seibert, personal communication on file at Easton Area Public Library, Easton, PA.
4. *Who's Who of American Women*, 4th ed. (Chicago: A. N. Marquis Company, Inc., 1966–67)

Singmaster, Elsie (124)
1. *Pennsylvania German Magazine,* December 1909, p. 633.
2. H. C. Long, "A Select Bibliography," *Pennsylvania German Magazine,* August 1910, pp. 470–476.
3. "Elsie Singmaster," Bookman, February 1931, pp. 621–626.
4. *The Gettysburg Times,* Gettysburg, PA, September 30, 1958.
5. *Gettysburg Seminary Bulletin,* Gettysburg, PA, August 1959, pp. 4–8.
6. Betty Gifford, friend, interview by Marilyn Culp Bollingner, October 16, 1982.

Sloan, Grace McCalmont (17)
1. A. J. Davis, *History of Clarion County, Pennsylvania, 1887 with historical supplement to 1969* (Rimersburg, PA: Record Press, 1968) pp. 150, 151.
2. Sylvester K. Stevens, *Pennsylvania: The Heritage of a Commonwealth,* (West Palm Beach, FL: American Historical Company, Inc., 1968) vol. 4, p. 15.

Soffel, Sara Mathlide, Judge (55)
1. "Pittsburgh Judge," *The Lamp,* November, 1950, pp. 22, 23.

Spencer, Mother Mary Agnes (95)
1. *Centenary of the Sisters of St. Joseph in the Diocese of Erie, 1860–1960.*
2. John Richie Schultz, "The History of Spencer Hospital," March 1, 1940, unpublished notes in the Spencer Hospital Archives, Meadville, PA.
3. *Erie Morning Dispatch,* Erie, PA, March 23, 1882.

Stokes, Madeline (148)
1. Paul B. Beers, *Profiles from the Susquehanna Valley* (Harrisburg: Stackpole Books, 1973) pp. 105, 106.
2. Millie Stroh Valentine, niece, interview by Ann Corby at Harrisburg, PA, October 1982 and January 12, 1983.
3. Scrapbooks located at the Hershey Museum of American Life, Hershey, PA, which were gifts of the estate of Alice Feaser Stroh, wife of Madeline's brother, and mother of Millie Stroh Valentine.

Sutton, Rachel McClelland (144)
1. Personal interviews by Martha L. Hunter, who was the artist's agent, 1982.
2. *Alumnae Recorder,* Chatham College, Pittsburgh, PA; vol. 50, no. 3, Spring 1982, p. 19.
3. WQED, videotape programs, Pittsburgh, PA. 1975, 1980.

Tarbell, Ida Minerva (62)
1. Ida M. Tarbell, *All In A Day's Work* (New York: Macmillan Co., 1939) pp. 79, 80, 239.
2. *The Villager,* Greenwich Village, NY, vol. 2, no. 41, January 13, 1944.
3. *The New York Times,* January 7, 1944.
4. Stanley J. Kunitz and Howard Haycraft, eds., *Twentieth Century Authors* (New York: The H. W. Wilson Co., 1942) p. 1383.
5. Frances G. Conn, *Ida Tarbell, Muckraker* (New York: Thomas Nelson, Inc., 1972) pp. 55, 117.

6. Alice Fleming, *Ida Tarbell, First of the Muckrakers* (New York: Thomas Y. Crowell Co., 1971) pp. 17, 24.
7. *The Derrick*, Oil City, PA, October 2, 1976 and November 6, 1976.

Tarnapowicz, Marie (39)
1. News files of *Post-Gazette*, Pittsburgh, PA.
2. News files of *The Pittsburgh Press*, Pittsburgh, PA.
3. Archives of The Polish Falcons of America, Pittsburgh, PA.
4. Ethnic Archives, Hillman Library, University of Pittsburgh, Pittsburgh, PA.
5. Archives of Western Pennsylvania Historical Society, Pittsburgh, PA.
6. Marie Tarnapowicz, personal conversations with Marie Iwanczyk.
7. Margie Carlen, "Hats Off To Tarney," *The Pittsburgh Press* Roto Magazine, Pittsburgh, PA, October 27, 1974.
8. Vicki Jarmulowski, "Nationality Group Gets Her Mementos," *Post-Gazette*, Pittsburgh, PA, June 19, 1980.
9. Jerry Vondas, "WW II Heroine Keeps Her Bond With Area Vets," *The Pittsburgh Press*, Pittsburgh, PA, July 20, 1980.

Taylor, Katherine Haviland (127)
1. Personal recollections of subject by her friend, Dorothy Baker, York, PA.
2. Betty Peckham, *The Story of a Dynamic Community-York, Pennsylvania* (York, PA: York Chamber of Commerce) pp. 40, 41.

Teagarden, Phoebe Jane, M.D. (44)
1. Miriam K. Dent and Elizabeth B. Gardner, interview by Anna Meighen, Waynesburg, PA, 1982.
2. Helen Elizabeth Vogt, *Descendants of Abraham Teagarden* (Berkeley, CA: 1967) p. 269.

Thorn, Sister Doloretta, Ph.D. (114)
1. *Erie Daily Times*, Erie, PA, September 1942.
2. *Lake Shore Visitor*, Erie, PA, July 8, 1966.
3. "The Integrator," *Journal of Engineering Societies Council*, May 9, 1975, p. 1.

Turnbull, Agnes Sligh (126)
1. Fred B. Millet, ed., *Contemporary American Authors* (New York: AMS Press, Inc. 1976) vol. 3.
2. *The New York Times*, November 26, 1972.
3. *Post-Gazette*, Pittsburgh, PA, February 2, 1982.
4. *The Tribune Review*, Greensburg, PA, February 2, 1982, February 4, 1982 and February 5, 1982.
5. *Who's Who In America*, 41st edition (Chicago: A. N. Marquis Company, Inc., 1980–81) vol. 2, p. 3338.
6. Stanley J. Kunitz and Howard Haycraft, *Twentieth Century Authors* (New York: H. W. Wilson Co., 1942) p. 1425.
7. Agnes Sligh Turnbull, *Out Of My Heart* (Boston: Houghton, Mifflin, 1958) p. 57.
8. Agnes Sligh Turnbull, *The Day Must Dawn* (New York: Macmillan, 1942) Forward, p. ix.
9. Alice Payne Hackett and James Henry Burke, *Eighty Years Of Best Sellers* (New York: R. R. Bowker, 1977) p. 148.

Vann Ausdall, Wealtha (145)
1. *The Derrick*, Oil City, PA, May 13, 1969.
2. *The News-Herald*, Franklin and Oil City, PA, February 22, 1969.

Waln, Nora (129)
1. Nora Waln, *House of Exile* (Boston: Little, Brown and Company, 1933)
2. Nora Waln, *Reaching for the Stars* (Boston: Little, Brown and Company, 1939)
3. Nora Waln, "I Saw Czechoslovakia," *Atlantic Monthly*, February, 1946.
4. Private files of George Scott, editor *emeritus*, *The Progress*, Clearfield, PA.

Warde, Mother Francis (94)
1. Sister M. Jerome McHale, *On the Wing: The Story of the Pittsburgh Sisters of Mercy 1843-1968*, pp. 27–34, 61.
2. The Reverend A. A. Lambing, *A History of the Catholic Church in the Dioceses of Pittsburgh and Allegheny*, p. 377.
3. *The Catholic*, July 15, 1865.
4. Mother Teresa Austin Carroll, *Leaves from the Annals of the Sisters of Mercy*, III, p. 66.
5. Sister M. Cornelius Meerwald, *History of the Pittsburgh Mercy Hospital 1847-1859*, pp. 43–46.
6. Kathleen Healy, *Francis Warde: American Founder of the Sisters of Mercy*, pp. 231, 232; 300.
7. Sister Pierre Jones, *Memoirs of the Pittsburgh Sisters of Mercy*, p. 56.

Welch, Martha McKeen (135)
1. Martha McKeen Welch, personal correspondence with Margaret D. Druse on file with the Easton Area Public Library, Easton, PA, 1982.
2. Greg Hanisek, "Her eye for nature got its start in local woods," *The Express*, Easton, PA, April 7, 1982.
3. *Who's Who of American Women*, 10th ed. (Chicago: A. N. Marquis Company, 1977) p. 926.
4. Martha McKeen Welch, *Sunflower!* (New York: Dodd, Mead and Co., 1980) book jacket.

Wheeler, Bessie S., The Reverend (93)
1. Joan Hellyer, "43 Year Pastor Does 'All Right,'" *Bucks County Courier Times*, Levittown, PA, January 18, 1980.
2. Karl Stark, "Rev. Wheeler Dies, Served for 45 Years," *Bucks County Courier Times*, Levittown, PA, October 21, 1981.
3. "Rev. Wheeler's Faith" (editorial), *Bucks County Courier Times*, Levittown, PA, October 21, 1981.

Wilson, Sarah (73)
1. W. Rush Gillan, "Personal Recollections of the Wilson Family," *Papers Read Before the Society from March 1905 to February 1908* (Chambersburg, PA: Kittochtinny Historical Society, 1908) vol. 5, pp. 200–222.
2. W. Rush Gillan, "Miss Sarah Wilson; a Biographical Sketch." Delivered before the faculty and students, October 7, 1922, *Wilson College Occasional Publications*, Chambersburg, PA, pp. 4–11.

3. Nettie Hesson Lloyd, *Forty Years of Wilson, as told by her Presidents, Faculty and Students* (Chambersburg, PA: Associate Alumnae, 1910) pp. 21–23.
4. Paul Swain Havens, "History of an Idea" (Portrait of Sarah Wilson, p. 4), *Wilson College Bulletin*, vol. 32, pp. 2–5, April 1969.
5. Gertrude B. Biddle and Sarah D. Lowrie, eds., *Notable Women of Pennsylvania* (Philadelphia: University of Pennsylvania Press, 1942) pp. 127, 128.

Wittenmyer, Annie (37)
1. Muriel E. Lichtenwalner, *Lower Pottsgrove, Crossroads of History* (Lower Pottsgrove Township, PA: Lower Pottsgrove Bicentennial Commission, 1979) pp. 116, 117.

Wolfe, Mary Moore, M.D. (48)
1. *American Women*, (Los Angeles: American Publications, Inc., 1939) vol. 3
2. *Encyclopedia of American Biography* (New York: Harper & Row, 1974)
3. File on Mary Moore Wolfe at the Bucknell University Archives, Lewisburg, PA.
4. Mary M. Wolfe, M.D., "The Relation of Feeble-Mindedness to Education, Citizenship and Culture." Reprinted from the Proceedings of the Forty–Ninth Annual Session of the American Association for the Study of the Feeble-Minded, Raleigh, NC, May 8–11, 1925.
5. Mary M. Wolfe, M.D., Sc.D., "President's Address to the American Association on Mental Deficiency," Chicago, April 26, 1935.
6. Mrs. Lois Kalp, wife of nephew, telephone interview by Elsbeth Steffensen, February 1983.
7. Mrs. Dorothy Ruhl, former employee at Laurelton, telephone interview by Elsbeth Steffensen, February 1983.
8. William Schooley, former employee, telephone interview by Elsbeth Steffensen, February 1983.
9. Jane Slack, librarian, Laurelton Center, Laurelton, PA, interview by Elsbeth S. Steffensen, February 1983.

Wotring, Margaret Frantz (41)
1. Charles Rhoads Roberts, et. al., *History of Lehigh County, Pennsylvania*, (Allentown: Lehigh Valley Publishing Co., Ltd., 1914) vol. 2, pp. 381–383.

Wright, Susanna (3)
1. *Journal*, Lancaster County Historical Society, Lancaster, PA, vol. 61, January 1957, pp. 1–3.
2. Marion Wallace Reninger, *Famous Women of Lancaster County Pennsylvania*, (Lancaster, PA: Lancaster County Historical Society) pp. 12–14.
3. John W. W. Loose, *The Heritage of Lancaster* (Woodland Hills, CA: Windsor Publications, 1978) p. 17.
4. *Journal*, Lancaster County Historical Society, Lancaster, PA, vol. 17, p. 226.
5. Gertrude B. Biddle and Sarah D. Lowrie, eds., *Notable Women of Pennsylvania* (Philadelphia: University of Pennsylvania Press, 1942) pp. 24, 25.

Wysor, Elizabeth (154)
1. *The Express*, Easton, PA, November 6, 1981.
2. Elizabeth Wysor and her sister, Virginia Purdy, interview by Cynthia Gordon and Margaret D. Druse, Easton, 1982.

Young, Patricia Kinkaid (88)
1. Patricia Kinkaid Young, telephone interview by Ethel DeVirgilis, Scranton, PA, March 6, 1983.
2. Patricia Kinkaid Young, telephone interview by Regina Petruskas, Scranton, PA, February 1983.
3. "World Food Day" (Washington, DC: National Committee for World Food Day, 1982)

APPENDIX C

Other Biographical Entries Submitted to the Division Project

This is a list of selected biographies which were not included in this volume, but which were submitted to the Division Project by the AAUW Branch indicated. All the original biographies and materials submitted are in the archives of the Pennsylvania Historical and Museum Commission in Harrisburg. Some research materials are also housed in the local archive of the submitting branch as indicated.

Aliquippa—Beaver County Historical Research Office, Resource and Research Center of Beaver County History, Beaver Falls.
Gladys L'Ashley Hoover....................... 1900–1980

Allentown
Ella Sophinisba Hergesheimer.................. 1873–1943
Frances C. Schaeffer, M.D...................... b. 1915
Alice Parker Tallmadge........................ 1890–1963

Bedford County
Lizzie Bain Lysinger.......................... 1862–1967

Bethlehem—Bethlehem Public Library
Catherine L. Barlieb.......................... 1889–1969
Adelaide Martin Bean.......................... 1883–1965
Hughetta E. Bender............................ b. 1905
M. Dolores White Caskey....................... b. 1920
Mary Crow..................................... b. 19-?
Grethe J. Goodwin............................. b. 1926
Sarah M. Hindman, M.D......................... 1913?–1972
Annie S. Kemerer.............................. 1865–1951
Rachel Mifflin Ullman......................... 189?–1976

Brookville Area—Rebecca M. Arthurs Memorial Library
Rebecca M. Arthurs............................ 1870–1955

Butler—Zelienople Historical Society
Gertrude M. Ziegler........................... b. 1919

Clearfield Area—Clearfield County Historical Society; Joseph and Elizabeth Shaw Public Library, Clearfield

Maria J. Bigler. 1816–1898
Inez Crandle. . . . . .18-?-1975
Jane S. Dietzel. 1913–1968
Jean M. Friday. 1898–1962
Ruth I. Moore. . . . . .b. 1888
Mary A. Rothrock. 1882–1979
Alice M. Sommerville. 1909–1978
Mandaine D. Walker. 1868–1947

DuBois—Library, DuBois Campus of the Pennsylvania State University

Nina Bentley Gray. 1905–1977

Eastern Delaware County

Mary H. Purcell. . . . . .b. 1926

Easton—Easton Area Public Library

Jacquelyn Rogers. . . . . .b. 19-?
June Stephanie Sprigg. . . . . .b. 1953

Elk County—Elk County Historical Society

Elizabeth D. Simons. . . . . .b. 1905

Erie—Mercyhurst College Archives

Laura G. Sanford. 1819–1907

Fox Chapel Area—Western Pennsylvania Historical Society, Pittsburgh

Ruth Dye Boyles. . . . . .b. 1907
Janet de Coux. . . . . .b. 1905
Mary Carson O'Hara Darlington. 1824–1915
Elsie Hilliard Hillman. . . . . .b. 1925
Ella Miller Meyer. 1877–1950
Lillian McCall Stofiel. 1864–1948

Franklin County—Wilson College; Kittochtinny Historical Society, Chambersburg

Lucy Benchoff. . . . . .b. 19-?
Margaret Criswell Disert. . . . . .b. 19-?

Harrisburg—Harrisburg AAUW

Alice R. Eaton. 1872–1968
Etta O. Engle. . . . . .b. 19-?
Lillie Coyle Hench Harris. 1873–1966
Katherine Elizabeth Landis. .1884–1964
Anne McCormick. 1881–1964
Gertrude Howard Olmsted McCormick. . . . . .1874–19?

Huntingdon—Hartslog Heritage Museum, Alexandria, Huntingdon County Historical Society (McMurtrie-only)

Elizabeth Dorsey. . . . . .17-?-1833
Solveig Wald Horn. 1914–1979

Clara McMurtrie. 1860–1952
Agnes Irvine Scott. 1799–1877

Lancaster–Lancaster County Library
Barbara Frietschie. 1766–1862
Ann S. Galbraith. . . . . 17-?-?
Barbara Ann Hackman Franklin O'Brecht. . . . . b. 1940

Lansdale–Montgomery County Federation of Historical Societies; Peter Wentz
Homestead, Worchester
Janet Mulvany Minehart. . . . . b. 1917
Selma Davis Neiburg. 1885–1978
Helen Newbury Ridington. 1898–1982
Helen Keller Ruth. . . . . b. 1917
Cora Sigafoos. . . . . b. 1893

Levittown-Lower Bucks County–Historic Langhorne Library-Museum
Anna Mary Williamson. 1836–1887

Makefield Area–Yardley-Makefield Library
Rachel Carver. 1876–1955

Pittsburgh–Western Pennsylvania Historical Society, Pittsburgh
Irene Pasinski Sailer. . . . . b. 19-?

Pottstown Area–Pottstown Library
Lena Kurtz Knauer. . . . . 1891?–1978

Punxsutawney–Punxsutawney Memorial Library
M. Virginia Beyer, M.D.. 1890–1954

Reading–Reading Public Library
Elizabeth Adams Hurwitz. 1903–1975

Scranton–Lackawanna Historical Society
Géné Brislin. . . . . b. 19-?
Marion Scranton Isaacs. b. 1908
Anne Vanko Liva. . . . . b. 19-?
Jeanne M. Martin. . . . . b. 1915
Mary B. McAndrew. 1887–1979
Sondra Myers. . . . . b. 1934
Mary C. Nivison, M.D.. 1834–1891
Carmel Sirianni. . . . . b. 1922
Frances Slocum. 1773–1847
Harriet Hollister Watres. 18-?–1900?

Shippensburg
Lucinda Piper. . . . . 17-?–17-?

State College
Marjorie W. Dunaway. . . . . b. 1920

Susquehanna Valley–Bucknell University, Archives, Lewisburg

Betty Cook..b. 1929
Gladys C. Cook, Ph.D...........................b. 1905
Jennie S. Erdley................................b. 1901
Elizabeth Zimmerman Farrow....................b. 1908
Edith Kelly Fetherston.........................1885–1972
Lois Geiger.......................................b. 1916
Nada Reichman Gray............................b. 1933
Jeannette Lasansky..............................b. 1943
Mildred Martin, Ph.D............................b. 1904
Nancy Adams Mosshammer Neuman.............b. 1936
Lystra Rogers...................................b. 1904
Thelma Johnson Showalter......................b. 1908
Mary Jane Stevenson...........................b. 1917
Martha Harris Zeller............................b. 1930

York–York County Historical Society

Jane M. Alexander.............................b. 1929
Doris Morrell Leader............................b. 1923
Nellie Leber Longsworth........................b. 1933
Margaret E. Moul...............................b. 1906
Janette D. Woolsey.............................b. 1904

APPENDIX D

Names of Submitting Branches and Project Chairmen

These are the names of the fifty-five branches which contributed to the Division Project and their Project Chairmen, or other submitting agents. An asterisk (*) designates an individual who submitted an entry requested by the Project Director from a branch without a chairman.

Aliquippa–Charlotte Bacon
Allentown–Camille S. Bucci
Annville–Nancy B. Hatz
Beaver Valley–Sarah P. Kenah
Bedford County–Mary Sue Whisker
Bethlehem–Polly Hinder
Bloomsburg–Florence Thompson*
Bradford–Joan Mansour
Brookville Area–Kathryn I. Wachob
Butler–Ruth B. Jones
Carlisle–Susan R. Gorsky*
Clarion–Helen Knuth
Clearfield Area–Norma G. Boykiw and Lois R. Gilmore
Doylestown–Anna E. Shaddinger
DuBois–Judy Furlow
Eastern Delaware County–Betty Moorhead*
Easton–Margaret D. Druse
Elk County–Joan Donovan
Erie–Sabina S. Freeman and Margaret L. Tenpas
Fox Chapel Area–Patricia Demase
Franklin County–Rachel Minick and Anne Vondra
Gettysburg–Donna M. Schaefer
Greensburg Area–Trish Smithson and Thelma Stack
Grove City–Carol Ann Gregg
Harrisburg–Margaret H. Davenport
Hawley–Honesdale Area–Anne Baschon
Hazleton–Patricia Conahan
Hershey–Betty V. Bartels

Huntingdon–Nancy R. Taylor
Indiana–Evelyn D. Landon
Johnstown–Mary Jo Novelli
Lancaster–Betty B. Duncan
Lansdale–Diane Brouillette and Kathy Sachs
Lawrence County–Mary Beth McLaughry
Levittown–Lower Bucks County–Jean M. Green
Makefield Area–Marie McGowan
Meadville Area–Rebecca Borthwick
Mt. Lebanon–South Hills–Elizabeth West
Murrysville–Carolyn Glick
Oil City–Franklin–Lois E. Follstaedt
Philadelphia–Ellen H. Moore
Pittsburgh–Doris M. Handy
Pottstown Area–Muriel E. Lichtenwalner
Punxsutawney–Betty H. Philliber
Reading–M. Susan Johns
Rices Landing–Ina P. Vance
Scranton–Ethel DeVirgilis and Judith D. Evans
Shippensburg–Carol Hozman
Southampton–Joan Frame
StateCollege–Martha Zeller (serving at-large)*
Susquehanna Valley–Lois Kalp
Valley Forge–Anne Odenweller
Waynesburg–Sarah Olmstead
West Chester–Mary S. Pinkney
York–Roseanne L. Garner